Reading Lists in Radical Social Science

Reading Lists in Radical Social Science

Editorial coordinators:
Mark Maier and Dan Gilroy

Monthly Review Press/
Union for Radical Political Economics

Copyright ©1982 by the Union for Radical Political Economics
All rights reserved

Library of Congress Cataloging in Publication Data
Main entry under title:

Reading lists in radical social science.

    1. Social Sciences — Bibliography. 2. Radicalism—Bibliography.
I. Maier, Mark. II. Gilroy, Dan.
III. Union for Radical Political Economics.
Z7161.R36 1982 [H85] 016.3 81-86025
ISBN 0-85345-616-X   AACR2

Monthly Review Press
62 West 14th Street
New York, N.Y. 10011

Manufactured in the United States of America

10 9 8 7 6 5 4 3 2 1

TABLE OF CONTENTS

Introduction and Acknowledgements vii

1. Introductory Courses 1
2. Marxism and Methodology 15
3. The State 35
4. Development and Regional Studies 49
5. Revolution 82
6. History 94
7. Women 101
8. Labor 126
9. Urban 138
10. The Corporation 143
11. Racism 148
12. Law and Crime 153
13. Miscellaneous

    Class 163

    Education 167

    Government Regulation 169

    Energy 171

    Health 173

    Hunger 177

What Is URPE 181

INTRODUCTION

These reading lists have been compiled with several purposes in mind. They are intended as a resource for students who are looking for readings within a perspective not covered by traditional social science courses. The lists also will be valuable to teachers as an aid in preparing course syllabi. Finally, we hope that the lists are helpful to those outside of formal educational settings who need assistance in their study groups and writing efforts.

In order to serve all of these readers we have chosen the lists so that they range from short introductory course outlines to more detailed graduate level course syllabi. The lists are organized by subject matter with most topics covered as separate chapters. Readings on some topics, however, will be found under sub-headings within various chapters. (Women's studies, for example, is both a separate chapter as well as a sub-heading in the "Labor" and "Development and Regional Studies" chapters.)

These Reading Lists are the fourth in a series dating back to 1971. The title has been changed from *Reading Lists in Radical Political Economics* to *Reading Lists in Radical Social Science*. Although past editions of the book contained outlines from courses not formally labelled as economics, the book's title perpetuated traditional fracturing of the social sciences. The new title is intended to reflect the interconnectedness of the social sciences and the need for radicals in all disciplines to break down barriers between their disciplines.

ACKNOWLEDGEMENTS

The title *Reading Lists in Radical Social Science* also points to the assistance received by URPE (the Union for Radical Political Economics) in preparing this book. In particular, MARHO: the Radical Historians Organization helped us in fundraising for the project. Members of MARHO, the Insurgent Sociologist Collective and the Anthropology Resource Center helped us contact several hundred teachers for their course outlines.

The reading lists printed in this volume represent only a small number of the lists submitted to us for consideration. The lists used were chosen in order to insure that the book would contain a variety of political perspectives, a number of different college programs and gradation of levels of difficulty. We thank everyone who sent us materials. We hope those whose lists are not reprinted will understand the difficult task we faced in making final selections from a large number of well thought-out course outlines. Suggestions for improving this book in its next edition are welcome and should be sent to the URPE National Office, 41 Union Square West, New York, NY 10003.

Many individuals helped assemble the lists including: Gordon Kiziway, Victoria DeGrazia, Marjorie Williams, Marty Oppenheimer and Michael Swerdlow. Members of the *Review of Radical Political Economics* Editorial Board, in their role as URPE's review body, made valuable suggestions concerning the preparation of the lists for publication. Typesetters Mary McHugh, Mike Prokosch, and Danny Williams are responsible for taking a hodge-podge of often difficult-to-read course outlines and turning them into these typeset pages.

Special thanks are due to Jules Geller and Susan Lowes of Monthly Review Press. Completion of the project is in large part the result of their expert advice and unflagging support.

Dan Gilroy
Mark Maier
Reading Lists Coordinators

INTRODUCTORY COURSES

Introductory Sociology

Hal Benenson
Sociology
Ramapo College of New Jersey
Fall 1980
Undergraduate

PART I—INTRODUCTION: THE PURPOSES OF SOCIAL ANALYSIS

A. INTELLECTUAL WORK. SOCIAL SCIENCE AND HUMAN VALUES

Paul Baran, "The Commitment of the Intellectual" (excerpt, mimeographed) from *The Longer View*, Monthly Review Press, N.Y. 1969.

Max Weber, "Science as a Vocation" (excerpt) from S.N. Eisenstadt, ed., *Max Weber on Charisma & Institution-Building*. Univ. of Chicago Press, Chicago. 1968. pp. 294-309.

Suggested Reading:

Jurgen Habermas, *Theory and Practice*. Beacon Press, Boston. 1974. pp. 253-256, 262-263.

Talcott Parsons, "Value-freedom and Objectivity" and M. Horkheimer and J. Habermas, "Comments" in O. Stammer, ed., *Max Weber and Sociology Today*. Harper and Row, N.Y. 1971. pp. 27-33, 46-53, 59-66.

Karl Marx, "Letter to Ruge" in *Writings of the Young Marx on Philosophy and Society*, eds. Easton and Guddat. Doubleday, Garden City, N.Y. 1967. pp. 212, 214-215.

Georg Lukacs, "On the Responsibility of Intellectuals" in *Marxism and Human Liberation*. Delta, N.Y. 1973. pp. 267-276.

Jurgen Habermas, *Knowledge and Human Interests* Beacon Press, Boston. 1972. pp. 301-317.

Barrington Moore, Jr. "Strategy in Social Science" in *Political Power and Social Theory*. Harper and Row, N.Y. 1962. pp. 111-125.

Leo Strauss, *Natural Right and History*. Univ. of Chicago Press, Chicago. 1953. Chapter Two.

B. THE "SOCIOLOGICAL IMAGINATION" AND INDIVIDUAL EXPERIENCE

C. Wright Mills, "The Promise" from *The Sociological Imagination*, Oxford University Press, N.Y. 1959.

George Jackson, *Soledad Brother*. Bantam Books, N.Y. 1970.pb pp. 9-37.

Richard Sennett and Jonathan Cobb, "Ricca Kartides" from *The Hidden Injuries of Class*, Random House, N.Y. 1973. pp. 46-50.

PART II—ECONOMIC STRUCTURE AND SOCIAL CLASS

A. THE DISTRIBUTION OF WEALTH AND INCOME

Statistical Tables (mimeographed) from G. Kolko, *Wealth and Power in America*, Praeger, N.Y. 1962.; F. Lundberg, *The Rich and the Super-Rich*, Bantam, N.Y. 1968; U.S. Bureau of the Census, *Statistical Abstract of the U.S.—1972 & 1973*, U.S. Government Printing Office, Washington, D.C.

B. THE THEORY OF CLASS

Karl Marx and Federick Engels, *The Communist Manifesto*. International Publishers, New York. 1949. Part I.

C. CLASSES IN AMERICAN SOCIETY

Paul Sweezy, "The American Class System" in Gillam, ed., *Power in Postwar America*, pp. 42-45.

Sennett & Cobb, *The Hidden Injuries of Class*.

Harry Braverman, *Labor and Monopoly Capital*, Monthly Review Press, N.Y. 1974.
Introduction, pp. 3-14, 31-41 only.
Chapter 1, "Labor and Labor Power" pp. 45-58
Chapter 4, "Scientific Management" pp. 85-123
Chapter 15, "Clerical Workers" pp. 293-358
Chapter 17, "The Structure of the Working Class" pp. 377-402.

G. William Domhoff, *The Higher Circles*, Random House, N.Y. 1970. Chapter 4, "Cohesion and Consciousness".

D. COMMUNITY CLASS STRUCTURE

PART III—THE STRUCTURE OF POWER IN AMERICAN SOCIETY

A. PLURALISM

Robert Dahl, "Power in New Haven," in R. Gillam, ed., *Power in Postwar America*. Little, Brown, Boston. 1971. pp. 23-31.

Arnold Rose, "The Multi-Influence Hypothesis" in Gillam, pp. 91-100.

Talcott Parsons, "The Distribution of Power in American Society" in Gillam, pp. 62-82.

B. POWER ELITE THEORY

C. Wright Mills, "The Structure of Power in American Society," in Gillam, pp. 49-62.

Floyd Hunter, "The Structure of Power in Regional City," in Gillam, pp. 13-24.

William Proxmire, "The Community of Interests in Our Defense Contract Spending," in Gillam, pp. 159-166.

C. MARXIST THEORY AND THE UPPER CLASS

Paul Sweezy, "The American Ruling Class," in Gillam, pp. 40-49.

G. William Domhoff, "Is the American Upper Class a Governing Class?" in Gillam, pp. 80-91.

Suggested Reading:

David Riesman, "The Theory of Veto Groups" in Gillam, pp. 32-40 (pluralist analysis)

Gabriel Kolko, "The American Military and Civil Authority" in Gillam, pp. 80-91 (Marxist critique of C. Wright Mills).

G.W. Domhoff, *The Higher Circles*. entire.

R. Miliband, *The State in Capitalist Society*. Basic Books, N.Y.

PART IV—INSTITUTIONAL RACISM AND THE POSITION OF BLACK PEOPLE IN AMERICAN SOCIETY

A. SOCIAL AND ECONOMIC POSITION OF BLACK PEOPLE—AN OVERVIEW

Statistical materials on Institutional Racism (mimeographed), from U.S. Bureau of the Census, *The Social and Economic Status of the Black Population of the U.S., 1971 & 1974*, U.S. Gov't Printing Office, Wash., D.C.; and *Statistical Abstract of U.S.*

B. INTERNAL COLONIALISM AND THE BLACK GHETTO

George Jackson, *Soledad Brother*. entire.

Robert Blauner, "Internal Colonialism and Ghetto Revolt" from *Social Problems*, XVI: 4, Spring 1969.

Eugene Genovese, "Class and Nationality in Black America," from *In Red and Black*. Vintage, New York. 1971. pp. 53-72.

Suggested Reading:

William Tabb, *The Political Economy of the Black Ghetto*. Norton. N.Y. 1970.

C. BLACK WOMEN AND THE BLACK FAMILY

"Black Women in Revolt" from *Lessons from the Damned*, Times Change Press, Washington, N.J. 1973. pp. 103-111.

Carol Stack, "Sex Roles and Survival Strategies in an Urban Black Community," in Rosaldo and Lamphere, eds., *Woman, Culture and Society*.

D. DEMOGRAPHIC AND ECONOMIC DIMENSIONS OF BLACK SOCIAL DEVELOPMENT

Karl and Alma Taueber, "The Black Population" in *The Black American Reference Book*.

Robert Hill, "The Illusion of Black Progress" in *The Black Scholar*, October 1978. pp. 18-24, 49-52.

Suggested Reading:

U.S. Bureau of the Census, *The Social and Economic Status of the Black Population of the U.S., 1974*. U.S. GPO, Washington. 1975.

A. Spear, *Black Chicago. The Making of a Ghetto*. Univ. Chicago Press. 1967.

E. RACISM AND RACE CONSCIOUSNESS

David Wellman, *Portraits of White Racism*. Oxford University Press, New York. 1978.

Allen Hunter and Jim Green, "Racism and Busing in Boston," *Radical America*, 8:6 (Nov-Dec 1974). New England Free Press pamphlet.

PART V—WOMEN, THE FAMILY AND WORK

A. THE ECONOMIC POSITION OF WOMEN—AN OVERVIEW

Statistical Tables on Women Workers (mimeographed), from Ilene Winkler, *Women Workers*, IS publications, N.Y.; and Lise Vogel, *Women Workers-Some Basic Statistics*, NEFP, Boston, 1971.

B. HISTORICAL BACKGROUND: THE INDUSTRIAL REVOLUTION, ECONOMIC CHANGE AND WOMEN'S WORK

Gerda Lerner, "The Lady and the Mill Girl," Bobbs-Merrill Reprint.

Ann Oakley, "Women and Industrialization" in *Woman's Work*. Vintage, New York. 1974. pp. 32-59.

S. Tobias & L. Anderson, "What Really Happened to Rosie the Riveter?" MSS.

H. Hayghe, "Families and the Rise of Working Wives," *Monthly Labor Review*, May 1976. pp. 12-19.

C. THE FAMILY, SOCIAL REPRODUCTION AND THE SEXUAL DIVISION OF LABOR

    Juliet Mitchell, "Women: the Longest Revolution" *New Left Review*, 40. New England Free Press pamphlet.

    Evelyne Sullerot, *Woman, Society and Change*. McGraw Hill, N.Y. 1974. pb
Introduction, pp. 7-17

Chapter 1, "The patriarchal system," pp. 19-42
Chapter 2, "Demography," pp. 43-77
Chapter 3, "Home and work," pp. 79-107
Chapter 4, "The economics of employment," pp. 109-133
Chapter 5, "Types of work," pp. 135-167
Conclusion, pp. 239-248

Suggested Reading: Chapters 6-9

Elements of Economics

Samuel Bowles
Department of Economics
University of Massachusetts-Amherst
Fall 1979
Undergraduate

COURSE OBJECTIVES:

Our main objective is to help you understand the manner in which the workings of the U.S. economy affect you: the way it structures your job(or why you can't find one), your standard of living, your health, the way it influences your schooling, your values, your community, your relations with others. Our approach is to offer a balance of facts (about the U.S. and world economies) and analytical tools (theoretical approaches, or ways of understanding these facts). The conceptual material in the course is designed to let you understand better what you already know (this is not your first encounter with the economy-you've been engaged with it since birth), and help you to be able to make economic judgements on your own. This knowledge, we believe, is essential to intelligent action and decision making—in your personal life as much as in your community participation.

BASIC TEXTS

    U.S. Dept. of Commerce and The Advertising Council, *The American Economic System...And Your Place in it.* (pamphlet)

    Popular Economics Press, *Why Do We Spend So Much Money?* (pamphlet)

    Popular Economics Press, *Q. What's Happening to Our Jobs?* (pamphlet)

    K. Marx, *Wage Labor and Capital.*

    President's Council of Economic Advisors, *Economic Report of the President 1979*, and *Report of the President's Council of Economic Advisors, 1979.*

    R. Edwards; T. Weisskopf, and M. Reich, *The Capital System.* (second edition) (ERW)

    Dollars and Sense, *Trade Wars.* (pamphlet)

    Milton Friedman and the Standard Oil Company. *The Economics of Freedom.* (pamphlet to be passed out in class)

    Mark Dowie, "Pinto Madness;" *Mother Jones*, Sept.-Oct., 1977 (pamphlet)

    Joseph Collins and Francis Moore Lappe, "Still Hungry After All These Years," *Mother Jones*, August, 1977. (This article is part of a pamphlet entitled, *The Myth of the Green Revolution*).

I. INTRODUCTION

INTRODUCTION: THE CURRENT ECONOMIC SITUATION

HUNGER: WHY THE 1972 FAMINE IN SENEGAL DID NOT DISRUPT ASPARAGUS EXPORTS TO FRANCE

ERW, ch. 1, pp. 3-35: "Still Hungry After All These Years."

YOUR CAR SPEAKS: AN ECONOMIC AUTOBIOGRAPHY

Why Do We Spend So Much Money (entire *What's Happening to Our Jobs?*) entire "Pinto Madness."

SOCIALISM IS NOT GOVERNMENT OWNERSHIP OF YOUR TOOTHBRUSH

ERW, pp. 517-528.

II. CAPITALISM, CLASSICAL LIBERALISM AND NEOCLASSICAL ECONOMICS

WHAT IS CAPITALISM (CAN DEFINITIONS LIE?)

ERW, Intro. to ch. 3, pp. 75-80. *ERW*, 2.2, 2.3, 2.4, pp. 49-69, *ERW*, 3.2, pp. 92-98.

THE INVISIBLE HAND: IS THE CASH REGISTER A BALLOT BOX?

The American Economic System, pp. 1-19.

SUPPLY AND DEMAND

The Economics of Freedom (entire)

FILM: CONTROLLING INTERESTS

TECHNOLOGY AND TASTES: ARE MOTHER NATURE AND HUMAN NATURE TO BLAME?

III. MARXIAN ECONOMICS

HISTORICAL MATERIALISM: AN OVERVIEW

ERW, Intro. to ch. 2, pp. 39-42. *ERW*, 2.1, pp. 42-49.

TWENTY YEARS OF SCHOOLING AND THEY PUT YOU ON THE DAY SHIFT: AN APPLICATION OF HISTORICAL MATERIALISM

ERW, 8.3, pp. 315-329.

VALUE AND SURPLUS VALUE: HOW CAPITALISM INVENTED TIME

ERW, 3.1, pp. 80-92.

COMPETITION, PROFIT AND THE RESERVE ARMY: HOW TO MAKE A MOUNTAIN OUT OF A MOLEHILL

Marx, *Wage Labor and Capital* (entire)

SUPER PROFITS, MONOPOLY CAPITAL AND IMPERIALISM

ERW, 3.3, pp. 99-105 and *ERW*, ch. 13, pp. 470-514.

CLASS CONFLICT: FILM—"THE INHERITANCE"

ERW, ch. 5, pp. 175-215.

BLUE MONDAY: THE LABOR PROCESS AND TECHNOLOGY

ERW, ch. 7, pp. 264-291.

INEQUALITY: THE INVISIBLE FINGER

ERW, intro. to ch. 8, 8.1, and 8.2, pp. 292-315.

SOME ARE MORE EQUAL THAN OTHERS: RACISM AND FREE ENTERPRISE

ERW, ch. 10, pp. 358-388.

WILL McDONALD'S LIBERATE WOMEN?

ERW, 2.5, pp. 69-73; 3.6, pp. 111-114; and ch. 9, pp. 330-358.

WAITING FOR UNCLE SAM (DON'T HOLD YOUR BREATH)

ERW, 3.5, pp. 108-110; intro. to ch. 6, 6.1, 6.2 and 6.3, pp. 216-242.

IV. THE U.S. ECONOMY TODAY: LIMPING CORNUCOPIA?

ECONOMIC GROWTH: WHEN IS MORE MORE? WHAT'S GROSS ABOUT THE GROSS NATIONAL PRODUCT?

ERW, pp. 391-409.
President's Economic Report, pp. 3-15.
Dollars and Sense, *Trade Wars*, pp. 3-23.

THE U.S. IN THE WORLD ECONOMY. (Q. IS THE GOOSE THAT LAID THE GOLDEN EGG REALLY DEAD? A. NO, I THINK IT'S LIVING IN S. KOREA)

Report of the President's Council of Economic Advisors, pp. 135-162.
Dollars and Sense, *Trade Wars*, pp. 3-23.

AGGREGATE SUPPLY AND DEMAND: WHEN IS ENOUGH ENOUGH?

ERW, ch. 12, pp. 426-469.

INFLATION, UNEMPLOYMENT, AND GOVERNMENT POLICY

Report of the President's Council of Economic Advisors, pp. 25-28; 36-47; 54-91.

WHICH WAY OUT OF THE STAGFLATION SWAMP: LAISSEZ FAIRE VS. CORPORATE STATE PLANNING?

Report of the President's Council of Economic Advisors, pp. 92-134.

THE INVISIBLE HAND AND THE IRON FIST: HAVE DEMOCRACY AND CAPITALISM REACHED A PARTING OF THE WAYS?

ERW, ch. 6.4 and 6.5, pp. 242-262.

SOCIALISM AND DEMOCRACY, PLUS FILM: *CAMPAMENTO*

ERW, 14.2 and 14.3, pp. 528-541.

Radical Perspectives on Economics

Thomas E. Weisskopf
American Association for the Advancement of Science/National Science Foundation Chautauqua-Type Short Course
1979-1980

Under each general topic heading I have listed a set of related readings, which vary in their importance and their degree of difficulty. Rather than try to characterize here each of the readings on the list, I will describe them briefly during the fall session so that you may decide which are the most appropriate for you to pursue. All readings are fully referenced, except that I have used the following notation for two frequently-cited volumes:

ERW-2: Richard Edwards, Michael Reich and Thomas Weisskopf, *The Capitalist System: A Radical Analysis of American Society* (Prentice-Hall, 2nd edition, 1978).

USCC: U.R.P.E., U.S. *Capitalism in Crisis* (U.R.P.E., 1978).

I. AN INTRODUCTION TO RADICAL POLITICAL ECONOMY

A. RADICAL CRITIQUES OF MAINSTREAM ECONOMICS

Review of Radical Political Economics, Vol. 3, No. 2, July 1971 (Special Issue on Radical Paradigms in Economics).

Duncan Foley, "Problems vs. Conflicts: Economic Theory and Ideology", *American Economic Review*, Vol. 65, No. 2, May 1975, pp. 231-236.

Ronald Meek, "Economics and Ideology", in Meek, *Economics and Ideology and Other Essays* (Chapman and Hall, 1967), pp. 196-224.

Edward Nell, "Economics: The Revival of Political Economy", in Robin Blackburn (ed.), *Ideology in Social Science* (Vintage, 1973), pp. 76-95.

Sue Himmelweit, "The Individual as Basic Unit of Analysis", and Ben Fine, "The Concept and Origin of Profit", in Francis Green and Peter Nore (eds.), *Economics: An Anti-Text* (MacMillan, 1977), pp. 21-35, 105-116.

Assar Lindbeck, *The Political Economy of the New Left: An Outsider's View* (Harper & Row, 2nd edition, 1977), especially pp. 9-27, 119-137, 148-183.

B. A RADICAL ALTERNATIVE: BASIC PREMISES OF MARXIAN POLITICAL ECONOMY

ERW-2, ch. 2, pp. 39-49.

John Gurley, *Challengers to Capitalism* (San Francisco Book Co., 1976), ch. 2, pp. 7-29 (excerpted in ERW-2, section 2.1, pp. 43-49).

M.C. Howard and J.E. King, *The Political Economy of Marx* (Longman, 1975), ch. 1, pp. 1-23, and ch. 2, pp. 24-45, 55-58.

Helmut Fleischer, *Marxism and History* (Harper & Row, 1969), especially ch. 2, pp. 38-63.

C. THE MARXIAN PERSPECTIVE ON CAPITALISM

ERW-2, ch. 2, pp. 49-69, and ch. 3, pp. 75-105.

John Gurley, *Challengers to Capitalism* (San Francisco Book Co., 1976), ch. 3, pp. 31-61 (excerpted in ERW-2, section 3.1, pp. 80-92).

Samuel Bowles and Herbert Gintis, *Schooling in Capitalist America* (Basic Books, 1976), ch. 3, pp. 53-68.

M.C. Howard and J.E. King, *The Political Economy of Marx* (Longman, 1975), chs. 4-6, pp. 93-235.

II. THE CAPITALIST MICROECONOMY: THE LABOR PROCESS

A. LABOR VS. LABOR POWER: THE PROBLEM OF CAPITALIST MANAGEMENT

Harry Braverman, *Labor and Monopoly Capital* (Monthly Review, 1974), Part I, especially chs. 1-2, pp. 45-69 (excerpted in ERW-2, section 3.2, pp. 92-98).

Herbert Gintis, "The Nature of the Labor Exchange and the Theory of Capitalist Production," *Review of Radical Political Economics*, Vol. 8, No. 2, Summer 1976, pp. 36-54.

Michael Reich and James Devine, "The Microeconomics of Conflict and Hierarchy in Capitalist Production," *Review of Radical Political Economics*, forthcoming 1980.

B. THE HISTORICAL ORIGINS OF THE HIERARCHICAL DIVISION OF LABOR

Samuel Bowles and Herbert Gintis, *Schooling in Capitalist America* (Basic Books, 1976), ch. 3, pp. 68-84 (excerpted in ERW-2, section 7.2, pp. 274-283).

Stephen Marglin, "What do Bosses Do? The Origins and Functions of Hierarchy in Capitalist Production," *Review of Radical Political Economics*, Vol. 6, No. 2, Summer 1974, pp. 60-112.

Richard Edwards, *Contested Terrain* (Basic Books, 1979), chs. 1-10, pp. 3-152, 163-199 (for a summary treatment of the main points, see *ERW-2*, sections 5.3-5.4, pp. 193-205).

C. CONTRADICTIONS OF THE LABOR PROCESS

Howard Wachtel, "Class Consciousness and Statification in the Labor Process," *Review of Radical Political Economics*, Vol. 6, No. 1, Spring 1974, pp. 1-31 (excerpted in *ERW-2*, section 7.3, pp. 283-291).

Andrew Zimbalist, "The Limits of Work Humanization," *Review of Radical Political Economics*, Vol. 7, No. 2, Summer 1975, pp. 50-59.

Richard Edwards, *Contested Terrain* (Basic Books, 1979), ch. 8, pp. 152-162, and ch. 11, pp. 200-216.

Samuel Bowles and Herbert Gintis, *Schooling in Capitalist America* (Basic Books, 1976), ch. 11, pp. 274-288.

III. THE CAPITALIST MACROECONOMY: ECONOMIC CRISES

A. GENERAL INTRODUCTION

ERW-2, ch. 12, pp. 427-441.

USCC, introduction, pp. 1-7, and article by David Gordon ("Up and Down the Long Roller Coaster"), pp. 22-35.

David Gordon, "Orthodox and Radical Economists: Differences in Analysis of the Current Crisis," in U.R.P.E., *Radical Perspectives on the Economic Crisis of Monopoly Capitalism* (U.R.P.E., 1975), pp. 138-142.

B. CYCLICAL DOWNTURNS

ERW-2, ch. 12, pp. 441-451.

Robert Heilbroner, *Beyond Boom and Crash* (Norton, 1978), chs. 2-4, pp. 18-37.

USCC, articles by Roger Alcaly ("An Introduction to Marxian Crisis Theory"), pp. 15-22, and Thomas Weisskopf ("Marxist Perspectives on Cyclical Crises"), pp. 241-260.

Raford Boddy and James Crotty, "Class Conflict and Macro-Policy: The Political Business Cycle", *Review of Radical Political Economics*, Vol. 7, No. 1, Spring 1975, pp. 1-19.

Howard Sherman, "Class Conflict and Macro-Policy," and Raford Boddy and James Crotty, "Wages, Prices and the Profit Squeeze," *Review of Radical Political Economics*, Vol. 8, No. 2, Summer 1976, pp. 55-67.

Thomas Weisskopf, "Marxian Crisis Theory and the Rate of Profit in the Postwar U.S. Economy," *Cambridge Journal of Economics*, Vol. 3, No. 4, December 1979.

C. INFLATION

ERW-2, ch. 12, pp. 451-455.

Robert Heilbroner, *Beyond Boom and Crash* (Norton, 1978), ch. 5, pp. 38-51.

Pat Devine, "Inflation and Marxist Theory," *Marxism Today*, Vol. 18, No. 3, March 1974, pp. 79-92.

John Goldthorpe, "The Current Inflation: Towards a Sociological Account," and Fred Hirsch, "The Ideological Underlay of Inflation," in Fred Hirsch and John Goldthorpe (eds.) *The Political Economy of Inflation* (Harvard University Press, 1978), pp. 186-214, 263-284.

R.E. Rowthorn, "Conflict, Inflation and Money," *Cambridge Journal of Economics*, Vol. 1, No. 3, September 1977, pp. 215-239.

D. THE ROLE OF THE STATE

ERW-2, ch. 6, pp. 217-225, 242-262.

Fred Block, "The Ruling Class Does Not Rule: Notes on the Marxist Theory of the State," *Socialist Revolution*, No. 33, May/June 1977, pp. 6-28.

Ian Gough, "State Expenditure in Advanced Capitalism," *New Left Review*, No. 92, July/August 1975, pp. 53-92.

Ian Gough, *The Political Economy of the Welfare State* (Humanities Press, 1979), especially chs. 4-7.

E. THE CURRENT CRISIS

Robert Heilbroner, *Beyond Boom and Crash* (Norton, 1978), chs. 1, 6-10, pp. 11-17, 52-89.

USCC, article by Arthur MacEwan ("The Development of the Crisis in the World Economy"), pp. 45-54 (excerpted in *ERW-2*, section 12.3, pp. 455-461).

James Crotty and Leonard Rapping, "The 1975 Report of the President's Council of Economic Advisers: A Radical Critique," *American Economic Review*, Vol. 65, No. 5, December 1975, pp. 791-811 (excerpted in *ERW-2*, section 12.4, pp. 461-469).

USCC, articles by Samuel Bowles ("The Trilateral Commission: Have Capitalism and Democracy Come to a Parting of Ways?"), pp. 261-265, and William Tabb ("Domestic Economic Policy Under Carter: The Imprint of Trilateralism"), pp. 265-275, and conclusion, pp. 331-342.

Samuel Bowles and Herbert Gintis, "The Crisis of Capital and the Crisis of Liberal Democracy: The Case of the United States," unpublished, University of Massachusetts at Amherst, October 1979.

IV. THE INTERNATIONAL CAPITALIST ECONOMY: IMPERIALISM

A. GENERAL INTRODUCTION

ERW-2, ch. 13, pp. 471-481, 492-499 (Hymer).

B.J. Cohen, *The Question of Imperialism* (Basic Books, 1974), chapters 1, 3.

S. Hymer, "The Multinational Corporation and the Law of Uneven Development," in J. Bhagwati (ed.), *Economics and World Order* (Macmillan, 1972).

M. Barratt-Brown, *The Economics of Imperialism* (Penguin, 1973).

R. Brenner, "The Origins of Capitalist Development: A Critique of Neo-Smithian Marxism," *New Left Review*, No. 104 (July/August 1977).

"Imperialism and the State," a special issue of *The Insurgent Sociologist*, Vol. 7, No. 2 (Spring 1977).

B. SOURCES OF IMPERIALISM IN THE CENTER

ERW-2, ch. 13, pp. 481-492 (MacEwan).

B.J. Cohen, *The Question of Imperialism* (Basic Books, 1974), chapters 2, 4, 7.

T.E. Weisskopf, "Theories of American Imperialism: A Critical Evaluation," *Review of Radical Political Economics*, Vol. 6, No. 3 (Fall 1974).

T. Kemp, "The Marxist Theory of Imperialism" and M. Barratt-Brown, "A Critique of Marxist Theories of Imperialism," in R. Owen and B. Sutcliffe, *Studies in the Theory of Imperialism* (Longman, 1974).

T. Moran, "Foreign Expansion as an 'Institutional Necessity' for Corporate Capitalism," *World Politics*, Vol. 25, No. 3 (April 1973).

C. IMPERIALISM AND UNDERDEVELOPMENT IN THE PERIPHERY

ERW-2, ch. 13, pp. 419-514 (Weisskopf).

P. Baran, "On the Political Economy of Backwardness," and A.G. Frank, "The Development of Underdevelopment," in R. Rhodes (ed.), *Imperialism and Underdevelopment* (Monthly Review, 1970).

B. Sutcliffe, "Imperialism and Industrialization in the Third World," in R. Owen and B. Sutcliffe (eds.), *Studies in the Theory of Imperialism* (Longman, 1974).

B. Warren, "Imperialism and Capitalist Industrialization," *New Left Review*, No. 81 (Sept./Oct. 1973), and critiques by P. McMichael *et al.* and A. Emmanuel in *New Left Review*, No. 85 (May/June 1974).

B.J. Cohen, *The Question of Imperialism* (Basic Books, 1974), chapters 5, 6.

P. Evans, *Dependent Development* (Princeton University Press, 1979), especially chapters 1, 6.

C. Wilber (ed.), *The Political Economy of Development and Underdevelopment* (Random House, 2nd edition, 1979), selected readings.

Economics I (P)

Political Economy Group
Department of Economics
University of Sydney, Australia
1981
Undergraduate

INTRODUCTION

This is a course in economics, emphasising different approaches to the subject, and the role of economics in the analysis of problems such as unemployment, inflation, inequality, and environmental deterioration. The P stands for Political Economy and denotes the orientaion of the course towards the study of actual economic systems and policy issues.

The Economics IP Course is designed as a general introduction to political economy, providing a basis for subsequent studies in economics, as well as a self-contained unit for students seeking a terminating course. Particular attention is paid to the role of economics in the analysis of current problems, and this is used as a vehicle for the introduction of such theory and technique as is demonstrably useful. The course is *not* mathematically oriented.

There will be three one-hour lectures per week and the course will be supported by seminars which will provide an opportunity for students to specialise in topics of their own choice. Additional tutorials will be provided for students who encounter difficulties with lectures or reading: these could be particularly useful for students who have not studied economics before.

WHY STUDY POLITICAL ECONOMY?

Whether we like it or not, economic issues are of great importance. As individuals we are all concerned with the material conditions of existence: securing an income, managing that income, and so on. At a more aggregated level, nations also face similar problems, since none has yet reached the utopian position in which material wants can all be satisfied. Economics concerns itself with the study of how these issues are confronted by individuals and by different types of society.

The conditions in the 1980's make some exposure to economic analysis even more imperative since many of the economic problems have intensified in recent years. The Australian economy and the global economy are in turmoil. Unemployment is high and rapid inflation is an ever-present threat. Answers that were acceptable in the seemingly prosperous days of the 1950's and 1960's are no longer appropriate.

However, Economics as a subject is itself in a state of crisis. A student coming to the subject for the first time will not find ready and simple answers to how our economic system functions. Instead, one finds a range of conflicting explanations of the operation and the problems of modern economies. Moreover, these varied explanations are typically linked with particular political positions.

Part of the reason for the crisis in the subject is the range of current economic problems. Another reason is that the subject has been increasingly dominated by a particular school of thought. An emphasis on formal model-building derived from the physical sciences has led this school into distorted answers to real problems and the emphasis on problems which are irrelevant or trivial—for example, that of the solitary Robinson Crusoe dividing his time between fishing and picking up coconuts.

The development of contemporary political economy is an attempt to cope with these dilemmas. It acknowledges the plurality of approaches to economics and the ideological foundations of these approaches. Moreover, it is committed to a realistic understanding of the complexity of modern economic systems and their historical development. As an essential part of such understanding, political economy recognises that political, social and economic aspects of the system cannot be treated separately but must ultimately be integrated.

SECTION I: AN OVERVIEW OF THE CURRENT ECONOMIC SITUATION

This opening section of the course seeks to sketch out some of the major problems of contemporary economic systems.

Lectures deal with an introduction to the study of political economy; Australia and the world economic crisis; multinational corporations and the third world; multinational corporations and the developed world; the changing balance of economic power between the third world and the developed world; the international trade and payments system; the role of the state in capitalist systems; neo-capitalism; socialist economic systems; the relationship between economic and ecological systems; and the political economy of "the arms race".

SECTION II: APPROACHES TO THE ANALYSIS OF THE CAPITALIST ECONOMIC SYSTEM.

Economics does not have a ready-made set of answers. There are substantial disagreements among economists on a whole range of matters. This part of the course considers the main traditions of thought on economics and their most important analytical techniques.

A. Introduction. The competing theories all purport to provide insights into the workings of the capitalist system. What is capitalism? What is the nature of economic theory? What are the most important paradigms in the history of economic thought? By providing a brief introduction to these issues these lectures lay a foundation for the subsequent consideration of the rival approaches to economic analysis.

B. Marxist economics. Marxist economics is a tradition of economic analysis which has its origins in the writings of Karl Marx. It has a distinctive methodology and theoretical structure and focusses on aspects of capitalist economies such as the social relations of production and the role of class-conflict in social and economic change. This short series of lectures provides a general introduction to Marxist economics. Lectures deal with the method of Marxism, the labour theory of value, surplus-value and exploitation; the accumulation process and the theory of crises; and analysis of the role of the state. Attention is paid to the application of Marxist analysis to current economic issues.

C. Neoclassical economics. This has been the dominant school of thought in economics since about 1870. It underwent a dramatic change after the 1930's depression as a result of the so-called Keynesian revolution which led to a distinction between microeconomics and macroeconomics being conventionally drawn. Although some economists claim that Keynes' contribution seriously undermined this approach, others such as Samuelson have proclaimed a "neoclassical synthesis" which purports to integrate Keynes' macroeconomic contribution within the neoclassical framework. This synthesis provides the subject matter of traditional courses in economics.

This set of lectures deals with microeconomics (macroeconomics being considered later in section 2(d)). Lectures deal with the historical origins of neoclassical economics; analysis of the market mechanism; forces behind supply and demand in price determination—consumer and producer behavior; forces behind supply and demand in wage determination; alternative market structures and their relative desirability; the properties of a market economy.

D. Keynesian economics. This provides the basis of conventional macroeconomic analysis and policy, though confidence in this approach has been badly shaken by the re-emergence of economic depression in the 1970's. Lectures deal with the general nature of Keynesian macroeconomics; income flow and basic national accounting quantities; an aggregate model of the economy; aggregate demand as the fundamental driving force; Keynesian theories of the determination of national income and of employment compared to previous ideas; the nature of money; post war macroeconomic policy; monetarism— the conservative counter-attack.

E. Institutional economics. This is a tradition of economic analysis which has its roots in the writings of Thorstein Veblen, and of which J.K. Galbraith and Gunnar Myrdal are the best known modern exponents. This short series of lectures deals with the focus of the institutionalists on ideas and value systems related to economic phenomena and on the institutions established to give expression to those ideas.

F. Competing approaches in economics: a reappraisal. An examination of the source of differences between the main schools of thought—philosophical and ideological. A brief comparison of the major emphasis of the alternative approaches—their advantages and limitations. The implications of these differences for the analysis of economic problems.

SECTION III: ANALYSIS OF CURRENT ECONOMIC PROBLEMS AND POLICIES

We are beset with a range of interconnected socio-economic problems: unemployment and inflation, structural problems associated with new technology and Australia's changing position in the international economy, inequality and poverty, imperialism and underdevelopment, and environmental degradation. The final section of the lecture programme considers a selection of these problems, drawing on the previously discussed bodies of theory. In each case the analysis will focus on the relative importance of market and extra-market forces, thus highlighting the importance of power relationships usually neglected in conventional economic analysis. Through this means, students are introduced to the contemporary political economist's approach to the analysis of economic problems and policy issues.

READING:

The text-books which are recommended for the course are:

E.K. Hunt and H.J. Sherman, *Economics: an Introduction to Traditional and Radical Views*, Harper and Row, 1972. (or any subsequent edition)

E.L. Wheelwright and Frank J.B. Stilwell, *Readings in Political Economy*, Volumes 1 and 2, Australia and New Zealand Book Co., 1976.

Hunt and Sherman's book is the nearest equivalent to a text-book for the course, though the examples are drawn largely from the American rather than the Australian economy. J. Robinson and J. Eatwell, *An Introduction to Modern Economics* is an alternative text but is not recommended to students with no previous study of economics. The two volumes of *Readings in Political Economy* were especially prepared by the staff teaching the Economics I (P) course at Sydney University and include a wide range of articles directly relevant to the course. (Incidentally, royalties from the sale of the *Readings* are donated to the Movement for Political Economy for the purpose of financing visiting speakers, conferences, a political economy newsletter, and similar enterprises of direct benefit to political economy students.)

All students are recommended to get in the habit of reading newspapers regularly (especially *Australian Financial Review*) taking note of government economic policy. This is extremely important for use in seminars during the year.

Students who have not studied economics before will find the following book useful preliminary reading: P. Donaldson, *Economics of the Real World*, Penguin Books, 1973.

The following notes are a guide to the best way of following the course in the text books. The headings refer to the different sections of the lecture programme. (The Chapter numbers in Hunt and Sherman refer to the third edition but students should note that the earlier editions of the book would be equally satisfactory for the course.)

SECTION I—MAJOR PROBLEMS OF CONTEMPORARY ECONOMIC SYSTEMS

Readings Vol. 1, Part One. Read as wide a range of articles from this section as you can find time for, so as to get a general idea of the nature and scope of political economy.

Hunt and Sherman, Part One. Less directly relevant to the material covered in lectures but provides a very useful historical perspective on economic analysis. Students intending to pursue their studies in economics beyond the first year level are advised to read this at some stage. Chapters 13, 22, 33, 34 and 35 touch more directly on matters dealt with in the opening lectures of the course. Also useful for this section of the course is R. Barnet & R. Mueller, *Global Reach*.

E.L. Wheelwright, *Capitalism, Socialism or Barbarism* contains chapters directly related to this section of the lecture programme.

SECTION II—APPROACHES TO THE ANALYSIS OF THE CAPITALIST ECONOMIC SYSTEM

A. INTRODUCTION

Readings Vol. 1, Chapter 48.

Additional reference:

D. Gordon, *Theories of Poverty and Underemployment*, Chapter 2. M. Dobb, *Studies in the Development of Capitalism*, Chapter 1 provides a more advanced treatment of the nature of the capitalist economy.

B. MARXIST ECONOMICS

Readings Vol. 1, Chapters 39-45.
Hunt and Sherman, chs. 6 and 16.
Additional references:

E. Mandel, *An Introduction to Marxist Economic Theory* is a useful short exposition of important fundamentals. So is Ben Fine *Marx's Capital* and P. Jalee, *How Capitalism Works*. P. Sweezy *The Theory of Capitalist Development* is a standard text for students seeking a fuller exposition.

C. NEOCLASSICAL ECONOMICS

Hunt and Sherman, Part Two, particularly chapters 14, 15, 18 & 19.
Readings, Vol. 1, chapters 24-27.
Alternative references:
There are literally dozens of standard texts which present the neoclassical approach to economic analysis. The most accessible are those by R. Dorfman, R. Leftwich, E. Mansfield, C. Tisdell, P. Samuelson, R. Lipsey, L. Reynolds and G. McConnell (the last four deal with macroeconomics as well as microeconomics). For a more critical approach see F.J.B. Stilwell, *Normative Economics: An Introduction to Microeconomics and Radical Critiques*.

D. KEYNESIAN ECONOMICS

Hunt and Sherman, Chapter 11 and Part Three, particularly chapters 22-30.
Readings, Vol. 1, chapters 24-27.
Additional reference:
M. Stewart, *Keynes and After*.

E. INSTITUTIONAL ECONOMICS

Readings, Vol. 1, chapters 28-38.
Additional references:

J.K. Galbraith, *The New Industrial State* or *Economics and the Public Purpose*. Either of these books can be recommended for students seeking a fuller elaboration of the views of this modern institutionalist. D. Ward, *Towards a Critical Political Economics* contains some discussion of Galbraithian and other views.

F. COMPETING APPROACHES IN ECONOMICS: A REAPPRAISAL

Readings, Vol. 1, chapters 46, 47 and 48.

SECTION III—ANALYSIS OF CURRENT ECONOMIC PROBLEMS AND POLICIES

Supplementary handouts will give further reading suggestions for this part of the course. Some of the sort of issues to be raised are as follows:

A. ENVIRONMENTAL DEGRADATION

Readings, Vol. 2, Chapters 20-24.
Hunt and Sherman, Chapter 33.

B. INFLATION AND UNEMPLOYMENT

Readings, Vol. 2, Chapters 5-10.
Hunt and Sherman, Chapters 28 and 31.

C. IMPERIALISM

Hunt and Sherman, Chapter 35.
P. Sweezy, *The Theory of Capitalist Development*, Chapter 17, or E. Mandel, *Marxist Economics*, Chapter 13.

D. INEQUALITY AND POVERTY

Readings, Vol. 2, Chapters 11-15 (plus Chapters 16-19 on the particular issue of discrimination as a source of inequality).
Hunt and Sherman, Chapters 15, 20 and 21.

E. STRUCTURAL CHANGE

J.G. Crawford, B. Inlgis, R.J. Hawke and N.S. Currie, *Report of the Study Group on Structural Adjustment*, Volume 1, March 1979, Parts 1 and 2.

The Economic Notes section of *Australian Left Review*, December 1979, March 1980 and June 1980.

It is hoped that all students will read a selection from this material. Lecturers and tutors will normally be happy to provide alternative or additional references on particular topics.

SEMINARS

Each student is expected to attend one seminar per week. These will begin in the second week.

Seminars can be used to serve a number of functions. They can be of a remedial nature, serving to sort out problems with lectures and reading. They can be used to develop themes briefly introduced in lectures. They can be used as general discussion groups. They can be used to deal with material completely separate from that considered in lectures. Different students may have different requirements and it is difficult to devise a system which caters for all needs. The seminar system proposed for Economics IP is an attempt to handle this situation by splitting the seminars into three parts as follows:

SEMINAR 1

Introductory Session. This first meeting provides an opportunity for students to meet each other and to talk with their tutor about their reasons for studying economics and about the nature and purpose of the seminar programme. Also, of course, students can raise any problems arising from the lectures to date.

SEMINAR 2

Ted Wheelwright's lectures have stressed that there is an economic crisis. This seminar is the first of three interconnected seminars in which we deal with this issue in more depth. This provides an opportunity for developing an understanding of the forces shaping the economic trends in the last three decades. We begin by examining the characteristics of the long boom of the 1950's and 1960's. The next seminar analyzes how this led to a generalized international downturn in the 1970's. Finally we assess how the Australian economy has been affected by the way in which corporations and governments have responded to the crisis.

Characteristics of the long boom

The period after the second world war was characterized by an unusually long period of sustained economic growth, high levels of employment and generally low rates of inflation in the advanced capitalist countries. What major factors were responsible for this long boom? (Students could consider such matters as war-linked technological developments; the international payments mechanism; the subduing of militant labour; the use of cheap resources from third-world countries, etc.)

References: K. Rowley, "The End of the Long Boom," *Intervention* No. 6, pp. 37-54; M. Brezniak & J. Collins, "The Australian Crisis: From Boom to Bust," *The Journal of Australian Political Economy*, No. 1, October 1977, pp. 8-16. A supplementary reference which deals particularly with international monetary arrangements is A. Gamble & P. Walton, *Capitalism in Crisis*, ch. 5, esp. pp. 148-158.

SEMINAR 3

World Economic Crisis. How do you identify an economic crisis/recession/slump? What are the characteristics of the present one? What are its causes? How do you assess the view that this is no ordinary recession but the "end of an era?"

References: E.L. Wheelwright, "The End of the Age of Growth," *The Journal of Australian Political Economy*, No. 1, October, 1977 (reprinted as ch. 2 in E.L. Wheelwright, *Capitalism, Socialism or Barbarism?*); K. Rowley, "The End of the Long Boom," *Intervention* No. 6, pp. 53-62. There are a number of possible supplementary references: see, for example, Wheelwright and Stilwell (eds) *Readings in Political Economy*. Volume 1, chapters 5-8 and 41. A historical perspective is provided by E. Hobsbawm, "Capitalist Crises in History," in R. Edwards, M. Reich and T. Weisskopf (eds) *The Capitalist System*, ch. 12-1.

SEMINAR 4

The Impact of the Current Economic Crisis on Australia

The Australian economy is experiencing a sustained depression which is reflected in high unemployment levels. To what extent is this the consequence of international forces (of the sort considered in the previous seminar)? To what extent does the Australian economy face special problems because of its position in relation to the new international division of labour? What has been the response of corporations and the government to the current economic crisis?

References: J. Alford, "Australian Labour, Multinationals and the Asia-Pacific Region," *The Journal of Australian Political Economy*, No. 6, November 1979, esp. pp. 1-11. This could be supplemented by M. Brezniak and J. Collins, "The Australian Crisis: from Boom to Bust," *J.A.P.E.* No. 1, October 1977, pp. 16-28. Additional references if necessary are K. Windshuttle, *Unemployment*, Chapter 1, and R. Catley and B. McFarlane, "An Australian Perspective on the New International Economic Order, *Australian Left Review*, No. 71, October 1979.

SEMINAR 5

This is the first of three seminars dealing with Marxist economics. Their general purpose is to clarify issues raised in the lectures on this topic, and to provide an opportunity for students to develop their understanding of this approach to economics.

Value and Exploitation. Work produces value. Part is returned to the workers as wages. Part is taken by the owners of capital and appears as profit, rent, interest, and so on. Marxist economists describe this as exploitation: one class (the owners of capital) exploits another (the workers). Profit is not due to the contribution of a particular factor of production but to the existence of certain social relations of production. This seminar is concerned with the theory of exploitation: this provides an opportunity to clarify basic concepts of Marxist economics: class, value, surplus value. An understanding of these concepts is fundamentally important for subsequent studies.

References: E. Mandel, *Introduction of Marxist Economics*, Section One; Ben Fine, *Marx's Capital*,

Chapters 3 and 4; or P. Jalee, *How Capitalism Works*, Chapters 3 and 4. A more advanced treatment is provided by P. Sweezy, *The Theory of Capitalist Development*, Ch. 4. Students interested in consulting Marx's original work are recommended to the pamphlet, *Wages, Price & Profit*. The labour theory of value is also discussed in Hunt and Sherman, *Economics*, Ch. 16.

SEMINAR 6

Capital accumulation. The accumulation of capital is the driving force in the capitalist system. The relentless search for surplus value leads capitalists to change the production process and the organization of work (e.g. through the introduction of new technology), to create new demands (e.g. through advertising) and to expand territorially across the globe (imperialism). Why is accumulation of capital so fundamentally important? What are the consequences of this accumulation? What are the impediments to continued accumulation?

References: B. Fine, *Marx's Capital*, Ch. 5; and P. Sweezy, *the Theory of Capitalist Development*, Chapter 5, provide a useful introduction to the issue of accumulation. These could be supplemented by Chapters 40 and 41 in Wheelwright & Stilwell, *Readings in Political Economy*, Vol. 1.

SEMINAR 7

Economic Crises. The hope of many economists has been that the capital accumulation process would inevitably lead to sustained economic growth. However, experience has shown that capitalist economies have not grown evenly, but have gone through cyclical patterns of boom and bust. This seminar is concerned with analysing this process. Why are economic crises a recurrent feature of capitalist system?

References: R. Alcaly, "The Relevance of Marxian Crisis Theory," in D. Mermelstein (ed.) *The Economic Crisis Reader* provides a useful survey. So too does Stuart Holland in the appendix to his book *The Socialist Challenge*. Other sources include B. Fine, *Marx's Capital*, ch. 8; P. Sweezy, *The Theory of Capitalist Development*, pp. 133-186; Ch. 41 in Wheelwright and Stilwell, *Readings in Political Economy*, Vol. 2, and P. Jalee, *How Capitalism Works*, Chapter 10.

SEMINAR 8

This is the first of four seminars which provide a back-up to the lectures on neoclassical economics. In each case the main objective is to put the theory into perspective by discussing its underlying assumptions and implications. Students should also take the opportunity to clarify any aspects of the lectures which they do not fully understand.

Consumers. Neoclassical economics assumes that consumers act in a rational self-interested manner and that their decisions collectively determine what is produced in a market economy. This assumption of "consumer sovereignty" has been challenged by institutional and Marxist economists. This seminar is concerned with exploring the competing arguments. How are consumers' tastes formed? In what sense, if any, are consumers' choices rational?

References: The first four articles in Wheelwright & Stilwell (eds.) *Readings in Political Economy*, Vol. 2, are the most obvious source for this topic. Galbraith's article raises the main issues in the critique of consumer sovereignty. Gintis' article is harder but worth making at least a start on because it shows the difference between the institutionalist approach to this issue and the Marxian view. Other sources include P. Donaldson, *Economics of the Real World*, Chap. 12 (fairly simple) and F. Green & P. Nore (eds.) *Economics: An Anti-text*, Chap. 4 (rather difficult). Students' personal experiences provide a useful input into this seminar.

SEMINAR 9

Firms. Neoclassical economics adopts a particular view of business behaviour. Firms are seen as responding to the demands of consumers. What they produce, how much they produce and the price they set for their products is determined by these demands and by the technological conditions which determine the costs of production. This seminar should consider the main features of the theory of the firm in neoclassical economics —in particular, the mechanics by which output and price are determined in a perfectly competitive firm. What impediments exist to applying this analysis to real-world firms concerned with long-run survival in conditions of uncertainty? (Note: this discussion links up with the more critical views considered in Seminar 15.)

References: On the theory of the firm see E.K. Hunt and H.J. Sherman, *Economics*, Chapter 19, particularly pp. 252-264, or the relevant section of any standard microeconomics text (see the list on page 6 of this handout), e.g. P. Samuelson, *Economics*, chapter 23A of the 2nd Australian edition (on the analysis of costs). On the behaviour of firms in the real world, see P. Baran & P. Sweezy, *Monopoly Capital*, Chapter 2, especially pp. 25-40 and 58-61, and/or Hunt and Sherman *Economics*, Ch. 18, pp. 238-248.

SEMINAR 10

Market Structures. Having spent the last two seminars looking at firms and consumers, we now put the two together by looking at the market situations in which firms interact in order to compete for consumers' demand. The neoclassical approach to this issue usually begins with perfect competition. This market structure has a central place in neoclassical analysis, because of its allegedly desirable properties: it is argued that the perfectly competitive market is impersonal, efficient, requires minimum government interference, and tolerates no monopoly profits in the long run. Other market structures (such as monopoly and oligopoly) are said to have less socially desirable characteristics.

This seminar is concerned with examining the allegedly desirable properties of perfectly competitive markets. Also there should be discussion of what meaning is attached to "efficiency" in this context, given that oligopolies are often said to be necessary in order to achieve economies of scale and rapid innovation.

References: P. Donaldson, *Economics of the Real World*, Ch. 13, provides a simple introduction to the issues. E. Jones, "Market Structure and the Firm in Economics," (article on closed reserve in Wolstenholme Library), pp. 1-10 is a useful reference. Supplementary sources are Hunt & Sherman *Economics*, Ch. 18, pp. 248-251 which discusses the social costs and benefits of monopoly power, and the last chapter in E. Mansfield, *Microeconomics*, which discusses some alleged advantages of oligopolistic market structures. Students seeking further references could consult R. Dorfman, *Prices and Markets*, ch. 6.

SEMINAR 11

Wages. This seminar is concerned with an examination and appraisal of the neoclassical approach to wage determination. The neoclassical theory of factor price determination centers upon the proposition that incomes of factors of production (labour, capital, land are treated similarly) are a price. Like any other price in a competitive market economy, factor incomes are thus determined by supply and demand. This general theory (known as the marginal productivity theory) is presented in various textbooks, e.g. Hunt & Sherman, *Economics*, Ch. 16, or P. Samuelson, *Economics*, ch. 26 and 29 in the second Australian edition.

In this seminar we are concerned with a more specific issue: the determination of wages between *different types of labour* (e.g. doctors, wharfies). Neoclassical theory sees the differentials as due to differences in supply and differences in demand (i.e. marginal productivity). Discuss the foundations and plausibility of this view. What about the difficulty of measuring productivity of certain types of labour, e.g., white-collar workers? What about other influences on wage differentials, e.g., the degree of bargaining power and how it is influenced by social conventions, restrictive practices, etc.

References: P. Samuelson, *Economics*, Ch. 28, pp. 631-4 and 641-9 in 2nd Australian edition. P. Donaldson, *Economics of the Real World*, Ch. 14, is a simple discussion of the principles of income distribution. In addition, students' personal experiences and observations on this topic are important.

SEMINAR 12

This is the first of three seminars which provide a back-up to the lectures on macroeconomics. They focus on policies of aggregate economic management and their underlying theory.

The Tendency to Macroeconomic Instability. Keynesian economics developed to explain the Great Depression of the 1930's, which could not be adequately explained with the existing theory. Keynes showed why there was no natural tendency for capitalism to generate full employment. What are the basic elements in this view of how capitalism works? Briefly consider the ideological role of this theory.

References: The simplest introduction to the issues (particularly suitable for students with no previous exposure to Keynesian economics) is P. Donaldson, *Economics of the Real World*, Chs. 2 and 3. Hunt and Sherman, *Economics*, chs. 11 and 24 and Wheelwright & Stilwell, *Readings in Political Economy*, Vol. 1, Ch. 25 are useful sources. A slightly more advanced but coherent treatment is provided by W. Barber, *A History of Economic Thought*, or see M. Stewart, *Keynes and After*, Ch. 4. Finally, on ideology see Wheelwright & Stilwell, *Readings in Political Economy*, Vol. 1, Ch. 24.

SEMINAR 13

Keynesian economic management. For many years, Keynesian econoics provided the rationale for government macroeconomic policy. What are the main instruments of conventional Keynesian monetary and fiscal policies? How have they been used? N.B. Where possible, these policies should be discussed with reference to examples drawn from recent Australian experience.

References: P. Donaldson, *Economics of the Real World*, Chapter 4 is a simple introduction to monetary and fiscal policy. See also Hunt and Sherman, *Economics*, Ch. 29 for a discussion of fiscal policy, and P. Samuelson, *Economics* (2nd Australian edition), Ch. 18, pp. 399-403 and 416-419; plus chs. 16B and 17 (for a discussion of monetary policy in the context of Australian institutions). *The Annual Report of the Reserve Bank of Australia* describes actual policies undertaken (copies will be placed on reserve in Wolstenholme Library). The article by Kalecki in Wheelwright & Stilwell *Readings in Political Economy*, Volume 2, Ch. 4, indicates some social and political limitations on macroeconomic management.

SEMINAR 14

The demise of Keynesianism and the rise of monetarism. The confidence in the view that governmental "fine tuning" of the aggregate economy could maintain full employment has now been shattered. Some economists have argued that, contrary to the views of Keynes, the government cannot or will not take remedial action because of the nature of the class interests which characterise capitalist societies. This left-wing response is based on the sort of crisis theory discussed in seminar 7. There has also been a significant right-wing response—and this is the topic of this seminar. The theories which Keynes criticized in the 1930's have recently been modified and developed by a group called "monetarists" of whom Milton Friedman is the best known member. This is an important development, both because Keynesian techniques have apparently failed, and because monetarists have been influential in the recent formulation of macroeconomic policy in countries like Chile, Great Britain, and Australia. Basically, Keynesians and monetarists differ over the mechanisms by which policy operates and hence the relative merits of fiscal policy and monetary policy for effective stabilisation. In summary, monetarists argue that discretionary fiscal policy is disruptive and that monetary policy should be limited to ensuring a slow and steady expansion of the money stock. This seminar is concerned with examining key points of the difference between these "liberal" and "conservative" approaches.

References: J.A. Trevithick, *Inflation*, Chs. 5 and 6. See also the article by Bruce MacFarlane in *Journal of Australian Political Economy*, No. 1, Oct. 1977. Regular public statements by the Reserve Bank and the Treasury, both sympathetic to monetarism, should be examined in this light.

SEMINAR 15

Institutional Economics. The lectures of institutional economics consider the origins of the institutional economic in the work of Veblen and its development through the modern writings of Galbraith. This seminar focuses on one recurrent theme of institutional economics: the changing power relationships assoicated with technological and institutional change within the modern corporation. Veblen stressed the growing importance of financial manipulators in business, as distinct from the productive engineers. Galbraith stresses the rise of the "technostructure" as the most powerful group in the contemporary economy. What is the technostructure? (Students are encouraged to give examples from firms of which they have some particular knowledge.) What is the significance of the alleged dominance of the technostructure (in terms of undermining consumer sovereignty? in terms of the goals and strategy of the modern corporation)?

References: J.K. Galbraith, *The New Industrial State*, esp. Chs. 5-8 is the principal reference, to be supplemented by Chapters 33-36 in Wheelwright & Stilwell (eds.) *Readings in Political Economy*, Volume 1; P. Baran & P. Sweezy *Monopoly Capital*, Ch. 2, provides a different view; D. Ward, *Towards a Critical Political Economics*, pp. 175-185 and 225-233 is another possible reference on comparing Galbraithian and other views. Where possible, students are encouraged to prepare for this seminar by digging out information on the organization and power structure of actual firms.

SEMINAR 16

Why can't economists agree? This seminar is an opportunity for an interim summing up. We have studied neoclassical orthodoxy and the contrasting analysis of the institutional and Marxian economists. What are the methodological and ideological bases for disagreements between these competing schools of economic thought?

References: Wheelwright & Stilwell (eds) *Readings in Political Economy*, Vol. 1, Chapters 46-8. Joan Robinson's article, which appears as Chapter 24 in the same volume, provides an illustration of competing paradigms. David Gordon, *Theories of Poverty and Unemployment* is a supplementary reference, containing a general discussion of competing frameworks (Chapter 2) and a summary of the Marxian approach. Reading number 31 in *Reading in Political Economy*, Vol. 1, discusses principal characteristics of institutionalism.

SEMINAR 17

Specialist seminars: introductory discussion. This final seminar in second term is an introduction to the specialist streams which occupy the third term. The group should discuss the objectives and structure of the seminar programme and make arrangements concerning which student is to introduce discussion on which topic, etc. *This is important:* the specialist seminar streams must get off to a quick and efficient start in the third term if they are to deal at all adequately with the issues.

Note: Throughout the seminar programme, students are encouraged to bring to the class any extracts from newspapers and so on, which show the relevance of economic analysis to matters currently in the news. These can be circulated in the class together with any accompanying notes and used as a basis for discussion.

MARXISM AND METHODOLOGY

Seminar in Economic Thought: Methodology

Jon D. Wisman
American University
Economics
Spring 1980

Reading List: *Means optional for the course but required for comprehensive.

I. INTRODUCTION

T.W. Hutchison, *Knowledge and Ignorance in Economics* (Chicago: Univ. of Chicago Press, 1977), Chapt. 1.

K.N. Prasad, "Economics As It Is Today" *Economic Affairs,* 20 (II), (Nov. 1975), pp. 451-460.

L. Boland, "Methodology as an Exercise in Economic Analysis," *Philosophy of Science,* 38 (March 1971), pp. 105-117.

Howard Sherman, "The Sad State of Orthodox Economics", *Journal of Economic Issues,* IX, 2 (June 1975), pp. 243-250.

Ralph W. Pfouts, "Some Proposals for a New Methodology for Economics", *Atlantic Economic Journal,* 1, 1 (Nov. 1973), pp. 13-22.

II. ISSUES IN THE PHILOSOPHY OF SCIENCE

A. THOMAS KUHN'S CONCEPT OF SCIENTIFIC REVOLUTIONS

Hutchison, chs. 2, 3.

Mark Blaug, "Kuhn versus Lakatos, or Paradigms versus Research Programmes in the History of Economics, "*History of Political Economy,* 7, 4, (Winter 1975), 399-433.

Stephen T. Worland, "Radical Political Economy as a 'Scientific Revolution' *Southern Economic Journal,* 39 (October 1972), pp. 274-284.

M.D. King, "Reason, Tradition, and the Progressiveness of Science", *History and Theory,* vol. 10, no. 1 (1970), pp. 1-32.

Joseph V. Remenyi, "Core dem-core interaction: toward a general theory of disciplinary and subdisciplinary growth", *History of Political Economy,* 11, 1, (Spring 1979), pp. 30-63.

*Ward, *What's Wrong With Economics?,* ch. 1-3, pp. 3-54.

*Thomas S. Kuhn, "Reflections on my Critics" in Imre Lakatos and Alan Musgrave (eds.), *Criticism and The Growth of Knowledge* (London: Cambridge University Press, 1970), pp. 231-278.

*Hyman R. Cohen, "Dialectics, and Scientific Revolutions," *Science and Society,* vol. XXXVII, no. 3 (Fall, 1973), pp. 326-336.

*Siegfried G. Karsten, "Dialectics and the Evolution of Economic Thought", *History of Political Economy,* vol. 5, no. 2 (Fall, 1973, pp. 399-419).

*A.W. Coats, "Is There a 'Structure of Scientific Revolutions' in Economic Thought?", *Kyklos,* vol. 22 (1969), pp. 289-294.

*Martin Bronfenbreaner, "The Structure of Revolutions in Economic Thought" *History of Political Economy,* vol, 3, no. 1 (Spring 1971), pp. 136-151.

*Thomas S. Kuhn, *The Structure of Scientific Revolution,* 2nd (ed.) (Chicago: University of Chicago Press, 1970).

B. VERIFICATION AND THE NATURE OF THEORIES

1. Formal Theories

Hutchison, chs. 4, 5.

Paul Diesing, *Patterns of Discovery in the Social Sciences,* ch. 1 and Part I, pp. 1-133.

Ben Ward, *What's Wrong With Economics,* ch. 10-11, pp. 143-177.

Fritz Machlup, "Operationalism and Pure Theory in Economics," in Sherman Roy Krupp, *The Structure of Economic Science,* pp. 53-67.

Lawrence A. Boland, "Conventionalism and Economic Theory" *Philosophy of Science,* 37 (June 1970), 239-248.

2. Participant Observation, Pattern Models and Ideal Types

Paul Diesling, *Patterns of Discovery in the Social Sciences,* Part II, pp. 137-288.

Ben Ward, *What's Wrong with Economics,* ch. 12.

Max Weber, "Ideal Types and Theory Construction", in *Brodbeck* pp. 496-507.

C. EXPLANATION

1. Introduction

McClelland, *Causal Explanation and Model Building*, Introduction and ch. 1, pp. 15-64.

2. Deductive Nomological Explanation and its critics

Carl G. Hempel and Paul Oppenheim, "The Covering Law Analysis of Scientific Explanation," in Krimerman, pp. 54-68; in *Feigl and Brodbeck*, pp. 319-362: in *Brody*, pp. 8-27.

John G. Gunnell, "Deduction, Explanation, and Social Scientific Inquiry, *American Political Science Review*, vol. LXIII, no. 4 (December 1969), pp. 1233-46 (Responses and a counter-response are optional, pp. 1347-62.)

Paul K. Feyerabend, "How to be a Good Empiricist—a Plea for Tolerance in Matters Epistemological," in *Brody*, pp. 8-27.

Karl Popper, "The Hypothetic-Deductive Methods and the Unity of Social and Natural Science," in *Krimerman*, pp. 47-53, and in *Braybrooke*, pp. 32-41.

Roy Bhaskar, "Feyerabend and Bachelard: Two Philosophies of Science," *New Left Review*, 94 (Nov.-Dec. 1975) 31-55.

3. Explanation in History

McClelland, *Causal Explanation and Model Building*, ch. 2 pp. 65-109.

Gareth Stedman Jones, "History: The Poverty of Empiricism" in Robin Blackburn (ed.), *Ideology in Social Science* (New York: Vintage Books, 1973), pp. 96-115.

*William Dray, *Laws and Explanation in History*, ch. 1-4 pp. 1-117.

4. Teleological (Functional) Explanation

Robert A. Solo, "What is Structuralism? Piaget's Genetic Epistemology and the Varieties of Structuralist Thought", *Journal of Economic Issues*, IX, 4 (December 1975), pp. 605-25.

W.G. Runciman, "What is Structuralism?", *British Journal of Sociology*, XX (1969), pp. 253-65; also in *Ryan*, pp. 189-202.

*Carl G. Hempel, "The Logic of Functional Analysis", in *Brodbeck*, pp. 179-210; in *Brody*, pp. 121-147; in *Aspects of Scientific Explanation*, pp. 297-330.

D. Explanation and Human Action

B.F. Skinner, "Is a Science of Human Behavior Possible?', in his *Science and Human Behavior*, (New York: The Macmillan Co., 1953), pp. 14-22; also in *Braybrooke*, pp. 19-26.

B.F. Skinner, "The Scheme of Behavior Explanations", in Braybrooke, pp. 42-52.

Paul Diesng, *Patterns of Discovery in the Social Sciences*, Part III, pp. 291-323.

Ben Ward, *What's Wrong With Economics?* ch. 7-9, pp. 95-139.

*Richard Bernstein, *Praxis and Action*, Part IV, pp. 230-304.

III. THEORIES AND CRITIQUES

A. Orthodox Economics

1. Introduction

McClelland, *Causal Explanation and Model Building*, ch. III pp. 105-45.

Sherman Roy Krupp, "Type of Controversy in Economics" in *Krupp*, pp. 39-52.

Martin Bronfenbrenner, "A 'Middlebrow' Introduction to Economic Methodology", in *Krupp*, pp. 5-29.

Robert A. Solo, "Neoclassical Economics in Perspective" *Journal of Economic Issues*, IX, 4 (December 1975), pp. 627-44.

2. The Role of Assumptions and Prediction in Economics

Milton Friedman, "The Methodology of Positive Economics" in *Essays in Positive Economics*. Also in May Brodbeck (ed) *Readings in The Philosophy of the Social Sciences*, pp. 508-528.

A. Coddington, "Positive Economics" *The Canadian Journal of Economy*, vol. V. No. 1, (Feb. 1972), pp. 1-15.

M.A. Karouzian, "Scientific Method and Positive Economics," Scottish Journal of Political Economy, XXI, 3 (Nov. 1974) pp. 279-87.

Diesing, pp. 299-303.

Robert Heilbroner, "On the Limits of Economic Prediction," *Diogenes* (April 1970). Reprinted in *Between Capitalism and Socialism*, Ch. 10.

*Charles K. Wilber and Jon D. Wisman, "The Chicago School: Positivism or Ideal Type," *Journal of Economic Issues*, IX, 4 (Dec. 1975), pp. 665-79; also in Warren J. Samuels (ed.), *The Chicago School of Political Economy* (East Lansing, Michigan, 1976).

*Jon D. Wisman, "The Naturalistic Turn of Orthodox Economics: A Study in Methodological Misunderstanding", *Review of Social Economy*, 36 (December 1978) 263-84 (Xerox on Reserve.)

*Stanley Wong, "The 'F-Twist' and the Methodology of Paul Samuelson" *American Economic Review*, vol. LXIII, no. 3, (June 1973), pp. 312-325.

3. Praxeology or Extreme Rationalism

Murray N. Rothbard, "In Defense of Extreme Apriorism" *Southern Economic Journal*, XXIII, (Jan. 1957), pp. 314-320.

Ludwig M. Lachmann, "From Mises to Shackle: An Essay on Austrian Economics and the Kaleidic Society", *Journal of Economic Literature*, XIV, 1 (March 1976), pp. 54-62.

Stephen Rosefielde, "Operational Economic Theory in the Excluded Middle Between Positivism and Rationalism," *Atlantic Economic Journal*, IV, 2 (Spring, 1976), pp. 1-8.

R.A. Gonce, "Natural Law and Ludwig von Mises' Praxeology and Economic Science" *Southern Economic Journal*, 39, 4, (April 1973), 490-507.

4. The "New" Economic History

McClelland, *Causal Explanation and Model Building*, ch. V. pp. 169-243.

J.D. Gould, "Hypothetical History," *Economic History Review*, XXII, (August, 1969), pp. 195-207.

B. INSTITUTIONALISM AND DARWINIAN CONCEPTIONS OF ECONOMIC SCIENCE

Earnest Nagel, "Mechanistic Explanation and Organismic Biology" in *Brody*, pp. 296-306.

Lawrence Nabbers, "The Positive and Genetic Approaches," in *Krupp*, pp. 68-82.

Charles K. Wilber with Robert S. Harrison, "The Methodological Basis of Institutional Economics: Pattern Model, Storytelling and Holism" *Journal of Economic Issues*, XII, 1 (March 1978).

C. MARXIAN ECONOMICS

1. Introduction

Anderson, *All*.

Donald Clark Hodges, "The Method of *Capital*" *Science and Society*, 31, 4 (1967) pp. 505-514.

David Goldway, "Appearance and Reality in Marx's *Capital*" *Science and Society* 31, 4 (1967) pp. 428-447.

Lucio Colletti, "Marxism and the Dialectic" *New Left Review*, 93 (Sept.-Oct. 1975) pp. 3-29.

*Jon D. Wisman, "Rereading Marx for the Non-Marxist Economist: On the Scope and Method of Scientific Economics", *Review of Social Economy*, 37 (Dec. 1979) (Xerox on Reserve).

2. The French "Structuralist" School

Louis Althusser, *For Marx*, (All).

Norman Geras, "Althusser's Marxism: An Assessment" *New Left Review* no. 71 (Jan-Feb. 1972); also in *Western Marxism*, pp. 232-272.

John O'Neill, "For Marx Against Althusser" in J.W. Freiberg (ed), *Critical Sociology: European Perspectives* (N.Y.: Wiley & Sons, 1979), 121-39.

Stephen Resnick and Richard Wolff, "The Theory of Transitional Conjunctions and The Transition from Feudalism to Capitalism in Western Europe", *Review of Radical Political Economics*, 11 (Fall 1979), 3-22. Also, Reply to Herb Gintis", *Ibid*. 32-36.

Herbert Gintis, "On the Theory of Transitional Conjunctions" *Ibid*, 23-31.

*Maurice Godelier, *Rationality and Irrationality in Economics* (All).

3. Heterodox Marxism: Lukaes, Gransci, Sartre, and Habermas

Gareth Stedman Jones, "The Marxism of the Early Lukacs," *New Left Review*, No. 70 (November-Dec. 1971) also in *Western Marxism*, pp. 11-60.

John Merrington, "Theory and Practice in Gramsci's Marxism" *The Socialist Register* (1968); also in *Western Marxism*, pp. 140-175.

Ronald Aronson, "The Social Theory of Jean-Paul Sartre" *Telos*, No. 16 (Summer 1973) also in *Western Marxism*, pp. 201-231.

Anthony Giddens, "Habermas' Critique of Hermenentics", in Freiberg (ed.), *Critical Sociology*, pp. 39-70.

Trent Schroyer, "The Dialectical Foundations of Critical Theory: Jurgen Habermas' Metatheoretical Investigations", *Telos*, no. 12 (Summer 1972), 93-114.

Goran Therborn, "The Frankfurt School", *New Left Review*, No. 63 (Sept.-Oct. 1970), and No. 67 (May-June 1971), also in *Western Marxism*, pp. 83-139.

*Lucio Colletti, "A Political and Philosophical Interview" *New Left Review*, no. 86 (July-Aug. 1974); also in *Western Marxism*, 315-50.

*Richard J. Bernstein, *The Restructuring of Social and Political Theory*, Part IV, pp. 171-236.

4. "Neo-Ricardianism"

Michael A. Lebowitz, "The Current Crisis of Economic Theory" *Science and Society*, 1974, 385-403.

Bob Rowthorn, "New Classicism, Neo-Ricardianism and Marxism," *New Left Review*, 86 (July-Aug. 1974) pp. 63-87.

Frank Roosevelt, "Cambridge Economics as Commodity Fetishism" *Review of Radical Political Economics*, vol. 7, no. 4 (Winter 1975), pp. 1-32.

IV. ECONOMICS AND OBJECTIVITY

A. VALUES AND IDEOLOGY

Ward, *What's Wrong With Economics?*, ch. 13-16, pp. 193-246.

D.K. Foley, "Problems versus Conflicts: Economic Theory and Ideology", *American Economic Review*, 65, 2 (May 1975) pp. 231-236.

*Denis Goulet, "An Ethical Model for the Study of Values," *Harvard Educational Review*, 41, 2 (May 1971) pp. 205-227.

*Jon D. Wisman, "Toward a Humanist Reconstruction of Economic Science" *Journal of Economic Issues* 13 (March 1979) 19-48.

B. ECONOMIC SCIENCE, LEGITIMATION, AND SOCIAL CONTROL

Joseph Ben-David, "Innovations and Their Recognition in Social Science" *History of Political Economy*, 7, 4 (Winter 1975) pp. 434-455.

Stephen Rousseas, "Paradigm Polishing Versus Critical Thought in Economics," *The American Economist*, vol. XVII, no. 2 (Fall, 1973), pp. 72-78.

*Jon D. Wisman, "Legitimation, Ideology-Critique, and Economics" *Social Research* 46 (Summer 1979) 291-320.

*Peter Berger and Thomas Luckman, *The Social Construction of Reality*.

V. APPEALING TO FREUD

Michael Maccoby, "'Winning' and 'Losing' in Work," *Spectrum (July 1973), pp. 39-48.*

Robert L. Heilbroner, "Marxism, Psychoanalysis, and The Problem of a Unified Theory of Behavior," *Social Research*, 42, 3 (Autumn 1975), pp. 414-432.

H. Jacoby, "Negative Psychoanalysis and Marxism, Toward an Objective Theory of Subjectivity," *Telos*, 14 (Winter 1972).

*Erich Fromm and Michael Maccoby, *Social Character in a Mexican Village.*

*Norman O. Brown, *Life Against Death*, Part V.

*Erick H. Erickson, *Childhood and Society*, ch. 3, 4.

Advanced Political Economy

Anwar Shaikh
Graduate Faculty, New School for
Social Research
Economics
Fall 1980/Spring 1981

Only starred readings on this list are optional. Editions of Marx's work referred to are: *Capital*, Vol. I-III, International Publishers, 1967; *Grundrisse*, Penguin, 1973; *Theories of Surplus Value (TSV)*, Progress Publishers.

I. REVIEWS

1. THE SCOPE OF MARX'S WORK IN ECONOMICS

R. Rosdolsky, *The Making of Marx's 'Capital,'* Pluto Press, London, 1977, Part One, Chs. I-V (on reserve).

Correspondence: Marx-Engels, Jan. 11, 1858 (not available in English); Marx-Engels, May 31, 1873 (not available in English).

D. Struik, "Marx and Mathematics," *Science & Society*, Vol. 12, 1948, pp. 181-96.

2. ISSUES OF METHOD

i. Historical Materialism

"Preface" to *A Contribution to the Critique of Political Economy*, International Publishers, N.Y. 1972, pp. 19-23.

Marx-Engels Selected Correspondence, Progress Publishers, Moscow, 1975 (Third Edition): Marx to Annenkov, Dec. 28, 1846.

Introduction to the *Grundrisse*, Sections 1-2 (This also appears as an appendix to *A Contribution—*, op. cit., pp. 205-214).

ii. On Method

Marx's Prefaces and Afterword to *Capital*, Vol. I.

Correspondence: Marx-Engels, Feb. 1, 1858; Marx-Kugelmann, March 6, 1868; Marx-Kugelmann, July 11, 1868; Marx-Engels, Oct. 10, 1868.

Introduction to *Grundrisse*, op. cit., Section 3: "The Method of Political Economy."

*L. Althusser, *Lenin and Philosophy*, Monthly Review Press, N.Y. 1971: "Lenin and Philosophy," Section 3, pp. 34-46; "Lenin and Hegel," pp. 107-125.

*L. Colletti, *From Rousseau to Lenin*, Monthly Review Press, N.Y. 1972: Ch. 3, "From Hegel to Marcuse."

3. MARX ON *CAPITAL*, VOLS. I—III

i. General

Correspondence, op. cit., Marx-Engels, April 2, 1858.

ii. Volume I

Ibid., Marx-Engels, Aug. 24, 1867; Marx-Engels, Jan. 8, 1868.

iii. Vols. II-III

Ibid., Marx-Engels, April 30, 1868.

iv. Some Connections in the Structure of the Argument in *Capital*

(Handout to be discussed in class.)

II. CONTRADICTIONS IN THE COMMODITY FORM: VALUE, MONEY

1. VALUE AND FORM-OF-VALUE

Capital, Vol. I, Ch. I.

First Edition of *Capital*, Vol. I: Ch. I and Appendix ("Forms of Value"), available as pamphlets from Labor Publications, U.S., 1972.

Marx, "Marginal Notes on Wagner" (on reserve).

2. MONEY AS DETERMINED BY THE CIRCULATION OF COMMODITIES

Capital, Vol. I, Chs. II-III.
A Contribution..., op. cit., Ch. II.
S. de Brunhoff, *Marx on Money*.

III. CONTRADICTIONS IN THE PRODUCTION OF CAPITAL

1. MONEY AS CAPITAL, LABOR-POWER AS COMMODITY

Capital, Vol. I, Chs. IV-VI.
Capital, Vol. I, Chs. XIX-XXI.

2. SURPLUS VALUE

Capital, Vol. I: Ch. VII (Labor Process and the Process of Producing Surplus Value).
Vol. I: Ch. XIV, XV: Sections 1-5 (The Capitalist Character of "Technical Change").
H. Braverman, *Labor and Monopoly Capital*, Monthly Review Press, N.Y., 1974.

3. ACCUMULATION OF CAPITAL

Capital, Vol. I, Ch. XXV (The General Law of Capitalist Accumulation).

4. RESULTS OF THE IMMEDIATE PROCESS OF PRODUCTION: APPENDIX IN THE PENGUIN EDITION OF *CAPITAL* I, INTRODUCED BY ERNEST MANDEL, PENGUIN BOOKS, 1976.

IV. CONTRADICTIONS IN THE CIRCULATION OF CAPITAL (DETERMINATIONS OF FORM WHICH SPRINGS FROM THE CIRCULATION OF CAPITAL)

1. CIRCUITS OF CAPITAL

Capital, Vol. II, Chs. I-IV.

2. TURNOVER OF CAPITAL (FURTHER DETERMINATIONS OF THE FORM OF CAPITAL-VALUE)

Capital, Vol. II, Chs. VII-IX, XII-XIV (Turnover, Fixed and Circulating Capital, Determinants of Time of Turnover).
Vol. II, Chs. XV-XVII (Effects of Turnover on the self-expansion of capital).

V. AGGREGATE CAPITAL AND SOCIAL REPRODUCTION

1. INTRODUCTION:

Capital, Vol. II, Chs. XVII-XIX and Retrospective.

2. SIMPLE REPRODUCTION:

Capital, Vol. II, Ch. XX.

3. EXTENDED REPRODUCTION:

Capital, Vol. II, Ch. XXI.

4. MODERN DISCUSSIONS

E. Mandel, *Late Capitalism*, New Left Books, 1975, Ch. I.
P. Sweezy, *The Theory of Capitalist Development*, Monthly Review Press, 1942: Chs. X-XI.
*A. Brody, *Proportions, Prices & Planning*, North-Holland, 1970; Ch. 1.1-1.2.

VI. THE TRANSFORMATION OF THE FORM-OF-VALUE (FORMATION OF A GENERAL RATE OF PROFIT)

1. GENERAL OUTLINE

Correspondence, op. cit., Marx-Engels, April 30, 1868; Marx-Kugelmann, July 11, 1868.

2. FORMATION OF THE GENERAL RATE OF PROFIT

Capital, Vol. III, Part II, Chs. VIII-IX.

3. MODERN DISCUSSIONS

i. The Traditional Presentation

P. Sweezy, op. cit., Ch. VII.
L. von Bortkiewics, "Value and Price in the Marxian System," *International Economic Papers*, No. 2, 1952.

ii. The Sraffa-von Neumann Tradition

I. Steedman, "Marx after Sraffa," New Left Books 1977, Ch. 2.
M. Morishima, *Marx's Economics: A Dual Theory of Value and Growth*, Cambridge, 1973: Ch. 4-5.
*P. Sraffa, *Production of Commodities by Means of Commodities*, Cambridge, 1963: Preface, Ch. I-IV, VI.
*F. Seton, "The Transformation Problem," *Review of Economic Studies*, Vol. 24, 1957.
*P. Samuelson, "Understanding the Marxian Notion of Exploitation: A Summary of the So-called Transformation Problem between Marxian Values and Competitive Prices," *Journal of Economic Literature*, June 1971.
*W. Baumol, "The Transformation of Values: What Marx 'Really Meant' (An Interpretation)," Journal of Economic Literature, March 1974.

iii. Modern Marxist Responses

L. Colletti, "Some Comments on Marx's Theory of Value" in *The Subtle Anatomy of Capitalism*, edited by Jesse Schwartz, Goodyear Publishing Co., California, 1977.
A. Shaikh, "Marx's Theory of Value and the Transformation Problem," in Schwartz, op. cit.
A. Medio, "Profits and Surplus Value: Appearance and Reality in Capitalist Production," in E.K. Hunt/J. G. Schwartz, *A Critique of Economic Theory*, Penguin Books, 1972.
A. Shaikh, "The Transformation from Marx to Sraffa," unpublished, on reserve.
*N. Okishio, "A Mathematical Note on Marxian Theorems," *Weltwirtschaftliches Archiv*, Vol. 91, 1963.

I. THE STRUCTURE OF MARXIST CRISIS THEORIES

Erik Olin-Wright, "Alternative Perspectives in the Marxist Theory of Accumulation and Crisis," in *The Subtle Anatomy of Capitalism*, (ed.) Jesse Schwartz, Goodyear Publishing Co., Santa Monica, California, 1977.

A. Shaikh, "An Introduction to the History of Crisis Theories," in *U.S. Capitalism in Crisis*, Union for Radical Political Economics, N.Y., 1978.

T. Weisskopf, "Marxist Perspectives on Cyclical Crises," in *U.S. Capitalism in Crisis*, op. cit.

II. THE FALLING RATE OF PROFIT

1. PROFIT AND RATE OF PROFIT

Marx-Engels Selected Correspondence, Progress Publishers, N.Y. (Third Revised Edition) 1975: Marx to Engels, April 30, 1868.

Capital, Vol. III, Chs. I-IV.

2. THE LAW OF THE RATE OF PROFIT

"The Law as Such," *Capital*, Vol. III, Ch. XIII.

"Expositions of the Internal Contradictions of the Law," op. cit., Ch. XV.

"The Most Important Law of Political Economy": *Grundrisse*, pp. 747-778.

Not Due to a Constantly Rising Wage (Value of Labor-Power), *Theories of Surplus Value*, Part II, Ch. XVI, Section 3, pp. 438-469.

Tendential Character of the Law: "Counteracting Influences," *Capital*, Vol. III, Ch. XIV.

3. DISCUSSION AND CRITICISM OF THE LAW

P. Sweezy, op. cit., Ch. VI.

M. Dobb, "The Falling Rate of Profit," *Science and Society*, 23(2) Summer 1959, pp. 97-103.

J. Robinson, "The Falling Rate of Profit," reprinted in *Economics and Ideology*, London, Chapman and Hall, 1967, pp. 120-130.

N. Okishio, "Technical Change and the Rate of Profit," Kobe University *Economic Review*, 1961, pp. 85-99.

N. Okishio, "A Formal Proof of Marx's Two Theorems," Kobe University *Economic Review*, 18 (1972), pp. 1-6.

A. Shaikh, "Political Economy and Capitalism: Notes on Dobb's Theory of Crisis," *Cambridge Journal*, June 1976, pp. 233-251.

M. Cogoy, "The Fall in the Rate of Profit and the Rate of Accumulation—A Reply to Paul Sweezy," *Bulletin of the Conference of Socialist Economists* (BCSE), Winter 1973, pp. 52-65.

Himmelweit, "The Continuing Saga of the Falling Rate of Profit—A Reply to Mario Cogoy," *BCSE* (9) Autumn 1974, pp. H 1-6.

P. Armstrong, "Accumulation of Capital, the Rate of Profit and Crisis," *BCSE IV 2(11)*, June 1975.

Geoff Hodgson, "The Theory of the Falling Rate of Profit," *New Left Review*, #84, March-April 1974.

III. CONCRETIZING INDIVIDUAL VALUE AND SOCIAL VALUE

1. THE TWO SENSES TO SOCIALLY NECESSARY LABOR-TIME

As the Average Amount of Abstract Labor-Time Required per Unit Output of a Given Commodity, Marx, *Capital*, Vol. I: Ch. I, Section 1, pp. 38-39; Ch. VII, Section 2, pp. 188-190.

As the Total Amount of Abstract Labor-Time Required in a Given Branch of Production, Marx, *Capital*, Vol. III: Ch. XXXVII, pp. 633 (last sentence)-636.

2. DIFFERENTIAL PROFITS

Competition Does Not Equalize Rates of Profit Within an Industry: Marx, *Capital*, Vol. III, Ch. X, pp. 180 (beginning with "For Commodities...")-195 (end with "...producers as such.")

Competition Forces a Lowering of Costs: A. Shaikh, "Political Economy and Capitalism: Notes on Dobb's Theory of Crisis," *Cambridge Journal of Economics*, March 1978: Section 4.

3. RENT

The Problem Stated

Marx-Engels Selected Correspondence: Marx to Engels, Jan. 7, 1851; June 18, 1862; August 2, 1862; Aug. 9, 1862.

Marx, *Capital*, Vol. III, Ch. XXXVII and XLVII.

Differential Rent

Ibid., Ch. XXXVII-XL.

Absolute Rent

Ibid., Ch. XLV.

Discussions

R. Murray, "Value and Theory of Rent: Part I," *Capital and Class*, Autumn 1977.

E. Mandel, *Marxists Economic Theory*, Monthly Review Press, 1968, Ch. 9.

National and International Values

A. Emmanuel, *Unequal Exchange*, Monthly Review Press, 1972, Ch. 2.

S. Amin, *End of a Debate*, U.N. African Institute for Economic Development & Planning, Dakar, Senegal, 1973.

A. Shaikh, "Foreign Trade and the Law of Value: Part II," *Science and Society*, Spring 1980, pp. 47-57.

IV. CONCRETIZING PRICES OF PRODUCTION

1. EQUALIZATION OF THE RATE OF PROFIT

General Outline: *Marx-Engels Correspondence*, Marx to Engels, April 30, 1868; Marx to Kugelmann, July 11, 1868.

Competition and the Equalization of the General Rate of Profit

Marx, *Capital*, Vol. III, Ch. X-XII.

2. COMMERCIAL CAPITAL AND PRICES OF PRODUCTION

Ibid., Ch. XVI-XVII.

3. COMPETITION AND MONOPOLY IN MARX

Illusions Created by Competition
Ibid., Ch. XVIII and Ch. L.

Production Relations and Distribution Relations
Ibid., Ch. LI, Ch. XLVIII-XLIX.

Competition and Monopoly

Marx-Engels Correspondence, Marx to Annekov, Dec. 28, 1846.

Marx, *Poverty of Philosophy*, Intl. Publishers, 1971, Ch. II, Section 3.

Marx, *Wage Labour and Capital* (any edition). This was written in 1847, and the section on competition is of particular interest.

Marx, *Wages, Prices and Profits* (any edition). This was written in 1865, two years before Vol. I of *Capital* was published. It is a summary of the major themes in *Capital*, Vols. I-III.

R. Rosdolsky, *The Making of Marx's Capital*, op. cit., Ch. IV, Sect. B.2.

4. MARXIST WRITERS ON MONOPOLY AND THE LAW OF VALUE

M. Dobb, *Political Economy and Capitalism*, Routledge & Kagan Paul, London, 1937, pp. 68-78.

P. Sweezy, *Theory of Capitalist Development*, Monthly Review Press, 1942, Ch. XIV-XV.

Baran & Sweezy, *Monopoly Capital*, Monthly Review Press, 1966, Ch. 1-3.

E. Mandel, *Marxist Economic Theory*, op. cit., Ch. 12.

M. Kalecki, *Theory of Economic Dynamics*, Monthly Review Press, N.Y., 1968, Ch. 1-2.

J. Steindl, *Maturity and Stagnation in American Capitalism*, Monthly Review Press, N.Y., 1976. Introduction, Ch. I-VII.

5. EMPIRICAL EVIDENCE

J. Steindl, op. cit., Ch. VIII.

H. Demsetz, *The Market Concentration Doctrine*, American Enterprise Institute for Public Policy Research, 1973 (Pamphlet).

J.M. Vernon, *Market Structure and Industrial Performance*, Allyn and Bacon, Inc., Boston, 1972, Ch. 3.

J. Bodoff, *Monopoly and Price Revisited*. Unpublished Ph.D. Dissertation, New School for Social Research, 1973.

W. Semmler, "Competition and Monopoly Power: Theories and Empirical Evidence," 1980, unpublished.

V. CONCRETIZING THE BASIC CATEGORIES

1. PRODUCTIVE/UNPRODUCTIVE LABOR

Marx, *Resultat* (Results of the Immediate Process of Production), Appendix, Penguin Edition of *Capital*, Vol. I, 1976: pp. 943-947, pp. 1023-1049. This reading is on reserve.

_____, *Capital*, Vol. II, Ch. V-VI.

_____, *TSV*, Part I.

a. First read the last paragraph in the Addenda (Section 125). Then read Sections 11-12.

b. Ch. IV, Sections 1-5, 20; Addenda, Section 11.

S. Coontz, *Productive Labour and Effective Demand*, Routledge & Kegan, Paul London, 1965, Ch I, II.

P. Bullock, "Defining Productive Labour for Capital," *BCSE*, Autumn 1974.

_____, "Productive and Unproductive Labor," *Journal of the Revolutionary Communist Group*, Issue 1, Jan. 1975.

Gardner, Himmelweit, Mackintosh, "Women's Domestic Labor," *BCSE*, June 1975.

I. Gough, "Marx's Theory of Productive and Unproductive Labour," *New Left Review*, Nov.-Dec. 1972.

Gough and Harrison, "Unproductive Labour and Housework Again," *BCSE*, Feb. 1975.

J. Harrison, "Productive and Unproductive Labour in Marx's Political Economy," *BCSE*, Autumn 1974.

*H. Minc, "On the Question of Productive and Unproductive Labor," Reprinted from *Communist Review*, London, Sept. 1948.

2. CIRCUITS OF CAPITAL AND REVENUE

Marx-Engels Correspondence, Marx to Engels, July 6, 1863.

Marx, *Capital*, Vol. II, Ch. XVIII-XIX.

Marx, *TSV*, Part I, Ch. VI, Section 1-3, 6.

3. AN EMPIRICAL INVESTIGATION OF THE MONEY-FORMS OF VALUE CATEGORIES (U.S., 1900-1972)

4. CRITIQUE OF PREVIOUS ATTEMPTS

J. Gillman, *The Falling Rate of Profits*, Cameron Assoc., N.Y., 1957: Ch. 1-7 (107 pages). The reading is not as long as it seems. Chs. 1-3 are introductions of Marxist concepts; the critical chapters are 4-7 (60 pages), and even a good part of these consists of charts and graphs.

S. Mage, *The Law of the Falling Tendency of the Rate of Profit* (unpublished Ph.D. dissertation, Columbia Univ., 1963): Glossary, Introduction, Chs. II, VI (pp. 161-175), Conclusions (62 pages).

V. Perlo, "Capital Output Ratio in Manufacturing," *Quarterly Review of Economics & Business*, 8, 3, Autumn 1968, pp. 29-42.

**Trends in American Capitalism*, Labor Research Assoc., International Publishers, N.Y., 1948, Ch. III-V (58 pages).

5. IMPLICATIONS FOR CRISIS THEORIES

Review Section I.2 (The Structure of Marxian Crisis Theories).

VI. KEYNESIAN THEORY AND THE ECONOMIC ROLE OF THE STATE

1. THE GENERAL PROBLEM

S. de Brunhoff, *The State, Capital and Economic Policy*, Pluto Press, London, 1978: Ch 3 (20 pages).

P. Mattick, *Marx and Keynes: The Limits of a Mixed Economy*, Merlin Press, London, 1969, Ch 1, 14 (38 pages).

2. THE STRUCTURE OF KEYNESIAN THEORY

L. Pasinetti, "The Economics of Effective Demand" (on reserve under the title). This is Ch. 11 of *Growth and Income Distribution*, L. Pasinetti, Cambridge, London, 1974.

P. Kenway, "Marx, Keynes, and the Possibility of Crisis," *Cambridge Journal of Economics*, 1980, 4, pp. 23-36.

3. THE DEBATE ABOUT KEYNESIAN THEORY

P. Garegnan, "Notes on Consumption, investment and effective demand: a reply to Joan Robinson, *Cambridge Journal*, 1979, 3, pp 181-187.

"An Analytical Framework for Federal Policies and Programs Influencing Capital Formation in the United States," Report to the Congress, Comptroller General of the U.S., Sept. 23, 1980, chs 1, ch 4-5 (27 pages).

A. Shaikh, "Towards A Critique of Keynesian Theory on The Role of the State," unpublished, Sept. 1980: pp 1-

---

Readings in European Marxist Theories Since Lenin

Theda Skocpol
Harvard
Sociology
Undergraduate
Fall 1974

Marxism—originally conceived as a science of bourgeois society committed to human liberation through proletarian revolution—has been "in crisis" since the 1920s. For by then it became apparent that the European working-class movement which had grown up with capitalism had failed to create socialism. Ever since, wedged between the barbarisms of fascism and Stalinism, and in constant contact and competition with professional academic traditions, theorists who remain within the Marxist tradition have grappled with the dilemmas of simultaneously defending and transforming the rich but not unambiguous Marxist theoretical legacy. Important questions have been raised and debated: In what sense, if any, is Marxism a science? *Can* there be a science of society(ies)? How should history be understood? What is the dialectic? How shall theory relate to practice? What are the roles of "consciousness" and "the superstructures" in society and history? Is revolution on the agenda for advanced industrial societies; if so, who will be the agents? The purpose of this Seminar is to begin to explore the complex and multifaceted debates of 20th-century Marxist theorists no only in order to comprehend why neo-Marxisms emerged and where they may be headed, but also so that we may better understand fundamental issues that all serious theories must face.

Week 1: INTRODUCTION AND ORGANIZATION

Week 2: THE INHERITANCE: FROM MARX THROUGH THE UPHEAVALS OF 1914-23

George Lichtheim, *Marxism: A Historical and Critical Study* (NY: Praeger, 1965).

Recommended

Shlomo Avineri, *The Social and Political Thought of Karl Marx* (Cambridge: At the University Press, 1968).

Background

Wolfgang Abendroth, *A Short History of the European Working Class* (NY: Monthly Review Press, 1972; orig. 1965).

E.H. Carr, *The Bolshevik Revolution, 1917-1923* (3 volumes) (Baltimore: Penguin Books, 1969 and 1971; orig. 1950, 1952 and 1953).

Lucio Colletti, "Bernstein and the Marxism of the Second International," pp. 45-110 in *From Rousseau to Lenin* (London: New Left Books, 1972; orig. 1969).

Lewis A. Coser, "Marxist Thought in the First Quarter of the 20th Century," *American Journal of Sociology* 78(1) (July, 1972).

Albert Fried and Ronald Sanders (eds.), *Socialist Thought: A Documentary History* (NY: Anchor Books, 1964).

Peter Gay, *The Dilemma of Democratic Socialism* (NY: Collier Books, 1970; orig. 1952).

D.C. Hodges, "Engels' Contribution to Marxism," *The Socialist Register, 1965.*

David McLellan, *Karl Marx: His Life and Thought* (NY: Harper and Row, 1973).

Arthur Rosenberg, *A History of Bolshevism from Marx to the First Five Years' Plan* (London, 1934).

A.J. Ryder, *The German Revolution of 1918* (Cambridge: At the University Press, 1967).

Carl E. Schorske, *German Social Democracy, 1905-1917* (NY: Harper and Row, 1972; orig. 19

Writings of: Eduard Bernstein; Karl Kautsky; Lenin; Marx; Rosa Luxembourg; and George Plekhanov.

Week 3: NIKOLAI BUKHARIN

N. Bukharin, *Historical Materialism: A System of Sociology.*

Background

Stephen E. Cohen, *Bukharin and the Bolshevik Revolution* (NY: Alfred A. Knopf, 1973).

A. Emery, "Dialectics versus Mechanics: A Communist Debate on Scientific Method," *Philosophy of Science* 2(1) (January, 1935): 9-38.

Sidney Heitman, "Between Lenin and Stalin: Nikolai Bukharin," in Leopold Labedz (ed.), *Revisionism: Essays on the History of Marxist Ideas* (NY: Praeger, 1962).

Week 4 GEORG LUKACS

Review of N. Bukharin's *Historical Materialism* (1925): *New Left Review* Number 39 (September, October, 1966); or pp. 134-146 in *Tactics and Ethics* (NY: Harper and Row, 1972).

History and Class Consciousness (Cambridge, MA: MIT Press, 1971): "What is Orthodox Marxism?" (1919); "Class Consciousness" (1920); "Reification and the Consciousness of the Proletariat" (1923); "Towards a Methodology of the Problem of Organization" (1922).

Recommended

Andrew Arato, "Lukacs' Theory of Reification," *Telos* Number 11 (Spring, 1972): 25-66.

Gareth Stedman Jones, "The Marxism of the Early Lukacs: An Evaluation," *New Left Review* Number 70 (November-December, 1971): 27-64.

The remainder of *History and Consciousness,* including the "Preface to the New Edition (1967)."

Background

Andrew Arato, "Georg Lukacs: The Search for a Revolutionary Subject," in Howard and Klare (eds.), *The Unknown Dimension.*

Alvin Gouldner, "Comments on History and Class Consciousness," pp. 414-424 in *For Sociolog* (NY: Basic Books, 1973).

George Lichtheim, *Georg Lukacs* (NY: Viking Press, 1970).

Maurice Merleau-Ponty, "Western Marxism," Chapter 2 of *Adventures of the Dialectic* (Evanston, Illinois: Northwestern University Press, 1973; orig. 1955); reprinted in *Telos* Number 6 (Fall, 1970).

Istvan Meszaros (ed.), *Aspects of History and Class Consciousness* (London: Routledge and Kegan Paul, 1971).

Istvan Meszaros, *Lukacs' Concept of Dialectic.*

G.H.R. Parkinson (ed.) *Georg Lukacs: The Man, His Work, and His Ideas* (MY: Vintage Books, 1970).

Telos Numbers 10 (Winter, 1971) and 11 (Spring, 1972): Special Lukacs Issue, Parts I and II.

Rudolf L. Tokes, *Bela Kun and the Hungarian Soviet Republic* (NY: Praeger, 1967).

Morris Watnick, "Relativism and Class Consciousness: Georg Lukacs," pp. 142-165 in Leopold Labedz (ed.), *Revisionism* (NY: Praeger, 1962).

Victor Zitta, *Georg Lukacs' Marxism: Alienation, Dialectics, Revolution* (The Hague, 1964).

"Lukacs on His Life and Work," Interview in *New Left Review* Number 68 (July-August, 1971): 49-58.

Week 5: ANTONIO GRAMSCI

Selections From the Prison Notebooks (NY: International Publishers, 1971):

I. Problems of History and Culture
    1. The Intellectuals
    2. On Education

II. Notes on Politics
    1. The Modern Prince
    2. State and Civil Society (selections to be recommended).

III. The Philosophy of Praxis
    1. The Study of Philosophy
    2. Problems of Marxism

"Soviets in Italy," *New Left Review* Number 51 (September-October, 1968): 22-58.

Recommended

John M. Cammett, *Antonio Gramsci and the Origins of Italian Communism* (Stanford, Cal.: Stanford University Press, 1967).

Alberto Martinelli, "In Defense of the Dialectic: Antonio Gramsci's Theory of Revolution *Berkeley Journal of Sociology* 13 (1968): 1-27.

Gramsci, "The Southern Question," pp. 28-58 in *The Modern Prince* (NY: International Publishers, 1970).

Background

Alastair Davidson, *Antonio Gramsci* (Sydney: Australian Left Review Publications, 1968).

Giuseppi Fiori, *Antonio Gramsci: Life of a Revolutionary* (NY: Schocken Books, 1973; orig. 1966).

Eugene D. Genovese, "On Antonio Gramsci," *Studies on the Left* 7(2) (March-April, 1967); reprinted in James Weinstein and David W. Eakins (eds.), *For a New America* (NY: Vintage Books, 1970).

Romano Giachetti, "Antonio Gramsci: The Subjective Revolution," pp. 147-168 in Howard and Klare (eds.), *The Unknown Dimension*.

John Merrington, "Theory and Practice in Gramsci's Marxism," pp. 145-176 in *The Socialist Register*, 1968.

A. Pozzolini, *Antonio Gramsci: An Introduction to his Thought* (London: Pluto Press, 1970).

Nigel Todd, "Ideological Superstructure in Gramsci and Mao Tse-tung," *Journal of the History of Ideas* 35(1) (January-March, 1974): 148-156.

Gwyn A. Williams, "The Concept of 'Egemonia' in the Thought of Antonio Gramsci...." *Journal of the History of Ideas* 21(4) (1960): 586-597.

Week 6: KARL KORSCH

Korsch, *Marxism and Philosophy* (NY: Monthly Review Press, 1970): "Introduction"; "Marxism and Philosophy" (1923); "The Present State of Marxism and Philosophy" (1930).

Stanley Aronowitz, "Left-Wing Communism: The Reply to Lenin," pp. 169-194 in Howard and Klare (eds.), *The Unknown Dimension*.

Paul Breines, "Praxis and Its Theorists: The Impact of Lukacs and Korsch in the 1920s," *Telos* Number 11 (Spring, 1972): 67-103.

Russell Jacoby, "Towards a Critique of Automatic Marxism: The Politics of Philosophy from Lukacs to the Frankfort School: *Telos* Number 10 (Winter, 1971): 119-146.

Recommended

Mihaly Vajda, "Karl Korsch's 'Marxism and Philosophy,'" pp. 131-146 in Howard and Klare (eds.), *The Unknown Dimension*.

Background

Erich Gerlach, "Karl Korsch's Undogmatic Marxism," *International Socialism* 19 (Winter, 1964-65): 22-27.

Karl Korsch, *Three Essays on Marxism* (reprinted) (London: Pluto Press, 1971).

Karl Korsch, *Karl Marx* (NY: Russell and Russell, 1963; orig. 1938).

Week 7: MAX HORKHEIMER AND THEODOR ADORNO

Horkheimer, "Notes on Science and the Crisis;" "The Latest Attack on Metaphysics;" and "Traditional Theory and Critical Theory" (essays from the late 1930s) in *Critical Theory* (NY: Herder and Herder, 1972).

Horkheimer and Adorno, "Introduction" and "The Concept of the Enlightment" in *Dialectic of Enlightenment* (NY: Herder and Herder, 1972; orig. 1944).

Recommended

A.J. Ayer, "Editor's Introduction" to *Logical Positivism* (NY: The Free Press, 1959) (Surveys the history and central theses of positivist philosophies in the twentieth century; helpful for understanding the object of Horkheimer and Adorno's criticisms).

Martin Jay, *The Dialectical Imagination: A History of the Frankfurt School of Social Research, 1923-1950* (Boston: Little Brown, 1973).

George Lichtheim, "Adorno;" "From Marx to Hegel;" and "From Historicism to Marxist Humanism in *From Marx to Hegel*.

Background

Martin Jay, "The Frankfurt School's Critique of Marxist Humanism," *Social Research* 39(2) (Summer, 1972): 285-305.

Goran Therbourn, "The Frankfurt School," *New Left Review* Number 63 (September-October, 1970).

Max Horkheimer, "The End of Reason," *Studies in Philosophy and Social Science* 9 (1941): 336-388.

Max Horkheimer, *The Eclipse of Reason* (NY: Seabury, 1974; orig. 1947).

Theodor Adorno, *Negative Dialectics* (NY: Herder and Herder, 1973; orig. 1966).

Week 8: HERBERT MARCUSE

Marcuse, *One-Dimensional Man* (Boston: Beacon Press, 1964).

Marcuse, "The Obsolescence of Marxism [?]," pp. 409-417 in Nicholas Lobkowicz (ed.) *Marx and the Western World* (Notre Dame, Indiana: University of Notre Dame Press, 1967).

Marcuse, "Freedom and the Historical Imperative" (1969), pp. 209-223 in *Studies in Critical Philosophy* (Boston: Beacon Press, 1973).

Recommended

Lucio Colletti, "From Hegel to Marcuse," pp. 111-140 in *From Rousseau to Lenin* (London: New Left Books, 1972; orig. 1969).

William Leiss, "Technological Rationality: Marcuse and His Critics," *Philosophy of the Social Sciences* 2(1) (March, 1972): 31-42.

Marcuse, "Some Social Implications of Modern Technology," *Studies in Philosophy and Social Science* 9 (1941): 414-439.

Marcuse, *Eros and Civilization* (Boston: Beacon Press, 1955).

Marcuse, "Industrialization and Capitalism in the Work of Max Weber" (1965), pp. 201-226 in *Negations* (Boston: Beacon Press, 1968).

Background

Paul Breines (ed.), *Critical Interruptions: New Left Perspectives on Herbert Marcuse* (NY: Herder and Herder, 1972).

Peter Clecak, "Herbert Marcuse: From History to Myth," Chapter 6 of *Radical Paradoxes: Dilemmas of the American Left: 1945-1970* (NY: Harper and Row, 1973).

Jerry Cohen, "Critical Theory: *The Philosophy of Marcuse,*" *New Left Review* Number 57 (September-October, 1969): 35-51.

Martin Jay, "How Utopian is Marcuse?" pp. 244-256 in George Fischer (ed.) *The Revival of American Socialism* (NY: Oxford University Press, 1971).

Alasdair Macintyre, *Herbert Marcuse: An Exposition and a Polemic* (NY: Viking Press, 1970.

Peter Sedgwick, "Natural Science and Human Theory: A Critique of Herbert Marcuse," *The Socialist Register,* 1966: 163-192.

Paul Walton and Andrew Gamble, "Herbert Marcuse," Chapter 4 of *From Alienation to Surplus Value* (London: Sheed and Ward, 1972).

Week 9: JURGEN HABERMAS

J.J. Shapiro, "The Dialectic of Theory and Practice in the Age of Technological Rationality, Herbert Marcuse and Jurgen Habermas," pp. 276-303 in Howard and Klare (eds.), *The Unknown Dimension.*

Habermas, "Knowledge and Human Interests: A General Perspective," pp. 301-317 in *Knowledge and Human Interests* (Boston: Beacon Press, 1971; orig. 1968).

Habermas, "Between Philosophy and Science: Marxism as Critique," pp. 195-252 in *Theory and Practice* (Boston: Beacon Press 1973).

Habermas, "Some Difficulties in the Attempt to Link Theory and Praxis," pp. 1-40 in *Theory and Practice.*

Habermas, "Dogmatism, Reason, and Decision: On Theory and Praxis in Our Scientific Civilization," pp. 253-282 in *Theory and Practice.*

Recommended

Sample additional parts of *Knowledge and Human Interests.*

Background

Habermas, "Toward a Theory of Communicative Competence," pp. 114-148 in Hans Peter Dreitze (ed.), *Recent Sociology No. 2: Patterns of Communicative Behavior* (NY: Macmillan, 1970).

Habermas, "Knowledge and Interest," *Inquiry* 9 (1966); reprinted in Dorothy Emmet and Alason Macintyre (eds.), *Sociological Theory and Philosophical Analysis* (NY: Macmillan, 1970).

Martin Jay, "Recent Developments in Critical Theory," *Berkeley Journal of Sociology* 18 (1973-74): 27-44.

Philosophy of Social Science 2(3) (September, 1972): Review Symposium on Habermas.

Trent Schroyer, "The Politics of Epistemology: A Marxist Perspective on Current Debates in German Sociology," *International Journal of Sociology* 1 (4) (Winter, 1971-72): 315-000

Jeremy Shapiro, "From Marcuse to Habermas," *Continuum* 8 (1970).

Goran Therbourn, "Jurgen Habermas: A New Eclecticism" *New Left Review* Number 67 (May-June 1971): 69-85.

Week 10: CRITICAL THEORY DEFENDED

Albrecht Wellmer, *Critical Theory of Society* (NY: Seabury, 1974; orig. 1969).

David Frisby, "The Popper-Adorno Controversy: The Methodological Dispute in German Sociology," *Philosophy of the Social Sciences* 2(2) (June, 1972): 8-119.

George Lichtheim, "Marx or Weber: Dialectical Methodology," pp. 200-218 in *From Marx to Hegel.*

Background

T.W. Adorno (ed.), *Der Positivismusstreit in der deutschen Soziologie* (Berlin: Neuwied, 1969).

Bryan Magee, *Karl Popper* (NY: Viking Press, 1973) (A good summary of the master's thought by a disciple).

Gerard Radnitzsky, *Contemporary Schools of Metascience* (Chicago: Henry Regnery, 1973; Third edition, enlarged).

Otto Stammer (ed.), *Max Weber and Sociology Today* (NY: Harper and Row, 1972; orig. 1965).

Week 11: CRITICAL THEORY APPLIED

Jurgen Habermas, "Technical Progress and the Social Life-World;" "The Scientization of Politics and Public Opinion;" and "Technology and Science as 'Ideology,'" pp. 50-000 in *Toward A Rational Society* (Boston: Beacon Press, 1970; orig. 1968).

Jurgen Habermas, "What Does a Crisis Mean Today?: Legitimation Problems in Late Capitalism," *Social Research* 40(4) (Winter, 1973): 643-667.

Trent Schroyer, "Toward a Critical Theory for Advanced Industrial Society," pp. 210-234 in Hans Peter Dreitzel (ed.), *Recent Sociology No. 2* (NY: Macmillan, 1970).

Claus Offe, "Political Authority and Class Structures—An Analysis of Late Capitalist Societies," *International Journal of Sociology* 2(1) (Spring, 1972): 73-108.

Background

Aspects of Sociology, by the Frankfurt Institute for Social Research (Boston: Beacon Press 1972; orig. 1956).

Boris Frankel, "Habermas Talking: *An Interview,*" *Theory and Society* 1(1) (1974): 37-58.

Trent Schroyer, *The Critique of Domination* (NY: George Braziller, 1973).

Week 12: LOUIS ALTHUSSER

Goran Therbourn, "The Frankfurt School," *New Left Review* Number 63 (September-October).

Goran Therborn, "Jurgen Habermas: A New Eclecticism," *New Left Review* Number 67 (May-June, 1971): 69-85.

Althusser, "The Object of Capital," Part II of *Reading Capital* (London: New Left Books, 1970; orig. 1968).

Althusser, "Marxism and Humanism" and "Contradiction and Overdetermination" in *For Marx* (NY: Vintage Books, 1970; orig. 1965).

Recommended

Althusser, Part I of *Reading Capital*.

Althusser, "Philosophy as a Revolutionary Weapon," Interview conducted by Maria Antonietta Macciocchi," pp. 11-22 in *Lenin and Philosophy* (NY: Monthly Review Press, 1971).

Robin Blackburn and Gareth Stedman Jones, "Louis Althusser and the Struggle for Marxism," pp. 365-387 in Howard and Klare (eds.), *The Unknown Dimension*.

George Lichtheim, "A New Twist in the Dialectic," pp. 143-159 in *From Marx to Hegel*.

Norman Geras, "Althusser's Marxism: An Account and an Assessment," *New Left Review* Number 7 (January-February, 1972).

Background

Michael Gane, "Althusser in English," *Theoretical Practice* 1 (January, 1971) (This is the journal of the English Althusserians).

Francois George, "Reading Althusser," *Telos* Number 7 (Spring, 1971): 73-98.

Radical America 3(5) (September, 1969): Special Issue on Louis Althusser.

Paul Walton and Andrew Gamble, "Louis Althusser and Structuralist Marxism," Chapter 5 of *From Alienation to Surplus Value* (London: Sheed and Ward, 1972).

Week 13: STRUCTURALIST MARXISM FURTHER EXPLICATED

Etienne Balibar, "The Basic Concepts of Historical Materialism," Part III of *Reading Capital*.

Maurice Godelier, "Comments on the Concepts of Structure and Contradiction," *International Journal of Sociology* 2(2-3) (Summer-Fall, 1972): 178-188.

Godelier, "Structure and Contradiction in Capital," *Socialist Register 1967*; reprinted in Robin Blackburn (ed.), *Ideology in Social Science* (NY: Vintage Books, 1973).

Godelier, "Functionalism, Structuralism and Marxism," Foreword to *Rationality and Irrationality in Economics* (London: New Left Books, 1972; orig. 1966).

Recommended

The Exchange between Godelier and Lucien Seve in *International Journal of Sociology* 2(2-3) (Summer-Fall, 1972): "Structuralism and Marxism: A Debate."

Background

Francois Furet, "The French Left: From Marxism to Structuralism," *Survey* Number 62 (January, 1967): 72-83.

Maurice Godelier, "La notion de mode de production asiatique et les schemas marxistes d'evolution des societes," pp. 47-100 in *Sur le Mode de Production Asiatique* (Paris: Editions Sociales).

H. Stuart Hughes, The Obstructed Path: *French Social Thought in the Years of Desperation 1930-1960* (NY: Harper and Row, 1966).

Michael Lane (ed.), *Introduction to Structuralism* (NY: Basic Books, 1970).

Emmanuel Terray, *Marxism and "Primitive" Societies* (NY: Monthly Review, 1972).

Week 14: STRUCTURALIST MARXISM APPLIED

Louis Althusser, "Ideology and Ideological State Apparatuses (Notes Toward an Investigation, pp. 127-186 in *Lenin and Philosophy* (NY: Monthly Review Press, 1971).

Nicos Poulantzas, *Political Power and Social Classes* (London: New Left Books, 1973; orig. 1968).

Recommended

Nicos Poulantzas, "The Problem of the Capitalist State" and Ralph Miliband, "Reply to Nicos Poulantzas," pp. 238-262 in Robin Blackburn (ed.), *Ideology in Social Science* (NY: Vintage Books, 1973).

Ralph Miliband, "Poulantzas and the Capitalist State," *New Left Review* Number 82 (November-December, 1973): 83-92.

Background

Amy Beth Bridges, "Nicos Poulantzas and the Marxist Theory of the State," *Politics and Society* 4(2) (Winter, 1974): 161-192.

Ralph Miliband, *The State in Capitalist Society* (NY: Basic Books, 1969).

Alan Wolfe, "New Directions in the Marxist Theory of Politics," *Politics and Society* 4(2) (Winter, 1974): 131-160.

Week 15: SUMMING UP

Whither Marxism?

So what for sociology/social theory?

Lucio Colletti, "Marxism as a Sociology," pp. 3-44 in *From Rousseau to Lenin* (London: New Left Books, 1972).

Background on Post-World War II Italian Marxism

Mario Montano, "The 'Scientific Dialectics' of Galvano Della Volpe," pp. 342-364 in Howard and Klare (eds.), *The Unknown Dimension*.

Lucio Colletti, "Power and Democracy in Socialist Society," *New Left Review* Number 56 (July-August, 1969): 18-26.

Galvano Della Volpe, "The Marxist Critique of Rousseau," *New Left Review* Number 49 (January-February, 1970): 97-109.

Lucio Magri, "Problems of the Marxist Theory of the Revolutionary Party," *New Left Review* Number 60 (March-April, 1970): 92-128.

Umberto Cerroni, "Italian Contributions to Marxian Research: Materialism and the Dialectic, *Social Research* 34(4) (Winter, 1967): 728-740.

Mario Montano, "On the Methodology of Determinate Abstraction...," *Telos* Number 7 (Spring, 1971): 30-49.

General Background: Additional attempts to situate Marx and Marxism in relation to sociology

Raymond Aron, *Main Currents in Sociological Thought* (2 volumes) (NY: Anchor Books, 1968 and 1970; orig. 1965 and 1967).

Peter Berger (ed.), *Marxism and Sociology: Views from Eastern Europe* (NY: Appleton-Century-Crofts, 1969).

Norman Birnbaum, "The Crisis in Marxist Sociology," *Social Research* (1968); reprinted in *Toward a Critical Sociology* (NY: Oxford University Press, 1971) and in Hans Peter Dreitzel (ed.), *Recent Sociology No. 1* (Toronto: Collier-Macmillan, 1969).

T.B. Bottomore, "Marxist Sociology," pp. 46-52 in Volume 10 of *The Encyclopedia of the Social Sciences* (1968).

Randall Collins, "Reassessments of Sociological History: The Empirical Validity of The Conflict Tradition," *Theory and Society* 1(2) (Summer, 1974): 147-178.

Anthony Giddens, *Capitalism and Modern Social Theory* (Cambridge: At the University Press 1971).

Lucien Goldmann, "Is there a Marxist Sociology?" *International Socialism* 34 (Autumn): 13-21.

Alvin Gouldner, *The Coming Crisis of Western Sociology* (NY: Avon Books, 1971; orig, 1970).

Alvin Gouldner, "The Two Marxisms," pp. 425-462 in *For Sociology* (NY: Basic Books, 1973).

Alvin Gouldner, "Marxism and Social Theory," *Theory and Society* 1(1) (1974): 17-35.

Henri Lefebre, *The Sociology of Marx* (NY: Vintage Books, 1969; orig. 1966).

Karl Mannheim, *Ideology and Utopia* (NY: Harcourt, Brace and World, 1936).

Robert Nisbet, *The Sociological Tradition* (NY: Basic Books, 1966).

Talcott Parsons, Chapter 3 of *The Structure of Social Action*, Vol. I (NY: The Free Press, 1968; orig, 1937).

Talcott Parsons, "Some Comments on the Sociology of Karl Marx," Chapter 4 of *Sociological Theory and Modern Society* (NY: The Free Press, 1967).

Irving Zeitlin, *Ideology and the Development of Sociological Theory* (Englewood Cliffs, New Jersey: Prentice-Hall, 1968).

Microeconomic Theory

Richard England
University of New Hampshire
Economics
Graduate
Fall 1981

TEXTS

There are two primary texts from which a substantial amount of required reading will be assigned:

William J. Baumol, *Economic Theory and Operations Analysis* (Prentice-Hall, 4th ed.), and

Frank Hahn and Martin Hollis, *Philosophy and Economic Theory* (Oxford Press, 1979).

For those with a background in mathematical economics, a recommended supplementary text is:

James Henderson and Richard Quandt, *Microeconomic Theory: A Mathematical Approach* (McGraw-Hill, 3rd ed.).

COURSE TOPICS

There are three basic objectives pursued in this course: 1) to introduce the student to the traditional content of microeconomics, 2) to discuss some recent developments in the field and to identify still unexplored theoretical questions, and 3) to critically assess the theoretical adequacy of microeconomics as a branch of economic theory.

The course begins with a brief introduction to neoclassical economic methododolgy, e.g. model construction, derivation of hypotheses, normative vs. positive propositions, etc. The development of the theory of consumer behavior comes next, with an emphasis on the transition from cardinal to ordinal conceptions of subjective utility. This section ends with a critical look at the commodity-consumption bias of utility analysis.

The theory of production begins with a look at the production function and isoquant devices which are commonly used to represent production processes. The need to take account of waste products as well as commodity outputs is emphasized in recognition of the natural law of mass-energy conservation. Theoretical problems involving the temporal aspects of production are also covered. Finally, the notion that production is a labor process wherein the efforts of some people are managed by others is seen to be missing from the microeconomic conception of production.

The theory of the firm raises questions about the goals pursued by private enterprises, e.g. profit-maximization vs. sales-maximization. These questions, in turn, raise theoretical questions about the adequacy of static models of the firm. The need for a developmental conception of the firm, i.e. an emphasis on the expansiveness and changes in structure which business firms typically display through history, is discussed.

An extensive section on various types of market structure follows. Microeconomics typically employs marginal revenue and marginal cost notions to make static comparisons of competitive, monopolistic and oligopolistic markets with respect to long-run profitability, price-cost margins, etc. Administered, markup pricing is inspected as a theoretical alternative to marginalist pricing models. The analytical problems posed by strategic interdependence of oligopolists are noted. Finally, the possibility that competition might produce market concentration historically is discussed.

Another major chunk of the course consists of theories of income distribution. The marginal productivity theory of input demand is presented as a leading contender, and the recent development of "human capital" theory is explored as a refinement of that earlier approach to income distribution. Critiques of both marginal productivity and human capital analyses are discussed.

The final topic is welfare economics, which discusses normative criteria by which to judge economic states of affairs.

*Denotes required reading.

1. ECONOMICS AS SCIENCE AND AS IDEOLOGY

*Hahn and Hollis, pp. 1-64.

*Paul Baran, "The Commitment of the Intellectual," ch. I of *The Longer View: Essays Toward a Critique of Political Economy*.

Martin Hollis and E.J. Nell, *Rational Economic Man*, pp. 1-43.

Lawrence Boland, "A Critique of Friedman's Critics," *J. of Econ. Lit.*, June 1979, pp. 503-22.

Nicholas Georgescu-Roegen, *The Entropy Law and the Economic Process*, pp. 22-52.

Maurice Dobb, *Theories of Value and Distribution Since Adam Smith*, ch. 1.

2. BASIC POSTULATES: RATIONALITY, OPTIMALITY, EQUILIBRIUM

*Baumol, ch. 1-4.

*Hahn and Hollis, pp. 65-109.

*Gary Becker, *The Economic Approach to Human Behavior*, ch. 1 and 8.

Martin Hollis and E.J. Nell, *Rational Economic Man*, pp. 47-64.

Thomas Schelling, *Micromotives and Macrobehavior*, pp. 11-33.

Joan Robinson, *Collected Economic Papers*, Vol. 4, ch. 27.

Nicholas Kaldor, "The Irrelevance of Equilibrium Economics," *Econ. J.*, December 1972, pp. 1237-1255.

3. THEORY OF CONSUMER BEHAVIOR

*Baumol, ch. 9, 10; pp. 343-64; ch. 17.

*Gary Becker, *The Economic Approach to Human Behavior*, ch. 7.

*Herbert Gintis, "Consumer Behavior and the Concept of Sovereignty," *Am. Econ. Rev.*, May 1972, pp. 267-278.

Martha Giminez, "Theories of Reproductive Behavior: A Marxist Critique," *Rev. of Rad. Pol. Econ.*, Vol. 11, No. 2 (1979), pp. 17-24.

Harvey Leibenstein, "An Interpretation of the Economic Theory of Fertility," *J. Econ. Lit.*, June 1974, pp. 457-479.

Kelvin Lancaster, "A New Approach to Consumer Theory," *J. Pol. Econ.*, April 1966, pp. 132-159.

Gary Becker, op. cit., ch. 5.

George Stigler and Gary Becker, "De Gustibus Non Est Disputandum," *Am. Econ. Rev.*, March 1977, pp. 76-90.

David Grether and Charles Plott, "Economic Theory of Choice and the Preference Reversal Phenomenon," *Am. Econ. Rev.*, September 1979, pp. 623-638.

4. THEORY OF PRODUCTION AND COST

*Baumol, ch. 11 + pp. 364-373.

*Robert Ayres and Allen Kneese, "Production, Consumption, and Externalities," *Am. Econ. Rev.*, July 1969, pp. 282-297.

*Nicholas Georgescu-Roegen, *Energy and Economic Myths*, ch. 2.

*Herbert Gintis, "The Nature of Labor Exchange and the Theory of Capitalist Production," *Rev. of Rad. Pol. Econ.*, Summer 1976, pp. 36-54.

E.R. Berndt and D.O. Wood, "Engineering and Econometric Interpretations of Energy-Capital Complementarity," *Am. Econ. Rev.*, June 1979, pp. 342-354.

Baumol, ch. 5, 6, and 12.

David P. Levine, *Economic Studies: Contributions to the Critique of Economic Theory*, ch. 7.

Donald Hay and Derek Morris, *Industrial Economics: Theory and Evidence*, ch. 2.

5. THEORY OF THE FIRM

*Michael Reich and James Devine, "The Microeconomics of Conflict and Hierarchy in Capitalist Production," *Rev. Rad. Pol. Econ.*, Winter 1981.

*Baumol, ch. 15.

*Kalman Cohen and Richard Cyert, *Theory of the Firm* (2nd ed.), pp. 399-453.

David P. Levine, *Op. cit.*, pp. 249-266.

Alfred Chandler, *Strategy and Structure*, pp. 19-50, 383-396.

Richard Caves, "Industrial Organization, Corporate Strategy and Structure," *J. Econ. Lit.*, March 1980, pp. 64-92.

Nina Shapiro, "The Neoclassical Theory of the Firm," *Rev. of Rad. Pol. Econ.*, Winter 1976, pp. 17-29.

Donald Hay, and Derek Morris, *op. cit.*, ch. 8-9.

H.A. Simon, "Rational Decision Making in Business Organizations," *Am. Econ. Rev.*, September 1979, pp. 493-513.

6. MARKET STRUCTURE: PERFECT COMPETITION

*Baumol, pp. 393-401.

*Cohen and Cyert, *op. cit.*, ch. 4 and 8.

Joan Robinson, *Collected Economic Papers*, Vol. 1, pp. 20-34.

B.T. McCallum, "Competitive Price Adjustments: An Empirical Study," *Am. Econ. Rev.*, March 1974, pp. 56-65.

7. MARKET STRUCTURE: PURE MONOPOLY

*Baumol, pp. 401-409.

*Cohen and Cyert, *op. cit.*, ch. 10.

*Robin Marris and Dennis Mueller, "The Corporation, Competition, and the Invisible Hand," *J. Econ. Lit.*, March 1980, Section III.

Donald Hay and Derek Morris, *op. cit.*, ch. 4.

8. MARKET STRUCTURE: MONOPOLISTIC COMPETITION

*Cohen and Cyert, *op. cit.*, ch. 11.

Joan Robinson, *Collected Economic Papers*, Vol. 2, Part III.

D. Capozza and R. Van Order, "A Generalized Model of Spatial Competition," *Am. Econ. Rev.*, December 1978, pp. 896-908.

Donald Hay and Derek Morris, *op. cit.*, pp. 10-20.

9. MARKET STRUCTURE: OLIGOPOLY

*Baumol, pp. 404-419 + ch. 18.

*Donald Hay and Derek Morris, *op. cit.*, ch. 5-7.

*Richard Edwards et al., *The Capitalist System* (2nd ed.), ch. 4.

F.M. Scherer, *Industrial Market Structure and Economic Performance* (2nd ed.), ch. 5-8, 13-15.

Gardiner Means, "The Administered-Price Thesis Confirmed," *Am. Econ. Rev.*, June 1972, pp. 292-306.

Leonard Weiss, "Stigler, Kindahl and Means on Administered Prices," *Am. Econ. Rev.*, September 1977, pp. 610-19.

Howard Sherman, "Monopoly Power and Stagflation," *J. Econ. Issues*, June 1977, pp. 269-284.

G.C. Harcourt and P. Kenyon, "Pricing and the Investment Decision," *Kyklos*, Vol. 29 (3), 1976, pp. 449-77.

10. MARGINAL PRODUCTIVITY, FACTOR PRICES AND INCOME DISTRIBUTION

*Baumol, ch. 24 and 26.

Carl Gerdes, "The Fundamental Contradiction in the Neoclassical Theory of Income Distribution," *Rev. Rad. Pol. Econ.*, Summer 1977, pp. 39-64.

Resad Kayali, "Neoclassical Theory Revisited," *Rev. Rad. Pol. Econ.*, Winter 1978, pp. 61-65.

Joan Robinson, *Collected Economic Papers*, Vol. 1 (pp. 1-19), Vol. 2 (pp. 114-158), Vol. 4 (pp. 129-138).

E.K. Hunt and J.G. Schwartz, eds., *A Critique of Economic Theory*, Part 3.

11. MORE ON INCOME DISTRIBUTION THEORY

*Gian Singh Sahota, "Theories of Personal Income Distribution: A Survey," *J. Econ. Lit.*, March 1978, pp. 1-55.

*Gilbert Gonzalez, "The Historical Development of the Concept of Intelligence," *Rev. Rad. Pol. Econ.*, Vol. 11, No. 2 (1979), pp. 44-54.

*Samuel Bowles and Herbert Gintis, "The Problem with Human Capital Theory—A Marxian Critique," *Am. Econ. Rev.*, May 1975, pp. 74-82.

F.L. Pryor, "Simulation of Impact of Social and Economic Institutions on the Size Distribution of Income and Wealth," *Am. Econ. Rev.*, March 1973, pp. 50-72.

12. WELFARE ECONOMICS AND GENERAL EQUILIBRIUM

*Baumol, ch. 20-22.

*Hahn and Hollis, pp. 110-169.

Maurice Dobb, *Welfare Economic and the Economics of Socialism*, ch. 1-6.

E.J. Mishan, "The Postwar Literature on Externalities: An Interpretative Essay," *J. Econ. Lit.* March 1971, pp. 1-28.

Amartya Sen, "The Welfare Basis of Real Income Comparisons: A Survey," *J. Econ. Lit.*, March 1974, pp. 1-45.

Arnold Harberger, "Three Basic Postulates for Applied Welfare Economics: An Interpretive Essay," *J. Econ. Lit.*, September 1971, pp. 785-797.

Dennis Mueller, *Public Choice*, Part II.

F.M. Scherer, *op. cit.*, ch. 2, 11, 17.

David P. Levine, *op cit.*, ch. 9.

Herbert Gintis, "A Radical Analysis of Welfare Economics and Individual Development," *Quarterly J. Econ.*, November 1972, pp. 572-599.

Marxist Approaches in Anthropology

P. Kohl, M Diskin
Wellesley College/
Massachusetts Institute of Technology
Anthropology

This course will consider concepts that derive from the body of Marxist writings as they are applicable to anthropological work. That will involve a historical survey of Marxist ideas as well as the development of anthropology as a separate discipline. The conditions for the exclusion of Marxist thought from anthropology as well as the current interest in this form of analysis will be examined as problems in the history of ideas as well as the sociology of knowledge. Contemporary ethnographic and archaeological work will be discussed in order to critically analyze the utility of Marxism in anthropology.

Required Books

Asad, Talal (ed.) *Anthropology and the Colonial Encounter.* Ithaca.
Engels, F. *The Origin of the Family, Private Property, and the State.* New World.
Hobsbawm, Eric (Marx) *Pre-Capitalist Economic Formations.* New World.
McLellan, David (ed.) *Karl Marx: Selected Writings.* Oxford.
Reiter, Rayna (ed.) *Toward an Anthropology of Women.* Monthly Review Press.
Seddon, David (ed.) *Relations of Production.* Cass.
Terray, E. *Marxism and "Primitive" Societies.* Monthly Review Press.

PART ONE

A. PRECURSORS AND ANTECEDENTS TO MARXIST THOUGHT-18TH AND 19TH CENTURIES

General Outline and Lecture Points

    The Enlightenment and the significance of idealism
    Progress and the perfectability of man through reason
    History as will
    Emergent materialism—anarchist denial
    Studies of human variability in fledgling anthropology
    The political configuration of the early 19th century
    Positivism
    Some biography about Marx and Engels

Required Readings

Harris: *Rise of Anthropological Theory*-the chapter on the Enlightenment.
    Malefijt: *Images of Man*-Chapters 5,6,7.
    Hobsbawm: *The Age of Capital: 1848-1875*, pp. 294-324.
    McLellan: 96-108, 129-190.

Optional Readings

    Kuhn: *The Structure of Scientific Revolution*, Chapter 7.
    Hirschman, Albert O.: *The Passions and the Interests*, Princeton, 1977.
    Manheim: *Ideology and Utopia*, Chapter 3.
    Edmond Wilson-on St. Simone, Hegel, Bruno, Vico, *To the Finland Station.*
    Marx; *Grundrisse*, Introduction, pp. 83-111.
    Philosophy of History-readings.

B. INTRODUCTION TO THE BASIC CONCEPTS AND WRITINGS OF MARX, ENGELS, AND LENIN

General Outline and Lecture Points

    General Biographical Information: The Men and Their Times
    The Intellectual Development of K. Marx and The Critique of Capitalism
    The Publication of Their Works and a Short History of Marxist Scholarship
    The Theory of Historical Materialism
    Marx and Engels' Relation to 19th Century Evolutionary Thought
    Lenin's Critique of Imperialism and the Nationalities Problem of the Young Soviet Union.

Required Readings

    E. Hobsbawm: "Introduction" in K. Marx: *Precapitalist Economic Formations.*
    D. McLellan: *Karl Marx: Selected Writings*, pp. 343-485.
    F. Engels: *The Origin of the Family, Private Property, and the State*, all except Chapter 2 and the Introduction; read Appendix, "The Part Played by Labor in the Transition from Ape to Man."

Optional Readings

    D. McLellan: *Karl Marx: Selected Writings*, pp. 156-191.

E. Terray: "Morgan and Contemporary Anthropology," in *Marxism and Primitive Societies.*

V.I. Lenin: *Karl Marx* (or Chapter 1, "Basic Principles" in *The Lenin Reader* by Possony).

V.I. Lenin: *What is to be Done?* and *The State and Revolution.*

C. THE INSTITUTIONALIZATION OF ANTHROPOLOGY AND ITS DIVORCE FROM THE MARXIST TRADITION IN EUROPE AND AMERICA

General Outline and Lecture Points

Marxian Analyses at the End of the 19th and Beginning of the 20th Century- Kautsky, Plekhanov, Bukharin.

The Development of the Social Sciences from Spencer to Weber and Their Reaction against Marxism

The Institutionalization of Anthropology in America: Boas and the Historical Particularist School (Lowie)

The Development of British Structural-Functionalism and the Beginnings of French Anthropology

Required Readings

M. Harris: *The Rise of Anthropological Theory,* Chapters 9, 13 and 19.

A.R. Radcliffe-Brown: *Structure and Function in Primitive Society,* Chapters 1, 6, 9, 10.

R. Lowie: *Primitive Society,* Chapters 8 ("The Position of Women"), 9 ("Property"), and 15 ("Conclusion").

R. Lowie: *Social Organization,* Chapters 3 ("Laws of Evolution...") and 2 ("Contemporary Western Civilization...").

M.E. Opler: "Cultural Evolution, Southern Athapaskans, and Chronology in Theory," *Southwestern Journal of Anthropology,* 1961, No. 1, and "Reply," op. cit., No. 4.

Optional Readings

E.E. Evans-Pritchard: *Theories of Primitive Religion,* Chapter 3 ("Sociological Theories").

F. Boas: *Race, Language, and Culture:* "The Methods of Ethnology" and "Some Problems of Methodology in the Social Sciences."

R. Lowie: *Origin of the State.*

G.W. Stocking: *Race, Culture and Evolution,* Chapters 6 and 9.

B. Malinowski: "Malinowski on the Kula," (Chap. 1) in *Economic Anthropology: Readings in Theory and Analysis,* ed. by E. LeClair and Schneider.

A. Kuper: *Anthropologists and Anthropology: The British School 1922-1972,* Chaps. 1-3.

Student Presentations

a. Franz Boas' concept of history.

b. The influence of E. Durkheim on British social anthropology.

D. THE DEVELOPMENT OF EVOLUTIONARY AND MATERIALIST CONCERNS IN ANTHROPOLOGY (MORGAN, FORDE, STEWARD, WHITE, CHILDE, AND HARRIS).

General Outline and Lecture Points

The Disappearance of Evolutionary Concerns in Social Anthropology

Periodization Models in Prehistory from the 19th to the early 20th Century

Geography, Ecology, and the Rebirth of Evolutionary Thought in Archaeology & Ethnology

The Apolitical Evolutionary Theories of L. White and J. Steward

Cultural Materialism Today

Required Readings

C. Daryll Forde: *Habitat, Economy, and Society,* "Introduction" and "Conclusion."

V. Gordon Childe: *History* (entire).

L. White: "The Concept of Evolution in Cultural Anthropology" in *Evolution and Anthropology: A Centennial Appraisal,* ed. by B. Meggers.

J. Steward: *Evolution and Ecology: Essays on Social Transformation,* Chapters 1,2,3,5.

M. Harris: *The Rise of Anthropological Theory,* Chapters 22, 23.

Optional Readings

L. White: *Evolution of Culture,* Chapters 1, 2, 12, and 13.

J. Steward: *Theory of Culture Change,* Chapters 1, 3, and 11.

E. Service: *Origins of the State and Civilization,* Chapters 2, 3, 4.

R. McC. Adams: "The Evolutionary Process in Early Civilizations" in *Evolution after Darwin: The Evolution of Man,* ed. by S. Tax.

J. Friedman: "Marxism, Structuralism, and Vulgar Materialism" in *Man* n.s 9(3): 444-469.

Student Presentations

The Vulgar Marxism of V. Gordon Childe: Fact or Fiction

The Non-Controversial Politics of L. White: An Enigma

Cutural Materialism and the Conscious Rejection of a Dialectical Approach

PART TWO

A. OVERVIEW OF MODERN MARXIST ANTHROPOLOGY

General Outline and Lecture Points

Constant tension between theory and praxis

Most Marxist classics written by activists

Anthropological concerns raised questions about situations not thought of in the original corpus (or perhaps for Euro-centric reasons not felt worthy?).

Events of May '68 broke relation between party and scholarship and redefined the epistemological basis of Marxist scholarship

Introduced mood making it acceptable to search for root meanings without specific formal definitions in the original (e.g. mode of production)

Required Readings

Godelier, *Perspectives in Social Anthropology*, pp. 99-126.

Firth in Bloch.

P.P. Rey, *Critique of Anthropology*, "the lineage mode of production," pp. 27-79, Spring 1975, No. 3.

Terray, E., "Marxism and 'Primitive' Societies," Part 2.

Optional Readings

Seddon, pp. 1-46.

Godelier in Bloch.

O'Laughlin Review article.

Althusser and Balibar-Reading Capital, Balibar Chap. 1.

Krader, L.: "Marx as Ethnologist," *Transactions of the N.Y. Academy of Sciences*, Series II, v. 35(4): 304-313.

Ethnological Notebooks of Karl Marx.

Student Presentations

Evolutionism in Marxian Writings

Neo-Marxian Epistemology

Expanded Definition of Mode of Production

B. MATERIALIST AND MARXIST APPROACHES IN ARCHAEOLOGY

General Outline and Lecture Points

The Nature of the Archaeological Record: Traditional and Contemporary Views

The New Archaeology as a Sociological Phenomenon

Dominant Trends in Contemporary Archaeology

Tentative Formulations of a Marxist-inspired Archaeology

Required Readings

L. Binford: "Archaeology as Anthropology" and "Archaeological Perspectives," in *An Archaeological Perspective*.

P.L. Kohl: "A Note on Chlorite Artifacts from Shahr-i Sokhta" in *East & West* 27 (1977).

P.L. Kohl: "The Balance of Trade in Southwestern Asia in the Mid-Third Millennium B.C.," in *Current Anthropology*, September 1978.

P.L. Kohl and R. Wright: "Stateless Cities: The Differentiation of Societies in the Near Eastern Neolithic" in *Dialectical Anthropology* 2(4).

M.J. Rowlands and J. Gledhill: "The Relation between Archaeology and Anthropology" in *Archaeology and Anthropology*, ed. by M. Spriggs; or *Critique of Anthropology* (6).

Optional Readings

P.J. Watson, S.A. LeBlanc, and C.L. Redman: "Archaeology as Social Science: Problems and Prospects," *Explanation in Archaeology* (Chapter 6).

M. Leone: *Contemporary Archaeology*, Chapters 1,2.

R. McC. Adams: "Anthropological Perspectives on Ancient Trade," in *Current Anthropology*, September 1974.

K.V. Flannery: "Archaeological Systems Theory and Early Mesoamerica," in *Prehistoric Agriculture* ed. by S. Streuver.

K.V. Flannery and J. Marcus: "Formative Oaxaca and the Zapotec Cosmos," in *American Scientist*, Vol. 64 (1976), pp. 374-382.

A. Gilman: "Bronze-Age Dynamics in Southeast Spain," in *Dialectical Anthropology* 1(4).

M. Tosi: "The Dialectics of State Formation in Mesopotamia, Iran, and Central Asia," in *Dialectical Anthropology* 1(2).

J. Friedman and M.J. Rowlands: *The Evolution of Social Systems* (article by editors).

Student Presentations

Positivism in the New Archaeology: Objectifying Prehistory

The Contemporary Staus of Social Archaeology

C. ANTHROPOLOGY AND THE COLONIAL ENCOUNTER

General Outline and Lecture Points

Anthropology could not handle colonialism (the very process that expanded the field was colonialism).

Pristine cultural examples were actually part of the world system (especially mercantile capitalism).

Anthropology lacked analytic categories large enough to include both the colonized (the studied) and the colonists (the anthropologists).

Required Readings

Maquet, J.: "Objectivity in Anthropology," *CA*, vol. 5(1), pp. 47-55.

Gough, K.: "New Proposals for Anthropologists," *CA*, vol. 9(5), pp. 403-407.

Murphy, R: "Tappers and Trappers..."

McLennan: pp. 332-337.

Laclau, E.: "Feudalism and Capitalism in Latin America," *New Left Review* 67.

Dupre and Rey in Seddon, pp. 171-209.

Asad, T.: Faris (153-172); Asad (103-120); Introduction (9-20); Forster (23-40); James (41-70); Feurchtwang (71-102); Marfleet (273-284).

Optional Reading

Wallerstein, E.: *The Capitalist World Economy* (Chapter 1, pp. 1-36).

Kay, G.: *Development and Underdevelopment* (pick a chapter).

Frank, A.G.: *Capitalism and Underdevelopment in Latin America* (Sects. A&B, pp. 1-19).

Oxaal, Barnett, and Booth (eds.): *Beyond the Sociology of Development* (pick a few).

Geertz, C.: *Agricultural Involution* (on the culture system).

Lenin: "National Questions," in Possony Reader, pp. 224-265.

Student Presentations

Larkner (pp. 123-152); Clammer (pp. 199-222); Owen; Willis; Ahmed.

D. MARXIST ETHNOGRAPHIC STUDIES

Guest Speaker: E. Terray.

Topics to be Discussed:

The Development of Marxist Anthropology in France

An Examination of Marxist Ethnographies and a Discussion of its Distinguishing Features

Required Readings

D. Seddon: *Relations of Production*, Part II.

E. Terray: "Long-Distance Exchange and the Formation of the State: The Case of the Abron Kingdom of Gyaman," *Economy and Society*, No. 3, 1974.

M. Bloch: *Marxist Analyses and Social Anthropology*, Articles by Bloch and Terray.

C. Meillassoux: *The Development of Trade and Indigenous Markets in West Africa* (Introduction).

M. Godelier: Perspectives in Marxist Anthropology (Chapter 5).

Optional Readings

C. Meillassoux: *The Development of Trade...*, op. cit., Chapters 4-7.

C. Meillassoux: "From Reproduction to Production," *Economy and Society*, No. 1(1).

Student Presentations

Godelier's article on Baruya salt money

Kinship-base or superstructure?

E. THE PEASANT DIALECTIC

General Outline and Lecture Points

Definitional Problem-the same for anthropology in general and for Marxist theory-part-whole controversy and participation in social change

One pole using primitive isolate (mir) and the other as some sort of proletarian or underclass in stratified society

Theoretical question is one of connections-articulation of modes of production

Reproduction of the peasantry as a distinct social type

Required Readings

Roseberry, W.: "Rent, Differentiation, and the Development of Capitalism Among Peasants," *AA* 78: 45-58.

Diskin, Martin: "Peasant Mode of Production and Reproduction," ms.

Mintz, S.: "The Rural Proletariat and the Problem of Rural Proletarian Consciousness," *JPS* 1:291-325.

Foster-Carter, Aidan: "Can We Articulate 'Articulation,'" *New Left Review*, 107.

Harrison, Mark: "The Peasant Mode of Production in the Work of A.V. Chayanov," *JPS* 4:323-337.

McLennan 43, pp. 576-580; 41, pp. 571-572.

Optional Readings

Lenin: *The Development of Capitalism in Russia*

Lenin: *To the Rural Poor*

Taussig: "Peasant Economics and the Development of Capitalist Agriculture in the Cauca Valley, Colombia."

F. MARXISM AND FEMINIST ANTHROPOLOGY

Guest Speaker: R. Rapp

Topics to be Discussed

Role of women (male/female relations) under different modes of production

Women's role in capitalist society

Male-bias in anthropology

Meaning of 'liberation'.

Required Readings

Rapp (ed): Introduction (pp. 11-19); Sacks (pp. 211-234); Rubbo (pp. 333-357); Remy (pp. 368-371); Diamond (pp. 372-395); Draper (pp. 77-109).

Rapp (article): "Family and Class in Contemporary America: Notes Toward an Understanding of Ideology."

Engels: *Origin of the Family*, Intro. by Leacock (pp. 7-68) and Ch. 2 (Family).

Optional Readings

Other articles in Rapp by Slocum, Gough, Rohrlich-Leavitt, Sykes, Weatherford, Faithron, Webster.

Latin-American Perspective, Women's Issue.

Report Topics

Significance of sexual division of labor in advanced capitalist society

Significance of women's work (housework)

Changing sense of family (contemporary political interest in the family)

G. MARXIST APPROACHES IN ARCHAEOLOGY AND ETHNOLOGY IN SOCIALIST AND THIRD WORLD COUNTRIES

Required Reading

S.P. and E. Dunn: "The Intellectual Tradition of Soviet Ethnography" in *Introduction to Soviet Ethnography*, ed. by Dunn and Dunn.

Yu. V. Bromley: "Subject Matter and Main Trends of Investigation of Culture by Soviet Ethnographers" in *Arctic Anthropology*, vol. XVI(1).

S.P. Dunn: "New Departures in Soviet Theory and Practice of Ethnicity" in *Dialectical Anthropology* 1(1).

G.P. Snesarev: "On Some Reasons for the Preservation of Some Religio-Customary Survivals among the Uzbeks of Khorezm" in *Introduction to Soviet Ethnography* (ISE), op. cit.

E. Dunn: "Post-Revolutionary Women in Soviet Central Asia" in *Canadian-American Slavic Studies*, vol. 9, 1975, no. 1, pp. 93-100.

E. and S.P. Dunn: "Ethnic Intermarriage as an Indicator of Cultural Convergence in Soviet Central Asia" in *The Nationality Question in Soviet Central Asia* ed. by E. Allworth.

Yu. V. Arutiunian: "A Preliminary Sociological Study of a Village" in *Soviet Sociology*, vol. X, 3-45, 153-190, 289-328, 411-435.

A. Vucinich: "the Peasants as a Social Class" in *The Soviet Rural Community*, ed. by J.R. Millar.

Optional Readings

D. Zilberman: "Ethnography in Soviet Russia" and "Replies" by S.P. and E. Dunn in *Dialectical Anthropology*, vol. 1, no. 2.

S.P. Tolstov and T.A. Zhdanko: "Directions and Problems of Soviet Ethnography" in *Soviet Anthropology and Archaeology*, III, no. 3.

M.A. Bikzhanova et. al.: "The Uzbeks: Social and Family Life" in ISE *op. cit.*

E. Dunn: "Russian Rural Women" in *Women in Russia* ed. by D. Atkinson, A. Dallin, and G.W. Lapidus.

W.W. Howells and P.J. Tsuchitani: *Paleoanthropology in the People's Republic of China*- articles by Keightley and Chang.

Student Presentations

The "Asian Mode of Production" Debate and its Influence on Soviet Ethnology

The Periodization of History and its Continuing Effect on Soviet Archaeology and Ethnology

The Influence of Contemporary Western Schools (structuralism, 'new' archaeology, etc.) on Soviet Ethnology and Archaeology

Nationalities' Policies and the Practice of Soviet Ethnology

Reports on the Contemporary Status of Women and Ethnic Minorities in the USSR

Chayanov's Theory of a Peasant Economy and its Current Status in Soviet Ethnology

H. MARXIAN INTERPRETATIONS OF IDEOLOGY AND RELIGION

General Outline and Lecture Points

Marx's View of Reality and False Consciousness

Religion and Ideology in Primitive Societies: Base or Superstructure?

Ideology and Objectivity in the Social Sciences

Economic Determinism and Reductionism in the Absence of Ideology

Required Readings

D. McLellan: *Karl Marx: Selected Writings*, pp. 159-171, 435-443.

M. Godelier: "Toward a Marxist Anthropology of Religion," *Dialectical Anthropology* 1(1).

M. Godelier: *Perspectives in Marxist Anthropology*, Part IV.

K. Mannheim: *Ideology and Utopia*, Chapter 2.

N. Harris: *Beliefs in Society*, Chapters 1, 2, 3, 7, 8.

S. Feuchtwang: "Investigating Religion" in *Marxist Analyses in Social Anthropology* ed. by M. Bloch.

B. Ollman: *Alienation*, Chapter 31.

E. Laclau: *Politics and Ideology in Marxist Theory*, Chapter 3.

Godelier, Levi-Strauss, and Auge: "Anthropology, History, and Ideology" in *Critique of Anthropology*, No. 6.

THE STATE

The Theory of the State

Erik Wright
University of Wisconsin
Sociology
Spring 1980
Graduate

This seminar is designed to provide a fairly comprehensive examination of alternative strategies for analysing the state within contemporary Marxist theory. Approximately two thirds of the sessions will focus on general theoretical and conceptual issues and about one third on more concrete historical problems.

The syllabus is divided into two sections: I. General Theoretical Perspectives on the State and Politics; II. Specific Topics. Five sessions will be selected from the list of 17 topics in this second section. Which of these we will discuss will be decided at the second seminar session. If there is sufficient interest in the seminar to have more than five of the special topics, then we may decide to have parallel sessions of the seminar meeting on certain weeks.

BACKGROUND READING FOR SEMINAR

1. Classics in the Marxist Tradition
    Marx, *The 18th Brumaire of Louis Napoleon*
    _____, *The Civil War in France*
    Engels, *The Origins of the Family, Private Property and the State*
    Lenin, *The State and Revolution*
    Gramsci, *The Modern Prince* and *State and Civil Society*

2. General Reviews of Recent Discussions of the State
    David Gold, Clarence Lo, and Erik Olin Wright, "Recent Developments in Marxist Theories of the State," *Monthly Review* October and November 1975. Reprinted in the xerox reader.
    Bob Jessop, "Recent Theories of the Capitalist State," *Cambridge Journal of Economics*, 1:4, 1977, pp. 353-373. Reprinted in xerox reader.
    Fred Block, "The Ruling Class Does Not Rule," *Socialist Revolution* #33, 1977. Reprinted in xerox reader.

3. General Overviews of the Marxist Theory of the State (textbooks)
    Ralph Miliband, *Marxism and Politics* (Oxford University Press, 1977).
    Albert Szymanski, *The Capitalist State and the Politics of Class* (Winthrop, 1978).

I. GENERAL THEORETICAL PERSPECTIVES ON THE STATE AND POLITICS

1. POSING THE PROBLEM: THE CAPITALIST STATE AND THE STRUGGLE FOR SOCIALISM

If the Marxist theory of the state is meant to accomplish anything it is to inform the struggle for socialism. The state is of such interest to Marxists because it plays such a decisive role in shaping struggles in capitalism. The capitalist state bears on the question of socialism; but all Marxists see the state as one of the central problems faced by the working class and socialist movements.

In this session of the seminar we will discuss one of the clearest and most provocative analyses of the relationship between the capitalist state and the struggles for socialism. Adam Przeworski's two essays define a series of objective dilemmas rooted in the structure of the capitalist state and the logic of capital accumulation which socialist movements in the advanced capitalist countries face as they attempt to transform capitalist society. Our discussion of these essays will hopefully help to set the agenda for the preoccupations of much of the rest of the semester.

Adam Przeworski, "The Material Bases of Consent: Economics and Politics in a Hegemonic System", in Maurice Zeitlin (ed) *Political Power and Social Theory* vol. I (JAI Press, 1979). Note: this will be distributed in class if the book is unavailable.

Adam Przeworski, "Social Democracy as a Historical Phenomenon" forthcoming in *New Left Review*. (In xerox reader).

Adam Przeworski, "From Proletariat into Class: the process of class formation from Kautsky's The Class Struggle to recent contributions," *Politics & Society*, vol. 7:4, 1977.

2. STATE POWER AND STATE APPARATUS: GORAN THERBORN

Theoretical discussions of the state are often extremely confusing because the use of terms is frequestly inconsistent or muddled. While an over-preoccupation with conceptual clarification can become an impediment to theorizing, some initial clarifications and definitions are needed if the debate is to procede in a coherent manner.

Goran Therborn's work on the state provides perhaps the clearest and most comprehensive map of the conceptual terrain of the Marxist theory of the state of any theorist. In particular, his extensive discussion of the distinction between state power and state apparatus is crucial, for this distinction makes it possible to theorize rigorously the contradictory character of the capitalist state. Therborn's comparative analysis of the feudal, capitalist and socialist state apparatuses is also interesting as a point of departure for discussion, but is somewhat less complete than some of his more general theoretical formulations.

Goran Therborn, *What Does the Ruling Class Do When It Rules?* (NLB, 1978). Read the entire book, but pay particular attention to the following pages: 23-48, 122-125, 129-161, 241-244.

Supplementary

Herbert Kitschelt, "Review of Goran Therborn, What Does...." *Kapitalistate* #7, 1979. Reprinted in xerox reader.

Goran Therborn, "Enterprises, Markets and States", unpublished manuscript, 1979. Reprinted in Xerox reader.

3. CRITICAL THEORY APPROACHES TO THE STATE: THE WORK OF CLAUS OFFE

Discussions of the state in the traditional of critical theory has been marked by two interconnected concerns: 1) the problem of state *rationality*; and 2) the problem of *legitimation*. Claus Offe's work on the state has been particularly preoccupied with the first of these.

He asks: given the formal, institutional separation of the state and economy in capitalist society, what (if anything) guarantees that the state will pursue policies that are rational from the point of view of the interests of the capitalist class? What structures and mechanisms define the possibility of state rationality? The essays below attempt in different ways to answer these questions within a framework which adheres to the traditional Marxist claims about the class character of the capitalist state.

Claus Offe, "Structural Problems of the Capitalist State: class rule and the political system. On the selectiveness of political institutions" in Von Beyme (ed) *German Political Studies*, vol. I (Sage, 1974). Reprinted in xerox reader.

"The Capitalist State and the Problem of Policy Formation", in Leon Lindberg (ed). *Stress and Contradiction in Contemporary Capitalism* (D.C. Heath). Reprinted in xerox reader.

Claus Offe and Volker Ronge, "Theses on the Theory of the State" *New German Critique* #6, Fall 1975. Reprinted in xerox reader.

Supplementary

Claus Offe: "Advanced Capitalism and the Welfare State" *Politics and Society*, Summer 1972.

"Laws of Motion of Reformist State Policies" (an empirical study applying the general theoretical ideas from the core readings), mimeo, 1976. Reprinted in xerox reader.

"The Abolition of Market Control and the Problems of Legitimacy", *Kapitalistate* #1 and #2, 1973-1974.

Industry and Inequality (London: Edward Arnold, 1976).

"Two Logics of Collective Action" in Zeitlin (ed) *Political Power and Social Theory*, vol. I, 1979.

John Keane, "The Legacy of Political Economy: Thinking with and against Claus Offe," *Canadian J. of Pol. & Soc. Theory*, 1978. Reprinted in Reader.

S. Sardei-Biermann et al, "Class Domination and the Political System: a critical interpretation of recent contributions by Claus Offe" *Kapitalistate* #1, 1973. In reader.

4. CRITICAL THEORY APPROACHES TO THE STATE: JURGEN HABERMAS

In the analyses of the state, Habermas's pivotal concerns have centered on the problem of legitimation and the tendency for contradictions in the economy to become displaced onto the political arena as the role of the state expands with capitalist development. The core of his work on the state thus concerns the dynamics of what he terms "crisis of legitimacy". Although the idiom of his analysis often seems closer to sociological systems theory than to Marxism, nevertheless the underlying theoretical problems are closely tied to traditional Marxist concerns with contradictions, capitalist development and revolutionary transformation.

Jurgen Habermas, *Legitimation Crisis* (Beacon Press, 1975) Read entire book, but especially Part II and III.

Supplementary

Tony Woodiwiss, "Critical Theory and the Capitalist State" *Economy and Society*, 7:2, 1978. Reprinted in xerox reader.

Jurgen Habermas, "The Public Sphere" in Telos 1:3, 1974.

Paul Connerton, *Critical Sociology* (London: Penguin, 1976), essay on legitimation by Habermas.

Goran Therborn, "A Critique of the Frankfurt School", *New Left Review #63, 1970*.

Other Work on the State in the Tradition of Critical Theory

Bertell Ollman, "State as a value Relation" in *Alienation* (Cambridge U.P. 1976, 2nd edition) pp. 212-220.

Alan Wolfe, "New Directions in the Marxist Theory of Politics" *Politics & Society*, 4:2, 1974. Reprinted in xerox reader.

5. THE SO-CALLED "STRUCTURALIST-INSTRUMENTALIST DEBATE"

Perhaps the most significant debate in the late 1960's and early 1970's around the theory of the state was between the French Marxist Nicos Poulantzas and the British Marxist Ralph Miliband. This debate has been characterized in a somewhat oversimplified way (by myself among others) as a confrontation between a structuralist position represented by Poulantzas and an instrumentalist position represented by Miliband. While this characterization in the end has proven rather misleading, nevertheless the debate itself was of considerable importance and set the stage for much of the theoretical work on the state over the past decade.

David Gold, Clarence Lo and Erik Olin Wright, "Recent Developments in Marxist Theories of the State", Monthly Review, October-November 1975. Reprinted in reader.

Erik Wright and Luca Perrone, "The Structuralist-Marxist Approach" part 3 of "The Structuralist-Marxist and Parsonsian Theories of Politics", unpublished mss. Reprinted in xerox reader. (along with reading guide to Poulantzas).

Nicos Poulantzas, "The Problem of the Capitalist State" *New Left Review* #58, 1969. Reprinted in xerox reader.

Ralph Miliband, "Poulantzas and the Capitalist State", *New Left Review* #82, 1973. Reprinted in xerox reader.

Supplementary

Nicos Pulantzas, *Political Power and Social Class* (New Left Books, 1973).

Ralph Miliband, *The State in Capitalist Society* (Basic Books, 1968).

Marxism and Politics (Oxford Univ. Press, 1977).

Fred Block, "The Ruling Class Does Not Rule" *Socialist Review*, May-June, 1977. Reprinted in reader.

6. THE DEVELOPED "STRUCTURALIST" APPROACH TO THE STATE

It would be difficult to exaggerate the importance of Nicos Poulantzas' contribution to the development of the Marxist theory of the state. While there is a great deal to criticize in his work, both in terms of the form of exposition and many of his specific formulations, still his ideas have systematically shaped the analysis of the state of both his critics and supporters for nearly a decade. Because of time constraints we will not be able to trace the development of Poulantzas's thought from his first important work, *Political Power and Social Class* (first published in France in 1968) to his last book, *State, Power, Socialism* (1978). Instead, we will focus our attention on this final work, and then turn to a series of critiques of Poulantzas's general framework.

Nicos Poulantzas, *State, Power, Socialism* (New Left Books, 1978) p. 7-165.

Supplementary

Nicos Poulantzas, *Political Power and Social Class* (NLB, 1973) Note: a reading guide to this book is duplicated in the xerox reader.

Fascism and Dictatorship (NLB, 1974).

Classes in Contemporary Capitalism (NLB, 1975).

7. CRITIQUES OF THE WORK OF POULANTZAS

As would be expected, some of the most hostile critiques of Poulantzas's work comes from other Marxists, some of whom consider him a bourgeois theorist in Marxist clothing (eg. Simon Clarke). Other critics (eg. LaClau) acknowledge the importance of Poulantzas's achievements but criticize him for various sorts of inconsistencies and incompleteness.

Ernesto LaClau, "The Specificity of the Political" in *Politics and Ideology in Marxist Theory* (NLB, 1977).

Simon Clarke, "Marxism, Sociology and Poulantzas' Theory of the State", *Capital and Class #2*, 1977. Reprinted in reader.

Amy Bridges, "Nicos Poulantzas and the Marxist Theory of the State" *Politics & Society* 4:2, 1974. Reprinted in xerox reader.

Supplementary

Simon Clarke, "Capital, Fractions of Capital and the State: 'Neo-Marxist' Analysis of the South African State", *Capital and Class* #5, 1978. Reprinted in xerox reader.

John Solomons, "The Marxist Theory of the State and the Problem of fractions: some theoretical and methodological remarks", *Capital and Class* #7, 1979. Reprinted in reader.

Gosta Esping-Anderson, Roger Friedland and Erik Wright, "Modes of Class Struggle and the Capitalist State", Kapitalistate #5, 1976. Reprinted in xerox reader.

Capitol Kapstate Group, "Typology and Class Struggle", *Kapitalistate* #6, 1977.

8. THE STATE AS A "CONDITION OF EXISTENCE" OF CAPITAL: BARRY HINDESS, PAUL HIRST AND "POST-ALTHUSSERIAN" BRITISH MARXISM.

The work of Poulantzas and Althusser has had an expecially important impact on certain tendencies within British Marxism. In particular, a group of Marxists commonly referred to as "post-Althusserians" (because of the way in which they have extended Althusser's analysis and in some ways carried it to a logical extreme) have had a major influence among academic Marxists in sociology and related disciplines. Within this group the work of Hindess and Hirst has been the most widely read and discussed. Their basic point in terms of the analysis of the state is that all attempts to derive an "essence" of the state from an analysis of class relations must be rejected. The state, they argue, cannot be understood in terms of the fulfilment of necessary functions dictated by the class structure of capitalism or as the ideal expression of those class relations. Rather, the state must be analysed in terms of the historically specific ways in which certain "conditions of existence" of capitalist production relations are secured. The securing of these conditions of existence, they argue, can never be taken for granted and is never guaranteed by the simple fact of capitalist class relations; rather, such conditions are produced by class struggles.

Barry Hindess, "Classes and Politics in Marxist Theory", in Littlejohn (ed) *Power and the State* (Croom Helm, 1978). Reprinted in xerox reader.

Barry Hindess and Paul Hirst, "Primitive Communism, politics and the state", pp. 21-41 in *Precapitalist Modes of Production* (Routledge & Kegan Paul, 1975). Reprinted in xerox reader.

Anthony Cutler, Barry Hindess, Paul Hirst and Athar Hussain, *Marx's Capital and Capitalism Today*, vol. I (Routledge & Kegan Paul, 1977), pp. 222-242 (Chapter 9, "Mode of Production, Social Formation, Classes), Reprinted in xerox reader.

9. THE "STATE DERIVATION" AND "CAPITAL LOGIC" PERSPECTIVES

Perhaps the least familiar tradition in the Marxist theory of the state in North America is the tradition which attempts to derive the central features of the capitalist state from the "logic" or "form" of the capital relation. This tradition has been particularly influential in West Germany and Scandanavia, but it has begun to have a certain influence in Britain as well. The essential thrust of the approach is to attempt to logically derive various characteristics of the capitalist state from the analysis of capital accumulation in *Capital*. Holloway and Picciotto provide a good overview of the approach in the introduction to their book, *State and Capital*, and the chapter by Hirsch is an example of the approach by one of the leading German proponents.

John Holloway and Sol Picciotto, "Towards a Materialist Theory of the State", Chapter 1 of *State and Capital* (University of Texas Press, 1978). Reprinted in xerox reader.

Joachim Hirsch, "The State Apparatus and Social Reproduction: Elements of a Theory of the Bouregois State" chapter 5 in *State and Capital*. Reprinted in reader.

Supplementary

John Holloway and Sol Picciotto, "Capital, Crisis and the State", *Capital and Class* #2, 1977. Reprinted xerox reader.

Margaret Fay, "Review of *State and Capital*", *Kapitalistate* #7, 1979. Reprinted in the xerox reader.

John Holloway, "The State and Everyday Struggle", unpublished manuscript, 1979. Reprinted in the xerox reader.

John Holloway and Sol Picciotto (eds). *State and Capital* (University of Texas Press, 1978): an anthology of essays in this tradition.

10. GRAMSCI AND THE STATE

Gramsci's fragmented work on the state has probably been more influential in shaping the thinking of recent Continental discussions of the state than any other writer of the first half of the twentieth century. Because of the conditions under which he wrote (in a Fascist prison in the 1920's and 30's) his work is often very difficult to decode, and the theoretical arguments are elliptic and ambiguous. Nevertheless, his discussions of hegemony, war of position/war of manoeuvre, civil society and the state, intellectuals, passive revolution and various other topics have helped to define the terrain of much contemporary work.

Antonio Gramsci, *Selections from the Prison Notebooks* (International Publishers, 1971), especially the following pieces: "Problems of Marxism: Economy and Ideology" (407-9); "The formation of intellectuals" (5-14); "The Modern Prince" (123-202); "The State and Civil Society" (206-275).

Supplementary

Carl Boggs, *Gramsci's Marxism* (Pluto Press, 1976).

C. Buci-Glucksman, *Gramsci et L'Etat* (Feyard, 1976).

Chantal Mouffe (ed) *Gramsci & Marxist Theory* (RKP, 1979).

Perry Anderson, "The Antinomies of Antonio Gramsci" *New Left Review* #100, 1977. Reprinted in Xerox reader.

II. SPECIFIC TOPICS

1. CAPITALISM AND REPRESENTATIVE DEMOCRACY

The empirical association between representative parliamentary institutions and capitalism has often been noted by both Marxist and nonMarxist theorists. Lenin characterized parliamentary democracy as the "best possible shell" for capitalism, as the form of the state most suited to the perpetuation of the dominance of the capitalist class. Milton Friedman, on the other hand, has argued that capitalism is a necessary condition for any form of democracy, since without freedom of economic transactions political freedom cannot be sustained.

In this session we will examine a number of works which attempt to explain the relation between capitalism and representative democracy, both as an historical problem and as a general theoretical problem in the analysis of the capitalist state.

V.I. Lenin, *The State and Revolution* (sections on bourgeois democracy).

Bob Jessop, "Capitalism and Democracy: The Best Possible Shell?" in Littlejohn, et. al. (eds) *Power and the State* (London: Croom Helm, 1978). Reprinted in xerox reader.

Goran Therborn, "The Rule of Capital and the Rise of Democracy" *New Left Review* #103, May-June 1977. Reprinted in xerox reader.

Supplementary

Ernesto LaClau, "Democratic Antagonisms of the Capitalist State" unpublished manuscript presented at the E.C.P.R. conference, April 1979. Reprinted in xerox reader.

Erik Olin Wright, "Bureaucracy and the State", chapter 4 in *Class, Crisis and the State* (NLB, 1978).

Barrington Moore, Jr. *The Social Origins of Dictatorship and Democracy* (Beacon, 1966).

Norberto Bobbio, "Are There Alternatives to Representative Democracy?" *Telos* #35, 1978. Reprinted in xerox reader.

Milton Friedman, *Capitalism and Freedom* (Univ. of Chicago Press, 1962).

Perry Anderson, "The Antinomies of Antonio Gramsci", *New Left Review* #100, 1977. *Reprinted in xerox reader.*

2. THE CRISIS OF LIBERAL DEMOCRACY

Has liberal/representative democracy outlived its "usefulness" for capitalism? This is a crucial question faced by the working class in the present era of capitalist development, for the answer may have important implications for the character of the political terrain for class struggles in the period to come. In the United States the discussion of the possible exhaustion of bourgeois democracy has centered around the work of the "Tri-lateral Commission", a group of well-known academics who have been investigating the problems faced by the "Western Democracies" in the last quarter of the century.

Alan Wolfe, "The Legitimacy Crisis of the State", c. 10 in *The Limits of Legitimacy* (reprinted in Quinney, *Capitalist Society*, Dorsey, 1979). Reprinted in xerox reader.

Sam Bowles and Herb Gintis, "The Crisis of Capital and the Crisis of Liberal Democracy: the Case of the United States", unpublished manuscript, 1979. Reprinted in xerox reader.

Nicos Poulantzas, "The Decline of Democracy: authoritarian statism", pp. 203-247 in *State, Power and Socialism* (NLB, 1978).

Supplementary

Michel Crozier, et. al. *The Crisis of Democracy* (New York University Press, 1975), the report of the Tri-lateral Commission.

Samuel Bowles, "Have Capitalism and Democracy Come to a Parting of the Ways?", in URPE, *Capitalism in Crisis* (URPE, 1978).

3. CORPORATISM: A NEW STRUCTURE OF REPRESENTATION IN ADVANCED CAPITALISM?

If traditional parliamentary forms of representation have become problematic in advanced capitalism, the question arises: what new forms of representation are likely to emerge? In this regard, considerable attention is being devoted to the study of "corporatism", a system of representation in which various social categories—unions, business, consumers, the handicapped, etc.—are represented on various government decision-making bodies. Instead of representing citizens as atomized individuals, corporatism thus is a structure of representing social categories, typically via representatives chosen from the formal organizations of those categories (i.e. unions send representatives to boards rather than workers as such electing representatives). There has been considerable debate over whether or not such systems of representation are becoming significant realities in bourgeois democracies, and if they are, whether they pose serious new contradictions for the capitalist state. The readings in this section explore some of these debates.

Leo Panitch, "Trade Unions and the Capitalist State: Corporatism and its Contradictions," unpublished manuscript. 1979. Reprinted in xerox reader.

P. Schmitter and L. Lehmbruch (eds.) *Trends Towards Corporatist Intermediation* (Sage, 1979), essays by Jessop and Panitch especially.

Supplementary

Leo Panitch, "Recent Theorizations of Corporatism: reflections on a growth industry", *British Journal of Sociology*, June 1980.

Claus Offe, "Two Logics of Collective Action," *Political Power and Social Theory*, vol. I (ed. by Zeitlin), 1979.

Bob Jessop, "Capitalism and Democracy: the Best Possible Political Shell?" (concluding section), reprinted in xerox reader.

J. Westergaard, "Class, Inequality and 'Corporatism'", in A. Hunt, *Class and Class Structure*, London: Laurence and Wishart, 1977.

4. SOCIAL DEMOCRACY AND THE WELFARE STATE

The welfare state is usually characterized by Marxists as a form of the capitalist state that attempts to respond to working class challenges by reform, cooptation and integration. The provision of basic social guarantees and benefits is seen as a strategy of the bourgeoisie for maintaining its hegemony. There is a tradition, however, which argues that the welfare state is a form of the capitalist state that in many ways prefigures—and may in fact initiate—the transition to socialism. This tradition is usually associated with social democratic political positions, but a variant of it which emphasizes the political reform of the capitalist state, is now appearing in various European Communist Parties as well (so-called "Eurocommunism"). In this section we will look at some of the arguments that see the welfare state as a possible bridge to socialism.

John D. Stephens, *The Transition from Capitalism to Socialism* (MacMillan, 1979).

Supplementary

Walter Korpi, *The Working Class in Welfare Capitalism* (RKP, 1978).

Walter Korpi, "Social Democracy in Welfare Capitalism" Institute for Research on Poverty Discussion Paper (Madison, Wisconsin), 1978.

Andrew Martin, "Is Democratic Control of Capitalist Economies Possible?" in Lindberg, et. al. *Stress and Contradiction in Modern Capitalism* (Lexington Books, 1975).

5. THE STATE AND CAPITAL ACCUMULATION

Recent discussions of the state have emphasized that the state is not simply a repressive apparatus which contains the class struggle. It is also an apparatus of economic regulation and intervention, an apparatus which provides many of the material preconditions for expanded accumulation. But while there is general agreement on the importance of such interventions, there is relatively little consensus on the appropriate way to characterize and explain such interventions. In this section we will examine a number of alternative accounts which variously explain the character of state intervention in accumulation on the basis of the theory of the rising organic composition of capital/falling rate of profit; tendencies towards underconsumption/overproduction; the need to regulate labor power and the rate of exploitation; the technological imperatives of infrastructure development; and other factors.

Erik Olin Wright, "Historical Transformations of Capitalist Crisis Tendencies", especially pp. 138-180, in *Class, Crisis and the State*.

Raford Boddy and James Crotty, "Class Conflict and Macro-Policy: the Political Business Cycle", *Review of Radical Political Economics*, 7:1, 1975. Reprinted in xerox reader.

David Yaffe, "The Marxian Theory of Crisis, Capital and the State", *Economy and Society*, vol. 2, 1973.

Suzanne de Brunhoff, *The State, Capital and Economic Policy.* (Pluto Press: London, 1978), especially: 5-36, 61-75, 81-100.

Supplementary

Thomas Weisskopf, "Marxist Perspectives on Cyclical Crises" in U.R.P.E. *U.S. Capitalism in Crisis*, pp. 241-260, especially part VI., "The Role of the State."

Ernest Mandel, *Late Capitalism* (NLB1975).

Clarence Lo, "The Functions of U.S. Military Spending", *Kapitalistate* No. 3, 1975.

Aboo Aumeeruddy, Bruno Lautier and Ramon Tortajada, "Labour Power and the State", *Capital and Class* #6, 1978.

6. THE FISCAL CRISIS OF THE STATE

Most investigations of the relationship of state to economy in Marxism have emphasized the impact of the state on economy (i.e. the "functions" of the state). More recently there has emerged a systematic discussion of the impact of the economy on the state. In part this is an extension of a long standing tradition of examining the effects of class struggle on the state. The recent work, however, goes beyond that in trying to establish the systematic character of the impact of accumulation on the state and the contradictions within the accumulation process on the conflicts within the state. Much of this work has revolved around what is called the "fiscal crisis of the state." As should become clear form our discussion of critical theory approaches to the study of the state, many of the issues raised in the analysis of fiscal crisis are closely tied to the more general problems posed by writers like Offe and Habermas concerning the displacement of economic contradictions to the political sphere.

James O'Connor, *The Fiscal Crisis of the State* (St. Martin's Press, 1973). Entire book, but especially: pp. 5-96, 203-260.

7. THE STATE AND THE LABOR PROCESS

The labor process constitutes one of the most fundamental categories of Marxist analysis, and yet there is very little theoretical or empirical work which attempts to link this category to the problem of the state. If the labor process defines the set of relations within which the working class is most fundamentally constituted and the state constitutes the arena within which class struggles are ultimately waged, then it is essential to theorize the relationship between these two structures of relations within Marxist theory. Michael Burawoy attempts to do this in his essay on the "Production of Politics and the Politics of Production" by introducing the distinction between the internal state and the global state.

Michael Burawoy: "The Production of Politics and the Politics of Production" in *Political Power and Social Theory*, vol. I (ed. by Zeitlin, JAI press, 1979). If this volume is unavailable, the essay will be distributed in class.

8. THE STATE AND THE INTERNATIONALIZATION OF CAPITAL

One of the most striking developments in the structure of capital since the Second World War has been the qualitative leap in international forms of organization of capitalist production. Yet political systems have remained almost exclusively organized on a national basis. The state remains national in form, while capitalist production becomes increasingly international. This contradiction has profound implications for the character of class struggles and for the capacity of nation states to regulate the conditions of accumulation on their own territories.

Alberto Martinelli and Eugenio Somaini, "Multinational corporations and the Nation State," *Kapitalistate* #1, 1973. Reprinted in xerox reader.

Nicos Poulantzas, "The Internationalization of Capitalist Relations and the Nation State" in *Classes in Contemporary Capitalism,* pp. 38-88. Reprinted in xerox reader.

9. THE STATE IN THE INTER-STATE SYSTEM

Marxists have generally insisted on the primacy of the state-class relation over the state-state relation in understanding the world system of states. Thus, for example, War tends to be understood as a result of interests pursued by competing ruling classes of different countries (i.e. inter-imperialist rivalry) rather than as a result of a distinct logic of inter-state interaction. States themselves do not have "interests", they are not "subjects"—at least in traditional Marxist theory. Theda Skocpol and others have challenged these assumptions and have argued that the inter-state system must be placed on an equal footing with the class system as a basis for understanding the character and actions of nation states.

Theda Skocpol, *States and Social Revolutions* (Cambridge University Press, 1979), general theoretical sections.

10. THE STATE IN THE TRANSITION FROM FEUDALISM TO CAPITALISM

Absolutism has always been something of a puzzle for Marxists. If states are always class states, then the Absolutist state must either be a feudal state, a capitalist state or some peculiar amalgam characteristic of a transition period. Yet none of these characterizations is entirely satisfactory. Of these positions, the sharpest lines of debate have been between those who see the state in this period as fundamentally feudal in character (eg. Perry Anderson) and those who see the Absolutist state as basically an early form of the capitalist state (eg. Wallerstein). In this section we will try to sort out the theoretical presuppositions of each position and examine the historical evidence for each.

Perry Anderson, *Linneages of the Absolutist State* (NLB, 1976) especially pp. 7-59, 195-235, 397-431.

Immanuel Wallerstein, *The Modern World System* (academic press, 1976).

11. THE FORMATION OF THE NATION STATE: THE UNITED STATES AS A CASE STUDY

The formation of a state is an ideal historical moment to examine the process by which institutional structures are formed, and thus potentially to see the process by which their class character is established. In this session we will examine the formation of the U.S. National State and see its relationship to the class relations and conflicts of the period.

Margit Mayer and Margaret A. Fay, "The Formation of the American Nation-State" *Kapitalistate* #6, 1977, pp. 39-90. Reprinted in the xerox reader.

12. THE STATE AND WOMEN'S OPPRESSION

The development of feminist theory in recent years has posed a significant challenge to Marxism. Is it possible to understand the specificity of the oppression of women within a theory that revolves around the concept of class without ultimately reducing sexual domination to an expression of class domination? Relatively little of the dialogue between Marxists and feminists has centered on the state, but in many ways the analysis of the state should be a fertile terrain for trying to understand these issues. The challenge to feminists in terms of the theory of the state would be: Can the state be understood as a form of patriarchal domination/relations? Can the state become a theoretical object within the conceptual framework of feminist theory as it now stands? In answering these questions it is not enough to simply describe the effects of the state in reproducing sexual domination (anymore than in the class theory of the state a description of such class-effects is sufficient). What is needed is a theory of the mechanisms which generate such effects.

The challenge of these issues for Marxists would be: Can a theory of the state which understands the structures, mechanisms and effects of the state in terms of class struggle provide an account of the state's role in the reproduction of sexual relations? Does such an attempt inevitably lead to a class functionalism within which sexual domination can be understood only in terms of the ways in which it contributes to class domination?

Mary McIntosh, "The State and the Oppression of Women," in Kuhn and Wolpe, *Feminism and Materialism* (RKP, 1978). Reprinted in xerox reader.

Jalna Hanmer, "Violence and the Social Control of Women" in Littlejohn, *Power and the State* (London: Croom Helm, 1978). Reprinted in reader.

Altina Grossman, "Abortion and the Economic Crisis," *New German Critique* #14. Reprinted in reader.

Supplementary

Lesley Caldwell, "Church, State and Family: the women's movement in Italy", in *Feminism and Materialism.*

Ann Corine Hill, "The Protection of Women Workers and the Courts: a legal case history" *Feminist Studies,* 5:2, pp. 247-274.

Linda Gordon, *Woman's Body, Woman's Right,* esp. pp. 313-402.

Diana L. Barker, "The Regulation of Marriage: repressive benevolence" in Littlejohn, op cit.

13. LAW AND THE STATE

The law and the legal system have rarely been systematically studied by Marxists. Most investigations have either collapsed the discussion of Law into the discussion of ideology, seeing the law as simply one variety of ideology. Or, the problem of law has been collapsed into the theory of the repressive state apparatus, seeing the legal system as simply the form through which repression is exercised in capitalist society. Relatively little attention has been given to law in its own right, as a structure or set of relations within which struggles take place and contradictions of a specific sort develop. This session will try to examine what some of the key elements of a Marxist theory of law should look like.

Bernard Edelman, *Ownership of the Image: Elements for a Marxist Theory of Law* (RKP, 1979).

Issac Balbus, "Commodity Form and Legal Form: an essay on the relative autonomy of the law", *Law & Society Review* 1977. Reprinted in xerox reader.

Supplementary

Pashukanis: Selected Writings on Marxism and Law, edited and introduced by P. Bierne and R. Sharlet (Academic Press, 1979).

Maureen Cain and Alan Hunt, *Marx and Engels on Law* Academic Press, 1979), paperback.

Colin Sumner, *Reading Ideologies: an investigation into the Marxist Theory of Ideology and Law* (Academic Press, 1979) paperback.

Issac Balbus, *The Dialectics of Legal Repression.*

Erik Olin Wright, *The Politics of Punishment* (Harper and Row, 1973).

Mark Tushnet, "A Marxist Analysis of American Law," *Marxist Perspectives* (1978).

14. THE STATE IN THE PERIPHERY

Most of the theorizing on the capitalist state has focussed on the state in advanced capitalist societies. Relatively little of a general character has been written on the state in the Third World. The analysis of the state in such societies is particularly complex because of the complexity of their class structures (particularly the continuing existence of precapitalist relations of production and large peasantries) and because of the dependent character of state activities which result from their subordination to international capital. In one session we cannot possibly hope to sort out the full range of problems concerning the state in the periphery, but we may be able to identify some of the salient issues which give these states their distinctive character.

W. Ziemann and M. Lanzendorfer, "The State in Peripheral Societies", *Socialist Register* 1977. Reprinted in xerox reader.

H. Alavi, "The State in Post-Colonial Societies—Pakistan and Bangladesh," NLR #74, 1972. Reprinted in xerox reader.

B.J. Berman and J.M. Lonsdale, "Crises of Accumulation, Coercion and the Colonial State: the Development of the Labor Control System in Keyna, 1919-1929" unpublished manuscript, 1979. Reprinted in xerox reader.

Supplementary

B. Harrison, "The Chilean State After the Coup", *The Socialist Register,* 1977.

G. Therbourn, "The Travail of Latin American Democracy", *New Left Review,* #113-114, 1979.

N. Hamilton, "The Limits of State Autonomy", chapter X in The Limits of State Autonomy, unpublished PhD dissertation, U.W. Madison, 1978.

C. Leys, "The Overdeveloped Post Colonial State: a re-evaluation" *Review of African Political Economy,* #5.

M. Mamdani, *Politics and Class Formation in Uganda* (M.R. Press).

G. O'Donnel, "Corporatism and the Question of the State" in *Authoritarianism and Corporatism in Latin America* ed. by Malloy, 1976.

15. CLASS COALITIONS IN THE POWER BLOC: AN APPLICATION OF POULANTZAS'S FRAMEWORK TO WEIMAR GERMANY

Poulantzas's work is often criticized for being so abstract to be useless for concrete investigation. David Abraham has completed an extremely important study of the shifting class alliances in Weimar Germany which explicitly uses Poulantzas's ideas concerning the power bloc and class alliances. The study is useful not only because of the way it illuminates the dynamics behind the political stalemate that facilitated the rise of German fascism and the destruction of the bourgeois democratic state, but also because it shows how one can do systematic historical research using Poulantzian concepts.

David Abraham, "State and Classes in Weimar Germany", *Politics & Society,* Vol. 7:3, 1977. Reprinted in reader.

16. QUANTITATIVE STUDIES ON THE STATE

Marxists have generally been quantophobic. Nevertheless, in recent years a number of interesting quantitative studies of state questions have emerged, many of them from the Wisconsin sociology department. These studies need critical assessment, especially since many students will probably want to do dissertations using such techniques. How faithful are these studies to the theoretical arguments which they advance? Does the theory get deformed by the attempts at quantification? Do we learn anything fundamentally new from the quantitative exercise, or does it mainly serve a polemical function?

Roger Friedland, "Class Power and Social Control: the War on Poverty", *Politics and Society,* 6:4, 1976. Reprinted in xerox reader.

Gosta Esping-Anderson, "Social Class, Social Democracy and the State: Housing Policy in Denmark and Sweden," *Comparative Politics,* Fall, 1978. Reprinted in xerox reader.

Alexander Hicks, et. al. "Class Power and State Policy" ASR, 43, 1978. Reprinted in xerox reader.

David R. Cameron, "The Expansion of the Public Economy: a Comparative Analysis", *APSR* 72:4, 1978. Reprinted in xerox reader.

17. POWER STRUCTURE RESEARCH

There is a tendency among Marxist theorists today to dismiss out of hand most "power structure research", on the grounds that it is based on an instrumentalist theory of the state. While it is certainly the case that such theoretical criticisms are warranted, nevertheless it is incumbent upon Marxists to try to incorporate into their theorizing the massive evidence about the power structures of the capitalist state compiled by people like Domhoff, Miliband, C.W. Mills and others. How can this information be comprehended theoretically? How can we understand the variability in forms of instrumental control (rather than simply the ubiquitousness of such control)? What is the relationship between structural determination and instrumental action in explaining the state? This research needs to be taken seriously and we need to establish what exactly we have learned from it.

G. William Domhoff (ed). *New Directions in Power Structure Research*, special issue of the *Insurgent Sociologist*, V:III, Spring, 1975.

Supplementary

C.W. Mills, *The Power Elite* (Oxford University Press, 1956).

G. William Domhoff, *Who Rules America* (Prentice-Hall, 1967); *The Higher Circles* (Vintage, 1970); *Who Really Rules: New Haven and Community Power Re-Examined* (Goodyear, 1978).

New Directions in Power Structure Research, vol II., Insurgent Sociologist, forthcoming.

Theories of the State

Michael H. Best
University of Massachusetts—Amherst
Economics
Spring 1980

BOOKS

S. Avineri, *Hegel's Theory of the Modern State*
O. Eckstein, *Public Finance*, 4th Editiion
B. Fay, *Social Theory and Political Practice*
J. Habermas, *Legitimation Crisis*
A. Hirschman: *The Passions and the Interests*
J. O'Connor, *Fiscal Crisis of the State*
C. Schultze, *Public Use of the Private Interest*
E. Wright, *Class Crisis and State*

PART ONE: THEORETICAL PERSPECTIVES

I. Neoclassical

A. Microeconomic—Virtues of the Market

1. Adam Smith—Market and Economic Freedom and Social Stability

A. Hirschman, Part One, pp. 3-66.

2. Chicago School—Free Market and Freedom

M. Friedman, *The Economics of Freedom*, Standard Oil handout, pp. 1-25.

G. Stigler, "The Economist Traditional Theory of the Economic Functions of the State" in Geo. Stigler, *The Citizen and the State* (Chicago, 1975) pp. 103-113. Reserve

M. Best and W. Connolly, *The Politicized Economy*, Ch., pp. 1-11. Reserve

3. General Equilibrium Theory/PPBS—Managed Market and Efficiency

O. Eckstein, *Public Finance*, Chs 1, 2, 5 and 6.

W. Baumol, *Economic Theory and Operation Analysis* (Prentice Hall, 1965) Ch. 16, "General Equilibrium and Welfare Economics." (Clear exposition of marginal conditions, optimality rules and "Fundamental Neoclassical Theorem.") Reserve

C. Schultze, *The Public Use of the Private Interest*, pp. 1-46.

C. Wright, "The Concept of a Program Budget," in H. Hinrichs and G. Taylor (eds) Program Budgeting and Benefit Cost Analysis (Goodyear, 1969) pp. 23-32. (Peruse articles by Enthoven, McNamara and Schlesinger in same volume for examples of technocratic planners and Hinrichs for a 'Primer' on cost benefit analysis). Reserve

C. Schultze, *Public Use of the Private Interest*, pp. 46-90.

B. Fay, *Social Theory and Political Practice*, Chs. 1-3, pp. 11-69.

W. Connolly, "The Public Interest and the Common Good," Reserve.

B. Macroeconomics—the Market and Economic Instability

O. Eckstein, Public Finance, Ch. 8.

A. Coddington, "Keynesian Economics," *Journal of Economic Literature*, Dec. 1976, pp. 1258-1273. Reserve

J. Keynes, *The General Theory*, Ch. 12, pp. 147-164. Reserve

S. Hymer "International Politics/International Economics," *Monthly Review* Vol. 29, No. 10, Mar. 1978, pp 15-35. Reserve

F. Hirsch, *Social Limits to Growth*, Parts I-IV, pp. 1-190.

II. Marxian

A. Hegel—Market (Civil Society) and the state

S. Avineri, *Hegel's Theory of the Modern State*, Chs. 1, 2, 5, 7, and 9.

B. Marx—Market Economy as Historical Stage

R. Jessop, "Recent Theories of the Capitalist State," *Cambridge Journal of Economics*, Vol. 1, No. 4, Dec. 1977, pp. 353-73. Reserve

L. Colletti, "Berstein and Marxism of the Second International" in L. Colletti, *From Rousseau to Lenin* (Monthly Review, 1972) pp. 45-108. Reserve

E. Wright, *Class, Crisis and State*, Ch. 3, "Historical Transformations of Capitalist Crisis Tendencies," pp. 111-180 also in *Insurgent Sociologist*, Vol. VI, No. 1, Fall 1975, pp. 5-40.

C. Instrumentalist/Structuralist Debate

N. Poulantzas, "The Problem of the Capitalist State" and R. Miliband, "Reply to Nicos Poulantzas" in R. Blackburn (ed) *Ideology in Social Science* (Vintage, 1973) pp. 238-262.

D. Capital Logic

J. Holloway and S. Picciotto, "Introduction: Towards a Materialist Theory of the State," in Holloway and Picciotto, *State and Capital* (Arnold, 1978) pp. 1-31. Reserve

E. Underspending and the Rise of the Welfare State

J. O'Connor, Fiscal Crisis of the State, Chs. 1, 2, 6, 8 and 9.

I. Gough, "State Expenditure in Advanced Capitalism," *New Left Review*, No. 92, July-August 1975, pp. 53-92. Reserve

C. Offe and V. Ronge, "Theses on the Theory of the State," *New German Critique*, No. 6, Fall 1975, pp. 137-47. Reserve

III. Political Economy

A. Structuralism

L. Althusser, "Ideological State Apparatuses," in L. Althusser, *Lenin and Philosophy* (Monthly Review, 1971) pp. 127-88. Reserve

M. Best and W. Connolly, "Structural Underdetermination: A Critique of Althusser," *Socialist Review*, No. 48.

B. Intersubjectivity

J. Habermas, *Legitimation Crisis*, Intro, Parts I and II.

B. Fay, *Social Theory and Political Practice*, Chs. 4 and 5.

W. Connolly, "Is the Welfare State Legitimate?" Chancellor's Lecture, 1978. Handout

C. Imperial State

S. Hymer "The Internationalization of Capital," *Journal of Economic Issues*, Vol. 6, No. 1, 1972, pp. 91-111.

J. Petras, "The Imperial State," mimeo.

D. Sociological Theories

J. Goldthorpe, "The Current Inflation: Towards a Sociological Account," pp. 186-213; and

C. Crouch, "Inflation and the Political Organization of Economic Interests," pp. 217-239; and

S. Brittan, "Inflation and Democracy" in F. Hirsch and J. Goldthorpe (eds) *The Political Economy of Inflation* (Martin Robertson, 1978) pp. 161-186.

PART TWO: HISTORICAL EXPERIENCES (SPECIFIC PERIODS TO BE DECIDED ON ACCORDING TO STUDENT AND INSTRUCTOR INTERESTS. SEVERAL POSSIBILITIES FOLLOW).

I. Role of state in 19th century England, particularly as gleaned from Marx's *Capital*.

II. Fascism in Germany and/or Italy, perhaps via W. Reich's *The Mass Psychology of Fascism*.

III. New Deal and the Emergence of the Warfare/Welfare state in the U.S.

IV. World War I and II Restructuring of the American economy to meet the exigencies of war. Could the U.S. economy be restructured and planned to meet the imperatives of production for social use based on renewable energy sources?

V. Internationalization of Capital in Post World War II period and the implications for the State.

VI. The State in dependent market economies or in poor countries in transition to socialism.

VII. The role of state planning boards in Western European countries.

Sociology of the State

Alan Wolfe
City University of New York—
Graduate Center
Sociology
Spring 1982
Graduate

To this day an understanding of the role of the state in both the development and the contemporary workings of modern society is incomplete. Minute attention has been paid to the economy, so that every tiny change has diverse immediate interpretations. Inordinate information exists about social structure, class, and occupation. Yet, in spite of the almost fantastic importance that the state has taken on in reproducing class structure, ideology, accumulation, and family relationships, political forces are often subsumed both by liberals and Marxists as a residue explained by other dynamics. In this seminar we will take the political as an area of importance in itself and seek to comprehend more fully the nature of public life in industrial societies. Most of the course will concern itself with capitalist politics, but there will also be material on the world economy and on socialist states.

The work of this seminar will proceed along two paths. For students who have not been exposed in depth to readings in the theory of the state, a reading list is included that contains most of the important statements currently under debate. Students may wish to read this material in advance of the seminar, for which purpose this list is being distributed early. This reading list will constitute the bulk of the seminar. But each week's assignments also includes an additional reading list, one designed for people who have already prepared work on the state. These additional readings have been chosen based on two criteria: either they represent advanced theoretical work done since the "classics" were written, or they attempt to apply theoretical insights to specific empirical research problems. Students who have already worked in the theory of the state may desire to take this seminar and concentrate on the additional readings.

The seminar will meet for one session each week. There will be a discussion of the readings at each session. In addition, readings and study groups will be created to meet in between each weekly session in order to facilitate the work of the seminar. In order to complete the requirement for the course, students will be expected to come to the seminars and participate. They will also be expected to prepare during the semester a research proposal that will attempt to apply a particular theoretical tradition in the theory of the state to a specific research interest.

FIRST WEEK: MARXIST CLASSICS

Basic reading:

Karl Marx, "Critique of Hegel's Philosophy of Right," any edition.

Karl Marx and Frederick Engels, *The German Ideology.*

Karl Marx, *The Eighteenth Brumaire.*

Karl Marx, *Capital,* Volume I., Chapter 10.

Additional reading:

Hal Draper, *Karl Marx's Theory of Revolution: State and Revolution* (New York: Monthly Review Press, 1977), Volume I, pp. 168-338.

Ralph Miliband, *Marxism and Politics* (New York: Oxford University Press, 1977), 1-117.

SECOND WEEK: WEBERIAN CLASSICS

Basic Reading:

Hans Gerth and C. Wright Mills, *From Max Weber* (New York: Oxford University Press).

Additional Reading:

Dennis Wrong, *Power* (New York: Harper & Row, 1975).

Robert Nisbet, *Twilight of Authority* (New York: Oxford University Press, 1975).

Reinhard Bendix, *Kings or People* (Berkeley: University of California Press, 1978).

THIRD WEEK: POST-MARXIST CONTROVERSIES

Basic Reading:

V.I. Lenin, *State and Revolution* (New York: International Publishers, 1943).

Antonio Gramsci, *Selections from the Prison Notebooks* (New York: International Publishers, 1971), 125-276.

Santiago Carillo, *Eurocommunism and the State* (Westport, Conn.: Lawrence Hill, 1978), pp. 7-109.

Additional Reading:

Ralph Miliband, *Marxism and Politics*, pp. 118-190.

Perry Anderson, "The Antimonies of Antonio Gramsci," New Left Review, #100.

Christina Bucci-Glucksman, *Gramsci et L'etat*, (Paris: Fayard, 1975).

Carl Boggs, *Gramsci's Marxism* (London: Pluto Press, 1977).

Norberto Bobbio, "Is There a Marxist Theory of the State?" and "Are There Alternatives to Representative Democracy?," *Telos* (Spring 1978), 3-30.

C.B. Macpherson, "Do We Need a Theory of the State?", *Archives Europeenes de Sociologie*, XVIII (1977), 223-244.

FOURTH WEEK: POST-WEBERIAN CONTROVERSIES

Basic Reading:

Joseph Schumpeter, *Capitalism, Socialism, and Democracy* (New York: Harper, 1962). Part IV, pp. 235-302.

Joseph Bensman, "Max Weber's Concept of Legitimacy: An Evaluation," in Arthur Vidich and Ronald Glassman (eds.), Conflict and Control (Beverly Hills: Sage Publications, 1979), 17-48.

Additional Reading:

Charles Lindblom, *Politics and Markets* (New York: Basic Books, 1977), pp. 17-62.

Peter Steinfela, *The Neo-Conservatives* (New York: Simon and Schuster, 1979).

Edward Tufte, *Political Control of the Economy* (Princeton: Princeton University Press, 1979).

Morris Janowitz, *Social Control of the Welfare State* (Chicago: University of Chicago Press, 1976).

FIFTH WEEK: POSTWAR MODIFICATIONS

Basic Reading:

Ralph Miliband, *The State in Capitalist Society* (New York: Basic Books, 1969), pp. 23-118.

Nicos Poulantzas, *Political Power and Social Classes* (London: Sheed and Ward, 1973), pp. 187-321.

Nicos Poulantzas, "The Problem of the Capitalist State," *New Left Review*, #58, pp. 67-78.

Ralph Miliband, "The Capitalist State," *New Left Review*, #59, pp. 53-60. Also published in Robein Blackburn, Ideology in Social Science (including preceding essay).

Ernesto Laclau, "The Specificity of the Political," *Economy and Society* (1975), pp. 87-110. Also included in Laclau's book published by NLR.

Nicos Poulantzas, "The Capitalist State," *New Left Review* #95, pp. 63-83.

David Gold, Clarence Lo, and Erik Olin Wright, "Recent Developments in Marxist Theories of the Capitalist State," *Monthly Review*, October and November 1975.

Additional Reading

Nicos Poulantzas, *Classes in Contemporary Capitalism* (London: New Left Books, 1975), 91-189.

Fred Block, "The Ruling Class Does Not Rule," *Socialist Revolution*, #33, pp. 6-28.

John Holloway and Sol Piccioto, "Introduction," *State and Capital: A Marxist Debate* (London: Edward Arnold, 1978), pp. 1-31.

Amy Beth Bridges, "Nicos Poulantzas and the Marxist Theory of the State," *Politics and Society*, Vol. 4, #2 (1974).

Goran Therborn, *What Does the Ruling Class Do When It Rules?* (London: New Left Books, 1978), 29-244.

SIXTH WEEK: ACCUMULATION/LEGITIMATION

Basic Reading:

Jurgen Habermas, *Legitimation Crisis* (Boston: Beacon Press, 1975), 33-94.

Claus Offe, "Structural Problems of the Capitalist State," in Klaus von Beyne (ed.), *German Political Studies* (Beverly Hills: Sage Publications, 1976).

Claus Offe, "The Theory of the State and the Problem of Policy Formation," in Leon Lindberg et al., *Stress and Contradiction in Modern Capitalism* (Lexington, Mass.: D.C. Heath, 1975), pp. 125-144.

Claus Offe and Volker Ronge, "Theses on the State," *New German Critique*, Vol. 2, #3 (1975), pp. 137-147.

James O'Connor, *The Fiscal Crisis of the State* (New York: St. Martin's 1973), Chaps. 1, 7, and 8.

Alan Wolfe, *The Limits of Legitimacy* (New York: Free Press, 1977), Introduction.

Additional Reading:

Ian Gough, "State Expenditure in Advanced Capitalism," *New Left Review*, #92, pp. 53-92.

Hugh Mosley, "Is There a Fiscal Crisis of the State?" *Monthly Review* (May 1978), 34-45.

David Wolfe, "The State and Economic Policy in Canada," in Lee Panitch (ed.), *The Canadian State* (Toronto: University of Toronto Press, 1977), 251-288.

SEVENTH WEEK: PROBLEMS IN THE THEORY OF THE STATE: HISTORICAL TRANSFORMATION

Basic Reading:

Immanuel Wallerstein, *The Origins of the Modern World System* (New York: Academic Press, 1974), pp. 224-357.

Theda Skocpol, *States and Social Revolutions* (Cambridge University Press, 1979).

Samuel P. Huntington, *Political Order in Changing Societies* (New Haven: Yale University Press, 1968), 93-139.

Additional Reading:

Charles Tilly, *The Formation of National States in Western Europe* (Princeton: Princeton University Press, 1975), esp. Chaps. 2, 3, 5, and 9.

Theda Skocpol and E.K. Trimberger, "Revolutions and the World Historical Development of Capitalism," *Berkeley Journal of Sociology*, XXII (1977-78), pp. 101-113.

Robert Brenner, "The Origins of Capitalist Development," *New Left Review*, #104 (July-August 1977), 25-92.

EIGHTH WEEK: PROBLEMS IN THE THEORY OF THE STATE: DEMOCRACY

Basic Reading:

Gosta Esping-Anderson, Roger Friedland, and Erik Olin Wright, "Modes of Class Struggle and the Capitalist State," *Kapitalistate,* #4-5 (Summer 1976), pp. 186-220.

Alan Wolfe, "Has Social Democracy a Future?" *Comparative Politics,* October 1978.

Nicos Poulantzas, *Classes in Contemporary Capitalism,* pp. 190-end.

Leo Panitch, Social Democracy and Industrial Militancy. (Cambridge: Cambridge University Press, 1976).

Additional reading:

Erik Olin Wright, "Contradictory Class Locations," *New Left Review,* #98, pp. 3-41.

Andrew Martin, *The Politics of Economic Policy in the United States* (Beverly Hills: Sage Publications, 1973).

Richard Scase, *Social Democracy in Capitalist Society* (London: Croom Held, 1977), Chap. 7.

Martin Rein and Peter Marris, "Equality, Inflation, and Wage Control," in Lindberg, *Stress and Contradiction,* pp. 199-213.

Fred Hirsch and John Goldthorpe (eds), *The Political Economy of Inflation* (Cambridge: Harvard University Press, 1978).

Robert Keohane, "Economics, Inflation, and the Role of the State," *World Politics,* forthcoming.

NINTH WEEK: PROBLEMS IN THE THEORY OF THE STATE: STATES IN A WORLD ECONOMY

Basic Reading:

Nicos Poulantzas, *Classes in Contemporary Capitalism,* pp. 38-88.

Claudia von Braunmuhl, "The Bourgeois Nation State Within the World Market," in Holloway and Piccioto, pp. 160-177.

Peter Katzenstein (ed.) *Between Power and Plenty* (Madison: University of Wisconsin Press, 1978), esp. the essays by Katzenstein, Blank, Maier, and Krasner.

Stephen Hymer, "International Politics and International Economics," in Lindberg, *Stress and Contradiction,* pp. 355-372.

James R. Kurth, "The International Politics of Postindustrial Societies," in Lindberg, *Stress and Contradiction,* pp. 373-392.

Alberto Martinelli and Eugenio Somaini, "Nation States and Multinational Corporations," *Kapitalistate,* 1 (1973), 69-78.

Additional readings:

Fred Block, *The Origins of International Economic Disorder* (Berkeley: University of California Press, 1977).

Franz Schurmann, *The Logic of World Power* (New York: Pantheon, 1974), pp. 3-200.

Immanuel Wallerstein, "The Rise and Future Demise of the World Capitalist Systems," *Comparative Studies in Society and History,* 16 (September 1974), 387-415.

TENTH WEEK: THE STATE IN THE THIRD WORLD

Basic Reading:

Alfred Stepan, *The State and Society: Peru in Comparative Perspectives* (Princeton: Princeton University Press, 1979).

Guillermo O'Donnell, Bureaucratic Authoritarianism Revisited," in David Collier (ed.), *The New Authoritarianism in Latin America* (Princeton: Princeton University Press, 1979).

Additional Reading:

Ellen Kay Trimberger, *Revolution from Above* (New Brunswick: Transaction Books, 1980).

Juan Linz and Alfred Stepan, *The Breakdown of Democratic Regimes* (Baltimore: Johns Hopkins, 1978).

Susan Eckstein, *The Poverty of Revolution* (Princeton: Princeton University Press, 1977.

Richard Fagen (ed.), *Capital and State in US-Latin American Relations* (Stanford: Stanford University Press).

ELEVENTH WEEK: PROBLEMS IN THE THEORY OF THE STATE: DELEGITIMATION

Basic Reading:

Claus Offe, "Political Authority and Class Structure," *International Journal of Sociology,* Vol. 2, #1, pp. 73-108.

Renate Mayntz, "Legitimacy and the Directive Capacity of the Political System," in Lindberg, *Stress and Contradiction,* pp. 261-274.

Walter Dean Burnham, "American Politics in the 1980s," *Dissent,* (Spring 1980), 149-160.

San Francisco Bay Area Kapitalistate Group, "Political Parties and Capitalist Development," *Kapitalistate,* 6 (Fall 1977), 7-38.

Alan Wolfe, *Limits of Legitimacy,* Part II.

Additional Reading:

Michel Crozier et al, *The Crisis of Democracy* (New York: New York University Press, 1976), esp. chapter by Huntington on the United States.

Alan Wolfe, *America's Impasse* (New York: Pantheon, 1981).

TWELFTH WEEK: PROBLEMS IN THE THEORY OF THE STATE: DISACCUMULATION

Basic Reading:

Joachim Hirsch, "The State Apparatus and Social Reproduction," in Holloway and Piccioto, pp. 57-107.

Larry Hirschhorn and Fred Block, "New Production Forces and the Contradictions of Contemporary Capitalism," *Theory and Society,* forthcoming.

James O'Connor, work to be distributed.

Additional reading:

Ernest Mandel, Late Capitalism (Atlantic Highlands, N.J.: Humanities Press, 1975), Chaps. 6, 7, and 15.

Karl Marx, The Grundrisse (New York: Vintage Books, 1973), pp. 690-751.

Joseph Schumpeter, *Capitalism, Socialism and Democracy,* Part II.

THIRTEENTH WEEK: THE STATE AND FOREIGN POLICY

Readings:

Alan Wolfe, "Resurgent Cold War Ideology," in Fagan (ed), *Capital and the State in US Latin American Relations*.

Alan Wolfe, *The Rise and Fall of the Soviet Threat* (Washington: Institute for Policy Studies, 1979).

Mary Kaldor, *The Disintegrating West* (New York: Pantheon, 1978).

Additional Readings:

Richard Barnet, *The Roots of War* (New York: Penguin).

Franz Schurmann, *The Logic of World Power* (New York: Pantheon, 1974).

FOURTEENTH WEEK: THE SOCIALIST STATE

Readings:

Severyn Bialer, *Stalin's Successors* (Cambridge: Cambridge University Press, 1980), Part I and Part III.

David Lane, *The Socialist Industrial State* (London: George Allen and Unwin, 1976).

Ernest Mandel, "The Nature of the Soviet State," *New Left Review*, #108, pp. 23-45.

Additional Readings:

Bogdan Denitch, *The Legitimation of a Revolution* (New Haven: Yale University Press, 1976).

Charles Bettleheim, *Class Struggles in the Soviet Union* (New York: Monthly Review Press).

FIFTEENTH WEEK: THE FUTURE OF STATE THEORY

Reading to be announced.

DEVELOPMENT AND REGIONAL STUDIES

Seminar on Development Studies

James Petras, Mark Selden
State University of New York—Binghamton
Department of Sociology
Fall 1979
Graduate

This seminar is a survey of social change, economic expansion, state organization and class formation in the periphery. The approach combines historical and contemporary sociological perspectives on pivotal processes, focusing on societal transitions and structural transformations. The first part of the course is designed to introduce graduate students to a variety of analytical perspectives on historical change and a critical review of the strengths and weaknesses of each. The second section deals with imperialism—the dynamic class relationship imposed by large-scale, long-term movements of western capital into peripheral societies—in its political and economic forms. The third and fourth parts are concerned with the processes and structural outcomes of transitions from pre-colonial to colonial societies and from the latter to post-colonial societies—and their varients. Part five focuses on various interpretations of peripheral industrialization processes—the principal features and future prospects. Agrarian and urban structures are considered in part six. Part seven considers the organization of the state—specifically differing conceptualizations of the state and the role of the military. Part eight focuses on class formation, especially the urban and rural bourgeoisie, the working class and the agrarian labor force and the inter-relationship of classes in formation.

I. PERSPECTIVES ON HISTORICAL CHANGE

A. WORLD HISTORICAL APPROACHES—Week 1

Paul Baran, *The Political Economy of Growth*, pp. 44-50, 134-162.

A. Gunder Frank, "The Development of Underdevelopment" in Rhodes, *Imperialism and Underdevelopment*, pp. 4-17.

I. Wallerstein, "Rise and Future Demise of the World Capitalist System," *Comparative Studies in History and Society*, Vol. 16, Sept. 1974.

Samir Amin, "Accumulation and Development: A Theoretical Model," *Review of African Political Economy*, No. 1, pp. 9-26.

James Petras and Kent Trachte, "Liberal, Structural and Radical Approaches to Political Economy: An Assessment," in J. Petras, *Critical Perspectives on Imperialism and Social Classes in the Third World* (Monthly Review: New York, 1979), pp. 13-62.

B. MODERNIZATION AND NATIONBUILDING APPROACHES TO DEVELOPMENT—Week 2

R. Bendix, *Nation-Building and Citizenship*, Ch. 1-4 and Ch. 8.

W.W. Rostow, *The Stages of Economic Growth*, Ch. 1-6, pp. 1-93.

Samuel Huntington, *Political Order in Changing Society*.

Schumpeter, *Imperialism and Social Classes*, essay on "Imperialism."

C. CRITICAL COMMENTARIES—Week 3

Baran and Hobsbawm, "The Stages of Economic Growth," *KYKLOS* XIV, pp. 234-242.

Robert Brenner, "The Origins of Capitalist Development," *New Left Review*, No. 104.

Victor Lippit, "The Development of Underdevelopment in China," *Modern China*, Vol. 4, July 1978, pp. 267-328.

A. Gunder Frank, "Sociology of Development or Underdevelopment of Sociology," in Johnson, Cockcroft and Frank (eds.), *Dependence and Underdevelopment*.

Colin Leys, "Underdevelopment and Dependency: Critical Notes," *Journal of Contemporary Asia*, Vol. 7, No. 1, pp. 92-107.

D. IMPERIALISM: ECONOMY AND STATE—Week 4

Lenin, *Imperialism*.

Harry Magdoff, "Imperialism: A Historical Survey," *Monthly Review*, Vol. 24, No. 1, May 1972, pp. 1-18.

Owen and Sutcliffe, *Studies in the Theory of Imperialism*, Ch. 1-4 and Ch. 6.

James Petras, "The Imperial State" (mimeo).

E. THE TRANSITION FROM PRE-COLONIAL TO COLONIAL AND SEMI-COLONIAL SOCIETIES—Week 5

Magdoff, *Imperialism: From the Colonial Age to the Present*, chapter on "Colonialism."

Owen and Sutcliffe, Ch. 5.

Andrew Nathan and Joseph Esherick, "Imperialism in China," *Bulletin of Concerned Asian Scholars*, Vol. 4, No. 4, pp. 3-16.

Jean Suret-Canale, "The Economic Balance Sheet of French Colonialism in West Africa," in Gutkind and Waterman, *African Social Studies Reader*, pp. 125-136.

F. THE TRANSITION FROM COLONIALISM TO NEO-COLONIALISM AND STATE CAPITALISM—Week 6

Colin Leys, *Underdevelopment in Kenya*.

Mark Selden, "Global Enterprise. The American Record in Asia," *Peace and Change*, Fall 1976, 20-33.

Gavan McCormack, "The South Korean Economy. GNP Versus the People," in *Korea North and South*, G. McCormack and M. Selden, eds., pp. 90-111.

George Lee, "Commodity Production and Reproduction Amongst the Malayan Peasantry," *Journal of Contemporary Asia*, Vol. 3, No. 4, pp. 441-455.

James Petras, "State Capitalism and the Third World," in Petras, *Critical Perspectives on Imperialism and Social Classes in the Third World*, pp. 84-102.

II. REVOLUTIONARY APPROACHES

A. NATIONAL AND SOCIAL REVOLUTIONARY MOVEMENTS—Week 7

Selden, "Revolution and Third World Development, People's War and the Transformation of Peasant Society," in Miller and Aya, *National Liberation*, pp. 214-248.

Allen Isaacman, *A Luta Continua. Creation of a New Society in Mozambique*, pp. 16-24.

Petras, "Toward a Theory of Twentieth Century Socialist Revolution," in Petras, *Critical Perspectives on Imperialism and Social Class*, pp. 271-314.

Return to the Source: Selected Speeches of Amilcar Cabral, pp. 39-74 (on culture and identity).

B. THE TRANSITION TO SOCIALISM—Week 8

Paul Sweezy and Charles Bettelheim, *On the Transition to Socialism*, pp. 3-76.

Ernest Mandel, "The Economy of the Transition Period," *Marxist Economic Theory*, Vol. 2, pp. 605-653.

Mark Selden, *The People's Republic of China*, pp. 27-65; 488-502.

Carl Riskin, "Maoism and Motivation: Work Incentives in China," *Bulletin of Concerned Asian Scholars*, Vol. 5, No. 1, July 1973, pp. 10-25.

"China: New Theories for the Old," *Monthly Review*, May 1979, pp. 1-19.

C. INDUSTRIALIZATION AND UNDERDEVELOPMENT—Week 9

Bob Sutcliffe, "Imperialism and Industrialization in the Third World," in *Studies in the Theory of Imperialism*, pp. 171-192.

Bill Warren, "Myths of Underdevelopment," *New Left Review*, No. 81, pp. 3-46.

McMichael, Petras and Rhodes, "Industrialization in the Third World," in Petras, *Critical Perspectives on Imperialism and Social Class in the Third World*, pp. 103-136.

Muto Ichiyo, "The Free Trade Zone and the Mystique of Export-Oriented Industrialization," in *Free Trade Zones and the Industrialization of Asia*, AMPO Japan Asia Quarterly Review, Summer 1977, pp. 9-32.

D. AGRARIAN STRUCTURES—Week 10

Ralph Thaxton, "Modernization and Peasant Resistance in Thailand," pp. 247-278 in M. Selden, ed., *Remaking Asia*.

Philip Huang, "Analyzing the Twentieth Century Chinese Countryside," *Modern China* I, 2, 1975, pp. 132-159.

John Saul and Roger Woods, "African Peasantry," in *African Social Studies Reader*, pp. 103-114.

Solon Barrachlough and Arthur Domike, "Agrarian Structures in Seven Latin American Countries," in R. Stavenhagen (ed.), *Agrarian Problems and Peasant Movements in Latin America*.

Petras, "The Latin American Agro-Transformation From Above and Outside," in Petras, *Critical Perspectives on Imperialism and Social Class in the Third World*, pp. 137-156.

E. URBAN STRUCTURES AND URBANIZATION—Week 11

Manuel Castells, *The Urban Question*, Ch. 1.

G. Soares, "The New Industrialization," in Petras and Zeitlin, *Latin America: Reform or Revolution*, pp. 186-201.

E. Petras, "Towards a Theory of International Migration: The New Division of Labor" (mimeo).

Kim Chang-so, "Marginalization and the South Korean Economy," *AMPO*.

F. THE STATE: MILITARY, CORPORATISM/FASCISM—Week 12

Hamzi Alavi, "The State in Post-Colonial Societies," in Gough and Sharmi (eds.) *Imperialism and the Revolution in South Asia*.

Colin Leys, "Post-Colonial State," *Review of African Political Economy*, No. 5, pp. 39-49.

Roger Murray, "Militarism in Africa," *New Left Review*, No. 38, July/August 1966. pp. 35-59.

Guillermo O'Donnell, "Corporatism and the Question of the State," in Malloy (ed.), *Authoritarianism and Corporatism in Latin America*.

Petras, "Neo-Fascism in the Third World: Social Demobilization, Economic Growth and the Permanent Purge" (mimeo).

III. SOCIAL STRUCTURE AND CLASS FORMATION

A. THE CAPITALIST CLASS—Week 13

Zeitlin, Ewen and Ratcliff, "New Princes for Old?," pp. 87-123 in *American Journal of Sociology*, Vol. 80, No. 1, July 1974.

Petras and Cook, "Dependency and the Industrial Bourgeoisie" and "Politics in a Non-democratic State," in Petras (ed.), *Latin America: From Dependence to Revolution*, pp. 143-194.

Jack Woddis, "Is There an African National Bourgeoisie," in Waterman and Gutkind, *African Social Studies Reader*, pp. 268-276.

James O'Connor, "International Corporations and Economic Underdevelopment," *Science and Society*, Vol. 34, No. 1, pp. 42-60.

Peter Evans, *Dependent Development: The Alliance of Multinational, State and Local Capital in Brazil*, pp. 101-163.

B. THE WORKING CLASS—Week 14

Petras, "Revolutions and the Working Class," *New Left Review*, No. 111, pp. 37-67.

Arrighi, "International Corporations, Labor Aristocracies and Economic Development in Tropical Africa," in Arrighi and Saul, *Essays on the Political Economy of Africa*.

Zeitlin, "Political Generations in the Cuban Working Class," in Petras and Zeitlin, *Latin America: Reform or Revolution*.

Petras and Zeitlin, "Miners and Agrarian Radicalism," in Petras and Zeitlin (eds.), *Latin America: Reform or Revolution*.

Petras, "Reflections on the Chilean Experience: The Petit Bourgeoisie and the Working Class," in Petras, *Critical Perspectives on Imperialism and Social Classes in the Third World*.

Selections from Robin Cohen, Peter Gutkind and Phyllis Brazier, *Peasants and Proletarians: The Struggles of Third World Workers*.

C. PEASANTRY—Week 15

T. Shanin, "Peasantry as a Political Factor," in Shanin (ed.), *Peasants and Peasant Society*, pp. 238-263.

D. Deal, "Peasant Revolts and Resistence in the Modern World: A Comparative View," *Journal of Contemporary Asia*, Vol. 5, No. 4.

Eric Wolf, "Peasant Rebellion and Revolutions," in Normal Miller and Rod Aya (eds.), *National Liberation Revolution in the Third World*.

Economic Development

Gita Sen
Department of Economics
Graduate Faculty, New School for Social Research
Fall/Spring 1980/81
Graduate

There is no text book for this course, but books such as C. Kindelberger's *Economic Development*, and G. Meier's *Leading Issues in Economic Development* are regarded as standard texts in this field and you should familiarize yourself with their basic arguments, and develop a critique of them. In addition, you are expected to keep abreast of such journals as the *Journal of Development Studies, World Development, Economic Development and Cultural Change, Journal of Development Economics*, as well as more region-specific journals as *CEPAL Review, Latin American Research Review, Review of African Political Economy, Latin American Perspectives, Economic and Political Weekly, Bulletin of Concerned Asian Scholars, Social and Economic Studies, MERIP Reports, Nacla Bulletin*, etc.

In addition, the UN and the World Bank put out numerous reports which are useful. The *World Development Reports* for 1978 and 1979 contain useful statistical appendices, are cheap, clue you to the latest positions of the international agencies, and can be obtained through Oxford University Press (200 Madison Avenue).

The second course in this sequence begins with a brief examination of 'surplus drain' explanations of the phenomena of underdevelopment. We then take up the debates on modes of production in Latin America and India which attempt to provide an alternative to dependency analysis. The main focus of the course is the capitalist transformation of Third World agriculture with special emphasis on peasantry. The differentiation of the peasantry (Chayanovian and Marxist), the problem of ground rent, barriers to the capitalist transition in agriculture, state policies and the nature of peasant struggles are explored in depth.

PART I
*Required Reading

1. INTRODUCTION—HISTORICAL PERSPECTIVE

Andre G. Frank, *World Accumulation, 1492-1789*, Monthly Review Press, NY, 1978.

*H. Magdoff, "Colonialism, 1763-c.1970," *Encyclopaedia Britannica*, 15th edition, 1974; also in *Imperialism: From the colonial age to the present*, NY, MR Press, 1978.

*Marx, *Capital*, International Publishers, NY, 1967, volume I, chapters 26-33.

E. Williams, *Capitalism and slavery*, NY, Capricorn Books, 1966, chapters 1-3.

W. Rodney, *How Europe underdeveloped Africa*, Bogle L'Ouverture, 1972.

A.G. Frank, *Capitalism and underdevelopment in Latin America*, MR Press, NY, 1969.

S. Amin, *Accumulation on a world scale*, vol I, NY, MR Press, ch 2.

P. Jalee, *The pillage of the third world*, NY, MR Press, 1968, ch 1,2.

E. Galeano, *Open veins of Latin America*, NY, MR Press, 1973.

*M. Dobb, *Studies in the development of capitalism*, International Publishers, NY, 1947, chs 1,5,6.

2. NEOCLASSICAL APPROACHES—THE BIG PUSH

Joyce and Gabriel Kolko, *The limits of power: the world and US foreign policy 1945-54*, NY, Harper and Row, 1972, ch 7.

*P.N. Rosenstein-Rodan, "Problems of industrialization of Eastern and South-Eastern Europe," *Economic Journal*, June Sept 1943; reprinted in A.N. Agarwala and S.P. Singh (eds) *The Economics of underdevelopment*, Oxford Univ Press, 1963.

_____, "Notes on the theory of the big push," in H. Ellis and H. Wallich (eds), *Economic development for Latin America*, NY, St Martin's Press, 1961.

*T. Scitovsky, "Two concepts of external economies," *JPE*, April 1954, in *Agarwala and Singh*.

H. Leibenstein, *Economic backwardness and economic growth*, NY, John Wiley, 1957, ch 8,9.

3. NEOCLASSICAL APPROACHES—VICIOUS CIRCLES AND BALANCED GROWTH

*R. Nurkse, *Problems of capital formation in underdeveloped countries*, Oxford Univ Press, NY, 1953, chs 1-3.

_____, "Some international aspects of the problem of economic development," *AER*, May 1952; also in *Agarwala and Singh*.

_____, *Equilibrium and growth in the world economy*, Cambridge 1961.

R.R. Nelson, "A theory of the low level equilibrium trap in underdeveloped economies," *AER*, Dec 1956.

*A.O. Hirschman, *The strategy of economic development*, Yale Univ Press 1958, chs 3-5.

H.W. Singer, "Balanced growth in economic development," in E. Nelson (ed), *Economic growth: rationale, problems, cases*, Austin, Univ of Texas Press.

T. Scitovsky, "Growth-balanced or unbalanced?" in M. Abramovitz et al, *The allocation of economic resources*, Stanford Univ Press, 1959.

P. Streeten, "Unbalanced growth," *OEP*, 1959, pp 167-190.

*R.B. Sutcliffe, "Balanced and unbalanced growth," *QJE*, 1964, pp 621-640.

M. Lipton, "Balanced and unbalanced growth in underdeveloped countries," *Economic Journal*, Sept 1962.

S. Paine, "Balanced development: Maoist conception and Chinese practice," *World Development*, April 1976.

4. NEOCLASSICAL APPROACHES—'TAKE-OFF'

*W.W. Rostow, *The stages of economic growth: a non-communist manifesto*, Cambridge Univ Press, 1960, chs 2,3,4,9,10.

_____, "The take off into self sustained growth," *EJ*, March 1956; also in *Agarwala and Singh*.

_____, "The stages of economic growth," *Economic History Review*, August 1959.

*S. Kuznets, "Notes on the take off," in W.W. Rostow (ed) *The economics of the take off*.

G. Meier, *Leading issues in economic development*, NY, Oxford Univ Press, 1964 (articles by Kuznets, Habbakuk et al).

I. Drummond, "The stages of economic growth: a non-communist manifesto," *Canadian Journal of Economic and Political Science*, Feb 1961.

A.K. Cairncross, "Essays in biography and criticism: the stages of economic growth," *Economic History Review*, April 1961.

*P.A. Baran and E. Hobsbawm, "The stages of economic growth: a review," in C.K. Wilber (ed) *The political economy of development and underdevelopment*, NY, Random House, 1973.

A.G. Frank, "The sociology of development and the underdevelopment of sociology," in J.D. Cockcroft, A.G. Frank & D.L. Johnson (eds), *Dependence and underdevelopment*, Garden City, Anchor, 1970.

5. DUALISM AND SURPLUS LABOR

J.H. Boeke, *Economics and economic policy of dual societies*, NY, Institute of Pacific Relations, 1953.

*W.A. Lewis, "Economic development with unlimited supplies of labor," *The Manchester School*, May 1954; also in *Agarwala and Singh*.

_____, *The theory of economic growth*, 1955.

_____, "Unlimited labor: further notes," *Manchester School*, 1958.

*J. Fei and G. Ranis, "A theory of economic development," *AER*, Sept 1961.

J. Fei and G. Ranis, *Development of the labor surplus economy*, Illinois 1964.

J. Weeks, "The political economy of labor transfer," *Science and Society*, Winter 1971.

J.R. Harris and M.P. Todaro, "Migration, unemployment and development: a two sector analysis," *AER*, March 1970.

*D.W. Jorgenson, "Surplus agricultural labor and the development of a dual economy," *OEP*, 1967, pp 288-312.

S. Enke, "Economic development with limited and unlimited supplies of labor," *OEP*, June 1962.

C.H.C. Kao, K.R. Anschel and C.K. Eicher, "Disguised unemployment in agriculture: a survey," in C.K. Eicher and L.W. Witt (eds), *Agriculture in economic development*, NY, 1964.

*A.K. Sen, "Peasants and dualism with or without surplus labor," *JPE* 1966, pp 425-450.

_____, *Employment, technology and development*, Oxford Univ Press 1975.

6. NEO-MALTHUSIAN THEORIES AND THE FOOD/POPULATION PROBLEM

C. Clark "Population growth and living standards," in *Agarwala and Singh*.

G. Myrdal, *Asian Drama: an inquiry into the poverty of nations*, vol 2, Random House, NY, 1968.

R.A. Easterlin, "Effects of population growth on the economic development of developing countries," *The Annals of the American Academy of Political and Social Sciences*, vol 369, Jan 1967.

*J.J. Spengler, "Was Malthus right?" *Southern Economic Journal*, July 1966.

H. Peter Gray and S.S. Tangri (eds), *Economic development and population growth: a conflict?* esp. introduction and essays by Gray and Myint.

M.B. Stamper, *Population and planning in developing nations: a review of sixty development plans for the 1970's*, NY, Population Council, 1977.

L. Tabeh (ed) *Population growth and economic development in the third world*, Dolhain, Ordina Editions, 1975.

*R. Meek, (ed), *Marx and Engels on the population bomb*, Ramparts Press, 1971.

Latin American Perspectives, Fall 1977, Section I, "Population & Imperialism."

B.T. Urlanis, *Wars and population*, Moscow, Progress Publ., 1971.

*S. Weissman, "Why the population bomb is a Rockfeller baby," *Ramparts* May 1970.

M. Mamdani, *The myth of population control: family, caste and class in an Indian village*, MR Press, 1972.

*H. Cleaver, "The contradictions of the green revolution," *Monthly Review*, July 1972.

_____, *The origins of the green revolution*, unpubl. Ph.D. thesis, Standford Univ.

C. Meillassoux, "Development or exploitation: is the Sahel famine good for business?" *Journal of African Political Economy*, #1, 1974.

*Susan George, *How the other half dies: the real reasons for world hunger*, Montclair, N.J., Allanheld, Osmun & Co. Publ. 1977.

*Robert J. Ledogar, *Hungry for profits: US food and drug multinationals in Latin America*, New York, IDOC-North America, 1975.

Roger Burback and Patricia Flynn, "Agribusiness targets in Latin America", *NACLA Report on the Americas*, vol 12, #1, Jan-Feb 1978.

F.M. Lappe and J. Collins, *Food first: beyond the myth of scarcity*, Boston, Houghton Mifflin, 1977.

Journal of Development Studies, vol 14, #4, July 1978, Special issue on *Population and Development* (see especially Alan MacFarlane, "Modes of reproduction").

7. FOREIGN CAPITAL AND FORGEIGN AID

*H.B. Chenery and A.M. Strout, "Foreign assistance and economic development," *AER* 1966, #4.

P.N. Rosenstein-Rodan, "International aid for underdeveloped countries," in J. Bhagwati and R.S. Eckaus (eds) *Foreign Aid*, Penguin, 1970.

M. Friedman, "Foreign economic aid: means and objectives," in *Bhagwati and Eckaus*.

R.S. Eckaus, "Economic criteria for foreign aid for economic development," in *Bhagwati and Eckaus*.

*J. Bhagwati, "The tying of aid," in *Bhagwati and Eckaus*.

T.W. Schultz, "Value of US farm surpluses to underdeveloped countries," in *Bhagwati and Eckaus*.

*T. Hayter, *Aid as imperialism*, penguin, 1973.

S. Weissman, *The trojan horse: a radical look at foreign aid*, Ramparts, 1974, chs 2-5.

D. Avramovic et all, *Economic growth and external debt*, IBRD, 1964.

*R. McKinnon, "Foreign exchange constraints in economic development," *Economic Journal*, June 1964.

H.J. Bruton, "The two-gap approach to aid and development: a comment," *AER*, June 1969.

D. Lal, "The foreign exchange bottleneck revisited," *EDCC*, July 1972.

W.E. Schmidt, "The economics of charity: loans versus grants," *JPE*, August 1974.

A. Carlin, "Project versus program aid," *EJ*, March 1967.

*K.B. Griffin and J.L. Enos, "Foreign assistance: objectives and consequences," *EDCC*, April 1970.

G. Papanek, "The effect of aid and other resource transfers on savings and growth in less developed countries," *EJ*, Sept 1972.

*T. Weisskopf, "The impact of foreign capital inflow on domestic savings in underdeveloped countries," *J of International Economics*, Feb 1972.

8. STRUCTURALISM AND MONETARISM

R. Prebisch, *The economic development of Latin America and its principal problems*, UN 1950.

*W. Baer, "Economics of Prebisch and ECLA," *Economic Development and Cultural Change*, Jan 1962, pp 169-182.

D. Seers, "Inflation and growth: the heart of the controversy," in W. Baer and I. Kerstenetzky (eds), *Inflation and growth in Latin America*, Homewood Illinois, R.D. Irwin, 1964.

*_____, "A theory of inflation and growth in underdeveloped economies based on the experience of Latin America," *OEP*, June 1962.

W. Baer, "The inflation controversy in Latin America: a survey," *Latin American Research Review*, Winter 1967.

R. Prebisch, "Economic development or monetary stability: the false dilemma," in G. Meier (ed) *Leading issues in economic development*, Oxford Univ Press, 1970.

R. de Oliveira Campos, "Economic development and inflation with special reference to Latin America," in *Meier*.

C. Furtado, *Development and underdevelopment: a structural view of the problems of developed and underdeveloped countries*, Univ of Calif Press, 1967.

*_____, *Obstacles to development in Latin America*, Anchor 1970.

Cheryl Payer, *The debt trap*, NY, MR Press, 1975.

Andre Gunder Frank, "An open letter about Chile to Arnold Harberger and Milton Friedman," *Review of Radical Political Economics*, vol 7, #2, Summer 1975.

Import Substitution versus export promotion

*L.E. Di Marco (ed) *International economics and development—essays in honor of Raul Prebisch*, New York, Academic Press, 1972.

*W. Baer, "Import substitution and industrialization in Latin America: experiences and interpretations," *Latin American Research Review*, Spring 1972.

*H. Bruton, "The import substitution strategy of economic development: a survey," *Pakistan Development Review*, Summer 1970.

A.O. Hirschman, "The political economy of import substituting industrialization," *QJE*, Feb 1968.

D.T. Healey, "Development policy: new thinking about an interpretation," *JEL*, Sept 1972.

D. Morawetz, "Employment implications of industrialization in developing countries: a survey," *EJ*, Sept 1974.

*Ian Little, Tibor Scitovsky and Maurice Scott, *Industry and trade in some developing countries*. London, Oxford University Press, (for OECD), 1970, especially ch 6 on direct controls on industrialization.

*Carlos Diaz Alejandro, "Trade policies and economic development," in Peter Kenen (ed) *International trade and finance: frontiers for research*, Cambridge University Press, 1975.

Anne Krueger, *Liberalization attempts and consequences*, Cambridge, Mass. Ballinger Publ. Co. 1978.

Jagdish Bhagwati, *Anatomy and consequences of exchange control regimes*, Cambridge, Mass. Ballinger Publ. Co. 1978.

(Both Bhagwati and Krueger are part of the NBER series on Foreign Trade Regimes and Economic Development).

B. Belassa et al, *The structure of protection in developing countries*, Baltimore, Johns Hopkins Press, 1971.

R. Thorp, "The post import substitution era: the case of Peru," *World Development*, vol 5, #1/2, 1977.

P. Malan & R. Bonelli, "The Brazilian economy in the 1970's: old and new developments," *World Development*, vol 5, #1/2, 1977.

Gary Sampson, "Contemporary protectionism and exports of developing countries," *World Development*, vol 8, #2, Feb 1980.

*G.K. Helleiner, "Manufacturing for export, multinational firms and economic development," *World Development*, July 1973.

*_____, "Transnational enterprises and neo-political economy of US trade policy," *OEP*, March 1977.

_____, "Structural aspects of Third World trade: some trends and some prospects," *Journal of Development Studies*, vol 15 #3, April 1979.

*Martin Landsberg, "Export led industrialization in the Third World: manufacturing imperialism," *RRPE*, vol 11, #4, Winter 1979 (Special issue on Imperialism).

T. Murray, "How helpful is the generalized system of preferences to developing countries?" *EJ*, June 1973.

9. SURPLUS DRAIN AND DEPENDENCE

*P.A. Baran, *The political economy of growth*, NY, MR. Press, 1957.

*A.G. Frank, *Capitalism and underdevelopment in Latin America*, NY, MR Press, 1969.

_____, *Latin America: Underdevelopment or revolution*, NY, MR Press, 1969.

_____, *Lumpenbourgeoisie: lumpendevelopment*, NY, MR Press, 1972.

O. Sunkel, "National development policy and external dependence in Latin America," *Journal of Development Studies*, Oct 1969.

_____, "Big business and dependencia: a Latin American view," *Foreign Affairs*, April 1972.

*N. Girvan, "The development of dependency economics in the Caribbean and Latin America: review and comparison," *Social and Economic Studies*, March 1973.

_____ & O. Jefferson, *The Political Economy of the Caribbean*.

J.D. Cockcroft, A.G. Frank and D.L. Johnson, *Dependence and underdevelopment: Latin America's political economy*, Anchor, 1972.

T. dos Santos, "The structure of dependence," *AER*, May 1970.

*_____, "The changing structure of foreign investment in Latin America," in J. Petras and M. Zeitlin (eds) *Latin America: reform or revolution?* NY, Fawcett, 1968.

*F.H. Cardoso, "Dependency and development in Latin America," *New Left Review*, July-Aug 1972.

_____, "Imperialism and dependency in Latin America," in F. Bonilla and R. Girling (eds) *Structures of dependency*, Stanford Institute of Political Studies, 1973.

_____, "Industrialization, dependency and power in Latin America," *Berkeley Journal of Sociology*, 1972-73.

_____ & E. Faletto, *Dependencia y desarrollo en America Latina*, Siglo Veintiuno, Mexico, 1969.

D. Ray, "The dependency model of Latin American underdevelopment: three basic fallacies," *Journal of InterAmerican Studies and World Affairs*, Feb 1973.

G. Gilbert, "Socialism and dependency," *Latin American Perspectives*, Spring 1974.

P. O'Brien, "A critique of Latin American theories of dependency," in I. Oxall, T. Barnett, D. Booth (eds), *Beyond the sociology of development*, 1975.

*B. Warren, "Imperialism and capitalist industrialization," *New Left Review*, 1973.

A. Foster Carter, "Neo-marxist approaches to underdevelopment," in E. de Kadt and G. Williams (eds) *The sociology of development*, 1973.

G.F. Papanek, "Development planners, ethics and objectives," in *Bulletin of the Institute of Development Studies*, Jan 1971.

D. Seers, "What types of governments should be refused what types of aid?" *Bulletin of IDS*, June 1972.

*S. Amin, *Accumulation on a world scale*, NY, MR Press, 1974, esp chapters 2,4,5.

S. Amin, *Unequal development*, NY, MR Press, 1977, ch 5.

A. Emmanuel, "Myths of development versus myths of underdevelopment," *New Left Review*, May-June 1974.

C. Leys, *Underdevelopment in Kenya, the political economy of neocolonialism*, Heinemann, London, 1975, esp ch 1.

10. IMPERIALISM

*K. Marx, *Capital*, vol II (ch 1), vol III (chs 13-15).

J.A. Hobson, *Imperialism*.

*R. Luxembourg, *The accumulation of capital*, MR Press, 1968, esp section III.

_____, *An anti-critique*, MR Press, 1972.

D.J. Harris, "On Marx's schemes of reproduction and accumulation," *JPE*, May-June 1972.

*B. Bradby, "The destruction of natural economy," *Economy and Society*, May 1975.

N. Bukharin, *Imperialism and world economy*, MR Press, 1973, esp chs 1,7,8,10,11.

*Lenin, *Imperialism—the highest stage of capitalism*, International Publ, NY, 1972.

P. Baran and P. Sweezy, "Notes on the theory of imperialism," in K.T. Fann and D.C. Hodges (eds) *Readings in US imperialism* Porter Sargent, Boston, 1971.

_____, *Monopoly Capital*, MR Press, 1966, relevant sections.

H. Magdoff, *The age of imperialism*, MR Press, 1969.

_____, *Imperialism: from the colonial age to the present*, MR Press, 1978.

T. Kemp, *Theories of imperialism*, Dennis Dobson, London, 1967.

J.A. Schumpeter, *Imperialism and social classes*, Meridian Books, NY, 1955, esp pp 64-98.

D.S. Landes, "Some thoughts on the nature of economic imperialism," *Journal of Economic History*, Dec 1961.

H. Alavi, "Imperialism old and new," *Socialist Register*, 1964.

R.I. Rhodes, (ed) *Underdevelopment and revolution*, MR Press, 1970.

R. Owen and B. Sutcliffe, (eds), *Studies in the theory of imperialism* London, Longman, 1972.

Special issue on Imperialism, *RRPE*, vol 11, #4, Winter 1979.

11. MULTINATIONAL FIRMS AND INTERNATIONAL INSTITUTIONS

*S. Hymer, "The multinational corporation and the law of uneven development," in H. Radice (ed) *International firms and modern imperialism*, Penguin, 1975.

C. Palloix, "The internationalization of capital and the circuit of social capital," in *Radice*.

*_____, "The self-expansion of capital on a world scale," *Review of Radical Political Economics*, Summer 1977.

G. Adam, "Multinational corporations and world wide sourcing," in *Radice*.

*R. Murray, "The internationalization of capital and the nation state," in *Radice*.

*B. Warren, "How international is capital?" in *Radice*.

M. Bienefeld and D. Innes, "Capital accumulation and South Africa," *Review of African Political Economy*, Sept-Dec 1976.

M. Tanzer, *The political economy of international oil and the underdeveloped countries*, Boston, Beacon Press, 1969.

*C. Payer, *The debt trap*, MR Press, 1975.

_____, (ed) *Commodity trade of the third world*, Halstead Press, 1976.

N. Girvan, *Corporate imperialism: conflict and expropriation*, NY, M.E. Sharpe, 1976.

T.H. Moran, *Multinational corporations and the politics of dependence: copper in Chile*, Princeton Univ Press, 1974.

A. Seidman, (ed), *Natural resources and national welfare: the case of copper*, NY, Praeger, 1974.

Industrial free trade zones as incentives to pro-mote export oriented industries, UNIDO, ID/WG, 112/3, Oct 1971.

*T. Takeo, "Free trade zones in Southeast Asia," *Monthly Review*, Feb 1978.

12. NEW INTERNATIONAL ECONOMIC ORDER

A. Fishlow et al, *Rich and poor nations in the world economy*, McGraw Hill, 1978.

*F.C. Bergsten, "The threat from the third world," *Foreign Policy*, Summer 1973.

_____, "The response to the third world," *Foreign Policy* Winter 1974-75.

*H. Chenery et al, *Redistribution with growth*, Oxford Univ Press, NY, 1974.

R.D. Hansen, "The political economy of North-South relations: how much change?" *International Organization*, Autumn 1975.

_____ et al, *The US and world development: agenda for action, 1976*, Praeger, 1976.

G.K. Helleiner (ed) *A world divided: the less developed countries in the international economy*, Cambridge Univ Press, NY, 1975.

*ILO, *Employment, growth and basic needs: a one-world problem*, Praeger NY, 1977.

N. Leff, "The new economic order—bad economics, worse politics," *Foreign Policy*, Fall 1976.

PART II

I. REVIEW OF 'SURPLUS DRAIN' AND ITS CRITIQUE

*P.A. Baran, *The Political Economy of Growth*, NY, MR Press, 1957.

A.G. Frank, *Capitalism and underdevelopment in Latin America*, NY, MR Press, 1969.

*_____, *Lumpenbourgeoisie: lumpendevelopment*, NY MR Press, 1972.

O. Sunkel, "National development policy and external dependence in Latin America," *J of Development Studies*, Oct 1969.

N. Girvan, "The development of dependency economics in the Caribbean and Latin America: review and comparison," *Social and Economic Studies*, March 1973.

*F.H. Cardoso, "Dependency and development in Latin America," *New Left Review*, July-August 1972.

*S. Amin, *Accumulation on a world scale*, NY, MR Press, 1974, esp chs 2,4,5.

*B. Warren, "Imperialism and capitalist industrialization," *New Left Review*, 1973.

P. O'Brien, "A critique of Latin American theories of dependency," in Oxall, Barnett, Booth (eds) *Beyond the sociology of development*, 1975.

A. Emmanuel, "Myths of development versus myths of underdevelopment," *New Left Review*, May-June 1974.

C. Leys, *Underdevelopment in Kenya, the political economy of neo-colonialism*, Heinemann, London, 1975, esp ch 1.

*R. Brenner, "The origins of capitalist development: a critique of neo-Smithian Marxism," *New Left Review*, July-Aug 1977.

J. Weeks and E. Dore, "International exchange and the causes of backwardness," *Latin American Perspectives*, Spring 1979.

II. DEBATES ON MODES OF PRODUCTION

A. Latin America

*E. Laclau, "Feudalism and capitalism in Latin America," *New Left Review*, #67, 1971.

R. Fernandez and J. Ocampo, "The Latin American revolution: a theory of imperialism, not dependence," *Latin American Perspectives*, vol 1, #1, 1974.

M. Sternberg, "Dependency, imperialism and the relations of production," *Latin American Perspectives*, vol 1, #1, 1974.

*A.G. Frank, "Dependence is dead, long live dependence and class struggle: an answer to critics," *Latin American Perspectives*, vol 1, #1 1974.

C. Leys, "Underdevelopment and dependency: critical and self-critical notes," mimeo on reserve.

*C. Kay, "Comparative development of the European manorial system and the Latin American hacienda system," *J of Peasant Studies*, Oct 1974.

B. Bradby, "The destruction of natural economy in Peru," *Economy and Society*, May 1975.

*J. Banaji, "Modes of production in a materialist conception of history," *Capital and Class*, Autumn 1977.

D.E. Goodman, "Rural structure, surplus mobilisation and modes of production in a peripheral region: the Brazilian north-east," *J of Peasant Studies*, Oct 1977.

*T. Meade, "The transition to capitalism in Brazil: notes on a third road," *Latin American Perspectives*, Summer 1978.

R. Harris, "Marxism & the agrarian question in L. America," *Latin American Perspectives*, Fall 1978.

B. India

*U. Patnaik, "Capitalist development in agriculture: a note," *Economic and Political Weekly*, Sept 25, 1971.

*P. Chattopadhyay, "On the question of the mode of production in Indian agriculture: a preliminary note," *EPW* March 25, 1972.

U. Patnaik, "On the mode of production in Indian agriculture: a reply," *EPW* Sept 30, 1972.

P. Chattopadhyay, "Mode of production in agriculture: an anti-kritik," *EPW* Dec 30 1972.

*J. Banaji, "For a theory of colonial modes of production," *EPW* Dec 23, 1972.

A.G. Frank, "On feudal modes, models and methods of escaping capitalist reality," *EPW* Jan 6 1973.

H. Alavi, "India and the colonial mode of production," *EPW* Aug 1975.

*H. Cleaver, "Internationalization of capital and the mode of production in agriculture," *EPW* March 27 1976.

R. Sau, "On the essence and manifestation of capitalism in Indian agriculture," *EPW* March 31 1973.

———, "Political economy of Indian agriculture: what is it all about?" *EPW* May 19 1973.

A. Rudra, et al, "In search of the capitalist farmer," *EPW June 27, 1970*.

D. McEachern, "The mode of production in India," *J of Contemporary Asia*, vol 6, #4, 1976.

*T. Shanin, "Measuring peasant capitalism," *EPW* Dec 19 1977.

III. PEASANTRY

A. Overview

*E. Wolf, *Peasants*, Englewood Cliffs, NJ, Prentice Hall 1966.

Ennew, Hirst and Tribe, " 'Peasantry' as an economic category," *J of Peasant Studies*, #4, 1977.

*A. de Janvry and C. Garramon, "The dynamics of rural poverty in Latin America," *J of Peasant Studies*, vol 4, #3, April 1977.

M. Duggett, "Marx on peasants," *J of Peasant Studies* Jan 1975.

B. The Peasant as Homo Economicus

*A.V. Chayanov, *The Theory of Peasant Economy*, Homewood, Ill., Richard D. Irwin, 1966.

*B. Kerblay, "Chayanov and the theory of peasantry as a specific type of economy," in T. Shanin (ed) *Peasants and peasant societies*, Penguin 1973.

D. Thorner, "Peasant economy as a category in economic history," in Shanin.

———, "A post-Marxian theory of peasant economy: the school of A.V. Chayanov," *EPW* Annual No. 1965.

T. Shanin, "The nature and logic of peasant economy," *J of Peasant Studies*, vol 1, #1 & 2, 1973-74.

*E. Archetti, "Peasant studies: an overview," in H. Newby (ed) *International research in rural studies: progress and prospects*, NY, John Wiley 1978.

D. Hunt, "Chayanov's model of peasant household resource allocation," *J of Peasant Studies* April 1979.

M. Lipton, "The theory of the optimising peasant," *J of Development Studies*, #4, 1968.

*M. Harrison, "Chayanov and the economics of the Russian peasantry," *J of Peasant Studies*, July 1975.

*U. Patnaik, "Neo-populism and Marxism: the Chayanovian view of the agrarian question and its fundamental fallacy," *J of Peasant Studies*, July 1979.

C. Differentiation of the Peasantry

*Lenin, *The development of capitalism in Russia*, Progress Publ 1974, ch 2,3.

*Kautsky, "The agrarian question," *Economy and Society* Feb 1976 selected parts (ed) J. Banaji.

Lenin, "Capitalism in agriculture," *Collected Works* vol 4, pp 105-159 (review of Kautsky).

*J. Banaji, "Chayanov, Kautsky, Lenin: considerations towards a synthesis," *EPW* Oct 2, 1976.

S. Solomon, *The Soviet agrarian debate: a controversy in social science 1923-29*, Boulder Colorado, 1977.

U. Patnaik, "Class differentiation within the peasantry," *EPW* Sept 1976.

S. Bhalla, "New relations of production in Haryana agriculture," *EPW*, March 27, 1976.

*H. Bernstein, "African peasantries: a theoretical framework," *J of Peasant Studies*, July 1979.

L. Cliffe, "Labour migration and peasant differentiation: Zambian experiences," *J of Peasant Studies* April 1978.

P. Raikes, "Rural differentiation and class formation in Tanzania," *J of Peasant Studies*, April 1978.

*C.D. Deere and A. de Janvry, "A conceptual framework for the empirical analysis of peasants," *American J of Agricultural Economics*, Nov 1979.

R. Stavenhagen, "Capitalism and the peasantry in Mexico," *Latin American Perspectives*, Summer 1978 (spl issue on peasants).

IV. GROUND RENT AND ITS TRANSFORMATION

*Marx, *Capital*, vol III, ch 37-47 (Part VI-The transformation of surplus profit into ground rent).

R. Murray, "Value and the theory of rent," *Capital and Class*, Autumn 1977.

S. Amin, "Capitalism and ground rent," in *Imperialism and Unequal development*, ch 2.

K. Kautsky, relevant section from "The agrarian question" *Economy and Society*, Feb 1976.

V. BARRIERS TO CAPITALIST AGRICULTURE

A. The Problem of the Internal Market

*Lenin, *Development of capitalism in Russia*, ch 1.

———, "On the so-called market question," *Collected Works*, vol 1, Progress Publ, 1972, pp 75-122.

———, "The heritage we renounce," *Selected Works*, vol 1, Progress Publ, 1975, pp 57-91.

B. Alternative Paths to Capitalist Transition in Agriculture

*Lenin, "The agrarian programme of social democracy in the first Russian revolution, 1905-1907," *Collected Works*, vol 13 (a summary of this also available in vol 15, pp 158-181).

———, "The agrarian question in Russia towards the close of the 19th century," *Collected Works*, vol 15, pp 69-147.

K. Vergopoulos, "Capitalism and peasant productivity," *J of Peasant Studies*, #5, 1978.

*S.A. Mann and J.M. Dickinson, "Obstacles to the development of a capitalist agriculture," *J of Peasant Studies*, July 1978.

C. Semi-Feudal Relations and Usury

Mao, "On new democracy," *Selected Works*, vol II, pp 339-384.

*A. Bottomley, "Interest rate determination in underdeveloped rural areas," *American J of Agricultural Economics*, 1975.

———, "The premium for risk as a determinant of interest rates in underdeveloped rural areas," *Quarterly J of Economics*, 1963 November.

*A. Bhaduri, "Agricultural backwardness under semi-feudalism," *Economic Journal*, March 1973.

*———, "On the formation of usurious interest rates in backward agriculture," *Cambridge J of Economics*, Dec 1977.

N.K. Chandra, "Farm efficiency under semi-feudalism: a critique of marginalist theories and some Marxist formulations," *EPW*, Aug 1974.

A. Rudra, "Semi-feudalism, usury capital, etc," *EPW* Nov 1974.

*Marx, *Capital*, vol 3, ch 36 ("Precapitalist relationships").

Introduction to Regional Planning

Ann Markusen
University of California, Berkeley
Department of City and Regional Planning
Winter Quarter 1981
Graduate

The Introduction to Regional Planning is a graduate lecture course which surveys the major conceptual, theoretical, empirical, planning and policy issues in regional planning. It is the first course in the graduate regional planning series and required for further work in regional planning within the department. The course is built around regional cases in the United States: Appalachia, the South, Native American reservations, the Northeast, the fast-growing West, the Bay Area. Through the set of diverse experiences, the course introduces analysis of regional structure, location theory, migration theory, growth and development theory. Planning issues covered include resource use, land use, employment generation, controls on capital mobility, boomtown growth, and metropolitan congestion and openspace. Several types of regional planning institutions are covered (regional councils, waterplanning institutions, etc.) Planning strategies covered include economic development planning, industry locational incentives, resource and land use controls, reindustrialization, national urban policy, and area redevelopment.

INTRODUCTION—REGIONS, REGIONALISM, AND REGIONAL PLANNING.

Richardson, Harry. "Introduction: Defining Regions," from *Regional Economics*, 1979, pp. 17-29.

Massey, Doreen. "In What Sense a Regional Problem?" *Regional Studies*, Vol. 13, 1979, pp. 233-243.

Hayes, Lynton. "Regionalism and Regional Institutions," from *Energy, Economic Growth and Regionalism in the West*, 1980, pp. 191-218.

*Markusen, Ann. "Regions and Regionalism: A Marxist View," Working Paper 326, Berkeley: Institute for Urban and Regional Development, 1980.

REGIONAL STRUCTURE AND LOCATION DECISIONS

Alonso, William, "Industrial Location and Regional Policy in Economic Development," from Alonso and John Friedmann, *Regional Policy: Readings in Theory and Applications*, 1975.

Morrison, Peter. "The Functions and Dynamics of the Migration Process," pp. 61-74: "Urban Growth and Decline in the United States: A Study of Migration's Effects in Two Cities," pp. 235-54, both from Alan Brown and Egon Neuberger, *Internal Migration A Comparative Perspective*, 1977.

Crowley, Ronald, "Population Distribution: Perspectives and Policies," in Brown and Neuberger, pp. 255-74.

REGIONAL GROWTH AND CHANGE

North, Douglass, "Location Theory and Regional Economic Growth," in Friedmann and Alonso, pp. 332-347.

Tiebout, Charles, "Exports and Regional Economic Growth," in Friedmann and Alonso, pp. 348-352.

North and Tiebout, "A Reply" and "A Rejoinder", op, cit., pp. 353-57.

Massey, Doreen and Richard Meegan, "Industrial Restructuring versus the Cities," in *Urban Studies*, Vol. 15, No. 3, October 1978, pp. 273-88.

Rees, J. and Norton, R.D., "The Product Cycle and the Spatial Decentralization of American Manufacturing" in Regional Studies, Vol. 13, pp. 141-51.

Frobel, Folker, Jurgen Heinrichs, and Otto Kreye, "Introduction" in *The New International Division of Labour: Structural Unemployment in Industrialized Countries and Industrialization in Developing Countries*, 1977. pp. 1-23.

SOUTHERN REGIONAL UNDER-DEVELOPMENT

Sydnor, Charles, "The Unawakened South," from *The Development of Southern Sectionalism 1819-1848*, pp. 1-32.

Genovese, Eugene, "The Slave South: An Interpretation," from *The Political Economy of Slavery*, pp. 13-39.

Mandle, Jay, "Obstacles to Black Migration," and "Migration North" from *The Roots of Black Poverty: The Southern Plantation Economy after the Civil War*, 1978, pp. 16-27, 71-83.

SOUTHERN REGIONAL PLANNING

Friedmann, John and Clyde Weaver, "The National Planning Board" and "The TVA and Comprehensive River Basin Development" from *Territory and Function: The Evolution of Regional Planning Doctrine*, 1979, pp. 62-86.

Whisnant, David, "How Green is Your Valley" and The TVA Saga" from *The Elements*, Nov.-Dec. 1976.

Hansen, Niles, "The Tennessee Valley" from *The Future of Nonmetropolitan America: Studies in the Reversal of Rural and Small Town Population Decline*, 1973, pp. 91-110.

APPALACHIAN REGIONAL UNDERDEVELOPMENT

Rothblatt, Donald, "The Origins of the Appalachian Regional Commission," from *Regional Planning: The Appalachian Experience*, 1971, pp. 1-23.

Simon, Rick, "The Labor Process and Uneven Development: the Appalachian Coalfields," *International Journal of Urban and Regional Research*, Vol. 4 No. 1, March 1980, pp. 46-71.

Brown, James and George Hillery, Jr., "The Great Migration, 1940-60," from Thomas Ford, ed. *The Southern Appalachian Region: A Survey*, 1962, pp. 54-78.

APPALACHIAN REGIONAL PLANNING

Cumberland, John, "The Appalachian Regional Commission," from *Regional Development Experiences in the United States of America*, 1971, pp. 91-103.

Burlage, Robb, "ARC's First Six-year Plan: A Critical Interpretation," from *People's Appalachia*, Vol. 1, No. 4, Nov. Sept. 1970, pp. 14-29.

Simon, Richard, and Roger Lesser, "A Regional Development Strategy for the Mountains," from *People's Appalachia*, Vol. III, No. 1, Spring 1973, pp. 9-16.

Tudiver, Neil, "Community Economic Development: Experiences in Central Appalachia" from *People's Appalachia*, Vol.III, No. 1, Spring 1973, pp. 28-31.

NATIVE AMERICANS AND U.S. REGIONAL FORMATION

Smaby, Beverly, "The Mormons and The Indians: Conflicting Ecological Systems in the Great Basin," *American Studies*, Vol. 16, No. 1, 1975, pp. 35-48.

RESERVATION DEVELOPMENT PLANNING

Robbins, Lynn, "The Navajo Nation and Industrial Developments," *Southwest Economy and Society*, Vol. 11, No. 3, Spring 1977, 47-69.

Owens, Nancy and Ken Peres, "Overcoming Institutional Barriers to Economic Development on the Northern Cheyenne Reservation," EDA Report, 1980, Ch. 2, "Anatomy of Past and Present Economic Ventures."

WESTERN REGIONAL DEVELOPMENT

Business Week, "The Angry West Versus the Rest," September 17, 1979, pp. 31-40.

Hayes, Lynton, "Toward Understanding the American West Experiences as a Region," and "Energy Resources in the American West," in *Energy, Economic Growth and Regionalism in the West*, pp. 51-74; 11-36.

Markusen, Ann, "Class, Rent and Sectoral Conflict: Uneven Development in Western U.S. Boomtowns," *The Review of Radical Political Economics*, Vol. 10, No. 3, Fall, 1978, pp. 117-129.

WESTERN PLANNING ISSUES: WATER AND BOOMTOWNS

Blundell, Williams, "New Rural Migration Overburdens and Alters Once-Sleepy Hamlets," *The Wall Street Journal*, Thursday, July 3, 1980.

Lou Cannon and Joel Kotkin, "Old Frontier Sees Bright New Future," and "Agriculture Losing the Contest for Western Water," *The Washington Post*, June 17-18, 1979.

Ingram, Helen, "The Political Economy of Regional Water Institutions," *American Journal of Agricultural Economics*, Feb. 1973, pp. 10-18.

Walker, Richard and Michael Storper, "The California Water System: Another Round of Expansion?" Berkeley, IGS *Public Affairs Report*, Vol. 20, No. 2, April 1979.

Western Water Educational Foundation, *Layperson's Guide to the Peripheral Canal*, 1979.

Massey, Garth, "Critical Dimensions in Urban Life: Energy Extraction and Community Collapse in Wyoming" *Urban Life*, Vol. 9, No. 2, July 1980, pp. 187-99.

Talagan, Rapp; Kneese; Rapp, Lang, "Mitigation of Social Impacts," in Federation of Rocky Mountain States, *Energy Development in the Rocky Mountain Region: Goals and Concerns*, 1975, pp. 71-82.

*Markusen, Ann, "Capital Accumulation, Capital Mobility and Regional Planning," Working Paper No. 313, Institute for Urban and Regional Development, Berkeley.

BAY AREA REGIONAL GROWTH

ABAG/Bay Area Council, *San Francisco Bay Area Economic Profile*, October 1979.

Saxenian, Anno, "Urban Contradictions: Shortages and Smog in Silicon Valley" from *Silicon Chips and Spatial Structure: The Industrial Basis of Urbanization in Santa Clara County, California*, Berkeley, M.C.P. thesis, 1980, pp. 86-113.

BAY AREA REGIONAL PLANNING AGENCIES AND ISSUES

*People for Open Space, "Endangered Harvest: The Future of Bay Area Farmlands," Report of the Farmlands Study, 1980.

*Bay Area Council, *Annual Report, 1979-80*.

Shipnuck, Les and Dan Feshbach, "Bay Area Council: Regional Powerhouse," in Pacific Studies Center, *Regionalism and the Bay Area*, 1972.

DECLINE IN THE NORTHEAST

Jusenius, Carol and Larry Ledebur, "Where Have All the Firms Gone: An Analysis of the New England Economy," U.S. Dept. of Commerce, EDA, 1977, pp. 1-22.

Sternlieb, George and James Hughes, "The Regional Futures," in *Revitalizing the Northeast*, D 78, pp. 109-127.

Bluestone, Barry and Bennett Harrison, "Plant Closings and Job Loss: The Magnitude of the Problem" in *Capital and Communities*, 1980, pp. 30-61.

PLANNING STRATEGIES FOR NORTHEASTERN REVIVAL

Harrison, Bennett and Sandra Kantor, "The Political Economy of States' Job Creation Business Incentives," *Journal of the American Institute of Planners* October 1978, pp. 424-35.

Stern, Robert, K. Haydn Wood and Tove Hellend Hammer, in *Employee Ownership in Plant Shutdowns*, 1979, pp. 9-34. "Communities and the National Economy."

Bluestone, Barry and Bennett Harrison, "Toward a New Agenda," in *Capital and Communities*, pp. 249-79.

REINDUSTRIALIZATION: THE NEW REGIONAL STRATEGY

Business Week, Special issue on the Reindustrialization of America, June 30, 1980.

Wiseman, Michael and Previn Varaiya, "Capital and Cities," Working Paper, Berkeley, Department of Economics, 1980.

Miller, S.M., "The Recapitalization of Capitalism," in *Social Policy*, November, December 1978, pp. 5-13.

NATIONAL URBAN AND REGIONAL POLICY

*Carter, Jimmy, "New Partnership to Conserve America's Communities," 1978.

*National Urban Policy Collective, "Carter's National Urban Policy: A Response" 1978.

*President's Commission on the '80's, *Final Report*, 1980.

Agricultural and Resource Economics

Alain de Janvry
University of California, Berkeley
Department of Agricultural and Resource Economics
Winter Quarter, 1980
Undergraduate

Required textbook: S. Amin, *Unequal Development* (New York: Monthly Review Press, 1976).

I. THE NEW INTERNATIONAL ECONOMIC ORDER AND THE DEVATE OF IMPERIALISM AND UNDERDEVELOPMENT

1.1 UNDERDEVELOPMENT AS A HISTORICAL PROCESS

S. Stein and B. Stein, *The Colonial Heritage of Latin America* (New York: Oxford University Press, 1970).

E. Galeano, *Open Veins of Latin America* (New York: Monthly Review Press, 1973).

P. Jalee, *The Pillage of the Third World* (New York: Modern Reader, 1968).

C. Leys, *Underdevelopment in Kenya* (Berkeley: University of California Pess, 1974).

P. Bairoch, *The Economic Development of the Third World Since 1900* (Berkeley: University of California Press, 1975).

1.2 THE NEW INTERNATIONAL ECONOMIC ORDER

D. Blake and R. Walters, *The Politics of Global Economic Relations* (Englewood Cliffs, N.J.: Prentice-Hall, 1976).

M. Harrington, *The Vast Majority: A Journey to the World's Poor* (New York: Simon and Schuster, 1978).

G. Barraclough, "Waiting for the New Order," *New York Review of Books*, Vol. 25, No. 16 (October, 1978).

N. Kaldor, "Inflation and Recession in the World Economy," *The Economic Journal*, Vol. 86 (December, 1976): 703-714.

1.3 EMPIRICAL EVIDENCE

World Bank, *World Bank Tables, 1976* (Washington, D.C.: World Bank, 1978).

M. Ahluwalia, "Income Inequality: Some Dimensions of the Problem," *Finance and Development* (September, 1974).

S. Kuznets, *Modern Economic Growth* (New Haven: Yale University Press, 1966).

I. Adelman and C. Morris, *Economic Growth and Social Equity in Developing Countries* (Stanford: Stanford University Press, 1973).

D. Morawetz, "Employment Implications of Industrialization in Developing Countries: A Survey," *The Economic Journal* (September, 1974): 491-542.

J. Poleman, "World Food: A Perspective," in P.H. Abelson (ed.), *Food: Politics, Economics, Nutrition, and Research* (Washington, D.C.: American Association for the Advancement of Science, 1975), pp. 8-16.

1.4 THE MODERNIZATION SCHOOL

I. Normal Patterns and Stages of Growth

H. Chenery and L. Taylor, "Development Patterns: Among Countries and Over Time," *Review of Economics and Statistics*, Vol. 50 (1967):174-182.

H. Chenery and M. Syrguin, *Patterns of Development, 1950-1970* (London: Oxford University Press, 1975).

W.W. Rostow, "The Take-Off into Self-Sustained Growth," *The Economic Journal*, Vol. 66, No. 261 (March, 1956):25-48.

P. Baran and E. Hobsbawn, "The Stages of Economic Growth: A Review," in C. Wilber (ed.), *The Political Economy of Development and Underdevelopment* (New York: Random House, 1973).

II. Malthusian Models, Big Push, and Balanced versus Unbalanced Growth

R. Nelson, "A Theory of the Low-Level Equilibrium Trap," *American Economic Review* (December, 1956): 894-908.

A. Hirschman, *The Strategy of Economic Development* (New York, Yale University Press, 1958).

B. Higgins, *Economic Development* (New York: W. Norton, 1959), Chapter 16.

A. Hirschman, "Generalized Linkages," *Economic Development and Cultural Change*, Special Issue (1978).

III. Comparative Advantages and Trade

H.G. Johnson, *Economic Policies toward Less-Developed Countries* (Washington, D.C.: Brookings Institution, 1967).

I. Little, T. Scitovsky, and M. Scott, *Industry and Trade in Some Developing Countries* (New York: Oxford University Press, 1970) Chapters 4,5, and 7.

D. Healy, "Development Policy: New Thinking about an Interpretation," *Journal of Economic Literature* (September, 1972).

IV. Dualism and Surplus Labor

W.A. Lewis, "Economic Development with Unlimited Supplies of Labor," in Agarwala and Singh (eds.), *The Economics of Underdevelopment* (New York: Oxford University Press, 1958), pp. 400-449.

G. Ranis and J. Fei, "A Theory of Economic Development," *American Economic Review*, Vol. 51, No. 4 (September, 1961): 534-565.

D. Jorgenson, "The Role of Agriculture in Economic Development: Classical versus Neo-Classical Models of Growth," in C. Wharton (ed.), *Subsistence Agriculture and Economic Development* (Chicago: Aldine Publishing Co., 1969), Chapter II.

C. Kao, K. Anschel, and C. Eicher, "Disguised Underemployment in Agriculture: A Survey," in Eicher and Witt (eds.) *Agriculture in Economic Development* (New York: McGraw-Hill, 1969), Chapter 7.

J. Weeks, "The Political Economy of Labor Transfers," *Science and Society*, Vol. 35, No. 4 (Winter, 1971): 463-480.

1.5 THE DEBATE ON THE TRANSITION TO CAPITALISM

H.K. Takahashi, "A Contribution to the Discussion," in *The Transition from Feudalism to Capitalism: A Symposium* (New York: Science and Technology, 1967).

R. Brenner, "Agrarian Class Structure and Economic Development in Pre-Industrial Europe," *Past and Present*, No. 70 (February, 1976).

S. Resnick and R. Wolff, "The Theory of Transitional Conjunctures and the Transition from Feudalism to Capitalism in Western Europe," University of Massachusetts, Amherst, 1977 (mimeographed).

M. Murray, "Recent Views on the Transition from Feudalism to Capitalism," *Socialist Review*, Vol. 34 (1977):64-67 and 73-86.

1.6 ELEMENTS OF THE THEORY OF CRISIS

E. Wright, "Alternative Perspectives on the Marxist Theory of Accumulation and Crisis," *Insurgent Sociologist* (Fall, 1975).

M. Lebowitz, "Marx's Falling Rate of Profit: A Dialectical View," *Canadian Journal of Economics*, Vo. 9, No. 2 (May, 1976):232-254.

J. Weeks, "The Sphere of Production and the Analysis of Crisis in Capitalism," *Science and Society*, Vol. 41, No. 3 (Fall, 1977):281-302.

R. Wolff, "Marxian Crisis Theory: Structure and Implications," *Review of Radical Political Economy*, Vol. 10, No. 1 (Spring, 1978):47-57.

URPE, U.S. *Capitalism in Crisis* (New York: URPE, 1978).

1.7 CLASSICAL THEORIES OF IMPERIALISM

R. Luxemburg, *The Accumulation of Capital* (New York: Monthly Review Press, 1964).

N. Bukharin, *Imperialism and World Economy* (New York: Monthly Review Press, 1973).

V.I. Lenin, *Imperialism: The Highest Stage of Capitalism* (Peking: Foreign Language Press, 1973).

L. Trotsky, *The Permanent Revolution and Results and Prospects* (New York: Merit Publishers, 1969).

T. Kemp, "The Marxist Theory of Imperialism," in R. Owen and B. Sutcliff (eds.), *Studies in the Theory of Imperialism, 1972.*

1.8 THE RADICAL STRUCTURALIST SCHOOL

I. The Monthly Review School

P. Baran, *The Political Economy of Growth* (New York: Monthly Review Press, 1957).

P. Sweezy, *The Theory of Capitalist Development* (New York: Monthly Review Press, 1942), Chapter 17.

P. Baran and P. Sweezy, *Monopoly Capital* (New York: Monthly Review Press, 1966), Chapter 7.

H. Magdoff, *The Age of Imperialism* (New York: Monthly Review Press, 1969).

H. Magdoff, *Imperialism: From the Colonial Age to the Present* (New York: Monthly Review Press, 1978).

II. The Development of Underdevelopment School

A.G. Frank, *Capitalism and Underdevelopment in Latin America* (New York: Monthly Review Press, 1969).

A.G. Frank, "The Development of Underdevelopment," in C. Wilber (ed.), *The Political Economy of Development and Underdevelopment* (New York: Random House, 1973).

I. Wallerstein, *The Modern World System*, (New York: Academic Press, 1974).

I. Wallerstein, "The Rise and Future Demise of Modern World System," *Comparative Studies in Sociology and History*, Vol. 16, No. 4 (1974):387-415.

III. The Dependency School

O. Sunkel, "National Development Policy and External Dependency," *Journal of Development Studies*, Vol 6, No. 1 (1969).

O. Sunkel, "Big Business and 'Dependencia'," *Foreign Affairs*, Vol. 50 (1972):517-531.

C. Furtado, *Economic Development of Latin America* (Cambridge, England: Cambridge University Press, 1970).

T. Dos Santos, "The Structure of Dependence," *American Economic Review*, Vol. 60 (May, 1970):231-236.

F.E. Cardoso, "Dependency and Development in Latin America," *New Left Review*, Vol. 74 (July-August, 1972).

P. O'Brien, "A Critique of Latin American Theories of Dependency," in Oxaal, et al. (eds.), *Beyond the Sociology of Development* (London: Routledge, 1975).

IV. Unequal Exchange

A. Emmanuel, *Unequal Exchange* (New York: Monthly Review Press, 1972).

S. Amin, "The End of a Debate," in *Imperialism and Unequal Development* (New York: Monthly Review Press, 1977).

V. Peripheral Capitalism and Bureaucratic Authoritarianism

S. Amin, *Unequal Development* (New York: Monthly Review Press, 1976).

S. Amin, "Accumulation and Development: A Theoretical Model," *Review of African Political Economy*, Vol. 1 (August-November, 1974):9-26.

J. Petras, "New Perspectives on Imperialism and Social Classes in the Periphery," *Journal of Contemporary Asia*, Vol. 5, No. 3 (1975).

G. O'Donnell, *Modernization and Bureaucratic Authoritarianism: Studies in South American Politics* (Berkeley: Institute of International Studies, University of California, 1973).

F.E. Cardoso, "Associated-Dependent Development: Theoretical and Political Implications," in A. Stepan (ed.), *Authoritarian Brazil* (New Haven: Yale University Press, 1973).

VI. Multinational Corporations and the Internationalization of Capital

S. Hymer, "The Internationalization of Capital," *Journal of Economic Issues*, Vol. 6, No. 1 (1972).

S. Hymer and S. Resnick, "International Trade and the Law of Uneven Development," in Bhagwati (ed.), *Economics and the World Order* (New York: Macmillan, 1972).

R. Muller, "The Multinational Corporation and the Underdevelopment of the Third World," in C. Wilber (ed.), *The Political Economy of Development and Underdevelopment* (New York: Random House, 1973).

G. Arroyo, "Institutional Constraints to Policies for Achieving Increased Food Production in Selected Countries," *World Food Conference* (Ames, Iowa: Iowa State University, 1977).

NACLA, *Agribusiness Targets in Latin America*, Vol. 12, No. 1 (January-February, 1978).

S. Lall, "Transnationals, Domestic Enterprises, and Industrial Structure in Host LDCs: A Survey," *Oxford Economic Papers*, Vol. 30, No. 2 (July, 1978):213-248.

1.9 THE MODES OF PRODUCTION SCHOOL

I. Critique of Stagnation

B. Warren, "Imperialism and Capitalist Industrialization," *New Left Review*, Vol. 81 (1973).

A. Szymanski, "Marxist Theory and Intentional Capital Flows," *Review of Radical Political Economy*, Vol. 6, No. 3 (Fall, 1974).

A. Szymanski, "A Response to A.G. Frank and M. Murray," *Review of Radical Political Economy* (Summer, 1976).

II. Critique of Unequal Exchange

C. Bettelheim, "Theoretical Comments," Appendix I in A. Emmanuel, *Unequal Exchange* (New York: Monthly Review Press, 1972).

G. Kay *Development and Underdevelopment: A Marxist Analysis* (New York: St. Martin's Press, 1975).

E. Mandel, *Late Capitalism* (London: New Left Books, 1975), Chapters 10 and 11.

III. Critique of Dependency and Underdevelopment

R. Brenner, "The Origins of Capitalist Development: A Critique of Neo-Smithian Marxism," *New Left Review*, No. 101 (July-August, 1977):25-93.

A. Philips, "The Concept of 'Development'," *Review of African Political Economy*, No. 8 (1977); 7-20.

S. Gerstein, "Theories of the World Economy and Imperialism," *The Insurgent Sociologist*, Vol. 7, No. 2 (Spring, 1977): 9-12.

E. Dore and J. Weeks, "International Exchange and the Causes of Backwardness," American University, Washington, D.C., 1978 (mimeographed).

IV. Unity-Rivalry Debate

R. Rowthorn, "Imperialism in the Seventies: Unity or Rivalry?" *New Left Review*, Vol. 69 (1971).

R. Murray, "The Internationalization of Capital and the Nation State," *New Left Review*, Vol. 67 (May-June, 1971).

B. Warren, "The Internationalization of Capital and the Nation State: A Comment," *New Left Review*, Vol. 68 (1971).

II. THE AGRARIAN QUESTION AND THE DEBATE ON PEASANTS

2.1 THE PROBLEMS OF FOOD AND RURAL POVERTY

L. Brown, *The Twenty-Ninth Day* (New York: W.W. Norton, 1978).

E. Feder, *The Rape of the Peasantry* (New York: Anchor Books, 1971).

S. Barraclough, "Agricultural Production Prospects in Latin America," *World Development*, Vol. 5, Nos. 5-7 (1977):459-476.

F. Lappe and J. Collins, *Food First* (Boston: Houghton-Mifflin, 1977).

NACLA, *U.S. Grain Arsenal*, Vol. 9, No. 7 (October, 1975).

M. Perelman, *Farming for Profit in a Hungry World* (Montclair, N.J.: Allanheld, 1977).

2.2 EMPIRICAL EVIDENCE

U.S. Economic Research Service, *Agriculture in the Americas* (1977).

U.S. Economic Research Service, *The World Food Situation and Prospects to 1985*, FAER no. 98, 1974.

United Nations, Food and Agriculture Organization, *Production Yearbooks*.

United Nations, Food and Agriculture Organization, *Assessment of the World Food Situation, 1974*.

OECD, *The Food Problem of Developing Countries, 1968*.

IFPRI, *Meeting Food Needs in Developing Countries*, Research Report No. 1, 1976.

2.3 THE CLASSICS IN THE DEVELOPMENT OF CAPITALISM IN AGRICULTURE

K. Marx, *Capital*, Vol. III (New York: International Publishers, 1967), Chapter 47.

K. Marx, "The Eighteenth Brumaire of Louis Bonaparte and the Class Struggle in France," in R. Tucker (ed.), *The Marx-Engels Reader* (New York: Norton, 1972), pp. 586-617; also, in T. Shanin (ed.), *Peasants and Peasant Societies* (Baltimore: Penguin Books, 1971, Chapter 18, "Peasants as a Class," pp. 229-339.

M. Duggett, "Marx on Peasants," *Journal of Peasant Studies*, Vol. 2, No. 2 (1975):159-182.

V.I. Lenin, *The Development of Capitalism in Russia* (Moscow: Progress Publishers, 1964), Chapters 1-5 and 8.

V.I. Lenin, "The Agrarian Program of the Social-Democracy in the First Russian Revolution," in *Selected Works*, Vol. III (New York: International Publishers), pp. 157-288.

K. Kautsky, *The Agrarian Question*, translation and summary of selected parts by J. Banaji in *Economy and Society*, Vol. 5, No. 1 (1976):1-49.

E. Preobrazhensky, "Peasantry and the Political Economy of the Early Stages of Industrialization," in T. Shanin (ed.), *Peasants and Peasant Societies* (Baltimore: Penguin Books, 1971), Chapter 17.

B. Bradby, "The Destruction of Natural Economy," *Economy and Society*, Vol. 4, No. 2 (1975): 127-161 (on Rosa Luxemburg).

2.4 ORGANIZATION OF THE PEASANT HOUSEHOLD

A.V. Chayanov, *The Theory of Peasant Economy*, D. Thorner, *et al.* (eds.) (Homewood, Ill.: Irwin, Inc., 1966).

B. Kerblay, "Chayanov and the Theory of Peasantry as a Specific Type of Economy," in T. Shanin, *Peasants and Peasant Societies* (Baltimore: Penguin Books, 1971), pp. 150-160.

M. Harrison, "Chayanov and the Economics of the Russian Peasantry," *Journal of Peasant Studies*, Vol. 2, No. 4 (1975):389-416.

C. Meillasoux, "From Reproduction to Production," *Economy and Society*, Vol. 1, No. 1 (1972):93-105.

J. Goody, *Production and Reproduction* (London: Cambridge University Press, 1976).

A. MacFarlane, "Modes of Reproduction," *Journal of Development Studies*, Vol. 14, No. 4 (July, 1978): 100-120

F. Edholm, O. Harris, and K. Young, "Conceptualizing Women," *Critique of Anthropology*, Vol. 3, Nos. 9 and 10 (1978):101-130.

C.D. Deere, "Rural Women's Subsistence Production in the Capitalist Periphery," *Review of Radical Political Economy*, Vol. 8, No. 1 (1976):9-17.

B. White, "The Economic Importance of Children in a Javanese Village," in M. Nag (ed.), *Population and Social Organization* (The Hague: Mouton, 1975):127-146.

E. Wolf, *Peasants* (Englewood Cliffs, N.J.: Prentice-Hall, 1966).

2.5 THE PEASANT MODE OF PRODUCTION SCHOOL AND THE ARTICULATION OF MODES OF PRODUCTION

M. Harrison, "The Peasant Mode of Production in the Work of A.V. Chayanov," *Journal of Peasant Studies*, Vol. 4, No. 4 (1977):323-336.

H. Wolpe, "Capitalism and Cheap Labour-Power in South Africa," *Economy and Society*, Vol. 1, No. 4 (1972):424-456.

R. Stavenhagen, *Social Classes in Agrarian Societies* (New York: Anchor Books, 1975).

K. Vergopoulos, "Capitalism and Peasant Productivity," *Journal of Peasant Studies*, Vol. 5, No. 4 (July, 1978):446-465.

J. Banaji, "Modes of Production in a Materialist Conception of History," *Capital and Class*, No. 3 (Fall, 1977):1-43.

B. Bradby, "The Destruction of Natural Economy," *Economy and Society*, Vol. 4, No. 2 (1975):127-161 (on P.P. Rey).

A. Foster-Carter, "The Modes of Production Controversy," *New Left Review*, pp. 47-77.

2.6 THE DEVELOPMENT OF CAPITALISM SCHOOL

E. Laclau, "Feudalism and Capitalism in Latin America," *New Left Review*, No. 67 (1971):19-38.

J. Ennew, P. Hirst, and K. Tribe, " 'Peasantry' as an Economic Category," *Journal of Peasant Studies*, Vol. 4, No. 4 (1977):295-322.

G. Littlejohn, "Peasant Economy and Society," in B. Hindess (ed.), *Sociological Theories of the Economy* (London: Macmillan, 1977).

W. Roseberry, "Peasants as Proletarians," *Critique of Anthropology*, Vol. 3, No. 11 (1978):3-18.

S. Mintz, "The Rural Proletariat and the Problem of Rural Proletariat Consciousness," *Journal of Peasant Studies*, Vol. 5, No. 1 (1977):291-325.

C. Kay, "Competitive Development of the European Manorial System and the Latin American Hacienda System," *Journal of Peasant Studies*, Vol. 2, No. 1 (October, 1974):69-98.

K. Duncan and I. Rutledge, *Land and Labour in Latin America* (Cambridge, England: Cambridge University Press, 1977).

A. Pearse, *The Latin American Peasant* (London: F. Cass, 1975).

2.7 THE STATE AND THE AGRARIAN QUESTION

A. Mitra, *Terms of Trade and Class Relations* (London: F. Cass, 1977).

E. Flores, "The Economics of Land Reform," in R. Stavenhagen (ed.), *Agrarian Problems and Peasant Movements in Latin America* (Garden City, N.Y.: Anchor Books, 1970), pp. 139-158.

M. Gutelman, "The Socialization of the Means of Production in Cuba," in R. Stavenhagen, *Agrarian Problems and Peasant Movements in Latin America* (Garden City, N.Y.: Anchor Books, 1970), pp. 347-369.

E. Feder, "The New World Bank Program for the Self-Liquidation of the Third World Peasantry," *Journal of Peasant Studies*, Vol. 3, No. 3 (April, 1976):343-354.

The Southern Appalachians: A Sociological Perspective

David Walls
University of Kentucky
Sociology, Anthropology
Spring 1982

BIBLIOGRAPHICAL RESOURCES:

The most comprehensive list of books on the region is *Bibliography of Southern Appalachia*, ed. Charlotte Ross (Boone: Appalachian Consortium, 1976). The major bibliography that includes books, articles, government publications, theses, etc., is *Appalachian Bibliography* (Morgantown: West Virginia Univ. Library, 1970, 1972, 1975, 1980). On coal mining, see Robert Munn, *The Coal Industry in America*, 2nd. ed. (Morgantown: WVU Library, 1977), and *Strip Mining* (Morgantown: WVU Library, 1973); also, Dorothy Campbell Tompkins, *Strip Mining for Coal* (Berkeley: Institute for Governmental Studies, 1973). The *Appalachian Journal*, 7 (Summer 1980) contains a detailed name and subject index to its first seven volumes.

I. HISTORICAL PERSPECTIVES: FROM THE FRONTIER TO THE EXPANSION OF INDUSTRIAL CAPITALISM

John C. Campbell, *The Southern Highlander and His Homeland* (1921), Chs. 2-5.

Harry Caudill, *Night Comes to the Cumberlands* (1962), pp. 3-215.

Alan J. Banks, "The Emergence of a Capitalistic Labor Market in Eastern Kentucky," *Appalachian Journal*, 7 (Spring 1980), 188-198; and "Land and Capital in Eastern Kentucky, 1890-1915," *Appalachian Journal*, 8 (Autumn 1980), 8-18.

II. APPALACHIA AS A SOCIAL PROBLEM AND A PROBLEM IN THE SOCIOLOGY OF KNOWLEDGE

Robert Munn, "The Latest Rediscovery of Appalachia," in *Appalachia in the Sixties*, ed. David Walls and John Stephenson (1972).

David Walls, "On the Naming of Appalachia," in *Appalachian Symposium*, ed. J.W. Williamson (1977).

Supplementary Reading:

Henry Shapiro, *Appalachia on Our Mind: The Southern Mountains and Mountaineers in the American Consciousness, 1870-1920* (1977).

"A Guide to Appalachian Studies," special issue of *Appalachian Journal*, 5 (Autumn 1977).

Dwight Billings and David Walls, "Appalachians," *Harvard Encyclopedia of American Ethnic Groups* (1980), pp. 125-128.

III. MODELS OF APPALACHIAN POVERTY AND UNDERDEVELOPMENT

A. GENETICS VS. ENVIRONMENT

John Fiske, *Old Virginia and Her Neighbours*, vol. 2 (1897), pp. 177-189, 311-321.

Arthur Estabrook, "Blood Seeks Environment," *Eugenical News*, 11 (August 1926), 106-114.

Harry Caudill, *A Darkness at Dawn* (1977), Chs. 1 and 2.

William G. Frost, "Our Contemporary Ancestors in the Southern Mountains," *Atlantic Monthly*, 83 (March 1899), pp. 311-319.

B. SUBCULTURE OF POVERTY MODEL

Jack Weller, *Yesterday's People* (1965), Chs. 3, 8 and Appendix.

Caudill, *Night Comes to the Cumberlands*, pp. 273-301.

Thomas Ford, "The Passing of Provincialism," Ch. 2 in *The Southern Appalachian Region: A Survey*, ed. Ford (1962).

Mike Maloney and Ben Huelsman, "Humanism, Scientism, and Southern Mountaineers," *Peoples' Appalachia*, 2 (July 1972), pp. 24-27.

Dwight Billings, "Culture and Poverty in Appalachia: A Theoretical Discussion and Empirical Analysis," *Social Forces*, 53 (December 1974), 315-323.

Stephen Fisher, "Victim-Blaming in Appalachia: Cultural Theories and the Southern Mountaineer," in *Appalachia: Social Context Past and Present*, ed. Bruce Ergood and Bruce E. Kuhre (1976), pp. 139-148.

C. REGIONAL DEVELOPMENT MODEL

Monroe Newman, *The Political Economy of Appalachia* (1972), Chs. 4-7.

Supplementary Reading

Niles Hansen, *Rural Poverty and the Urban Crisis* (1970), Ch. 4.

Annual Reports of the Appalachian Regional Commission.

D. INTERNAL COLONIALISM MODEL

Helen Lewis, "Fatalism or the Coal Industry?" in *Appalachia*, ed. Ergood and Kuhre, pp. 153-162.

Helen Lewis, Sue Kobak, and Linda Johnson, "Family, Religion and Colonialism in Central Appalachia," in *Growin' Up Country*, ed. Jim Axelrod (1973), pp. 131-153.

James Branscome, "Annihilating the Hillbilly," in *Growin' Up Country*, pp. 90-106.

Supplementary Reading:

Charles Valentine, *Culture and Poverty* (1968).

Robert Blauner, "Internal Colonialism and Ghetto Revolt," *Social Problems*, 16 (Spring 1969), 393-408; rpt. as Ch. 3 in Blauner, *Racial Oppression in America* (1972).

Latin American Perspectives, 1 (Spring 1974), Special Issue on Dependency Theory: A Reassessment.

Colonialism in Modern America: The Appalachian Case, ed. Helen Lewis, Linda Johnson, and Don Askins (1978).

E. INTERNAL PERIPHERY/ADVANCED CAPITALISM MODEL

David Walls, "Central Appalachia: A Peripheral Region within an Advanced Capitalist Society," *Journal of Sociology and Social Welfare*, 4 (November 1976), 232-247; or "Internal Colony or Internal Periphery?" in *Colonialism in Modern America*, pp. 319-349.

Supplementary Reading:

Jürgen Habermas, *Legitimation Crisis* (1973), pp. 33-41.

James O'Connor, *The Fiscal Crisis of the State* (1973), Introduction and Ch. 1.

David A. Gold, Clarence Y.H. Lo, and Erik Olin Wright, "Recent Developments in Marxist Theories of the Capitalist State," *Monthly Review*, 27 (October 1975), pp. 29-43, and (November 1975), pp. 36-51.

Ian Gough, "State Expenditure in Advanced Capitalism," *New Left Review*, No. 92 (July-August 1975), pp. 53-92; or Chs. 3 and 4 in Gough, *The Political Economy of the Welfare State* (1979).

Immanuel Wallerstein, "Dependence in an Interdependent World," *African Studies Review*, 17 (April 1974), 1-26; rpt. as Ch. 4 of Wallerstein, *The Capitalist World-Economy: Essays* (1979), pp. 66-94.

IV. COMMUNITY AND CULTURE

A. KINSHIP AND COMMUNITY STRATIFICATION

Campbell, *Southern Highlander*, pp. 81-89.

John Stephenson, *Shiloh* (1968), Chs. 1-3.

Harry Schwarzweller, James Brown, and J.J. Mangalam, *Mountain Families in Transition* (1971), pp. 23-58.

Robert Coles, *Migrants, Sharecroppers, Mountaineers* (1972), Chs. 5-6.

B. CULTURAL CONFIGURATIONS

Campbell, *Southern Highlander*, Chs. 6-9.

Stephenson, *Shiloh*, Chs. 4-6.

Schwarzweller, et al., *Mountain Families*, pp. 58-70.

Coles, *M,S,M*, Chs. 9-12.

C. DEMOGRAPHICS

Articles by Brown, Montgomery, in *Appalachia in the Sixties*, pp. 130-157.

Schwarzweller, et al., *Mountain Families*, Chs. 4,5,8,10 and 11.

Robert Coles, *The South Goes North* (1972), Ch. 6.

Supplementary Reading:

Todd Gitlin and Nanci Hollander, *Uptown* (1970).

The Invisible Minority: Urban Appalachians, ed. William W. Philliber and Clyde B. McCoy (1981).

V. CLASS, STATUS, POWER

A. COAL AS A DOMINANT INDUSTRY

Articles by Wakefield, Millstone, Bethell, Franklin, Trillin, and Brooks, in *Appalachia in the Sixties*, pp. 10-25, 69-129.

Richard Simon, "Uneven Development and the Case of West Virginia," *Appalachian Journal*, 8 (Spring 1981), 165-186.

Supplementary Reading:

Harry Caudill, *My Land is Dying* (1973).

J. Davitt McAteer, *Coal Mine Health and Safety: The Case of West Virginia* (1973).

Kai Erikson, *Everything in Its Path: Destruction of Community in the Buffalo Creek Flood* (1976).

B. SUBORDINATE STATUS GROUPS

Carter G. Woodson, "Freedom and Slavery in Appalachian America," *Journal of Negro History*, 1 (April 1916), 132-150.

Fayetta Allen, "Blacks in Appalachia," *The Black Scholar* (June 1974), pp. 42-51.

Paul Nyden, *Black Coal Miners in the United States* (1974).

"Special Cherokee Issue," *Appalachian Journal*, Summer 1975.

Edward Price, "The Melungeons: A Mixed-Blood Strain of the Southern Appalachians," *The Geographical Review*, 41 (April 1951), 256-271.

Kathy Kahn, *Hillbilly Women* (1974).

Sharon B. Lord and Carolyn Patten-Crowder, *Appalachian Women* (1979).

C. SOCIAL MOVEMENTS

Articles by Lee, Rasmussen, Good, Trillin, and West in *Appalachia in the Sixties*, pp. 164-216.

Supplementary Reading:

Brit Hume, *Death and the Mines* (1971).

Huey Perry, *They'll Cut Off Your Project* (1972).

Bill Peterson, *Coaltown Revisited* (1972).

Richard Couto, *Poverty, Politics and Health Care: An Appalachian Experience* (1975).

Harry Caudill, *The Watches of the Night* (1976).

Various issues of *United Mine Workers Journal* since 1973, and *Mountain Life & Work* since 1970.

Thomas J. Schoenbaum, *The New River Controversy* (1979).

David Whisnant, *Modernizing the Mountaineer: People, Power and Planning in Appalachia* (1980).

John Gaventa, *Power and Powerlessness: Quiescence and Rebellion in an Appalachian Valley* (1980).

VI. ALTERNATIVES FOR THE FUTURE

Caudill, *Night Comes to the Cumberlands*, pp. 365-392; and *A Darkness at Dawn*, Ch. 4.

Articles by Fetterman, Young, Caudill, and Burlage in *Appalachia in the Sixties*, pp. 232-258.

Richard Simon and Roger Lesser, "A Working Community Commonwealth," *Peoples' Appalachia*, 3 (Spring 1973), pp. 9-15.

ADDITIONAL RESOURCES:

The most comprehensive list of materials on Appalachia available by mail order from a single source is the *Bibliography/Catalog on the Appalachian South*, which lists approximately 1000 books, records, pamphlets and films, available for $2.50 from the Appalachian Bookstore, 104 Center Street, Berea, Kentucky 40403.

A catalog of documentary films and a list of June Appal recordings is available free from Appalshop, Inc., Box 743, Whitesburg, Kentucky 41858.

Latin American Economics

Andrew Zimbalist
Smith College
Department of Economics
Spring 1980
Undergraduate

Asterisked readings are optional. The readings constitute only a small sampling of available work on each subject and country. Students should consult me regarding readings on topics and countries not listed. Students may also be interested in consulting *Latin America Weekly Report* in the periodical room of the library, a British weekly on current economic and political affairs in Latin America. Finally, students who have never travelled or lived in an underdeveloped country might wish to familiarize themselves with the different cultural and sociological environments of these areas by reading one of the following: O. Lewis, *The Children of Sanchez* or *Pedro Martinez*; Gabriel Garcia Marquez, *One Hundred Years of Solitude*; or O. Barrios de Chungara, *Let Me Speak!*.

TEXTS

J. Swift, *Economic Development in Latin America* (EDLA)
Barnet and Muller, *Global Reach*
A.G. Frank, *Lumpenbourgeoisie: Lumpendevelopment*

I. (Week 1) INTRODUCTION: UNDERDEVELOPMENT-WHAT IS IT?

B. Higgins, *Economic Development*, Ch. 1, "The Worldwide War Against Poverty," pp. 3-33.

J. Swift, *EDLA*, Chs. 1,2,6.

Statistical Handout.

II. (Week 2) INFLATION: THE STRUCTURALIST-MONETARIST CONTROVERSY

A. Hirschman, *Journeys Toward Progress*, Ch. 3 on "Inflation in Chile," pp. 159-223.

G. Meier (ed.), *Leading Issues in Economic Development*, "Inflation in Latin America," pp. 203-210, 219-225.

A. Hirschman (ed.), *Latin American Issues*, "Two Views on Inflation in Latin America," pp. 69-123.

J. Swift, *EDLA*, Ch. 8.

C. Furtado, *Economic Development of Latin America*, pp. 27-42, 75-92, 93-104.

III. (Week 3) LAND REFORM

S. Barraclough and A. Domike, "Agrarian Structure in Seven Latin American Countries," in R. Stavenhagen (ed.), *Agrarian Problems and Peasant Movements in Latin America*, pp. 41-96.

C. Furtado, *op. cit.*, pp. 51-58, 114-123, 214-230.

J. Petras, "The Latin American Agro-Transformation from Above and Outside," in Petras, *Critical Perspectives on Imperialism and Social Class in the Third World*, pp. 137-156.

J. Swift, *EDLA*, Ch. 7.

E. Feder, *The Rape of the Peasantry: Latin America's Landholding System*, pp. 239-258.

J. Petras and R. LaPorte, *Cultivating Revolution*, pp. 11-32, 125-232.

J. Collins, "Agrarian Reform and Counter-Reform in Chile," *Monthly Review*, November 1979.

IV. INTERPRETATIONS OF UNDERDEVELOPMENT

A. (Week 4) DEPENDENCY AND FOREIGN INVESTMENT

S. Bodenheimer, "Dependency and Imperialism: The Roots of Latin American Underdevelopment," in Fann and Hodges (eds.), *Readings in U.S. Imperialism*, pp. 155-182.

T. Dos Santos, "The Structure of Dependence," *American Economic Review*, May, 1970.

T. Weisskopf, "Capitalism and Underdevelopment in the Modern World," in Edwards *et. al.* (eds.), *The Capitalist System*, pp. 442-457.

K. Griffin, *Underdevelopment in Spanish America*, Ch. 3 ("Importation of Capital and National Development") and Ch. 4 ("Mixed Enterprises and Foreign Investment").

"Latin America Opens and Door to Foreign Investment Again," *Business Week*, August 9, 1976.

B. (Week 5) DEPENDENCY, MULTINATIONALS AND FOREIGN AID

R. Barnet and R. Muller, *Global Reach*, pp. 123-212 and (213-253).

Latin American Perspectives, Winter 1976, articles by Erickson and Peppe, and Spalding, pp. 19-69. Instead of Spalding article you can substitute Ch. 6 (pp. 251-276) in his book, *Organized Labor in Latin America*.

H. Magdoff, *The Age of Imperialism*, Ch. 4, "Aid and Trade," pp. 115-172.

R. Scott, "Economic Aid and Imperialism in Bolivia," *Monthly Review*, May 1972, pp. 48-60.

J. Swift, *EDLA*, pp. 66-80.

H. Wachtel, *The New Gnomes: Multinational Banks in the Third World*.

C. (Week 6) HISTORICAL OVERVIEW

A.G. Frank, *Lumpenbourgeoisie—Lumpendevelopment*

J. Swift, *EDLA*, pp. 39-63.

Stein and Stein, *The Colonial Heritage of Latin America: Essays on Economic Dependence in Perspective*.

D. (Week 7) THE DEBATE

F. Cardoso, "Dependency and Development," *New Left Review*, No. 74, July-August 1972.

B. Warren, "Myths of Underdevelopment," *New Left Review*, No. 81, pp. 3-46.

McMichael, Petras and Rhodes, "Industry in the Third World," *New Left Review*, No. 85, pp. 83-104.

V. CASE STUDIES

A. (Week 8) CHILE

N. Girvan, "Corporate Imperialism and Copper in Chile," in Girvan's *Corporate Imperialism: Conflict and Expropriation*, pp. 52-97 Or A.G. Frank, *Capitalism and Underdevelopment in Latin America*, Ch. 1 on Chile.

Espinosa and Zimbalist, *Economic Democracy: Workers' Participation in the Management of Industrial Enterprises in Chile, 1970-73*, Ch. 3 on "The Chilean Context," pp. 57-73.

P. Rosenstein-Rodan, "Why Allende Failed," *Challenge*, May-June, 1974.

Stallings and Zimbalist, "The Political Economy of the *Unidad Popular*," in *Latin American Perspectives*, Spring 1975.

Petras and Morley, *The United States and Chile*.

K. Griffin, *Underdevelopment in Spanish America*, Ch. 4 on "Mixed Enterprises and Foreign Investment."

B. (Week 9) CUBA

E. Boorstein, *The Economic Transformation of Cuba*, Ch. 1.

Bray and Harding, "Cuba," in Chilcote and Edelstein (eds.), *Latin America: The Struggle with Dependency and Beyond*.

A. Zimbalist, "Worker Participation in Cuba," *Challenge*, Nov-Dec. 1975.

D. Lehman, "The Cuban Economy in 1980," *Cambridge Journal of Economics*, Fall 1979.

A. Ritter, *Economic Development in Revolutionary Cuba*.

C. Mesa-Lago, *Cuba in the 1970s*, Chs. 1, 2, and 5.

Latin American Perspectives, issue on Cuba, Vol. II, No. 4 (1975).

A. Zimbalist, "The Prospects for U.S.-Cuban Trade," *Challenge*, Nov.-Dec. 1977.

Southern Africa in World Politics

Barbara B. Brown
Mount Holyoke College
Politics
Spring 1981
Undergraduate

Southern Africa is one of the most exciting—and terrrifying—areas of the world today. It is also a complex region and we cannot expect to cover all aspects in 13 weeks. The course will concentrate on major regional and international issues, with primary attention given to U.S.-South African relations.

You are expected to participate actively in class, raising questions, clarifying issues, criticizing analyses and promoting new and better analyses. You are also expected to keep up-to-date on southern African news. Do not rely only on the *New York Times*. There are many important events that this paper hardly touches on, so you should skim through *Africa News* (a weekly) every week and also *Southern Africa* magazine every month.

BOOKS

American Policy in Southern Africa
The Kissinger Study
South Africa: Foreign Investment and Apartheid
Southern Africa: The Continuing Crisis
U.S. Military Involvement in Southern Africa

PAMPHLETS

"General Motors in Southern Africa"
"Confidential Diplomatic Cable"
"The Soviets in Africa" (may be in short supply)
"Apartheid: A Threat to Peace"
"Taking Stock of Divestment"

I. THE PRESENT SITUATION: AN INTRODUCTION TO WHITE MINORITY RULE

A. RACE AND CLASS: A THEORETICAL OVERVIEW

Dobb, M. "The Essence of Capitalism," in Edwards, Reich and Weisskopf, *The Capitalist System* [hereafter referred to as ERW].

Baran, P. and Sweezy, P. "Monopoly Capital and Race Relations," in ERW.

Johnstone, F.A. "White Prosperity and White Supremacy in South Africa Today," *African Affairs*, 69, 1970, pp. 124-40.

B. SOUTH AFRICA

Callinicos, A. and Rogers, J. *Southern Africa after Soweto*, pp. 10-40.

Carter, Gwen. "South Africa," in Carter and O'Meara, eds., *Southern Africa: The Continuing Crisis* [hereafter referred to as Carter and O'Meara].

II. UNITED STATES POLICY TOWARD THE WHITE-RULED STATES

A. THEORETICAL OVERVIEWS

Isaacs, H. "Race and Color in World Affairs," in G. Shepherd, ed., *Racial Influences on American Foreign Policy*.

MacEwan, A. "Capitalist Expansion, Ideology and Intervention," in ERW.

Magdoff, H. "Imperialism without Colonies," in Magdoff, *Imperialism: from the Colonial Age to the Present*.

B. U.S. POLICY

1. pre-1974

El-Khawas and Cohen, eds., *The Kissinger Study of Southern Africa*, pp. 1-85 and 105-09.

Isaacman and Davis, "U.S. Policy toward Mozambique, 1946-1976," in Lemarchand, ed., *American Policy in Southern Africa* [hereafter referred to as Lemarchand].

2. 1974—

A. Government Policy

Houser, G. "Carter's Africa Policy," pamphlet.

Lockwood, E. "The Future of the Carter Policy," in Lemarchand

Root, Chris. Two articles on Reagan's South African Policy in the *Guardian,* Jan. 14 and 21, 81.

"South Africa Joins the Nuclear Club," in *Dollars and Sense,* Dec. 1979, pp. 12-13.

Gervasi, S. "Breakdown of U.S. Arms Embargo," in *U.S. Military Involvement in Southern Africa,* ed. by the Western Mass. Association of Concerned African Scholars [hereafter referred to as U.S. Military].

"Hot Shells," transcript of WGBH-TV (PBS station) program aired Jan. 16, 1980.

B. Corporations

Litvak, L. et al. *South Africa: Foreign Investment and Apartheid,* all.

Makgetla, Neva and Seidman, Ann. "U.S. Transnational Corporations in South Africa's Military-Industrial Complex," in *U.S. Military,* pp. 197-220

"General Motors in South Africa: Secret Contingency Plan for Unrest," pamphlet.

C. The U.S. Press' Presentation of Southern African News

Southern Africa (magazine) Aug. 1977, pp. 6-9 and January 1980, p. 7 ff. and Dec. 1978, p. 5 ff.

III. WHAT CAN BE DONE IN THE WEST TO END APARTHEID?

A. WHAT CAN BE DONE?

Nolutshugu, S. "The Impact of External Opposition on South African Politics," in Thompson and Butler, eds., *Change in Contemporary South Africa,* pp. 369-99.

Ferguson, C. and Cotter, W. "South Africa: What is to Be Done," *Foreign Affairs,* 56, 2, Jan. 1978, pp. 253-74.

"Taking Stock of Divestment," pamphlet.

Houser, G. "Polaroid's Dramatic Withdrawal from South Africa," pamphlet.

B. WHO WILL ACT?

The U.S. Government?

Foltz, W. "U.S. Policy toward Southern Africa," in Lemarchand.

Davis, H. "U.S. Policy toward Southern Africa: A Dissenting View," in Lemarchand.

Black Americans?

Weil, M. "Can the Blacks Do for Africa What the Jews Did for Israel?" in Lemarchand.

Lemelle, T. "American Black Constituencies: A Rejoinder," in Lemarchand.

Shuster, M. "Advocates for Africa on Capitol Hill," *Southern Africa,* Jan. 1980 p. 4 ff.

Students, Churches, Community Groups?

Myers, D. *U.S. Business in South Africa,* pp. 127-42.

Anti-Apartheid Organizing on Campus, pp. 9-28.

IV. SOCIALIST AND AFRICAN COUNTRIES' POLICIES ON APARTHEID

A. AFRICA

Grundy, K. "Economic Patterns in the New Southern African Balance," in Carter and O'Meara.

Mazrui, Ali and Gordon, D. "Independent African States and the Struggle for South Africa," in Seiler, ed., *Southern Africa Since the Portuguese Coup* [hereafter, Seiler].

Grundy, K. *Confrontation and Accommodation,* pp. 152-70 and 191-212.

B. SOCIALIST STATES

Roger, S. and Vickery, K. "The Soviets in Africa: Fiction and Fact," pamphlet.

Stevens, C. "The Soviet Role in Southern Africa," in Seiler.

Halperin, M. "The Cuban Role in Southern Africa," in Seiler.

Shepherd, G. "Socialist State Strategy and Arms in Southern Africa, *Issue,* 9, ½, 1979, pp. 47-51.

V. SOUTH AFRICA'S DEFENSE OF ITS INTERESTS

A. DOMESTIC CONTROL

Review Carter article.

B. RELATIONS WITH THE WEST

Barber, W. *South Africa's Foreign Policy,* pp. 273-308.

Minty, Abdul. "Apartheid: A Threat to Peace," pamphlet.

Articles on the S. Afr. Information Department scandal in *Southern Africa,* January 1980, p. 25 and May 1979, pp 10-11 and ff. (read the 1980 article first).

C. RELATIONS WITH SOUTH AFRICA'S BLACK NEIGHBORING STATES

Brown, Barbara. "South Africa's Foreign Policy toward its Black Neighbors," pp. 146-280.

VI. ZIMBABWE: THE STRUGGLE FOR INDEPENDENCE

O'Meara, P. "Rhodesia/Zimbabwe," in Carter and O'Meara.

Raeburn, M. *We Are Everywhere,* pp. 3-67 and 141-91.

Bratten, M. "Structural Transformation in Zimbabwe," *Journal of Modern African Studies,* April 1977, pp. 600-611 only.

VII. NAMIBIA: THE NEXT TO INDEPENDENCE?

Landis, Elizabeth and Davis, M. "Namibia," in Carter and O'Meara.

Using *Africa News* and *Southern Africa,* bring your knowledge up to date, following on the period since Sept. 1980.

Johns, S. "Obstacles to Guerrilla Warfare," *Journal of Modern Africa Studies*, June 1973, pp. 267-303.

VIII. ANGOLA

Marcum, J. "Angola," in Carter and O'Meara.

Minter, W. *Portuguese Africa and the West*, pp. 13-36, 74-143.

Stockwell, J. *In Search of Enemies: A CIA Story*, pp. 9-69.

"Why Is Gulf Still in Angola?" *Dollars and Sense*, May-June, 1979, 3 pp.

IX. MOZAMBIQUE VS. BOTSWANA: SOUTH AFRICA'S HOSTAGES OR INDEPENDENT STATES?

Morgan, P. "Botswana," in Carter and O'Meara.

Hodges, T. "Mozambique," in Carter and O'Meara, pp. 74-92 *only*.

Isaacman, A. "Transforming Mozambique's Rural Economy," *Issue*, 8,1, 1978, pp. 17-24.

Mittleman, J. "State Power in Mozambique," *ibid*, pp. 4-11.

Culture and Social Change in Modern Africa

P.C.W. Gutkind
McGill University
Department of Anthropology
Winter/Spring 1977
Undergraduate

The study of Modern Africa requires some background knowledge of "traditional" African civilization. Thus those who have come into this course without such background would do well to do some extra reading. Such as:

Bohannan, P. and Curtin, P., *Africa and Africans* (Revised Edition), Natural History Press, 1971.
Ayisi, E. O. *An Introduction to the Study of African Culture*, Heinemann, 1972.
Maquet, J. *Africanity: the Cultural Unity of Black Africa*. Oxford University Press 1972.
Skinner, E. P. (ed.). *Peoples and Cultures of Africa*. Natural History Press, 1973.
Steward, J.H. (ed.). *Contemporary Change in Traditional Societies, Vol 1, Introduction and African Tribes*. University of Illinois Press, 1967.
Middleton, J. (ed.). *Black Africa Its People and Cultures Today*. Macmillan, 1970.
Klein, M.A. and Johnson, G.W. (eds.) *Perspectives on the African Past*, Boston, Little, Brown and Company, 1972.

MODERN AFRICA

The literature on contemporary Africa is enormous. Much of it is worthless as it is written from a strongly Eurocentric and ethnocentric point of view. Most fundamentally, however, a great deal of the literature is devoid of any critical historical approach, ignorant of, or insensitive to, the realities of colonialism. These limitations, while now being systematically corrected, must be kept in mind. To cover all aspects of Modern Africa is simply impossible in the course of a few lectures. All that can be done is to skim over the top, to bring out the highlights. Students with a real interest who wish to penetrate a subject more deeply should see me.

REQUIRED READINGS

There is no ONE good book on Africa although that by Walter Rodney, *How Europe Underdeveloped Africa* is superb in many respects—and you *must* read it in its entirety (as well as some of the *very important* reviews of it). A more precise case study is the fine book by Colin Leys, *Underdevelopment in Kenya* which has received wide acclaim. This too is required reading. A major theme of the course will be the transition—often to the worse—from colonialism to the pernicious condition of neo-colonialism. Hence you are required to read to Samir Amin's, *Neo-Colonialism in West Africa*. Two more general books, also required reading, are Peter Lloyd's, *Africa in Social Change* (1967), and Basil Davidson's, *Can Africa Survive?*

Some *important* supplementary reading.

Crowder, M., *West Africa Under Colonial Rule*, Evanston, Northwestern U.P. 1968.
Wallerstein, I. (ed.) *Social Change: The Colonial Situation*, New York, Wiley, 1966.
Davidson, B., *Which Way Africa*, Penguin Books, 1971.
Arrighi, E. and Saul, J.S., *Essays on the Political Economy of Africa*, New York, Monthly Review Press, 1973.
Wallerstein, I. *Africa: the Politics of Unity*. New York, Random House, 1967.

TOPIC 1

It is appropriate that we begin the course with the view that the African continent has, in recent historic times, i.e. since at least the 15th century, been part of a *World System* in economic and political terms.

Wallerstein, I., "Africa in a Capitalist World", *Issue*, vol. 3, No. 3, Fall 1973, pp. 1-11.

_____, "Three Stages of African Involvement in the World-Economy", in *The Political Economy of Contemporary Africa*, Gutkind, P.C.W. and Wallerstein, I. (eds.), Beverley Hills, Sage Publications, 1976, pp. 30-57.

_____, "The Present State of the Debate on World Inequality" in *World Inequality: Origins and Perspectives on the World System*, Wallerstein, I. (ed.), Montreal, Black Rose Press, 1975, pp. 9-28.

Hopkins, A.G. *An Economic History of West Africa*, London, Longmans, 1973.

Rodney, W., *op. cit.*

Amin, S. "Underdevelopment and Dependence in Black Africa: Historical Origins", *Journal of Peace Research*, No. 2, 1972, pp. 105-119.

TOPIC 2

Colonialism transformed the totality of African *society*. The most significant transformation being the total loss of political autonomy, the subordination of the continent to the economic needs and demands of the colonial powers and the destruction of social and cultural institutions and values, and the emergence of contemporary *stratification*.

Colson, E. "African Society at the time of the scramble", in *Colonialism in Africa 1870-1960*, Vol. 1, Gann, L.H. and Duignan, P. (eds.), Cambridge U.P. 1969, pp. 27-65.

Little, K.L. "African Culture and Western Intrusion", *Journal of World History*, Vol. 3, No. 4, 1956, pp. 941-964.

Tuden, A. and Plotnicov, L. (eds.), *Social Stratification in Africa*, New York, Free Press, 1970.

Magubane, B. "A Critical Look at Indices Used in the Study of Social Change in Africa", *Current Anthropology*, Vol. 12, Nos. 4-5, Oct-Dec. 1971, pp. 419-430.

Dyson-Hudson, N. "Factors Inhibiting Change in an African Pastoral Society: The Karimojong of Northeast Uganda", *Transactions of the New York Academy of Sciences*, Vol. 24, No. 7, May 1962, pp. 771-801.

Fallers, L.A. "The Predicament of the Modern African Chief: An Instance from Uganda", *American Anthropologist*, Vol. 57, No. 2, April 1955, pp. 290-305.

Middleton, J. "Some Effects of Colonial Rule Among the Lugbara" in *Colonialism in Africa 1870-1960*, Vol. 3, Turner, V. (ed.), London, Cambridge University Press, 1971, pp. 6-48.

Ajayi, J.F.A. "The continuity of African institutions under colonialism", in *Emerging Themes of African History*, Ranger, T.O. (ed.), London, Heinemann, 1968, pp. 189-200.

Wallerstein, I. "The Colonial Era in Africa: Changes in the Social Structure", in *Colonialism in Africa 1870-1960*, Vol. 2, Gann, L.H. and Duignan, P. (eds.), London, Cambridge University Press, 1970, pp. 399-421.

Davidson, B. "The Development of People", in *Can Africa Survive?*, London, Heinemann, 1975, pp. 144-180.

Cohen, A. "The Social Organization of Credit in a West African Cattle Market", *Africa*, Vol. 35, No. 1, 1965, pp. 8-19.

TOPIC 3

However the African continent entered the world economic system via the brutalization of her people: the *slave trade*.

Curtin, P.D. *The Dimensions of the Slave Trade*, Madison, U. of Wisconsin Press, 1969.

Rodney, *op. cit.* pp. 103-112.

_____, *West Africa and the Atlantic Slave Trade*, Nairobi, E.A. Publishing House, 1967.

Alpers, E. *The East African Slave Trade*, Nairobi, E.A. Publishing House, 1967.

Anene, J.C. "Slavery and the Slave Trade", in *Africa in the Nineteenth and Twentieth Centuries*, Anene, J.C. and Brown, G.N. (ed.), Ibadan, Ibadan University Press, 1966, pp. 92-109.

Centre of African Studies, University of Edinburgh, *The Transatlantic Slave Trade from West Africa*, Proceedings of a Seminar, 1965.

Rodney, W. "African Slavery and Other Forms of Social Oppression of the Upper Guinea Coast in the Context of the Atlantic Slave-Trade" *Journal of African History*, vol. 7, 1966, pp. 431-443.

Alpers, E.A. "The Growth and Impact of the Slave Trade after 1810" in *Ivory and Slaves in East Central Africa*, London, Heinemann, 1975, pp. 209-263.

TOPIC 4

Perhaps fundamental to Africa-Non-Africa relations is the historic attitude to the continent. It is not merely one of exploitation but of *racism* and *ethnocentricity*.

Fanon, F. *Black Skin, White Masks*, New York, Grove Press, 1967.

———, "Racism and Culture" in *Toward the African Revolution (Political Essays)*, New York, Grove Press, 1967, pp. 29-44.

George, K. "The Civilized West Looks at Primitive Africa: 1400-1800, A Study in Ethnocentrism", *Isis*, Vol. 49, No. 155, March 1958, pp. 62-72.

Mphalele, E. *Down Second Avenue*, London, Faber and Faber, 1959.

Mannoni, O. *Prospero and Caliban: The Psychology of Colonization*, New York, Praeger, 1956.

Adam, H. *Modernizing Racial Domination: The Dynamics of South African Politics*, Berkeley, University of California Press, 1971.

Burawoy, M. "Race, Class and Colonialism" *Social and Economic Studies*, Vol. 23, No. 4, Dec. 1974, pp. 521-550.

Gann, L.H. and Duignan, P. *Burden of Empire: An appraisal of Western Colonialism in Africa South of the Sahara*, New York, Praeger, 1967.

TOPIC 5

The Imperialists, naturally, competed among themselves for the spoils which the African continent provided. Thus the prelude to conquest was the *scramble* for and the *partition* of Africa.

Hargreaves, J.D. *Prelude to the Partition of Africa*, London, Macmillan, 1966.

Gifford, P. and Louis, W.R. (eds.), *France and Britain in Africa Imperial Rivalry and Colonial Rule*, New Haven, Yale University Press, 1971.

Centre of African Studies, University of Edinburgh, *The Theory of Imperialism and the European Partition of Africa*, Proceedings of a Seminar, 1968.

Crowder, M. *West Africa under Colonial Rule*, Evanston, Northwestern University Press, 1968 pp. 45-161.

Robinson, R. and Gallagher, J. (with A. Denny), *Africa and the Victorians: the Official Mind of Imperialism* New York, St. Martin's Press, 1961. (For a critique see 6 below).

Louis, W.R. (ed.), *Imperialism The Robinson and Gallagher Controversy*, New York, Watts, 1976.

Rodney, W. "The Imperialist Partition of Africa", *Monthly Review*, Vol. 21, No. 11, April 1970, pp. 103-114.

TOPIC 6

The colonial masters did not have it all their own way. Africans *reacted* sharply to the *encounter*.

Lloyd, P.C. 1967, *op cit*. pp. 51-67.

Ajayi, J.F. "The Continuity of African Institutions under Colonialism", in *Emerging Themes of African History*, Ranger, T.O. (ed.), Nairobi, E.A. Publishing House, 1968, pp. 189-200.

Person, Y. "Samori and Resistence to the French", in *Protest and Power in Black Africa*, Rotberg, R. and Mazrui, A.A. (eds.), New York, O.U.P., 1970, pp. 80-112.

Iliffe, J. "The Organization of the Maji-Maji Rebellion", *Journal of African History*, Vol. 8, No. 3, 1967, pp. 495-512.

Ranger, T.O. "African Reactions to the Imposition of Colonial Rule in East and Central Africa", in *Colonialism in Africa 1870-1960* Vol. 1, Gann, L.H. and Duignan, P. (eds.), Cambridge U.P. 1969, pp. 293-324.

Balandier, G. "The Colonial Situation: A Theoretical Approach", in *Social Change the Colonial Situation*, Wallerstein, I. op. cit. 1966, pp. 34-61.

Rotberg, R.I. and Mazrui, A.A. (eds.), *Protest and Power in Black Africa*, New York, O.U.P. 1970.

Ranger, T.O. "Connexions Between 'Primary Resistance' Movements and Modern Mass Nationalism in East and Central Africa", *Journal of African History* Vol. 9, No. 3, 1968, pp. 437-453, No. 4, pp. 631-641.

Henderson, I. "Wage-earners and Political Protest in Colonial Africa: The Case of the Copper Belt", *African Affairs*, Vol. 72, No. 288, July 1973, pp. 288-299.

Davidson, A.B. "African Resistance and Rebellion Against the Imposition of Colonial Rule", in *Emerging Themes of African History*, Ranger, T.O. (ed.), London, Heinemann, 1968, pp. 177-188.

Ranger, T.O. (ed.) *Aspects of Central African History*, London, Heinemann, 1968.

TOPIC 7

The Europeans claimed that they brought 'civilization' to Africa. What were their *colonial policies*?

Perham, M., *The Colonial Reckoning*, New York, Knopf, 1962.

Anderson, P. "Portugal and the End of Ultra-Colonialism", *New Left Review*, No. 15, May-June 1962, pp. 83-102.

Gifford, P. and Louis, W.R. (eds.), *France and Britain in Africa: Imperial Rivalry and Colonial Rule*, New Haven, Yale U.P. 1971, pp. 409-784.

Post, K.W.J., "British Policy and Representative Government in West Africa, 1920-1951", in *Colonialism in Africa 1870-1960*, Vol. 2. Gann, L.H. and Duignan, P. (eds.), Cambridge U.P. 1970, pp. 31-57.

Ballard, J.A. "The Colonial Phase in French West Africa" in *A Thousand Years of West African History*, Ajayi, J.F.A. and Espie, I. (ed.), Ibadan, Ibadan University Press, 1969, pp. 431-455.

Crowder, M. "Indirect-Rule-French and British Style", *Africa*, Vol. 34, No. 3, July 1964, pp. 197-205.

Cohen, A. *British Policy in Changing Africa*, London, Routledge and Kegan Paul, 1959.

Suret-Canale, J. *French Colonialism in Tropical Africa 1900-1945*, New York, Pica Press, 1971.

TOPIC 8

Neo-Colonialism, economic *dependency* and exploitation, despite political independence, continues to be the critical issue for Africa (as for most of the "Third World"—other than, perhaps, the "oil-rich nations"). The issue is *capitalism* and its control and operations in Africa.

Emmanuel, A. "White-Settler Colonialism and the Myth of Investment Imperialism", *New Left Review,* No. 73, May-June 1973, pp. 35-57.

National Christian Council of Kenya, *Who Controls Kenya Industry,* Nairobi, East African Publishing House, 1968.

Boavida, A. *Angola: Five Centuries of Portuguese Exploitation,* Richmond, LSM Information Center, 1972.

Nkrumah, K. *Neo-Colonialism The Last Stage of Imperialism,* New York, International Publishers, 1965.

Green, R. and Swidman, A. *Unity or Poverty: The Economics of Pan-Africanism,* Baltimore, Penguin Books, 1968.

Ehrensaft, P. "Semi-Industrial Capitalism in the Third World", *Africa Today,* Vol. 18, No. 1, Jan. 1971, pp. 40-67.

Hopkins, A.G., *An Economic History of West Africa,* London, Longman, 1973.

Amin's, "Capitalism and Development in the Ivory Coast", in *African Politics and Society* Markovitz, I.L. (ed.), New York, Free Press, 1970, pp. 277-288.

Langdon, S. "Multinational Corporations, Taste Transfer and Underdevelopment: A Case Study from Kenya", *Review of African Political Economy,* No. 2, 1975, pp. 12-35.

Shivji, I. "Capitalism Unlimited: The Public Corporations in Partnership with Multi-National Corporations", *The African Review,* Vol. 3, No. 3, 1973, pp. 359-384.

Hopkins, A.G. "On Importing A.G. Frank into Africa", *African Economic History Review,* Vol. 2, No. 1, 1975, pp. 13-21.

Galtung, J. "A Structural-Theory of Imperialism", *The African Review,* Vol. 1, No. 4, April 1972, pp. 93-138.

Bauer, P.T. "British Colonial Africa: Economic Retrospect and Aftermath" in *Colonialism in Africa 1870-1960,* Vol. 4, Duignan, P. and Gann, L.H. (eds.), London, Cambridge University Press, 1975, pp. 632-654.

Leys, C. *Underdevelopment in Kenya The Political Economy of Neo-Colonialism* Berkeley, University of California Press, 1974.

Davidson, B. "The Force of Economics" in *Can Africa Survive?,* London, Heinemann, 1975, pp. 72-104.

Schatz, S.P. "Crude Private Neo-Imperialism: A New Pattern in Africa", *Journal of Modern African Studies,* Vol. 7, No. 4, Dec. 1969, pp. 677-688.

Widstrand, C. (ed.) *Multi-National Firms in Africa,* Uppsala, Scandinavian Institute of African Studies, 1975.

Suret-Canale, J. *French Colonialism in Tropical Africa 1900-1945,* New York, Pica Press, pp. 155-306.

TOPIC 9

There are those who insist that the most significant transition in Africa is the rapid growth of *towns* and *cities,* a development produced primarily by *migration, urban associations.*

Gluckman, M. "Tribalism, ruralism and urbanism in South and Central Africa", in *Colonialism in Africa 1870-1960,* Vol. 3, *op. cit.* pp. 127-166.

Southall, A.W. "The impact of imperialism upon urban development in Africa", see 1 above, pp. 216-255.

Lloyd, P.C. *op cit.* 1967, pp. 92-124, 193-213.

Epstein, A.L. "Urbanization and Social Change in Africa", *Current Anthropology,* Vol. 8, No. 4, Oct. 1967, pp. 275-295.

Magubane, B. and O'Brien, J. "The Political Economy of Migrant Labor: a Critique of Conventional Wisdom or a Case Study in the Functions of Functionalism", *Critical Anthropology,* Vol. 2, No. 2, 1972, pp. 88-103.

Mitchell, J.C. "The Causes of Labour Migration", *Bulletin Inter-African Labour Institute,* Vol. 6, 1959, pp. 12-46.

Skinner, E.P., "Strangers in West African Societies", *Africa,* Vol. 33, No. 4, Oct. 1963, pp. 307-320.

Peil, M., "The Apprenticeship System in Accra", *Africa,* Vol. 40, No. 2, April 1970, pp. 137-150.

Meillassoux, C. *Urbanization of an African Community: Voluntary Associations in Bamako,* Seattle, Washington University Press, 1968.

Mabogunje, A.L. *Urbanization in Nigeria,* London, University of London Press, 1968.

Cohen, A. *Custom and Politics in Urban Africa A Study of Hausa Migrants in Yoruba Towns,* London, Routledge and Kegan Paul, 1969.

Osoba, S.O., "The Phenomenon of Labour Migration in the Era of British Colonial Rule: A Neglected Aspect of Nigeria's Social History", *Journal of the Historical Society of Nigeria,* Vol. 4, No. 4, June 1969, pp. 515-538.

Ekwensi, C. *People of the City,* London, Heinemann, 1964.

Paden, J.N. "Communal Competition Conflict and Violence in Kano", in *Modernization and the Politics of Communalism,* Melson, R. and Wolpe, H. (eds.), East Lansing, Michigan State University Press, 1971, pp. 113-144.

Mabogunje, A.L. "Urbanization and Change" in *The African Experience Vol. 1, Essays*, Paden, J.N. and Soja, E.W. (eds.), Evanston, Northwestern University Press, 1970, pp. 331-358.

TOPIC 10

Non-Africans have characterised the African continent and polity as *"tribal"* and *"tribalism"* as the bane of Africa. They claim that there are no real nations but only antagonistic Tribes. They ignore the historical truth that the colonial powers created "tribes" where none existed or created and exploited inter-ethnic tensions where these existed.

Mafeje, A. "The Ideology of Tribalism", *Journal of Modern African Studies*, Vol. 9, No. 2, August 1971, pp. 253-262.

_____, "A Chief Visits Town", *Journal of Local Administration Overseas*, Vol. 2, 1963, pp. 88-99.

Lloyd, P. *op. cit.*, 1967, pp. 288-303.

Banton, M. "Urbanization and the colour line in Africa", *Colonialism in Africa 1870-1960*, Vol. 3, *op. cit.* pp. 256-285.

Epstein, A.L. "Tribal Elders to Trade Unions", in *Africa in Transition*, Smith, P. (ed.), London Reinhardt, 1958, pp. 97-105.

Mitchell, J.C. *Tribalism and the Plural Society*, London, O.U.P. 1960.

Cohen, R. and Middleton, J. "Introduction", in *From Tribe to Nation in Africa: Studies in Incorporation Processes*, Scranton, Chandler Publishers, 1970, pp. 1-34.

Gulliver, P.H. (ed.), *Tradition and Transition in East Africa: Studies of the Tribal Element in Modern Africa*, London, Routledge and Kegan Paul, 1969.

Gluckman, M. "Tribalism in British Central Africa" *Cahiers d'etudes Africaines*, Vol. 1, 1960, pp. 55-70.

Gutkind, P.C.W. (ed.), *The Passing of Tribal Man in Africa*. Special Issue of the *Journal of Asian and African Studies*, Vol. V, Nos. 1-2, Jan-April 1970, 128 pp.

Skinner, E. "Group Dynamics in the Politics of Changing Societies: The Problem of 'Tribal' Politics in Africa" in *Essays on the Problem of Tribe*, Helm, J. (ed.), American Ethnological Society, Seattle, University of Washington Press, 1968, pp. 170-185.

Apthorpe, R.J. *"Does Tribalism Really Matter?"*, *Transition*, Vol. 7, No. 37, 1968, pp. 18-22.

TOPIC 11

Most significant is the rise of new soico-economic and political *classes* and *class struggles*.

Cohen, R. "Class in Africa: Analytical Problems and Perspectives" in *The Socialist Register 1972*, Miliband, R. and Saville, J.C. (eds.), London, Merlin Press, 1972, pp. 231-55.

xxx (Samir Amin) "The Class Struggle in Africa" *Revolution*, Vol. 1, No. 9, 1964, pp. 23-47.

Gerard-Libois, J. "The New Class and Rebellion in the Congo", *The Socialist Register 1966*, Miliband, R. and Saville, J.C. (eds.), London, The Merlin Press, 1966, pp. 267-280.

Kitching, G.N. "The Concept of Class and the Study of Africa", *The African Review*, Vol. 2, No. 3, 1972, pp. 327-350.

Seidman, A. "Class stratification and Economic Development in Africa", *Pan-African Journal*, Vol. 5, No. 1, Spring 1972, pp. 7-26.

Wallerstein, I. "Class and Conflict in Africa," *Monthly Review*, Vol. 26, No. 9, February 1975, pp. 34-42.

Lloyd, P.C. *Classes, Crises and Coups*, London, Paladin, 1973.

Cruise O'Brien, D.B. "Cooperators and Bureaucrats: Class Formation in a Senegalese Society" *Africa*, Vol. 41, No. 4, Oct. 1971, pp. 263-278.

Cabral, A. "The Weapon of Theory", in *Revolution in Guinea*, New York, Monthly Review Press, 1968, pp. 90-111.

Chodak, S. (ed.) *Social Stratification in Africa*, Special Issue of the *Canadian Journal of African Studies*, Vol. 7, No. 3, 1973.

Sanda, A.O. "Education and Social Change in Africa: Some Problems of Class Formation", *Ufahamu*, Vol. 3, No. 1, Spring 1972, pp. 73-86.

Wallerstein, I. "Social Conflict in Post-Independence Black Africa: The Concepts of Race and Status-Group Reconsidered", in *Racial Tensions and National Identity*, Campbell, E.Q. (ed.), Nashville, Vanderbilt University Press 1972, pp. 207-226.

Grundy, K. "The Class Struggle in Africa: An Examination of Conflicting Theories", *Journal of Modern African Studies*, Vol. 2, No. 3, Nov. 1964, pp. 379-393.

Ottaway, M. "Social Classes and Corporate Interest in the Ethiopian Revolution", *Journal of Modern African Studies*, Vol. 14, No. 3, Sept. 1976, pp. 469-486.

Rodney, W. "Class Contradictions in Tanzania", *The Pan-Africanist*, No. 6, June 1975, pp. 15-28.

Suret-Canale, J. "Tribes, Classes and Nations in Tropical Africa", *World Marxist Review*, Vol. 12, No. 11, Nov. 1969, pp. 75-81.

MacRae, P. "Race and Class in Southern Africa", *The African Review*, Vol. 4, No. 2, 1974, pp. 237-257.

Kilson, M.L. "Nationalism and Social Classes in British West Africa", *Journal of Politics*, Vol. 20, No. 2, May 1958, pp. 368-387.

Manghezi, A. *Class, Elite and Community in African Development*, Uppsala, Scandinavian Institute of African Studies, 1976.

Arrighi, G. "Rhodesia: Class and Power", *New Left Review*, No. 39, Sept-Oct. 1966, pp. 35-65.

_____, and Saul, J.S. "Nationalism and Revolution in Sub-Saharan Africa" in *The Socialist Register 1969*, Miliband, R. and Saville, J. (eds.), London, Merlin Press, 1969, pp. 137-188.

Toyo, E. *The Working Class and the Nigerian Crises*, Ibadan, The Sketch Publishing Co., 1967.

TOPIC 12

Classes in Africa, as everywhere else, are (antagonistic) groupings which range along the spectrum from those who have nothing but their labour power, to those who buy and control labour. Hence we have a simple division between the *workers* (including *peasants*) and the *elites*.

Sandbrook, R. and Cohen, R. (eds.) *The Development of an African Working Class Studies in Class Formation and Action*, London, Longman, 1975.

Van Onselen, C. *Chibaro:African Mine Labour in Southern Rhodesia 1900-1933*, London, Pluto Press, 1976.

Grillo, R.D. "Toward An African Proletariat", in *African Railwaymen Solidarity and Opposition in an East African Labour Force*, Cambridge, University Press, 1973, pp. 36-64.

Loudon, J.B. *White Farmers and Black Labour-Tenants: A Study of a Farming Community in the South African Province of Natal*, African Social Research Documents No. 1, African Studies Centre, Cambridge University, 1970.

Gutkind, P.C.W. *The Emergent African Urban Proletariat*, Occasional Paper No. 8, Centre for Developing Area Studies, McGill University, Montreal, 1974.

Sandbrook, R. *Proletarians and African Capitalism: The Kenyan Case 1960-1972*, London, Cambridge University Press, 1975, pp. 123-191.

Miller, R.A. "Elite Formation in Africa: Class, Culture, and Coherence", *Journal of Modern African Studies*, Vol. 12, No. 4, Dec. 1974, pp. 521-542.

Lloyd, P.C. (ed.) *The New Elites of Tropical Africa*, London, O.U.P. 1966.

Ajandele, E.A., *The Educated Elite in the Nigerian Society*, Ibadan, Ibadan University Press, 1974.

Hinchliffe, K. "Labour Aristocracy—A Northern Nigerian Case Study", *Journal of Modern African Studies*, Vol. 12, No. 1, March 1974, pp. 57-67.

Lloyd, P.C. *op. cit.* 1967, pp. 125-153.

Allen, V.L. "The Meaning of the African Working Class", *Journal of Modern African Studies*, Vol. 10, No. 2, July 1972, pp. 169-189.

Waterman, P. "The Labour Aristocracy in Africa: Introduction to a Debate", *Development and Change*, Vol. 6, No. 3, July 1975, pp. 57-73.

Arrighi, G. "International Corporations, Labour Aristocracies, and Economic Development in Tropical Africa", in *Imperialism and Underdevelopment: a reader*, Rhodes, R.I. (ed.), New York, Monthly Review Press, 1970, pp. 220-267.

Peace, A. "Industrial Protest in Nigeria", in *Sociology and Development*, De Kadt, E. and Williams, G. (eds.), London, Tavistock Publications, 1974, pp. 141-167.

Cohen, R. *Labour and Politics in Nigeria*, London, Heinemann, 1974.

Thoden Van Velzen, H.U.E. *Staff, Kulaks and Peasants: A Study of a Political Field*, Medelingen Afrika-Studiencentrum No. 3, Leiden, 1970.

Cohen, R. "From Peasants to Workers in Africa" in *The Contemporary Political Economy of Africa*, Gutkind, P.C.W. and Wallerstein, I. (eds.), Beverly Hills, Sage Publications, 1976, pp. 155-168.

Beer, C.E.F. and Williams, G. "The Politics of the Ibadan Peasantry", *The African Review*, Vol. 5, No. 3, 1975, pp. 235-256.

Davidson, B. "African Peasants and Revolution", *Journal of Peasant Studies*, Vol. 1, No. 3, April 1974, pp. 269-290.

Awiti, A. "Class Struggle in Rural Society of Tanzania", *Maji Maji*, No. 7, Oct. 1972, pp. 1-39.

Lloyd, P.C. "The Rise of new indigenous elites", in *Colonialism in Africa 1870-1960*, Vol. 4, Duignan, P. and Gann, L.H. (eds.), London, Cambridge University Press, 1975, pp. 546-564.

Kilson, M. "The Emergent Elites of Black Africa, 1900 to 1960", in *Colonialism in Africa 1870-1960*, Vol. 2, Gann, L.H. and Duignan, P. (eds.), London, Cambridge University Press, 1970, pp. 351-398.

Odhiambo, A. "The Rise of the Kenya Peasant, 1888-1922", in *Developmental Trends in Kenya*, Allen, C. and King, K. (eds.) Edinburgh Centre of African Studies, 1972, pp. 27-37.

TOPIC 13

Change is often seen best by looking at a structure very central to social life and organization such as *marriage* and *family* patterns.

Colson, E. "Family Change in Contemporary Africa", *Annals of the New York Academy of Sciences*, Vol. 96, No. 2, Jan. 1962, pp. 641-652.

Goody, J. "Marriage Policy and Incorporation in Northern Ghana", in *From Tribe to Nation in Africa*, Cohen, R. and Middleton, J. (eds.) Scranton, Chandler Publishing, 1970, pp. 114-149.

Lloyd, P.C. *op. cit.* 1967, pp. 171-192.

Marris, P. *Family and Social Change in an African City*, London, Routledge and Kegan Paul, 1961.

Smith, M.F. *Baba of Karo: A Woman of the Muslim Hausa*, New York, Praeger, 1964.

Caldwell, J.C. "The Erosion of the Family—a Study of the Fate of the Family in Ghana", *Population Studies*, Vol. 20, 1966, pp. 5-26.

Clignet, R. "Urbanization and Family Structure in the Ivory Coast", *Comparative Studies in Society and History*, Vol. 8, 1966, pp. 385-401.

Harries-Jones, P., "Marital Disputes and the process of Conciliation in a Copperbelt Town", *The Rhodes-Livingstone Journal*, Vol. 35, 1964, pp. 29-72.

Okediji, F.O. and Okediji, O.O. "Marital Stability and Social Structure in an African City" *Nigerian Journal of Economic and Social Studies*, Vol. 8, 1966, pp. 151-163.

Parkin, D. "Types of Urban Marriage in Kampala (Uganda)", *Africa*, Vol. 36, 1966, pp. 269-285.

TOPIC 14

Until recently students of Africa, alongside those with other interests, have ignored the role played by *women* in the historical process.

Bay, E. and Hafkin, N. (eds.), *Women in Africa*. Special issue of *The African Studies Review*, Vol. 18, No. 3, Dec. 1975.

Wipper, A. (ed.), *The Roles of African Women: Past, Present and Future*. Special issue of the *Canadian Journal of African Studies*, Vol. 6, No. 2, 1972.

Bujra, J.M. "Women 'Entrepreneurs' of Early Nairobi", *Canadian Journal of African Studies*, Vol. 9, No. 2, 1975, pp. 213-234.

Kratochvil, L. and Shaw, S. (Comp.) *African Women: A Select Bibliography*, Cambridge (U.K.), African Studies Centre, University of Cambridge, 1974.

African Women Today, Special issue of *Ufahamu*, Vol. 6, No. 1, 1975, pp. 5-64.

Paulme, D. (ed.), *Women of Tropical Africa*, Berkeley, University of California Press, 1963.

TOPIC 15

In very recent times the study of Africa has, at last, turned to the application of a different model from those used in what has come to be known as "Mainstream Social Science". This is the model of *political economy*. It is usually associated with Marxist writers, but actually it predates Marx quite considerably. The following use this approach in dealing with a wide range of topics.

Arrighi, G. and Saul, J.S. *Essays in the Political Economy of Africa*, New York, Monthly Review Press, 1973.

Gutkind, P.C.W. and Wallerstein, I. (eds.), *The Political Economy of Contemporary Africa*, Beverley Hills, Sage Publications, 1976.

Shivji, I. *Class Struggles in Tanzania*, London, Heinemann, 1975.

Widstrand, C. (ed.), *Multi-National Firms in Africa*, Uppsala, Scandinavian Institute of African Studies, 1975.

Harris, R. (ed.) *The Political Economy of Africa*, Cambridge, Mass. Schenkman, 1975.

Lofchie, M. "Political and Economic Origins of African Hunger", *Journal of Modern African Studies*, Vol. 13, No. 4, Dec. 1975, pp. 551-567.

Ball, N. "Understanding the Causes of African Famine", *Journal of Modern African Studies*, Vol. 14, No. 3, Sept. 1976, pp. 516-522.

Hiwet, A. *Ethiopia: From Autocracy to Revolution*, Occasional Paper No. 1, Review of African Political Economy, 1975.

TOPIC 16

Since the end of the Second Imperialist War and into the 1960's the colonial powers have had to come to terms with the fight for independence by the African people. This struggle was generally referred to as the rise of *nationalism* (by "nationalists") rather than as National Liberation. The former label, when applied to the oppressed and exploited, conveyed a "primitive" and chauvinistic quality, while the latter revealed a historical experience.

Hodgkin, T. "Nationalism in Colonial Africa: Theories and Myths" in *Nationalism in Colonial Africa*, New York, New York University Press, 1957, pp. 169-184.

James, C.L.R. "Colonialism and National Liberation in Africa: The Gold Coast Revolution", in *National Liberation: Revolution in the Third World*, Miller, N. and Aya, R. (eds.), New York, The Free Press, 1971, pp. 102-136.

Wallerstein, I. *Africa: The Politics of Unity*, London, Pall Mall, 1968.

Ajayi, J.F.A. "Nineteenth Century Roots of Nigerian Nationalism", *Journal of the Historical Society of Nigeria*, Vol. 2, 1961, pp. 196-210.

Afigbo, A.E. "The Masses and Nationalism: Some Observations on the Nigerian Example", *Ikorok*, Vol. 1, No. 2, 1971, pp. 47-64.

Sklar, R.L. "The Contribution of Tribalism to Nationalism in Western Nigeria", *Journal of Human Relations*, Vol. 8, Nos. 3-4, Spring-Summer 1960, pp. 407-415.

Potekhin, I. "The Formation of Nations in Africa", *Marxism Today*, Vol. 2, No. 10, 1958, pp. 308-314.

Lonsdale, J.M. "Some origins of nationalism in East Africa", *Journal of African History*, Vol. 9, No. 1, 1968, pp. 119-146.

Paden, J.N. "African Concepts of Nationhood" in *The African Experience Vol. 1, Essays*, Paden, J.N. and Soja, E.W. (eds.), Evanston, Northwestern University Press, 1970, pp. 403-433.

Sithole, N. *African Nationalism*, London, O.U.P. 1962.

TOPIC 17

The struggle in Africa for political independence and freedom from oppression and exploitation is far from over. Not only is it a fight against neo-colonialism but also the more basic *armed struggle* against hegemony. These *African liberation movements* are now restricted to Southern Africa—yet they must also be seen historically.

Gibson, R. *African Liberation Movements: Contemporary Struggles Against White Minority Rule*, London, O.U.P. 1972.

Davidson, B. *The Liberation of Guinea*, Harmondsworth, Penguin Books, 1969.

Fanon, F. *Toward the African Revolution (Political Essays)*. New York, Grove Press, 1967.

Nkrumah, K. *Handbook of Revolutionary Warfare*, London, Panaf Press, 1968.

Shamuyarira, N.M., *Crisis in Rhodesia*, London, Deutsch, 1965.

Grundy, K.W. *Guerilla Struggle in Africa: An Analysis and Preview*, New York, Grossman, 1971.

Davidson, B., Slovo J. and Wilkinson, A.R. *Southern Africa: The New Politics of Revolution*, Harmondsworth, Penguin Books, 1976.

Mandela, N. *No Easy Walk to Freedom*, London, Heinemann, 1965 (and 1973).

Shamuyarira, N.M. *Essays on the Liberation of Southern Africa*. Studies in Political Science No. 3, Dept. of Political Science, University of Dar-es-Salaam, Tanzania Publishing House, 1975.

Berman, S. "African Liberation Movements: A Preliminary Bibliography", *Ufahamu*, Vol. 3, No. 1, Spring 1972, pp. 107-128.

Cabral, A. "A Brief Report on the Situation of the Struggle (January-August 1971)", *Ufahamu*, Vol. 2, No. 3, Winter 1972, pp. 5-25.

Mohan, J. "African Liberation Struggle: In Continental and International Perspective", *Economic and Political Weekly* (Bombay), Vol. 11, No. 4, January 24, 1976.

Venter, A.J. *Portugal's War in Guinea-Bissau*, Munger Africana Library Notes No. 19, April 1973.

Cabral, A. *Revolution in Guinea: An African People Struggle*, London, Stage 1, 1969.

Henriksen, T.H. "People's War in Angola, Mozambique, and Guinea-Bissau", *Journal of Modern African Studies*, Vol. 14, No. 3, Sept. 1976, pp. 377-399.

Chaliand, G. *Armed Struggle in Africa: with the guerrillas in 'Portuguese' Guinea*, London, 1969.

Paul, J. *Mozambique: Memoirs of a revolution*, Harmondsworth, Penguin Books, 1975.

TOPIC 18

As everywhere else, political ideologies and structures in Africa are expressed largely through institutionalization, i.e. *political parties* and movements (the former tend to be from the top down and the latter from the grassroots upward). *Political development* and *political thought*.

Hodgkin, T. *African Political Parties*, Harmondsworth, Penguin Books, 1961.

_____, *Nationalism in Colonial Africa*, New York, New York University Press, 1968 (9th Imp.), pp. 139-168.

Suret-Canale, J. "The End of Chieftaincy in Guinea" in *African Politics and Society*, Markovitz, I.L. (ed.), New York, Free Press, 1970, pp. 96-117.

Cartey, W. and Kilson, M. (ed.), *The Africa Reader: Independent Africa* New York, Random House, 1970.

Drake, St. C. and Lacy, L.A. "Government Versus the Unions: The Sekondi-Takoradi Strike, 1961", in *Politics in Africa 7 Cases*, Carter, G.M. (ed.), New York, Harcourt, Brace and World, 1966, pp. 67-118.

Abraham, W.E. *The Mind of Africa*, London, Weidenfeld and Nicolson, 1962.

Hyden, G. *Tanu Yajenga Nchi: Political Development in Rural Tanzania*, Lund Political Studies 8, Lund, 1968.

Chilcote, R.H. "The Political Thought of Amilcar Cabral", *Journal of Modern African Studies*, Vol. 6, No. 3, October 1968, pp. 373-388.

Butler, J. and Castagno, A.A. (eds.), *Boston University Papers on Africa: transition in African Politics*, Boston, 1968.

Mutiso, G.C.M. and Rohio, S.W. (eds.), *Readings in African Political Thought*, London, 1975.

Skurnik, W.A.E. (ed.) *African Political Thought*, Denver, University of Denver, 1968.

Dowse, R.E. "Ghana: one party or totalitarian", *British Journal of Sociology*, Vol. 18, No. 3, Sept. 1967, pp. 251-268.

Mohan, J. "A Whig Interpretation of African Nationalism", *Journal of Modern African Studies*, Vol. 6, No. 3, Oct. 1968, pp. 389-409.

Centre of African Studies, University of Edinburgh, *Political Theory and Ideology in African Society*. Proceedings of a Seminar, February 1970.

Davidson, B. "The Heritage of Politics", in *Can Africa Survive?*, London, Heinemann, 1975, pp. 36-71.

Nyerere, J.K. "Democracy and the Party System" in *Freedom and Unity: A Selection From Writings and Speeches*, London, O.U.P., 1967, pp. 195-203.

Saul, J.S. "Africa", in *Populism its Meaning and National Characteristics*, Ionescu, G. and Gellner, E. (eds.), London, Weidenfeld and Nicolson, 1970, pp. 122-150.

Coleman, J.S. and Rosberg, C.G. (eds.), *Political Parties and National Integration in Tropical Africa*, Berkeley, University of California Press, 1964.

Le Vine, V. *Political Leadership in Africa*. Hoover Institution Studies 18, Stanford, The Hoover Institution, Stanford University, 1967.

Nyerere, J.K. "One Party System", *Spearhead*, Vol. 2, No. 1, January 1963, pp. 1 and pp. 12-23.

Legum, C. "What Kind of Radicalism for Africa", *Foreign Affairs*, Vol. 43, Jan. 1965, pp. 237-250.

Fallers, L. "Equality, modernity and democracy in the new states", in *Old Societies and New States*, Geertz, C. (ed.) New York, The Free Press, 1963, pp. 158-219.

TOPIC 19

There are two kinds of "incorporation" taking place in Africa—as elsewhere in much of the world. It is a complex process which involves *micro* and *macro* analysis. There is the incorporation of a small unit, a cultural and language group, into a larger *regional* setting and, secondly, the incorporation of such units, into a *nation*. This whole process is sometimes referred to as *nation-building*—a rather "unique" North American conceptualization.

Cohen, R. and Middleton, J. (eds.), *From Tribe to Nation in Africa*, Scranton, Chandler Publishing, 1970.

Lofchie, M.F. (ed.), *The State of the Nations: Constraints on Development in Independent Africa*, Berkeley, University of California Press, 1971.

Tessler, M.A., O'Barr, W.M. and Spain, D.H., *Tradition and Identity in Changing Africa*, New York, Harper and Row, 1973.

Mazrui, A.A. *Towards a Pax Africana: A Study of Ideology and Ambition*, Chicago, University of Chicago Press, 1967.

Gellar, S. *State-Building and Nation-Building in West Africa.* Occasional Papers No. 2, International Development Research Center, Bloomington, Indiana University, Dec. 1972.

Post, K.W.J. *The New States of West Africa*, Baltimore, Penguin Books, 1968 (Revised Ed.).

Jordan, R.S. and Renniger, J.P., "The New Environment of Nation-Building", *Journal of Modern African Studies*, Vol. 13, No. 2, June 1975, pp. 187-207.

Ajayi, J.F.A. "The Place of African History and Culture in the Process of Nation-Building in Africa South of the Sahara", *Journal of Negro Education*, Vol. 30, No. 3, 1960, pp. 206-213.

Davidson, B. "A Continental Crisis" in *Can Africa Survive?*, London, Heinemann, 1975, pp. 3-35.

Zolberg, A. "Patterns of Nation-Building" in *The African Experience Vol. 1, Essays*, Paden, J.N. and Soja, E.W. (eds.), Evanston, Northwestern University Press, 1970, pp. 434-451.

TOPIC 20

How can the contradictions and so-called tensions be overcome? How can the independence revolution be converted to an on-going transformation which places the power of the state where it belongs—into the hands of the people. Hence the issue is *socialism, regionalism and pan-Africanism*.

Onuoha, B. *The Elements of African Socialism*, London, Deutsch, 1965.

Senghor, L.S., *On African Socialism*, London, Pall Mall Press, 1964.

Republic of Kenya, *African Socialism and its Application to Planning in Kenya*, Nairobi, Government Printer, 1965. (see item 9).

Arrighi, G. and Saul, J.S. "Socialism and Economic Development in Tropical Africa", *Journal of Modern African Studies*, Vol. 6, No. 2, June 1968, pp. 141-169.

Mohiddin, A. "Reflections on Socialist Tanzania", *East Africa Journal*, Vol. 9, No. 11, Nov. 1972, pp. 26-37.

Friedland, W.H. and Rosberg, C. (eds.), *African Socialism*, Stanford, Stanford University Press, 1964.

Langley, J.A. *Pan-Africanism and Nationalism in West Africa, 1900-1945: a study in ideology and social class*, London, Oxford U.P. 1973.

Legum, C. *Pan-Africanism: a short political guide*, New York, Praeger, 1965.

Dubula, S. "A Socialist Label for Bourgeois Thinking—A Critical Examination of the Kenya Sessional Paper on 'African Socialism'", *The African Communist*, No. 22, 3rd Quarter, 1965, pp. 24-40.

Grundy, K.W. "African Explanations of Underdevelopment", *Review of Politics*, Vol. 28, Jan. 1966, pp. 62-75.

Hazard, J.N. "Marxian Socialism in Africa", *Comparative Politics*, Vol. 2, No. 1, Oct. 1969, pp. 1-15.

Murray, R. "The Ghanian Road", *New Left Review*, No. 32, July-August 1965, pp. 63-71.

Rodney, W. "Tanzanian Socialism and Scientific Socialism", *The African Review*, Vol. 1, No. 4, 1972, pp. 61-76.

Padmore, G. *Pan-Africanism or Communism*, New York, Roy Publishers, 1956.

Desfosses, H. and Levesque, J. (eds.) *Socialism in the Third World*, New York, Praeger, 1975, pp. 163-251.

TOPIC 21

The place of the non-African *minorities* in Africa continues to be a problematical issue. On a non-racial basis there would appear to be a future for them; as racialists not, while African racialism—if such it is—also stands condemned.

West, R. *The White Tribes of Africa*, London, Macmillan, 1965.

Twaddle, M. (ed.), *Expulsion of a Minority: Essays on Ugandan Asians.* Commonwealth Papers 18, Institute of Commonwealth Studies, University of London, London, Athlone Press, 1975.

Mangat, J.S. *The History of the Asians in East Africa, 1886-1945.* London, O.U.P. 1969.

Gann, L.H., *A History of Southern Rhodesia*, London, 1965.

Morris, H.S. *The Indians in Uganda*, Chicago, University of Chicago Press, 1968.

Cruise O'Brien, R. "Lebanese Entrepreneurs in Senegal: economic integration and the politics of protection", *Cahiers d'etudes africaines*, vol. 15, No. 1, 1975.

Dotson, F. and L.O. "The Economic Role of Non-Indigenous Minorities in Colonial Africa", in *Colonialism in Africa 1870-1960*, Vol. 4. Duignan, P. and Gann, L.H. (eds.), London, Cambridge University Press, 1975, pp. 565-631.

Crowder, M. "The White Chiefs of Tropical Africa"[on colonial administrators], in *Colonialism in Africa 1870-1960, Vol. 2*, Gann, L.N. and Duignan, P. (eds.), London, Cambridge University Press, 1970, pp. 320-350.

Gann, L.H. and Duignan, P. *White Settlers in Tropical Africa*, Harmondsworth, Penguin Books, 1962.

Ghai, D.P. (ed.) *Portrait of a Minority*, London, Oxford University Press, 1965.

Levine, R.A. "Anti-European Violence in Africa: A Comparative Analysis", *Journal of Conflict Resolution*, Vol. 3, 1959, pp. 420-429.

Jahoda, G. *White Man: A Study of the Attitudes of Africans to Europeans in Ghana Before Independence*, London, O.U.P. 1961.

O'Brien, R. *White Society in Black Africa: The French in Senegal*, London, Faber and Faber, 1972.

Rogers, C.A. and Frantz, C. *Racial Themes in Southern Rhodesia—The Attitudes of the White Population*, New Haven, Yale University Press, 1962 (of historical interest only).

Gussman, B. *Out in the Midday Sun*, London, 1963 (For amusement only!).

Rothchild, D. "African Nationalism and Racial Minorities", *East Africa Journal*, Vol. 2, No. 8, Dec. 1965, pp. 14-22.

Trillin, C. "Letter From Salisbury", *New Yorker Magazine*, 12 Nov. 1966, pp. 139-193.

Orlik, P.B. "Divided Against Itself: South Africa's White Polity", *Journal of Modern African Studies*, vol. 8, No. 2, July 1970, pp. 199-212.

TOPIC 22

Despite rapid changes, or because of them, sometimes for reasons both natural and sensible (but at times an impediment to further transformation and action), there is opposition to departing from "Traditionality". While *belief systems* change, like anything else, to predict their direction is, perhaps, more difficult than to project economic and political change. Millenarian and syncretistic movements flourish in Africa.

Lanternari, V., *The Religions of the Oppressed*, New York, New American Library, 1965.

Lloyd, P.C. *Op. cit.* 1967, pp. 244-263.

Messenger, J.C., "Reinterpretations of Christian and Indigenous Belief in a Nigerian Nativstic Church", *American Anthropologist*, vol. 62, No. 2, April 1960, pp. 268-78.

Banton, M. "African Prophets", *Race*, vol. 5, No. 2, 1963, pp. 42-55.

Kobben, A.J.F. "Prophetic movements as an expression of social protest", *International Archives of Ethnography*, Vol. 49, 1960, pp. 117-164.

"Religion in Africa", Special issue of *Ufahamu*, Vol. 6, No. 3, 1976.

Marwick, M. "The Continuance of Witchcraft Beliefs" in *Africa in Transition*, Smith, P. (ed.), London, Reinhardt, 1958, pp. 106-114.

Brain, J.L. "Witchcraft in Africa: A Hardy Perennial", in *Colonialism and Change: Essays Presented to Lucy Mair*, Owusu, M. (ed.), The Hague, Mouton, 1975, pp. 179-201.

Balandier, G. "Messianism and Nationalism in Black Africa", in *Africa, Social Problems of Change and Conflict*, Van Den Berghe, P. (ed.), San Francisco, Chandler, 1965, pp. 443-460.

Rotberg, R.I. "The Lumpa Church of Alice Lenshina", in *Protest and Power in Black Africa*, Rotberg, R.I. and Mazrui, A.A. (eds.), New York, O.U.P., 1970, pp. 513-568.

Scotch, N.A. "Magic, Sorcery and Football among the Urban Zulu: a case of reinterpretation under acculturation" *Journal of Conflict Resolution*, Vol. 5, 1964, pp. 70-74.

Hodgkin, T. "Prophets and Priests" in *Nationalism in Colonial Africa*, New York, New York University Press, 1957, pp. 93-114.

Adjei, A. "Imperialism and Spiritual Freedom: An African View", *American Journal of Sociology*, Vol. 50, No. 3, Nov. 1944, pp. 189-198.

Fernandez, J.W. "African Religious Movements—Types and Dynamics," *Journal of Modern African Studies*, Vol. 2, No. 4, Dec. 1964, pp. 531-549.

Welbourn, F.B. *East African Rebels: A Study of some Independent Churches*, London, S.C.M. Press, 1961.

TOPIC 23

All change, be it slow or rapid, desired or resisted, radical or reformist, is likely to produce a reaction—therein lies the dynamic of transformation, of revolution or stagnation. These reactions are sometimes referred to as "rising expectations" or *tensions of development*. The latter in particular is an inept label to describe historical processes, of thesis—antithesis—synthesis....contradiction and resolution....

Beattie, J. "Democratization in Bunyoro: The Impact of Democratic Institutions and values on a Traditional African Kingdom", *Civilizations*, Vol. 11, No. 1, 1961, pp. 8-20.

Melson, R. "Nigerian Politics and the General Strike of 1964" in *Protest and Power in Black Africa*, Rotberg, R.I. and Mazrui, A.A. (eds.), New York, O.U.P. 1970, pp. 771-787.

Murray, R., "Militarism in Africa", *The New Left Review*, No. 38, July-August, 1966, pp. 35-59.

A.R.F. "Pan-Africanism in the Era of Neo-Colonialism", *African Red Family*, Vol. 2, Nos. 1-2, 1974, pp. 2-48.

Wallerstein, I. "The Colonial Era in Africa: Changes in the Social Structure", in *Colonialism in Africa 1870-1960*, Vol. 2, *op. cit.*, pp. 399-421.

Rotberg, R.I. and Mazrui, A.A. (eds.), *Protest and Power in Black Africa*, New York, O.U.P. 1970.

AKE, C. "Explaining Political Instability in New States", *Journal of Modern African Studies*, Vol. 11, No. 3, Sept. 1973, pp. 347-359.

First, R. *The Barrel of a gun: political power in Africa and the coup d'etat*, Harmondsworth, Penguin Books, 1970.

Decalo, S. "Military Coups and Military Regimes in Africa", *Journal of Modern African Studies*, Vol. 11, No. 1, March 1973, pp. 105-127.

Levine, V. *Political Corruption in Ghana*, Stanford, Hoover Institution, 1974.

Lloyd, P.C. *Classes, Crises and Coups: Themes in the Sociology of Developing Countries*, London, Paladin, 1973.

Gutkind, P.C.W. "The Energy of Despair: Social Organization of the Unemployed in Two African Urban Areas: Lagos and Nairobi. A Preliminary Account", *Civilizations*, Vol. 17, No. 3, 1967, pp. 184-214 and Vol. 17, No. 4, 1967, pp. 380-405.

_____, "From the Energy of Despair to the Anger of Despair: The Transition from Social Circulation to Political Consciousness Among the Urban Poor in Africa", *Canadian Journal of African Studies*, Vol. 7, No. 2, 1973, pp. 179-198.

Cruise O'Brien, D.B. "Modernization, Order and the Erosion of a Democratic Ideal", *Journal of Development Studies*, Vol. 8, No. 4, July 1972, pp. 352-378.

Ankomah, K., "The Colonial Legacy and African Unrest", *Science and Society*, Vol. 34, No. 2, Summer 1970, pp. 129-145.

Smith, M.G., "Historical and Cultural Conditions of Political Corruption among the Hausa", *Comparative Studies in Society and History*, Vol. 6, No. 2, Jan. 1964, pp. 164-194.

Nyerere, J.K., *Man and Development: Binadamu Na Maendeleo*, London, O.U.P. 1974.

Nduka, O., "The Anatomy of 'Rationalisation'", *Nigerian Opinion*, Vol. 7, No. 1, January 1971, pp. 7-12.

Diamond, S. "Modern Africa: The Pains of Birth", *Dissent*, Vol. 10, 1963, pp. 169-179.

Leys, C., "What is the problem about corruption", *Journal of Modern Africa Studies*, Vol. 3, No. 2, August 1965, pp. 215-230.

Armah, A.K., *The Beautiful Ones Are Not Yet Born*, London, Heinemann, 1969.

Achebe, C., *Man of the People*, London, Heinemann, 1966.

_____, *Things Fall Apart*, London, Heinemann, 1959.

Peil, M. "The Common Man's Reaction to Nigerian Urban Government", *African Affairs*, No. 296, Vol. 74, July 1975, pp. 300-313.

TOPIC 24

Destablization is not only externally produced. It is also the consequence of *civil* and *internal war*.

Kariuki, J.M. *'Mau Mau' Detainee*, Harmondsworth, Penguin Books, 1964.

Rumah, K. *Handbook of Revolutionary Warfare*, New York, International Publishers, 1969.

Badal, R.K. "The Rise and Fall of Separatism in Southern Sudan", *African Affairs*, Vol. 75, No. 301, Oct. 1976, pp. 463-474.

Wallerstein, I. *Africa: The Politics of Unity*, New York, Random House, 1967, pp. 43-65, 83-108.

Fanon, F. *A Dying Colonialism*, New York, Grove Press, 1967.

Ojukwu, C.O. *Biafra: Selected Speeches by C. Odumegwu Ojukwu General of the People's Army*, New York, Harper Row, 1969.

_____, *Biafra: Random Thoughts of C. Odumegwu Ojukwu General of the People's Army Vol. 2*, New York, Harper Row, 1969.

Nwanko, A.A. and Ifejika, S.U. *The Making of a Nation: Biafra*, London, C. Hurst, 1969.

Widstrand, C.G. (ed.), *African Boundary Problems*, Uppsala, Scandinavian Institute of African Studies, 1969.

Grundy, K.W. *Guerrilla Struggle in Africa: An Analysis and Preview*, New York, Grossman, 1971.

Roden, D. "Regional Inequality and Rebellion in the Sudan", *Geographical Review*, Vol. 64, No. 4, Oct. 1974, pp. 498-516.

Chaliand, G. *Armed Struggle in Africa*, New York, Monthly Review Press, 1969.

Barnett, D.L. and Karari, N. *Mau Mau from Within*, New York, Monthly Review Press, 1966.

Lemarchand, R. and Martin, D. *Selective Genocide in Burundi*, Minority Rights Group Report No. 20, 1974.

TOPIC 25

Neo-colonialism and dependency are not the only enemies of the African people (whose own agents are not infrequently in league with these enemies). *External agents*, political and academic, contribute to the *"destabilisation."* Extreme right-wing interpretations should also be taken into account; some of these have been exposed.

Lemarchand, R. "The C.I.A. in Africa: How Central? How Intelligent?", *Journal of Modern African Studies*, Vol. 14, No. 3, September 1976, pp. 401-426.

Bauer, P.T. "Western Guilt and Third World Poverty", *Commentary* (New York) Vol. 61, January 1976, pp. 31-38.

Gann, L.H., "Neo-Colonialism, Imperialism and the 'New Class'", *The Intercollegiate Review*, Winter 1973-74, pp. 13-27.

Echenberg, M. "Paying the Blood Tax: Military Conscription in French West Africa", *Canadian Journal of African Studies*, Vol. 9, No. 2, 1975, pp. 171-192.

Karioki, J.N. "African Thinkers versus Ali Mazrui", *Transition*, Vol. 9, No. 45, 1974, pp. 55-63. (See reply: Mazrui, A.A., "Africa, My Conscience and I", *Transition*, Vol. 9, No. 46, 1974, pp. 67-71).

El-Khawas, M.A. and Cohen, B. (eds.), *The Kissinger Study of Southern Africa (Secret), National Security Study Memorandum 39*, Westport, Lawrence Hill, 1976.

REVOLUTION

Comparative Sociology of Revolution

Hal Benenson
Sociology
Ramapo College of New Jersey
Fall 1979
Undergraduate

I. THEORY AND METHODOLOGY

A. THEORIES OF REVOLUTION

Karl Griewank, "Emergence of the Concept of Revolution" (mimeographed), from Heinz Lubasz, ed., *Revolutions in Modern European History*, Macmillan. N.Y. 1966, pp. 55-62.

Walter Laqueur, "Revolution" (reprint), from *International Encyclopedia of the Social Sciences*, ed. D. Sills. Macmillan, N.Y. 1968.

Karl Marx, "Preface" to *A Contribution to the Critique of Political Economy*, Charles H. Kerr, Chicago. 1904. (mimeographed)

Karl Marx & Friedrich Engels, *The Communist Manifesto*, International Publishers, N.Y. 1948. pb.

Suggested Reading:

Crane Brinton, *Anatomy of Revolution*, Vintage, N.Y. 1965. (revised ed.) pb esp. Chapter 9, pp. 237-264. (Library reserve)

B. COMPARATIVE APPROACHES

Eric Wolf, *Peasant Wars of the 20th Century*, Harper & Row, N.Y. 1969. pb Preface, pp. ix-xv; and Conclusion, pp. 276-302.

Barrington Moore, Jr., *The Social Origins of Dictatorship and Democracy: Lord and Peasant in the Making of the Modern World*, Harper & Row, N.Y. 1966. pb Preface, pp. xi-xviii.

Sheila Rowbotham, *Women, Resistance and Revolution*, Vintage, New York, 1974. pb Introduction (pp. 11-13), Ch. 4 (p. 98 only) and Ch. 8 (pp. 244-247 only).

Suggested Reading:

B. Moore, Chapters 7, 1 and 3.

Hamza Alavi, "Peasants and Revolution" (New England Free Press pamphlet, Library Reserve), from R. Miliband & J. Saville, eds., *The Socialist Register—1965*. Merlin Press, London. 1965.

Nicos Poulantzas, "The Models of Bourgeois Revolution," in *Political Power and Social Classes*. New Left Books, London. 1973. pp. 168-184. (Library reserve).

Juliet Mitchell, "Women and Equality," in J. Mitchell & A. Oakley, eds., *The Rights and Wrongs of Women*. Penguin, N.Y. 1976. pp. 379-399. (Library reserve).

Marilyn Boxer and Jean Quataert, "The Class and Sex Connection," in Boxer and Quataert, eds., *Socialist Women*, Elsevier, New York. 1978. pp. 1-18. (Library reserve).

Ros Petchesky, "Dissolving the Hyphen" in Z. Eisenstein, *Capitalist Patriachy*, Monthly Review. N.Y. 1978. pp. 373-389. (Library reserve).

II. THE FRENCH REVOLUTION

A. GENERAL ANALYSES

Georges Lefebvre, *The Coming of the French Revolution*, Princeton University Press, Princeton, N.J. 1947. pb entire.

Albert Soboul, "VI. The French Revolution and Napoleon, 1789-1815, in 'France, History of—' " in *Encyclopaedia Brittanica. Macropaedia*. 1974. 15th edition. (mimeographed).

B. Moore, Chapter 2.

Alfred Cobban, "The Myth of the French Revolution," (mimeographed) from *Aspects of the French Revolution*. Braziller, N.Y. 1968.

B. THE POPULAR MOVEMENT

George Rude, "Paris on the Eve of the French Revolution," (mimeographed) from *The Crowd in the French Revolution*. Oxford University Press, N.Y. 1959. pb.

Albert Soboul, "The Popular Movement and Bourgeois Revolution," (mimeographed) from *The Parisian Sans-Culottes and the French Revolution, 1793-1794*. Doubleday, Garden City, N.Y. 1964. pb.

C. THE ROLE OF WOMEN

Elizabeth Racz, "Women's Rights in the French Revolution," (mimeographed) from *Science & Society*. Spring 1952, Vol. XVI: No. 2.

Olwen Hufton, "Women in Revolution, 1789-1794," (mimeographed) from *Past & Present.* No. 53, November 1971.

S. Rowbotham, Chapter 2 (pp. 50-56 only) & Chapter 5 (pp. 103-107, 116-122).

Suggested Background Readings:

For general histories of the Revolution, see: F. Furet & D. Richet (Macmillan, 1970); G. Lefebvre (Columbia Univ. Press, 2 vol., 1962-64); A. Mathiez (Grosset & Dunlap, 1964); A. Soboul (Vintage, 1974).

A. DeTocqueville, *The Old Regime & the French Revolution.* Doubleday, Garden City, N.Y. 1955.

R. Greenlaw, ed., *The Economic Origins of the French Revolution (1967) & The Social Origins.. Role of the Middle Classes* (1975). D.C. Heath, Lexington, Mass.

D. Johnson, ed., *French Society & the Revolution.* Cambridge Univ. Press, Cambridge. 1976. (essays from *Past & Present).*

F. Kafker & J. Laux, eds., *The French Revolution: Conflicting Interpretations.* Random House, N.Y. 1968.

J. Kaplow, ed., *New Perspectives on the French Revolution.* John Wiley, New York. 1965.

F.L. Ford, *Robe & Sword.* Harper & Row, New York. 1965.

O. Hufton, *The Poor in 18th C. France.* Oxford Univ. Press. N.Y. 1976.

R. Cobb, *The Police & the People.* Oxford Univ. Press, N.Y. 1970.

G. Lefebvre, *The Great Fear.* Vintage, N.Y. 1973.

C.L.R. James, *The Black Jacobins.* Vintage, N.Y. 1963.

R.B. Rose, *The Enrages.* Melbourne Univ. Press, 1963, see esp. Ch. 5-6 on women's movements, see articles by: S. Lytle, *Jl. of Mod. History,* (XXVII: 1, 14-26); J. Ahray, *Amer. Hist. Review* (Feb. 1975); and M. George, *Science & Society* (XL: 4, 410-437).

C. Tilly, *The Vendee.* Harvard Univ. Press, Cambridge. 1976.

III. THE RUSSIAN REVOLUTION

A. SOCIAL BASES OF REVOLUTION

E. Wolf, Chapter 2

V.I. Lenin, "Lecture on the 1905 Revolution," *Collected Works,* Progress Publishers, Moscow. 1956 edition. v. 23 (Library reserve).

Suggested Reading:

William Chamberlin, 'Social Forces in Russian History" in *The Russian Revolution.* Grosset & Dunlap, N.Y. 1965. (Library reserve).

Leon Trotsky, "The Proletariat and the Peasantry" in *History of the Russian Revolution.* Gollancz, London. 1965. (Library reserve).

B. THE OCTOBER REVOLUTION

Arthur Rosenberg, "March to October 1917" in *A History of Bolshevism.* Doubleday, Garden City, N.Y. 1967. pp. 91-116. (Library reserve).

V.I. Lenin, "Letters from Afar—1st letter" and "April Theses (The Tasks of the Proletariat in the Present Revolution)" (excerpt), *Selected Works in 3 Volumes.* v. 2. Progress Publishers, Moscow. 1975. pp. 19-28, 29-31. (Library reserve).

Isaac Deutscher, *The Unfinished Revolution. Russia, 1917-1967.* Oxford University Press, N.Y. 1967. Chapters 1-2.

C. THE TRANSFORMATION OF SOVIET SOCIETY: CLASSES, FAMILY AND WOMEN'S POSITION

Deutscher, Chapters 3-6.

S. Rowbotham, Chapter 6 (pp. 134-169)

B.G. Rosenthal, "Love on the Tractor: Women in the Russian Revolution and After," in Bridenthal & Koontz, eds., *Becoming Visible.* (Library reserve).

R. Zelnick, *Labor and Society in Tsarist Russia.* Stanford University Press, Stanford, California. 1971.

Jerome Blum, *Lord and Peasant in Russia from the 9th to the 19th Century.* Princeton University Press, Princeton, N.J. 1961. pb.

G.T. Robinson, *Rural Russia under the Old Regime.* University of California Press, Berkeley and Los Angeles. 1969. pb.

M. Raeff, *Origins of the Russian Intelligentsia: The 18th Century Nobility.* Harcourt. Brace. N.Y. 1966. pb.

F. Venturi, *Roots of Revolution.* Grosset & Dunlap, N.Y. 1966. pb.

N.G. Chernyshevsky, *What is to Be Done?* Vintage N.Y. 1961. pb.

B. Engel & C. Rosenthal, eds., *5 Sisters. Women Against the Tsar.* Knopf, N.Y., 1975.

J.L.H. Keep, *The Rise of Social Democracy in Russia.* Oxford University Press, N.Y. 1963.

R. Pipes, *Social Democracy and the St. Petersburg Labor Movement, 1885-1897.* Harvard University Press, Cambridge, Mass. 1963.

O. Anweiler, *The Soviets, 1905-1921.* Pantheon, N.Y. 1974.

M. Ferro, *The Russian Revolution of February 1917.* Prentice-Hall, Englewood Cliffs, N.J. 1972.

R. Stites, *The Women's Liberation Movement in Russia.* Princeton Univ. Press. Princeton, N.J. 1977.

B.E. Clements, *Aleksandra Kollantai.* Indiana UP, Bloomington, Ind. 1979.

A. Bobroff, "Bolsheviks and the Working Women, 1905-1920," *Soviet Studies,* (October, 1974), pp. 540-567.

A. Kollontai, *Selected Works.* Lawrence Hill, Westport, Conn. 1978.

IV. THE CHINESE REVOLUTION

A. GENERAL ANALYSES

E. Wolf, Chapter 3.

B. Moore, Chapters 4, 9 and Epilogue (pp. 496-508).

Mao Tse-Tung, "Analysis of the Classes in Chinese Society" (pamphlet) and "Report on An Investigation of the Peasant Movement in Hunan" (pamphlet), *Selected Works*. v. 1. Foreign Languages Press, Peking. 1965.

B. WOMEN, THE TRADITIONAL FAMILY SYSTEM AND REVOLUTION

Jack Belden, "Goldflower's Story" (NEFP pamphlet), from *China Shakes the World*. Monthly Review Press, N.Y. 1970 pb.

Judith Stacey, "When Patriarchy Kowtows: The Significance of the Chinese Family Revolution for Feminist Theory," *Feminist Studies*, Vol. 2, No. 2/3. 1975. pp. 64-112. (Library reserve) or in Z. Eisenstein, ed., *Capitalist Patriarchy*, Monthly Review, N.Y. 1978 (Lib. res.).

Rowbotham, Chapter 7 (pp. 170-199).

E. Balazs, *Chinese Civilization and Bureaucracy*. Yale, New Haven. 1972.

R.H. Tawney, *Land and Labour in China*. Beacon Press, Boston. 1964.

K. Wittfogel, *Oriental Despotism*. Yale, New Haven. 1957. pb.

Chung-Li Chang, *The Chinese Gentry*. Univ. of Washington, Seattle. 1974.

Ping-ti Ho, *The Ladder of Success in Imperial China*. Columbia University Press, N.Y. 1962.

A. Feuerwerker, *China's Early Industrialization*. Harvard, Cambridge, 1958.

J. Chesneaux, *Peasant Revolts in China*. W.W. Norton, N.Y. 1973. pb.

F. Michael, *The Taiping Rebellion*. v. 1. Univ. of Washington, Seattle. 196

V.Y.C. Shih, *The Taiping Ideology*. Univ. of Washington, Seattle. 1967.

Siang-tseh Chiang, *The Nien Rebellion*. Univ. of Wash., Seattle. 1954.

M.C. Wright, *The Last Stand of Chinese Conservatism*. Stanford University Press, Stanford, California. 1957. pb.

M.C. Wright, ed., *China in Revolution, 1900-1913*. Yale, New Haven. 1971.

H. Schiffrin, *Sun Yat-sen and the Origins of the Chinese Revolution*. University of California Press, Berkeley. 1968. pb.

W. Franke, *A Century of Chinese Revolution, 1851-1949*. Harper & Row, N.Y. 1970. pb.

L. Bianco, *Origins of the Chinese Revolution*. Stanford, 1971. pb.

C. Johnson, *Peasant Nationalism & Communist Power*. Stanford, 1962. pb.

J. Chesneaux, *The Chinese Labor Movement*. Stanford, 1968.

H. Isaacs, *The Tragedy of the Chinese Revolution*. Atheneum, N.Y. 1961.

Chow Tse-tung, *The May 4th Movement*. Harvard, Cambridge. 1960.

J. Israel, *Student Nationalism in China*. Stanford, 1966.

R. Hofheinz, *Peasant Movement and Rural Revolution*. PhD., Harvard. 1966.

M. Selden, *The Yenan Way in Revolutionary China*. Harvard, Camb. 1971.

O. Lang, *Chinese Family & Society*. Archon, N.Y. 1968.

W. Hinton, *Fanshen*. Vintage, N.Y. 1966. pb.

D. Davin, *Woman-Work*. Oxford Univ. Press, London. 1976.

E. Croll, *Women's Movement in China, 1949-73*. SACU, London. 1974. pb.

C.K. Yang, *Chinese Communist Society: Family & Village*. MIT, Camb. 1965.

M. Levy, *Family Revolution in Modern China*. Atheneum, N.Y. 1968. pb.

R. Sidel, *Families of Fengsheng*. Penguin, Baltimore. 1974. pb.

Background readings on France, Russia, China and the Comparative Analysis of Revolutionary Change:

I. THE FRENCH REVOLUTION

1. GENERAL HISTORIES

Norman Hampson, *A Social History of the French Revolution*. University of Toronto Press, Toronto. 1963. pb

Georges Lefebvre, *The French Revolution, from its origins to 1793*. Columbia Univ. Press, N.Y. 1962. pb.

Georges Lefebvre, *The French Revolution, from 1793 to 1799*. Columbia Univ. Press, N.Y. 1964. pb.

Albert Mathiez, *The French Revolution*. Grosset & Dunlap. N.Y. 1964. pb.

Albert Soboul, *The French Revolution, 1787-1799*. Random House, N.Y. 1975 pb.

2. SOCIAL ASPECTS

Richard Cobb, *The Police and the People. French Popular Protest 1789-1820*. Oxford Univ. Press, N.Y. 1970. pb Parts II & III.

Alexis de Tocqueville, *The Old Regime and the French Revolution*. Doubleday, Garden City, N.Y. 1955. pb.

C.L.R. James, *The Black Jacobins. Toussaint L'Ouverture and the San Domingo Revolution*. Random House, N.Y. 1963. (revised edition) pb.

Georges Lefebvre, *The Great Fear of 1789. Rural Panic in Revolutionary France*. Random House, N.Y. 1973. pb.

George Rude, *The Crowd in the French Revolution*. Oxford Univ. Press, N.Y. 1959. pb.

Albert Soboul, *The Sans-Culottes. The Popular Movement and Revolutionary Government, 1793-1794*. Doubleday, Garden City, N.Y. 1972. pb.

3. IN LITERATURE

Georg Buechner, *Danton's Death*. Chandler publishers, N.Y. 1961. pb.

II. THE RUSSIAN REVOLUTION

1. THE OLD REGIME AND 19th CENTURY POPULISM

Geroid T. Robinson, *Rural Russia under the Old Regime. A History of the Landlord-Peasant World and a Prologue to the Peasant Revolution of 1917.* University of California Press, Berkeley. 1969. pb.

Franco Venturi, *Roots of Revolution. A History of Populist and Socialist Movements in 19th Century Russia.* Grosset & Dunlap. N.Y. 1966. pb.

Reginald Zelnick, *Labor and Society in Tsarist Russia, 1855-1870.* Stanford Univ. Press, Stanford. 1971. h.

2. FICTIONAL AND BIOGRAPHICAL ACCOUNTS

N.G. Chernyshevsky, *What is to be done?* Random House, N.Y. 1961. pb.

Barbara Engel & Clifford Rosenthal, eds. *Five Sisters—Women Against the Tsar.* Alfred A. Knopf, N.Y. 1975 h.

Vera Figner, *Memoirs of a Revolutionist.* Greenwood Press, Westport, Conn. 1968 (Reprint of 1927 ed.) h.

3. THE REVOLUTIONS OF 1905 and 1917

Oskar Anweiler, *The Soviets—The Russian Workers', Peasants', and Soldiers' Councils, 1905-1917.* Pantheon, N.Y. 1975. h.

E.H. Carr, *The Bolshevik Revolution, 1917-1923.* Vol. 1. Penguin, Baltimore. 1966. pb.

Marc Ferro, *The Russian Revolution of February 1917.* Prentice-Hall, Englewood Cliffs, N.J. 1972. h.

History of the Communist Party of the Soviet Union (Bolsheviks). Short Course. 1939 edition. Proletarian publishers, Chicago. 1975. pb.

John Reed, *10 Days that Shook the World.* Random House, N.Y. 1961. pb.

Arthur Rosenberg, *A History of Bolshevism.* Doubleday, Garden City, N.Y. 1967. pb.

S.M. Schwarz, *The Russian Revolution of 1905. The Workers' Movement and the Formation of Bolshevism.* University of Chicago Press, Chicago. 1967. h.

Leon Trotsky, *The Russian Revolution.* (abridged edition) Doubleday, Garden City, N.Y. pb.

4. BIOGRAPHIES

Isaac Deutscher, *Trotsky: The Prophet Armed, 1879-1921.* Random House, N.Y. 1965. pb.

Louis Fischer, *The Life of Lenin.* Harper & Row. N.Y. 1964. pb.

N.K. Krupskaya, *Reminiscences of Lenin.* International publishers, N.Y. 1970. pb.

5. IN LITERATURE

F.V. Gladkov, *Cement.* Ungar, N.Y. 1969. pb.

Maxim Gorky, *Mother.* Macmillan, N.Y. 1962. pb.

Anton Makarenko, *The Road to Life.* Oriole Editions, N.Y. 1973 (Reprint of 1951 ed) h.

Vladmir Mayakovsky, *The Bedbug & Selected Poetry.* Meriden, N.Y. 1960 pb.

Vladmir Mayakovsky, *Complete Plays.* Simon & Shuster. N.Y. 1971. pb.

Mikhail Sholokhov, *And Quiet Flows the Don.* Random House, N.Y. 1934. ph.

III. THE CHINESE REVOLUTION

1. BACKGROUND TO REVOLUTION

Jean Chesneaux, *Peasant Revolts in China, 1840-1949.* Norton, N.Y. 1973. pb.

Jean Chesneaux, *The Chinese Labor Movement, 1919-1927.* Stanford Univ. Press, Stanford. 1968. h.

Franz Michael, *The Taiping Rebellion.* vol. 1. University of Washington Press, Seattle. 1966. pb.

R.H. Tawney, *Land and Labour in China.* Octagon, N.Y. 1964. h.

Mary C. Wright, *China in Revolution. The First Phase, 1900-1913.* Yale University Press, New Haven. 1968. pb.

2. THE DEVELOPMENT OF THE COMMUNIST REVOLUTION (1921-1949)

William Hinton, *Fanshen.* Random House, N.Y. 1968. pb.

Harold Isaacs, *The Tragedy of the Chinese Revolution.* (2nd edition) Stanford University Press, Stanford. 1961. pb.

Marc Selden, *The Yenan Way in Revolutionary China.* Harvard Univ. Press, Cambridge. 1971. pb.

3. THE COMMUNIST REVOLUTION—FIRST-HAND ACCOUNTS AND DOCUMENTS

Jack Belden, *China Shakes the World.* Monthly Review, N.Y. 1970. pb.

Elisabeth Croll, *The Women's Movement in China. A selection of readings.* SACU, London. 1974. pb. (available from China Books, 125 Fifth Ave. NYC).

Edgar Snow, *Red Star over China.* Grove Press, N.Y. 1968 (revised ed). pb.

4. BIOGRAPHY

Stuart Schram, *Mao Tse-Tung.* Pelican, Baltimore. 1967. pb.

Agnes Smedley, *The Great Road—The Life and Times of Chu Teh.* Monthly Review, N.Y. 1972. pb.

Han Suyin, *Birdless Summer.* Putnam, N.Y. 1968. h.

Han Suyin, *The Crippled Tree.* Putnam, N.Y. 1965. h.

Han Suyin, *A Mortal flower.* Putnam, N.Y. 1965. h.

Ning L. T'ai-T'ai, *Daughter of Han: Autobiography of a Chinese Working Woman.* ed. Ida Pruitt. Stanford Univ. Press, Stanford. 1945. pb.

Nym Wales, *Red Dust. Autobiographies of Chinese Communists as told to Nym Wales* (Helen Foster Snow). Stanford Univ. Press, Stanford. 1952. h.

5. IN LITERATURE

Lu Hsun, *Selected Stories.* Foreign Languages Press, Peking. 1963. pb.

Lu Xun, *Silent China.* Oxford Univ. Press, N.Y. 1973. pb. (both collections of Lu Hsun's writings are avialable from China Books, see above)

Andre Malraux, *Man's Fate.* Random House, N.Y. 1969. pb.

IV. COMPARATIVE ANALYSIS OF REVOLUTIONARY PROCESSES, EUROPEAN SOCIETIES (Annotated bibliography).

A. THE PROBLEM OF BOURGEOIS REVOLUTION

Crane Brinton, *Anatomy of Revolution.* Random House, New York. 1957 (revised edition). pb Comparative analysis of revolutions that points to the common stages and logic of revolutionary conflicts, and minimizes the distinguishing economic and class contexts of different revolutionary situations.

E.J. Hobsbawm, *The Age of Revolution, 1789-1848.* New American Library, New York. 1967. pb. Explores the transformation of Western societies in the wake of the "dual revolution," the French Revolution of 1789 and the British industrial revolution.

Heinz Lubasz, ed., *Revolutions in Modern European History.* Macmillan, New York. 1966. pb. A valuable collection of short selections that range from discussion of urban revolts in 17th Century France to articles on the Russian Revolution of 1917.

Karl Marx, *The 18th Brumaire of Louis Bonaparte.* International Publishers, New York. 1963. pb. Marx's classic analysis of the conditions underlying the parliamentary and the dictatorial modes of rule in bourgeois society.

Barrington Moore, Jr., *Social Origins of Dictatorship and Democracy—Lord and Peasant in the Making of the Modern World.* Beacon Press, Boston. 1966 pb. A comparative study of patterns of capitalist development, change in class structure and political revolution in European and Asian societies.

Charles Moraze, *The Triumph of the Middle Classes.* Doubleday, Garden City, New York. 1968. pb. Explores the impact of the rise of the European bourgeoisie in the 19th Century of Western and non-Western societies.

Henri Pirenne, *Early Democracies in the Low Countries. Urban Society and Political Conflict in the Middle Ages and the Renaissance.* Harper and Row, New York. 1963 (Reprint of 1915 edition).

Nicos Poulantzas, *Political Power and Social Classes.* New Left Books, London. 1975. pp. 168-184, "The Models of Bourgeois Revolution." Poulantzas argues that the French Revolution should not be considered the "typical" case, from the standpoint of Marxist theory, of bourgeois revolution. The English Revolutions of the 17th Century were more successful, from the point of view of furthering the development of the national capitalist economy.

George Rude, *The Crowd in History, 1730-1848.* John Wiley and Sons, New York. 1964. pb. Analyses of the role of the common people of France and England in economic protests and larger revolutionary upheavals.

George Rude, *Revolutionary Europe, 1789-1815.* Harper and Row, New York. 1964. pb.

B. THE RISE OF THE WORKING CLASS AND SOCIALIST MOVEMENTS

Wolfgang Abendroth, *A Short History of the European Working Class.* Monthly Review Press, N.Y. 1972. pb. The best short, comparative history; useful discussion of 20th century developments.

Louis Chevalier, *Laboring Classes and Dangerous Classes in Paris during the first half of the 19th Century.* H. Fertig, N.Y. 1973. A study of social conditions and culture of the Parisian poor in period of upheaval.

Frederick Engels, *The Condition of the Working Class in England in 1844.* Stanford Univ. Press, Stanford, Cal. 1958. pb.

M.W. Flinn and T.C. Smout, eds., *Essays in Social History.* Oxford Univ. Press, N.Y. 1974. pb. Excellent collection, includes essays by E.P. Thompson, Asa Briggs, J. Foster and R.M. Titmuss.

J.L. and Barbara Hammond, *The Village Labourer, 1760-1832.* Augustus M. Kelley, New York. Reprint of 1913 edition.

E.J. Hobsbawm, *Labouring Men, Studies in the History of Labour.* Doubleday, Garden City, New York. 1964. A collection of Hobsbawn's essays, including his essays on the standard of living of the British working class in the early 19th century and the British labor aristocracy.

Jurgen Kuczynski, *The Rise of the Working Class.* McGraw-Hill, New York. 1967. pb. An excellent discussion of the impact of the industrial revolution on the work situation and social life of workers, with a comparative survey of the varied experiences of the British, American, French and German working classes.

Karl Marx, *The Civil War in France.* International Publishers, New York. 1968. pb. Marx' analysis of the significance and lessons of the Paris Commune of 1871, the first revolutionary government established by workers.

Karl Marx, *Class Struggles in France, 1848-1850.* International Publishers, New York. 1964. pb. Marx' analysis of the economic conflicts that underlay the political struggles of 1848, and the lessons of the defeats suffered by the French working class.

Ivy Pinchbeck, *Women Workers in the Industrial Revolution, 1750-1850.* Augustus M. Kelley, New York. 1969. (Reprint of 1930 edition).

Arthur Rosenberg, *Democracy and Socialism. A Contribution to the Political History of the Past 150 Years.* Beacon Press, Boston. A study that encompasses the history of bourgeois democracy, the popular democratic movements of 1848, Marxism and the European working class, and 20th century fascism.

Arthur Rosenberg, *A History of Bolshevism.* Doubleday, Garden City, N.Y. 1967. pb. An analysis of the Russian Revolution that places Marx, Lenin, Rosa Luxemburg and Social Democracy in the context of developments in the European working class.

Sheila Rowbotham, *Women, Resistance and Revolution. A History of Women and Revolution in the Modern World.* Random House, New York. 1972. pb. An analysis of women's role and consciousness in a variety of revolutions (in England, France, Russia, China, Cuba, Algeria and Vietnam) and in working class and radical movements.

Carl Schorske, *German Social Democracy, 1905-1917.* John Wiley & Sons, New York. 1965. pb. A study of the origins and basis of political reformism in the German working class movement.

Edith Thomas, *The Women Incendiaries.* George Brazziler, New York. 1966. A history of the role of women in the Paris Commune of 1871.

E.P. Thompson, *The Making of the English Working Class.* Random House, New York. A history of the traditions, culture, struggles, political consciousness and economic life of British workers in the period of the industrial revolution.

Charles, Louise and Richard Tilly, *The Rebellious Century, 1830-1930.* Harvard University Press, Cambridge, Mass. 1975.

Franco Venturi, *Roots of Revolution. A History of the Populist and Socialist Movements in 19th Century Russia.* Grosset & Dunlap, New York. 1960 pb.

Edmund Wilson, *To the Finland Station.* Doubleday, New York. 1974. (Revised edition). A study of revolutionary traditions from 19th century historians of the French Revolution to Lenin and Trotsky in 1917.

Transition to Socialism I: Revolutionary Movements

James Petras
Department of Sociology
State University of New York-Binghamton
Spring 1980

The seminar will be divided into two parts.

In part one, we will discuss the classical Marxist writings on national and social revolutions in dependent capitalist countries. Specifically, we will critically analyze the ambiguities, changes, polemics and contradictions in the writings of Marx, Lenin, Trotsky and Stalin. We will examine Marx's rather unsystematic writings on the relationship between imperialism and capitalist development, as well as his efforts to link the colonial revolution to revolutions in the imperial countries. In the writings of Lenin, we will critically examine the assumptions and conceptions that informed his discussion of the relationship between social and national revolutions. Specifically, we will examine the impact that imperialism was perceived to have had in class formation in the colonial and semi-colonial countries and the kinds of social forces which were envisioned as playing a central role in the colonial liberation movements. Trotsky's writings will be examined to focus on the historical debate over the relationship between the national and social dimensions of revolutionary change. Specific attention will be paid to the notion of the "permanent revolution" and the social dynamics underlying it. The second section within part one is composed of a series of writings on various themes that relate to social and national revolutions.

Part two is made up of a series of case studies involving national and social revolutions. The cases include Russian, Chinese, Cuban and Vietnamese revolutions. Within each case we will consider the social and economic changes that lead up to the revolution, the political and social struggles that culminate in the revolution and some of the immediate problems. We will focus specifically on the impact of capitalist industrialization, imperialist wars and the transformation of agriculture as the central processes creating the social forces leading to revolution. The relationship of classes to political organization will also be considered a central ingredient to the process of change which is envisioned as occurring within a world historic framework.

PART I

Week One: THE CLASSICAL MARXIST TRADITION ON THE NATIONAL-COLONIAL QUESTION

S. Avineri, ed., *Karl Marx on Colonialism and Modernization*, Introduction, 1-34 and Part II.

Sami Mustafa, Marx on India (mimeo)

Week Two:

Rosa Luxemburg, *The National Question: Selected Writings*, 121-291.

J.P. Nettl, *Rosa Luxemburg* (abridged ed.), 500-20.

V.I. Lenin, *National Liberation, Socialism and Imperialism*.

Leon Trotsky, *The Permanent Revolution and Results and Prospects*, 37-122.

Joseph Stalin, *Marxism and the National/Colonial Question*, 15-48.

Week Three: COMMENTARIES AND CURRENT CONTROVERSIES

Horace B. Davis, *Nationalism and Socialism: Marxist and Labor Theories of Nationalism to 1917*.

V. Kiernan, "On the Development of a Marxist Approach to Nationalism," *Science and Society* XXXIV, 1, 92-98.

Michael Lowy, "Marxists on the National Question," *New Left Review*, 96, 81-100.

Tom Nairn, "Marxism and the Modern Janus," *New Left Review*, 94, 3-30.

Philip McMichael, "The Relations Between Class and National Struggle: Lenin's Contribution," *Journal of Contemporary Asia*, 7, 2, 200-12.

E.J. Hobsbawm, "On the Break-Up of Britain," *New Left Review*, 105, 3-24.

Regis Debray, "Marxism and the National Question," *New Left Review*, 105, 25-41.

T. Skocpol and E.K. Trimberger, "France, Russia, China: A Structural Analysis of Social Revolution," *Comparative Studies in Society and History*, 18, 1976, 175-210.

James Petras, "Toward a Theory of Twentieth Century Socialist Revolutions," *Journal of Contemporary Asia*, Summer 1978.

PART II

Week Four: RUSSIA-SOCIAL AND ECONOMIC BACKGROUND

Roger Portal, "The Industrialization of Russia," in M. Postan and J.J. Habakkuk, eds., *The Cambridge Economic History of Europe*, Vol. VI, Part 2, 801-70.

Gregory Grossman, "Russia and the Soviet Union," in C.M. Cipolla, ed., *The Fontana Economic History of Europe*, Vol. 4, 2, 486-531

Tom Kemp, "The Modernization of Tsarist Russia," in T. Kemp, *Industrialization in Nineteenth Century Europe*, 119-159.

Maurice Dobb, "Russian Economic Development Prior to the First World War," Ch. 2 of *Soviet Economic Development Since 1917*.

Leon Trotsky, *A History of the Russian Revolution*, Ch. 1.

Week Five: SOCIAL FORCES IN THE RUSSIAN REVOLUTION

G.V. Rimlinger, "Autocracy and the Factory Order in Early Russian Industrialization," *Journal of Economic History*, V.XX, 1960.

G.V. Rimlinger, "The Expansion of the Labour Market in Capitalist Russia," *Journal of Economic History*, V.XXI, 1961.

Leopold Haimson, "The Problem of Social Stability in Urban Russia, 1905-1917," *Slavic Review*, 23, 3, and 24, 1.

G.W. Phillips, "Urban Proletarian Politics in Tsarist Russia: Petersburgh and Moscow, 1912-1924," *Comparative Urban Research*, V.III, 3, 11-20.

Arthur P. Mendel, "Peasant and Worker on the Eve of the First World War," *Slavic Review*, V.XXIV, 1, 1965.

Reginald E. Zelnick, "Essay Review," *Journal of Social History*, 6, 2, 214-36.

Maureen Perrie, "The Russian Peasant Movement of 1905-1907: Its Social Composition and Revolutionary Significance," *Past and Present*, 57, 1972, 123-55.

Solomon M. Schwarz, *The Russian Revolution of 1905: The Workers' Movement and the Formation of Bolshevism and Menshevism*.

Week Six: THE RUSSIAN REVOLUTION AND ITS AFTERMATH

A.

Alexander Rabinowitch, *The Bolsheviks Come to Power*.

Marcel Liebman, *The Russian Revolution*.

E.H. Carr, *The Bolshevik Revolution*, Vol. 2.

Issac Deutscher, *The Unfinished Revolution*.

Leon Trotsky, *The Revolution Betrayed*.

Ted Uldricks, "The 'Crowd' in the Russian Revolution: Towards Reassessing the Nature of Revolutionary Leadership," *Politics and Society*, 4, 3, 1974.

B. THE COMINTERN

Fernando Claudin, *The Communist Movement* (Penguin 1975), "The Colonial Experience," 242-70.

Stephen White, "Colonial Revolution and the Communist International," *Science and Society*, V.XL, 2. Useful collection of documents.

Jane Degras, ed., *The Communist International*, 1919-1943, Vol. I and II.

Helmut Gruber, ed., *International Communism in the Era of Lenin* and *Soviet Russia Masters the Comintern*.

Week Seven: CHINA: ECONOMIC AND SOCIAL BACKGROUND

R.H. Tawney, *Land and Labor in China* (chapters on land ownership, usury, etc.).

J. Chesneaux, et. al., *China From the Opium Wars to the 1911 Revolution.*

J. Chesneaux, *Peasant Revolts in China.*

J. Chesneaux, *The Chinese Labor Movement*, 3-150.

Week Eight: SOCIAL FORCES IN THE CHINESE REVOLUTION

R. Hofheinz, *The Broken Wave: The Chinese Communist Peasant Movement, 1922-1928*, 3-110.

J. Chesneaux, *The Chinese Labor Movement*, 151-414.

Suggested Reading:

Joseph Esherick, *Reform and Revolution in China: The 1911 Revolution in Hunan and Hubei.*

Week Nine: THE REVOLUTION AND ITS AFTERMATH

Edgar Snow, *Red Star Over China* (129-440 of paper edition).

Mark Selden, *The Yenan Way in Revolutionary China.*

Chalmers Johnson, *Peasant Nationalism and Communist Power.*

Elinor Lerner, "The Chinese Peasantry and Imperialism: A Critique of C. Johnson's *Peasant Nationalism...*," *Bulletin of Concerned Asian Scholars*, 6, 2, 1974, 43-56.

Eric Wolf, *Peasant Wars of the Twentieth Century*, Ch. 3.

Week Ten: CUBA-SOCIAL AND ECONOMIC BACKGROUND

R.F. Smith, *The United States and Cuba.*

James O'Connor, *The Origins of Socialism in Cuba* (excerpts).

Dennis B. Wood, "The Long Revolution: Class Relations and Political Conflict in Cuba," *Science and Society*, 34, 1, 1-41.

H.A. Spalding, Jr., "The Workers' Struggle, 1850-1961," *Cuba Review*, V.IV, No. 1, 3-10.

Luis Aguilar, *Cuba 1933—Prologue to a Revolution*, Ch. 8-16.

Boris Goldenberg, "The Rise and Fall of the Cuban Communist Party," *Problems of Communism*, July-Aug. 1970.

Week Eleven: CUBA—THE REVOLUTION AND ITS AFTERMATH

R. Bonachaea and M. San Martin, *The Cuban Insurrection.*

K.S. Karol, *Guerillas in Power*, Ch. 2.

G.C. Alroy, "The Peasantry in the Cuban Revolution, *Review of Politics*, Jan. 1967, 87-99.

Maurice Zeitlin, *Revolutionary Politics and the Cuban Working Class*, Ch. 11.

Week Twelve: VIETNAM-SOCIAL AND ECONOMIC BACKGROUND

David G. Marr, *Vietnamese Anticolonialism.*

Jean Chesneaux, "The Historical Background of Vietnamese Communism," *Government and Opposition*, Winter 1969, 118-35.

Gareth Proter, "Imperialism and Social Structure in Vietnam," Ph. D. Dissertation, Cornell University, 1976.

Ngo Vinh Long, *Before the Revolution: Vietnamse Peasants Under the French.*

Jean Chesneaux, "Stages in the Development of the Vietnam National Movement," *Past and Present*, 1955.

Week Thirteen: THE REVOLUTION AND ITS AFTERMATH

John T. McAlister, *Vietnam: The Origins of Revolution*, Ch. 4-8.

Jeffrey Race, *War Comes to Long An: Revolutionary Conflict in a Vietnamese Province.*

Pierre Rousset, "The Vietnamese Revolution and the Role of the Party," *International Socialist Review*, No. 35, Apr. 1974, 4-25.

Alexander B. Woodside, *Community and Revolution in Modern Vietnam.*

W. Burchett, *Vietnam: Inside Story of the Guerilla War*, Section 2.

Twentieth Century Revolutions in the Third World

Mark Selden
Department of Sociology
State University of New York-Binghamton
Fall 1979
Undergraduate

* = Main texts used

I. CAPITALISM, IMPERIALISM, THE MODERN WORLD SYSTEM: THIRD WORLD PERSPECTIVES. PEASANT SOCIETY AND THE DIVERSITY OF THIRD WORLD EXPERIENCE

*Gerard Chaliand, *Revolution in the Third World*, Forward, Preface, 1-32.

*Eric Wolf, *Peasant Wars of the Twentieth Century*, Preface.

*V.I. Lenin, "Imperialism: The Highest Stage of Capitalism," in Tucker, *Lenin Anthology*, 204-74.

Supplement:

Eric Wolf, *Peasants*.

Andre Gunder Frank, "The Development of Underdevelopment," in Charles Wilber, ed., *The Political Economy of Development and Underdevelopment*, 94-104.

Eduardo Galeano, "Open Veins of Latin America," *Monthly Review*, Dec. 1978, 12-35.

Harry Magdoff, "The American Empire and the U.S. Economy," *The Age of Imperialism*, Ch. 5.

John Gurley, "Marxism and Capitalism," "The Triumph of Capitalism," and "Marx and the Critique of Capitalism," in *Challengers to Capitalism, Marx, Lenin and Mao*, 1-62.

Frantz Fanon, *The Wretched of the Earth*, 68-147, 311-16.

II. NATIONAL LIBERATION AND PEOPLE'S WAR. SOCIALIST AND CAPITALIST STRATEGIES OF DEVELOPMENT

Chaliand, *Revolution in the Third World*, 33-165.

Lenin, "Two Tactics of Social-Democracy in the Democratic Revolution," in Tucker, *Lenin Anthology*, 120-47.

*Mao Tse-tung, "Some Questions Concerning Methods of Leadership," "Get Organized!" "Serve the People," "The Foolish Old Man Who Removed the Mountains," *Selected Readings*, 287-305, 310-12, 320-23.

Supplement:

Barrington Moore, "Peasants and Revolution," in *Social Origins of Dictatorship and Democracy*, 453-83.

Karl Marx, "Peasantry as a Class," Teodor Shanin, "'Peasantry as a Political Factor," in T. Shanin, ed., *Peasants and Peasant Societies*.

William Pomeroy, *Guerrilla Warfare and Marxism*. Introduction (9-49), Engels (68-72), Lenin (77-84, 109-15), Mao (177-93), Ho & Giap (203-8), Guevara (287-90).

Paul Sweezy and Charles Bettelheim, *The Transition to Socialism*.

Samir Amin, "Self-Reliance and the New International Economic Order," *Monthly Review* July/August 1977, 1-21.

James Petras, "Towards a Theory of Twentieth Century Socialist Revolutions," *Journal of Contemporary Asia*, 8, 2, 1978, 167-95.

RUSSIA

III. CLASS AND SOCIETY IN RUSSIA. RUSSIAN MARXISM, LENIN AND THE ORIGINS OF REVOLUTION

Wolf, *Peasant Wars*, 51-99.

Robert Tucker, "Lenin and Revolution, xxv-lxiv; *Lenin Anthology*.

Lenin, "Tasks of the Russian Social-Democrats," (3-12); "What is to be Done?" (excerpts) 23-33, 46-59, 112-14; "Two Tactics of Social-Democracy in the Democratic Revolution" (120-47); "Left-Wing Communism—An Infantile Disorder" (550-618), *Lenin Anthology*.

Supplement:

John Gurley, "Lenin and the Revolution Against Capitalism," *Challengers to Capitalism*, 63-96.

Christopher Hill, *Lenin and the Russian Revolution*.

Saul Silverman, ed., *Lenin* (excerpts, topically arranged).

Rolf Theen, *Lenin: Genesis and Development of a Revolutionary*.

IV. THE ROAD TO POWER: EARLY PHASES OF REVOLUTIONARY TRANSFORMATION. THE FIRST SOCIALIST REVOLUTION AND BUREAUCRACY: THE LIMITS OF CHANGE

Lenin, "The State and Revolution," (311-99); "The Dictatorship of the Proletariat" (489-91); "Communism and Electrification" (492-95); "Introducing the New Economic Policy" (503-10); "The Importance of Gold Now and After the Complete Victory of Socialism" (511-17); "Communism and the East: Theses on the National and Colonial Questions" (619-25), *Lenin Anthology*.

Paul Sweezy, "Bettelheim on Revolution From Above: The USSR in the 1920's," *Monthly Review*, October 1977, 1-20; "Is There a Ruling Class in the USSR?" *Monthly Review*, October 1978, 1-17.

Supplement:

Charles Bettelheim, *Class Struggles in the Soviet Union 1917-23*.

Robert Tucker, *Stalin as Revolutionary 1879-1929*.

Stephen Cohen, *Bukharin and the Russian Revolution*.

Merle Fainsod, *How Russia is Ruled*.

E.H. Carr, *The Bolshevik Revolution*.

CHINA

V. CLASS AND SOCIETY IN TRADITIONAL CHINA. THE IMPACT OF IMPERIALISM. REFORM, NATIONALISM AND THE ORIGINS OF CHINESE COMMUNISM

Wolf, *Peasant Wars*, 103-55.

Mao Tse-tung, "Report on an Investigation of the Peasant Movement in Hunan," (23-39), *Selected Readings from the Works of Mao Tse-tung*.

Andrew Nathan, "Imperialism's Effects on China," and Joseph Esherick, "Harvard on China: The Apologetics of Imperialism," *Bulletin of Concerned Asian Scholars* IV, 4 (1972), 2-18.

Supplement:

Victor Lippit, "The Development of Underdevelopment in China," *Modern China* 4, 3 (1978), 251-328.

Jean Chesneaux, *Peasant Revolts in China 1840-1949*.

Philip Huang, "Analyzing the Twentieth-Century Chinese Countryside," *Modern China* 1, 2 (1975), 132-59.

Jean Chesneaux, *The Chinese Labor Movement, 1919-1927*, 3-146.

Stuart Schram, *Political Thought of Mao Tse-tung*, 236-59.

Lucien Bianco, *Origins of the Chinese Revolution, 1915-1949*

VI. PEOPLE'S WAR AND THE TRANSFORMATION OF THE PEASANT SOCIETY. SOCIALIST TRANSFORMATION I: THE SOVIET MODEL

*William Hinton, *Fanshen*, as much as possible, but especially 3-45, 103-60, 190-209, 251-311, 360-66, 400-16, 454-58, 488-508, 528-34, 601-13.

Mao Tse-tung, "Current Problems of Tactics in the Anti-Japanese United Front" (182-93); "Some Questions Concerning Methods of Leadership" (287-94); "Get Organized" (295-305); "On the People's Democratic Dictatorship," (371-88), *Selected Readings From the Works of Mao Tse-tung*.

Supplement:

Mark Selden, "Revolution and Third World Development: People's War and the Transformation of Peasant Society," N. Miller and R. Aya, eds., *National Liberation*.

Franz Schurmann, "Villages," *Ideology and Organization in Communitst China*, 404-42.

John Wong, *Land Revolution in China*.

John Gurley, "The Formation of Mao's Economic Strategy, 1927-1949," in *China's Economy and the Maoist Strategy*, 20-92.

VII. SOCIALIST TRANSFORMATION II: BUREAUCRACY, THE GREAT PROLETARIAN CULTURAL REVOLUTION AND CHINA'S MODERNIZATION

Mao, "On the Question of Agricultural Cooperation (389-420), "Selections from the Introductory Notes in the Socialist Upsurge in China's Countryside" (421-31); "On the Correct Handling of Contradictions Among the People" (432-79), "Where Do Correct Ideas Come From?" (502-4), *Selected Readings From the Works of Mao Tse-tung*.

Kojima Reiitsu and Mark Selden, "The Great Leap Forward and the Chinese Road to Socialist Development" (mimeo), 24 pp.

Supplement:

Stephen Andors, *China's Industrial Revolution*.

David and Nancy Milton, *The Wind Will Not Subside. Years in Revolutionary China*.

Jack Chen, *Inside the Cultural Revolution*.

Bill Brugger, *Contemporary China*.

Stuart Schram, ed., *Chairman Mao Talks to the People*.

Charles Bettelheim, "The Great Leap Backward," *Monthly Review*, July-August 1978, pp. 38-130.

"The Cultural Revolution" in David Milton, Nancy Milton and Franz Schurmann, eds., *People's China*, 217-393; also see 93-177.

Mark Selden, *The People's Republic of China. A Documentary History of Revoluionary Change*.

VIII. CLASS, SOCIETY AND COLONIALISM IN VIETNAM. THE ORIGINS OF COMMUNISM. PEOPLE'S WAR AND THE UNITED STATES IN VIETNAM

Wolf, *Peasant Wars*, 159-210.

*Nguyen Khac Vien, *Tradition and Revolution in Vietnam*, Forward to 74, esp. "Confucianism and Marxism in Vietnam."

Gabriel Kolko, *The Roots of American Foreign Policy*, Ch. 4, Epilogue.

Supplement:

Bernard Fall, ed., *Ho Chi Minh on Revolution*.

David Hunt, "Organizing for Revolution in Vietnam," *Radical America*, 8, 1-2.

Michael Klare, *War Without End. United States Planning for Future Vietnams*.

Committee of Concerned Asian Scholars, *The Indochina Story*.

Ngo Vinh Long, "The Indochinese Communist Party and Peasant Rebellion in Central Vietnam, 1930-1931," *Bulletin of Concerned Asian Scholars*, 10, 4, (1978), 15-35.

George Kahin and John Lewis, *The United States in Vietnam.*

Virginia Brodine and Mark Selden, *Open Secret: The Kissinger-Nixon Doctrine in Asia.*

IX. THE VIETNAMESE ROAD TO SOCIALISM. VIETNAM AND THE NEW INTERNATIONAL RELATIONS OF EAST ASIA

Vien, *Tradition and Revolution in Vietnam,* 75-169.

"Two Views on the Vietnam-Kampuchea War," *Southeast Asia Chronicle,* No. 64, 1-30.

Supplement:

Gerard Chaliand, *The Peasants of North Vietnam.*

Christine White, *Land Reform in Vietnam.*

Kathleen Gough, *Ten Times More Beautiful. The Rebuilding of Vietnam.*

Le Duan and Pham Van Dong, *Toward Large-Scale Socialist Agricultural Production.*

CUBA

X. CLASS, SOCIETY AND IMPERIALISM IN PRE-REVOLUTIONARY CUBA. GUERRILLA WARFARE: THE ROAD TO POWER

Wolf, *Peasant Wars,* 251-73.

George Lavan, ed., *Che Guerara Speaks,* 9-15, 18-23, 74-91.

Supplement:

James O'Connor, "On Cuban Political Economy," in James Petras and Maurice Zeitlin, eds., *Latin America Reform or Revolution?,* 486-500.

Che Guevara, *Guerrilla Warfare.*

Regis Debray, *Revolution in the Revolution?*

James O'Connor, *The Origins of Socialism in Cuba.*

Lowry Nelson, *Rural Cuba.*

XI. THE CUBAN ROAD TO SOCIALISM. SELF-RELIANCE AND THE INTERNATIONAL ECONOMIC ORDER. CUBA AND THE EXPORT OF REVOLUTION

Lee Lockwood, *Castro's Cuba, Cuba's Fidel.*

Che Guevara Speaks, 26-46, 61-67, 121-59.

Supplement:

Leo Huberman and Paul Sweezy, *Socialism in Cuba.*

Richard Fagen, *The Transformation of Political Culture in Cuba.*

K.S. Karol, *Guerrillas in Power. The Course of the Cuban Revolution.*

Edward Boorstein, *The Economic Transformation of Cuba.*

William Kenner and James Petras, eds., *Fidel Castro Speaks,* especially 171-98.

Theodore Draper, "What is Castroism?," in *Castroism, Theory and Practice,* 3-57.

GUINEA-BISSAU

XII. CLASS, SOCIETY AND IMPERIALISM IN GUINEA-BISSAU

*Gerard Chaliand, *Armed Struggle in Africa,* Introduction to 27.

*Amilcar Cabral, *Revolution in Guinea,* introduction (7-10), "Guinea and Cabo Verde against Portuguese Colonialism," (11-23) "Brief Analysis of the Social Structure in Guinea" (56-75).

Supplement:

Basil Davidson, *The Liberation of Guinea.*

William Minter, *Portuguese Africa and the West.*

Samir Amin, *Neo-Colonialism in West Africa.*

Frantz Fanon, *The Wretched of the Earth.*

Giovanni Arrighi and John Saul, eds., *Essays on the Political Economy of Africa.*

XIII. PEOPLE'S WAR AND SOCIALIST DEVELOPMENT IN GUINEA-BISSAU

Chaliand, *Armed Struggle in Africa,* 29-139.

Cabral, *Revolution in Guinea,* "The Weapon of Theory," (90-111), "Development of the Struggle" (112-26), "Practical Problems and Tactics" (134-51).

Supplement:

Return to the Source: Selected Speeches of Amilcar Cabral.

Allen Isaacman, *A Luta Continua. Creating a New Society in Mozambique.*

Eduardo Mondlane, *The Struggle for Mozambique.*

Immanuel Wallerstein, *Africa. The Politics of Independence.*

XIV. SUMMING UP. IMPERIALISM, NATIONAL LIBERATION AND SOCIALIST TRANSITION IN THE THIRD WORLD

Chaliand, *Revolution in the Third World,* 167-95.

Wolf, *Peasant Wars,* 276-302.

Sociology of Protest Movements

Theda Skocpol
Department of Sociology
Harvard
Spring 1978-1979
Undergraduate

Why, how, and when do movements that demand change emerge? Under what conditions can such movements achieve—or partially achieve—their declared goals? What obstacles stand in the way of success, causing movements quite often to fail altogether? This course will explore some of the many (often contradictory) theories that have been developed by contemporary social scientists to characterize, explain, and guide research on movements for change. The focus will be expecially upon movements by and for exluded or relatively less powerful groups in society. Most of the actual movements discussed in the readings have occurred in U.S. history since the 1930s. Hence we shall also gain a certain familiarity with debates about the limits and possibilities for protest and change afforded by the contemporary political system of the United States.

Week 1: INTRODUCTION TO THE COURSE

I. AN OLD THEORY AND SOME EVIDENCE

Week 2

William Kornhauser, *The Politics of Mass Society*.

Week 3

Donald Von Eschen, Jerome Kirk, and Maurice Pinard, "The Organizational Substructure of Disorderly Politics" *Social Forces* 49 (4) (June 1971): 529-44.

Maurice Jackson, et al., "The Failure of an Incipient Social Movement" *The Pacific Sociological Review* 3(1) (Spring 1960): 35-40.

Jo Freeman, "The Origins of the Women's Liberation Movement" *American Journal of Sociology* 78 (4) (January 1973): 792-811.

II. THE GROUP BASES OF POLITICAL ACTION

Week 4

Mancur Olson, *The Logic of Collective Action: Public Goods and the Theory of Groups*.

Week 5

Charles Tilly, *From Mobilization to Revolution*, chapters 1-5, 8.

III. THEORIES OF SOCIETY AND NONINSTITUTIONALIZED PROTEST

Week 6

Neil Smelser, *Theory of Collective Behavior*, chapters 1-5, 9-11

Week 7

Michael Schwartz, *Radical Protest and Social Structure: The Southern Farmers' Alliance and Cotton Tenancy, 1880-1890*.

IV. U.S. POLITICS AND THE STRATEGIES OF CHALLENGERS

Week 8

William Gamson, *The Strategy of Social Protest*.

Week 9

Frances Fox Piven and Richard Cloward, *Poor People's Movements: Why They Succeed and How They Fail*.

Week 10

David J. Garrow, *Protest at Selma: Martin Luther King, Jr., and the Voting Rights Act of 1965*.

Michael Lipsky, "Rent Strikes: Poor Man's Weapon," *Transaction* 6 (February 1969): 10-15. (See also, for the official version of this argument, written in more obscure and academic language: Lipsky, "Protest as a Political Resource," *The American Political Science Review* 62(4) (December 1968): 1144-58).

Week 11

J. Craig Jenkins and Charles Perrow, "Insurgency of the Powerless: Farm Worker Movements (1946-1972)," *American Sociological Review* 42 (2) (April 1977): 249-68.

J. Craig Jenkins, "Farm Workers and the Powers: Insurgency and Political Conflict (1946-1972)," parts to be announced.

V. Grass-Roots Organizing

Week 12

Saul D. Alinsky, *Reveille for Radicals*, part II.

John H. Mollenkopf, "On the Causes and Consequences of Neighborhood Political Mobilization."

Week 13

Discussion of (all or parts of) a Senior Thesis by Adair Damann, Stephanie Van Dyke, Susan Eaton, Sarah Royce, and Karen Scharff.

HISTORY

Precapitalist Economy and Society

Stephen A. Marglin
Harvard University
Economics
Undergraduate
Spring 1980

*indicates supplementary reading

I. THE ORIGINS OF FEUDALISM

J. Strayer and R. Coulbourn, "Feudalism" in R. Coulbourn (ed.), *Feudalism in History*.

J. Strayer, "Feudalism in Western Europe," in R. Coulbourn (ed.), *Feudalism in History*.

M. Bloch, *Feudal Society*, ch. 11-17.

*F. Ganshof, *Feudalism*.

L. White, *Technology and Social Change in the Middle Ages*, ch. 1.

R. Hilton and P. Sawyer, "Technological Determinism: The Stirrup and the Plough," *Past and Present*, April 1963, pp. 90-95.

II. THE ORIGINS OF SERFDOM AND THE MANOR

M. Bloch, *Feudal Society*, ch. 18-20.

G. Duby, *Rural Economy and Country Life in the Medieval West*, Ch. 2.

*M. Postan (ed.), Cambridge Economic History of Europe, Vol. I, *The Agrarian Life of the Middle Ages* (2nd ed.), ch. 4 and 6.

M. Bloch, *French Rural History: Its Basic Characteristics*, ch. 2-3, part I, pp. 21-77.

M. Postan, *The Medieval Economy and Society*, ch. 5.

*R. Hoffman, "Medieval Origins of the Common Fields" in W. Parker and E. Jones (eds.), *European Peasants and Their Markets*.

III. THE MANORIAL ECONOMY AT ITS HEIGHT

H.S. Bennett, *Life on the English Manor*, Prologue, ch. 5-8.

*E. DeWindt, *Land and People in Holywell Cum Needingworth*, ch. 1-2.

*F. & J. Gies, *Women in the Middle Ages*, ch. 8.

M. Postan, *Medieval Society and Economy*, ch. 6-10.

M. Bloch, *French Rural Society: Its Basic Characteristics*, ch. 3, part II; ch. 4, part I and II; ch. 5.

J. Raftis, *Tenure and Mobility*, ch. 4-5.

*F. Maitland (ed.), "Introduction" to *Select Pleas in Manorial and Other Seignorial Courts*, Vol. I, (Publications of the Selden Society, Vol. II, 1889).

*D. Oschinsky, *Walter of Henley and Other Treatises on Estate Management and Accounting*.

*E. Kosminsky, *Studies in the Agrarian History of England in the Thirteenth Century*.

IV. THE LARGER SOCIETY: THE GROWTH OF TOWNS, INDUSTRY AND COMMERCE

J. LeGoff, "The Town as an Agent of Civilization" in C. Cipolla (ed.), *The Fontana Economic History of Europe*, Vol. I, The Middle Ages.

S. Thrupp, "Medieval Industry 1000-1500," in C. Cipolla (ed.), *The Fontana Economic History of Europe*.

*J. Bernard, "Trade and Finance in the Middle Ages 900-1500" in C. Cipolla (ed.), *The Fontana Economic History of Europe*.

M. Postan, *Medieval Society and Economy*, ch. 11-12.

F. & J. Gies, *Women in the Middle Ages*, ch. 9.

*M. Dobb, *Studies in the Development of Capitalism*, ch. 2, part IV, and ch. 3.

V. THE LARGER SOCIETY: THE DEVELOPMENT OF THE MEDIEVAL STATE AND CHURCH

M. Bloch, *Feudal Society*, ch. 30-31.

J. Strayer, *On the Origins of the Modern State*, ch. 1-2.

C. Petit-Dutaillis, *The Feudal Monarchy in France and England*, Book 2, ch. 2 and 4.

*E. Miller, "Government Economic Policies and Public Finance 1000-1500" in C. Cipolla (ed.), *The Fontana Economic History of Europe*, Vol. I.

*G.L. Harriss, *King Parliament and Public Finance in Medieval England to 1369*.

R. Southern, *Western Society and the Church in the Middle Ages*, ch. 1-2.

R. Southern, *The Making of the Middle Ages*, ch. III, part III, pp. 154-169.

*B. Bolton, "Mulieres Sanctae," in S. Stuard (ed.), *Woman in Medieval Society*.

VI. THE LARGER SOCIETY: THE MIND AND THE SPIRIT

*M. Bloch, *Feudal Society*, ch. 5-7, 26 (pp. 345-52).

R. Southern, *The Making of the Middle Ages*, ch. 4-5.

H.S. Bennett, *Life on the English Manor*, ch. 1 and 12.

D. Herlihy, "Alienation in Medieval Culture and Society," in F. Johnson (ed.), *Alienation: Concept, Term, and Meanings.*

*G. Leff, *Heresy in the Later Middle Ages.*

*F. & J. Gies, *Women in the Middle Ages*, ch. 4.

D. Herlihy (ed.), *Medieval Culture and Society*, pp. 95-103, 190-207, 126-153, 254-269, 234-254.

VII. THEORIES OF MANORIAL ECONOMY AND ITS DECLINE

E. Domar, "The Causes of Slavery or Serfdom: A Hypothesis," *Journal of Economic History*, 1970, pp. 18-32.

L. White, *Technology and Social Change in the Middle Ages*, Ch. 2.

R. Hilton and P. Sawyer, "Technological Determinism: The Stirrup and the Plough," *Past and Present*, April 1963, pp. 95-100.

H. Pirenne, *Medieval Cities*, ch. 8.

D. North and R. Thomas, "The Rise and Fall of the Manorial Economy: A Theoretical Model," *Journal of Economic History*, 1971, pp. 777-803.

M. Dobb, *Studies in the Development of Capitalism*, ch. 2, parts I-III.

*R. Hilton, M. Dobb et al (eds.), *The Transition from Feudalism to Capitalism.*

R. Brenner, "Agrarian Class Structure and Economic Development in Pre-Industrial Europe," *Past and Present*, no. 70, Feb. 1976.

The Anonimalle Chronicle, "The Peasants Revolt of 1381" in A.R. Myers (ed.), *English Historical Documents 1327-1485*, pp. 127-140.

R. Hilton, *Bond Men Made Free*, Part II.

The Transition from Feudalism to Capitalism

Robert Brenner
Graduate Faculty, New School for Social Research/University of California
Economics
Fall 1981

Weeks I-III: INTRODUCTION TO HISTORICAL MATERIALISM: "THE MODE OF PRODUCTION"

K. Marx, "Preface" to *The Critique of Political Economy (1859).*

K. Korsch, "The Materialistic Scheme of Society", in *Karl Marx* (1938), pp. 183-188.

K. Marx, "The Genesis of Capitalist Ground Rent", in *Capital*, III, part IV, chapter 47.

K. Marx, "Historical Facts about Merchants" in *Capital*, III, part IV, chapter 20.

K. Marx, *Pre-Capitalist Economic Formations*, pp. 97-120.

K. Marx, "The So-Called Primitive Accumulation of Capital" in *Capital*, I, part VIII.

J. Banaji, "Modes of Production in a Materialist Conception of History", *Capital and Class*, no. 3 (1977).

Optional

E. Balibar, "The Basic Concepts of Historical Materialism", in L. Althusser and E. Balibar, *Reading Capital* (1968, 1970).

E.J. Hobsbawm, "Introduction" to Marx' *Pre-Capitalist Economic Formations.* pp. 9-66.

J. Cohen, "The Achievements of Economic History: The Marxist School" *Journ. Econ. Hist.*, XXXVIII (March 1978), pp. 29-57.

G.A. Cohen, *Karl Marx' Theory of History* (1978).

Week IV: THE ORIGINS OF FEUDALISM

P. Anderson, *Passages from Antiquity to Feudalism* (1974), pp. 107-146, and esp. pp. 147-153.

G. Duby, *The Early Growth of the European Economy* (1973, 1974), pp.

J.R. Strayer, "Feudalism in Western Europe" in *Lordship and Community in Western Europe*, ed. F.L. Cheyette (1968), pp. 12-21.

O. Hintze, "The Nature of Feudalism" in *Lordship and Community in Western Europe*, ed. F.L. Cheyette (1968), pp. 22-31.

Optional

M. Weber, "The Social Causes of the Decline of Ancient Civilization" in *The Agrarian Sociology of Ancient Civilizations* (1976), pp. 387-412.

O. Brunner, "Feudalism: The History of a Concept" in *Lordship and Community in Western Europe*, ed. F.L. Cheyette (1968), pp. 32-63.

Weeks V-VII: FEUDAL DYNAMICS AND FEUDAL CRISIS

P. Anderson, *Passages from Antiquity to Feudalism* (1974), pp. 147-212.

M. Dobb, "The Decline of Feudalism and the Growth of Towns" in *Studies in the Development of Capitalism* (1946), pp. 33-70.

P. Sweezy, "Critique of Dobb" in *The Transition From Feudalism to Capitalism*, ed. R.H. Hilton (1976).

M. Dobb, "Reply"; M. Dobb, "A Further Comment"; P. Sweezy, "A Rejoinder"; in *The Transition from Feudalism to Capitalism*, ed. R.H. Hilton (1976).

R. Brenner, "Agrarian Class Structure and Economic Development: A Reply to Critics", *Past & Present* (1981, forthcoming) *Manuscript*.

J.L. Bolton, *The Medieval English Economy 1150-1500* (1980)
Optional

J. Merrington, "Town and Country in the Transition to Capitalism" in *The Transition From Feudalism to Capitalism*, ed. R.H. Hilton (1976).

R. Brenner, "Agrarian Class Structure and Economic Development in Pre-Industrial Europe", *Past & Present*, no. 70 (1976).

Replies to Brenner by Postan and Hatcher, by Croot and Parker, by H. Wunder, by E. Le Roy Ladurie, by G. Bois, by R. Hilton, by J.P. Cooper in *Past & Present*, nos. 78-80 (1978).

Weeks VIII-X: THE WORLD MARKET AND THE EARLY MODERN EUROPEAN ECONOMY

See, again, R. Brenner, "Reply to Critics."

I. Wallerstein, *The Modern World System* (1974), pp. 14-129.

R. Brenner, "The Origins of Capitalism: A Critique of Neo-Smithian Marxism" *New Left Review*, no. 104 (July-August 1977).

M. Malowist, "Poland, Russia, and Western Trade in the 15th and 16th Centuries", *Past & Present*, no. 10 (Nov. 1956).

J. Topolski, "Economic Regression in Poland in the 16th and 17th Centuries" in *Essays in European Economic History*, ed. P. Earle (1970).

M. Bloch, *French Rural History* (1966), pp. 102-149.

D.C. Coleman, *The Economy of England, 1450-1750* (1977), pp.
Optional

C. Hill, *From the Reformation to the Industrial Revolution*

R.H. Tawney, *The Agrarian Problem of the 16th Century* (1912), pp.

J. Thirsk, "Seventeenth Century Agriculture and Social Change" *Agricultural History Review*, XVIII (1970).

Weeks XI-XII: STATE AND ECONOMY IN EARLY MODERN EUROPE: "ABSOLUTISM"

P. Anderson, *Lineages of the Absolutist State* (1974), pp. 7-142, 195-235.

H. Rosenberg, "The Rise of the Junkers", *American Hist. Rev.*, XLIX (Oct. 1943), pp. 1-22, XLIX (Nov. 1944), pp. 228-242.

J.H.M. Salmon, "Venality of Office and Popular Sedition in 17th Century France", *Past & Present*, no. 37 (July 1967).

P. Deyon, "Relations Between the Fench Nobility and the Absolute Monarchy During the First Half of the Seventeenth Century" in *State and Society in Seventeenth Century France*, ed. R. Kierstead (1976) pp. 25-43.

Weeks XIII-XIV: THE BOURGEOIS REVOLUTION

L. Stone, *The Causes of the English Revolution*

L. Stone, "Power" in *The Crisis of the Aristocracy*

W.T. MacCaffrey, "The Crown and the New Aristocracy", *Past & Present*, no. 30 (1965).

R.H. Tawney, "The Rise of the Gentry", *Econ. Hist. Rev.* (1941).

H.R. Trevor-Roper, "The General Crisis of the 17th Century", *Past & Present*, no. 16 (1959).

J.H. Hexter, "Storm Over the Gentry" in *Reappraisals in History* (1961).

C. Russell, *The Crisis of Parliaments*
Optional

C. Hill, "Recent Interpretations of the English Civil War", *History*, (1956).

Week XV: FROM THE BOURGEOIS REVOLUTION TO THE INDUSTRIAL REVOLUTION

J. DE VRIES, *Crisis and Change in the European Economy, 1600-1750*

E. Hobsbawm, "The General Crisis of the 17th Century", *Past & Present*, nos. 5-6 (1953).

I. Wallerstein, "The Seventeenth Century Economy" Crisis or Transition?" *New Left Review*, no. 109

E. Hobsbawm, *Industry and Empire* (1968), pp. 23-78.

D. Landes, *Unbound Prometheus* (1969), pp. 41-80.
Optional

D.C. Coleman, *The English Economy 1500-1750*,

American Economic History

David Kotz
University of Massachusetts-Amherst
Economics
Spring 1980

Note: An asterisk (*) means that a reading is supplementary.

I. APPROACHES TO ECONOMIC HISTORY

Carr, E.H., *What is History*, Ch. 4,5.

Cornforth, M., *Historical Materialsim*, Ch. 2-5.

Mao Tsetung, *On Contradiction*.

Resnick, S., and Wolff, R., "The Theory of Transitional Conjunctures and the Transition from Feudalism to Capitalism in Western Europe," *Review of Radical Political Economics*, v.11, n.3, (Fall, 1979), pp. 3-13 only.

Williamson, H.F., "The Process of Economic Development," in Williamson, *Growth of the American Economy*, 2nd Ed.

North, Douglass, *Growth and Welfare in the American Past*, Ch. 1.

II. THE COLONIAL PERIOD AND THE WAR FOR INDEPENDENCE

A. COLONIAL ECONOMY AND CLASS STRUCTURE

Farnie, D.A., "The Commercial Empire of the Atlantic, 1607-1738," *Economic History Review*, v. 15 n. 2, Dec. 1962, pp. 205-17.

Morris, Richard, "The Organization of Production During the Colonial Period," in Williamson, *Growth of the American Economy*, ch. 4.

Nash, Gary, *Class and Society in Early America*, ch. 15-19.

Main, Jackson, *The Social Structure of Revolutionary America*, ch. 2,5.

Merrill, Michael, "Cash is Good to Eat: Self-Sufficiency and Exchange in the Rural Economy of the U.S.," *Radical History Review*, Winter 1976-77, pp. 42-71.

*Hacker, Louis, *Triumph of American Capitalism*, ch. 8-10.

*Kulikoff Allan, "The Progress of Inequality in Revolutionary Boston," *William and Mary Quarterly*, v. 28, pp. 375-411.

*Bailyn, Bernard, *The New England Merchants in the 17th Century*, ch. 8.

*Robertson, Ross, *History of the American Economy*, 3rd Edition, ch. 2,3.

*Williamson, H., *Growth of the American Economy*, ch. 2,3.

*Bining, A.C., and Cochran, T.C., *The Rise of American Economic Life*, ch. 205.

*Tryon, Rolla, *Household Manufactures in the U.S., 1640-1860*, ch. 3.

B. THE WAR FOR INDEPENDENCE

Harper, Lawrence, "Mercantilism and the American Revolution," in Nash, Gerald, *Issues in American Economic History*, 2nd ed.

Hacker, Louis, "The First American Revolution," in Nash, Gerald, *Issues in American Economic History*, 2nd Ed.

*Lynd, Staughton, "The Mechanics in New York Politics, 1774-88," *Labor History*, Fall 1964.

*Hacker, Louis, *Triumph of American Capitalism*, ch. 11-12.

*Williams, W.A., *The Contours of American History*, pp. 75-117.

*Lynd, Staughton, "Who Should Rule at Home," in Scheiber, Harry, *U.S. Economic History*, ch. 4.

*Aptheker, Herbert, *The American Revolution, 1763-1783*, ch. 1-6.

III. THE DEVELOPMENT OF INDUSTRIAL CAPITALISM BEFORE 1860

A. OVERVIEW

Montgomery, David, "The Working Classes of the Pre-Industrial American City, 1780-1830," *Labor History*, v. 9, pp. 3-22.

Pessen, Edward, "The Egalitarian Myth and American Social Reality: Wealth, Mobility, and Equality in the Era of the Common Man," *American Historical Review*, v. 76, pp. 375-412.

North, Douglass, *Economic Growth of the U.S., 1790-1860*, ch. 6, 7, 12.

Taylor, George R., *The Transportation Revolution, 1815-1860*, ch. 16; ch. 2*-8*.

*Warner, Sam Bass, *The Private City*, part 2.

*Williamson, *Growth of the American Economy*, ch. 7,8,17.

B. THE FACTORY AND WAGE LABOR

Ware, Caroline, *The Early New England Cotton Manufacture*, ch. 1-4.

Ware, Norman, *The Industrial Worker, 1840-1860*, ch. 1-7.

Gitelman, H.M., "The Waltham System and the Coming of the Irish," *Labor History*, Fall 1967, pp. 227-53.

*Tryon, Rolla, *Household Manufactures in the U.S.*, ch. 7,8.

*Rosenberg, Nathan, *Technology and American Economic Growth*, ch. 3,4.

*Williamson, *Growth of the American Economy*, ch. 10.

*Robertson, R., *History of the American Economy*, 3rd Ed., ch. 8.

C. RESISTANCE AND CLASS STRUGGLE

Ware, Norman, *The Industrial Worker, 1840-1860*, ch. 8-15.

*Commons, J.R., *History of Labor in the U.S.*, Vol. I, Parts 1-4.

IV. THE SLAVE SYSTEM

A. U.S. SLAVERY IN WORLD CONTEXT

Genovese, Eugene, *The World the Slaveholders Made*, part 1.

Degler, Carl, "Slavery in the U.S. and Brazil: An Essay in Comparative History," *American Historical Review*, April, 1970.

*Williams, Eric, *Capitalism and Slavery*.

B. U.S. SLAVERY AS A MODE OF PRODUCTION

Hindess, Barry, & Hirst, Paul, *Pre-Capitalist Modes of Production*, Intro. and ch. 3.

Genovese, *Political Economy of Slavery*, ch. 1,2,4,6,10.

Moore, Barrington, *The Social Origins of Democracy and Dictatorship*, ch. 3.

*Genovese, E., *Roll, Jordan, Roll: The World the Slaves Made*, books 1,4.

*North, Douglass, *Economic Growth of the U.S., 1790-1860*, ch. 10.

*Stampp, Kenneth, *The Peculiar Institution*.

*Aptheker, Herbert, *American Negro Slave Revolts*.

*Gray, Lewis, *History of Agriculture in the Southern U.S. to 1860*.

C. NEW ECONOMIC HISTORY OF SLAVERY

Fogel, R.W., and Engerman, S., *Time on the Cross*, vol. 1.

David, P.A., et. al., *Reckoning with Slavery*.

Elbert, Sarah, "Good Times on the Cross: A Marxian Review," *Review of Radical Political Economics*, v.7, n.3, Fall 1975, pp. 55-66.

Aptheker, H., "Heavenly Days in Dixie, or the Time of their Lives," *Political Affairs*, June-July, 1974.

V. FROM COMPETITIVE TO MONOPOLY CAPITALISM

A. AGRICULTURE AND AGRARIAN DISCONTENT

Shannon, Fred, *The Farmers Last Frontier*, ch. 1,3,6,7,8,13,15.

Higgs, Robert, *The Transformation of the American Economy, 1865-1914*, ch. 4.

North, D., *Growth and Welfare in the American Past*, ch. 11.

*Faulkner, Harold, *The Decline of Laissez Faire*, ch. 13,14.

*Williamson, *Growth of the American Economy*, ch. 18,20.

*Mayhew, Anne, "A Reappraisal of the Causes of Farm Protest in the U.S., 1870-1900," *Journal of Economic History*, v.32, June 1972, pp. 464-75.

*Bogue, Allan, *From Prairie to Corn Belt*.

B. THE RISE OF BIG BUSINESS

Sweezy, Paul, *Theory of Capitalist Development*, ch. 14,15.

Josephson, Matthew, *Robber Barons*, ch. 2,5,7,9,12.

Kirkland, Edward, *Industry Comes of Age*, ch. 3,7,8,10,13*.

Chandler, Alfred D., "The Beginnings of Big Business in American Industry," in Scheiber, H., *U.S. Economic History*, ch. 13.

*Myers, Gustave, *History of the Great American Fortunes*, part 3.

*Williamson, *Growth of the American Economy*, ch. 19,23-25,31.

*Cochran, Thomas, and Miller, William, *Age of Enterprise*, ch. 7,8.

*Lenin, V.I., *Imperialism: The Highest Stage of Capitalism*, ch. 1-3.

C. FINANCE CAPITAL AND THE CENTRALIZATION PROCESS.

Kotz, David, *Bank Control of Large Corporations in the U.S.*, pp. 23-51.

Corey, Lewis, *House of Morgan*, ch. 23-25.

Nelson, Ralph, *Merger Movements in American Industry*, ch. 4.

Edwards, Richard, "Capital Accumulation and Corporate Power in the Transition to Monopoly Capitalism," photocopy on reserve.

Kolko, Gabriel, *Triumph of Conservatism*, ch. 1 2.

Faulkner, H., *The Decline of Laissez Faire*, ch. 6,7,8.

*Josephson, Matthew, *Robber Barons*, 16-18.

*Passer, H.C., "The Development of Large-Scale Organization Electrical Manufacturing Around 1900," *Journal of Economic History*, Autumn 1952.

*Navin, T., and Sears, Marion, "The Rise of a Market in Industrial Securities," *Business History Review*, 1955, pp. 105-38.

*Brandeis, Louis, *Other People's Money*.

Campbell, E.G., *The Reorganization of the American Railway System*.

*Moody, John, *The Truth About the Trusts*.

*Moody, John, *Masters of Capital*.

*Williamson, *Growth of the American Economy*, ch. 28,29,32.

D. THE LABOR PROCESS AND THE WORKING CLASS

Braverman, Harry, *Labor and Monopoly Capital*, ch. 1-10; 15*-20*.

Gordon, David, et. al., *Labor Segmentation in American Capitalism*, ch. 2-6.

Stone, Katherine, "The Origins of Job Structures in the Steel Industry," in Edwards, Richard, et. al., *Labor Market Segmentation*.

Kessler-Harris, Alice, "Women, Work, and the Social Order," in Edwards et. al., *Labor Market Segmentation*.

Davies, Marjory, "Woman's Place is at the Typewriter: The Feminization of the Clerical Labor Force," *Radical America*, v.8, Summer 1974, pp. 1-28.

Edwards, Richard, *Contested Terrain*, ch. 2,4,6-11.

*Ozanne, Robert, *A Century of Labor-Management Relations at International Harvester*.

*Chandler, Alfred D., *Strategy and Structure*.

*Nelson, Daniel, *Managers and Workers*, ch. 1-3.

*Gutman, H., "Work, Culture, and Society in Industrializing America, 1815-1919," *American Historical Review*, v. 78, pp. 531-88.

E. THE WORKERS' MOVEMENT AND CLASS STRUGGLE

Boyer, Richard, and Morais, Herbert, *Labor's Untold Story*, ch. 2-8.

Brecher, Jeremy, *Strike!* ch. 1,2.

Grob, Gerald, "Organized Labor and the Negro Worker, 1865-1900," *Labor History*, Spring 1960, pp. 164-76.

Green, James, "The Brotherhood of Timberworkers, 1910-13," *Past and Present*, August, 1973.

Weinstein, James, "The IWW and American Socialism," *Socialist Revolution*, Sept./Oct. 1970, pp. 3-42.

Montgomery, David, "The 'New Unionism' and the Transformation of Workers' Consciousness in America, 1909-22.

*Weinstein, James, *Decline of Socialism in America*, ch. 1,2.

*Brody, David, *Steelworkers in America*, The Non-Union Era.

*Grob, G., *Workers and Utopia*.

*Laslett, John, *Labor and the Left...*, ch. 1-5.

*Ginger, Ray, *Eugene V. Debs: A Biography*.

*Montgomery, David, *Beyond Equality*, ch. 1,6, App. A.

F. THE STATE

Kolko, Gabriel, *Triumph of Conservatism*, ch. 3-10.

Hays, Samuel, "Municipal Reform in the Progressive Era: Whose Class Interest?," *Pacific Northwest Quarterly*, v. 60, October 1964, pp. 157-69.

Weinstein, James, *The Corporate Ideal in the Liberal State*.

*Hofstadter, Richard, *Age of Reform*.

*Williams, W.A., *Contours of American History*, pp. 390-412.

VI. IMPERIALISM AND U.S. ECONOMIC DEVELOPMENT

Lenin, V.I., *Imperialism: The Highest Stage of Capitalism*, ch. 4-10.

Sweezy, Paul, *Theory of Capitalist Development*, ch. 16, 17, Appendix B.

Magdoff, Harry, *The Age of Imperialism: The Economics of U.S. Foreign Policy*, ch. 2,3*.

Williams, William A., *The Roots of the Modern American Empire*, ch. 1-3.

Crapol, Edward P., & Schonberger, Howard, "The Shift to Global Expansion," in Williams, W.A. (ed.), *From Colony to Empire*, ch. 4.

LaFeber, Walter, "The Background of Cleveland's Venezuelan Policy: a Reinterpretation," in Scheiber, *U.S. Economic History*, ch. 14.

Williams, William A., *Tragedy of American Diplomacy*, ch. 1-5.

*Williamson, *Growth of the American Economy*, ch. 27, 41.

*Gardner, Lloyd, *Economic Aspects of New Deal Diplomacy*.

*Nearing, Scott, and Freeman, Joseph, *Dollar Diplomacy*.

*Wilkins, Mira, *The Emergence of Multinational Enterprise: American Business Abroad from the Colonial Era to 1914*.

*Wilkins, Mira, *The Maturing of Multinational Enterprise: American Business Abroad from 1914-1970*.

*Weisskopf, T., Theories of American Imperialism: A Critical Evaluation," *Review of Radical Political Economics*, v.6 n.3.

*LaFeber, Walter, *The New Empire: An Interpretation of American Expansion 1860-1898*.

*Van Alstyne, R.W., *The Rising American Empire*.

*Kolko, Gabriel, *Roots of American Foreign Policy*.

*Beard, Charles, *The Idea of National Interest*.

VII. ECONOMIC CRISES UNDER MONOPOLY CAPITALISM

Sweezy, P., *Theory of Capitalist Development*, ch. 8-12.

Baran, P., and Sweezy, P., *Monopoly Capital*, ch. 3,4,8.

Keller, R., "Monopoly Capital and the Great Depression," *Review of Radical Political Economics*, v.7 n.4.

Gordon, R.A., *Economic Instability and Growth: The American Record*, ch. 1-3.

Williamson, H.F., *Growth of the American Economy*, ch. 34,48.

*Steindl, Josef, *Maturity and Stagnation in American Capitalism*, ch. 9-14.

*Smith, Walter B., & Cole, Arthur H., *Fluctuations in American Business 1790-1860*.

*Kindleberger, C., *The World in Depression, 1929-39*.

*Galbraith, J.K., *The Great Crash*.

*Friedman, M., & Schwartz, A., *A Monetary History of the U.S., 1867-1960*.

*Klein, L., *Economic Fluctuations in the U.S., 1921-1941*.

*Corey, Lewis, *The Decline of American Capitalism*.

*Temin, Peter, *Did Monetary Forces Cause the Great Depression?*

WOMEN

Sexual Inequality

Barrie Thorne
Michigan State Univ.
Sociology
Spring 1981

This seminar will start with the fact of sexual inequality and explore it from diverse sociological perspectives—theoretical and empirical, macro and micro, structural and experiential. We will begin with cross-cultural issues: the varying nature of sex/gender systems in different times and places, debate over the universality and origins of male dominance (including questions about the usefulness of these debates), and biosociology and its critics. Engels, who drew on anthropological materials to theorize about the evolution and structure of women's oppression, provides a transition to the next part of the course: efforts to account for sexual inequality by combining Marxist and Feminist perspectives. This has been called the "unhappy marriage of Marxism and Feminism," a tension we will examine both through Marxist theories which have emphasized men's control of women's labor, and through Radical Feminist theories, which emphsize men's control of women's bodies (sexuality, reproduction, violence against women). We will then discuss the interior dynamics of patriarchy: recent theories, based on psychoanalytic and object relations theory, of gender differentiation in personality and experience, including the question of women's vs. men's anger; and research on sex similarities and differences in verbal and nonverbal communication. Sexual inequality is intricately related to inequalities of social class and race—complex patterns we will explore through case studies of the organization of sex and gender as it varies by class and race in contemporary society. Finally, we will discuss sexual inequality in socialist countries, and the politicization of sex and gender in recent U.S. history, including feminist movements and the New Right. Throughout the course we will ask about the implications of each theory for practice, for strategies to eliminate inequality.

I. CROSS-CULTURAL PERSPECTIVES ON SEXUAL INEQUALITY

A. CROSS-CULTURAL VARIATION IN THE DEGREE AND KIND OF SEXUAL INEQUALITY, AND THE SEARCH FOR A GENERAL THEORY

Review essays:

Louise Lamphere, "Review Essay: Anthropology," *Signs* 2(3), spring 1977: 612-27;

Michelle Z. Rosaldo, "The Use and Abuse of Anthropology: Reflections on Feminism and Cross-Cultural Understanding," *Signs* 5(3), spring 1980: 389-417;

Rayna Rapp, "Review Essay: Anthropology," *Signs* 4(3), spring 1979: 497-513;

Naomi Quinn, "Anthropological Studies of Women's Status," in Bernard J. Siegel, ed., *Annual Review of Anthropology* 6 (Oct. 1977): 181-225;

Susan Rogers, "Woman's Place: A Critical Review of Anthropological Theory," *Comparative Studies in Society and History* 20 (1): 123-73.

In Rayna R. Reiter, ed., *Toward an Anthropology of Women*. Monthly Review Press, 1975: Patricia Draper, "!Kung Women: Contrasts in Sexual Egalitarianism in Foraging and Sedentary Contests," 77-109. Judith Brown, "Iroquois Women: An Ethnohistoric Note," 235-252. Gayle Rubin, "The Traffic in Women: Notes on the 'Political Economy' of sex," 157-210.

Michelle Z. Rosaldo and Louise Lamphere, eds., *Woman, Culture and Society*, Stanford Univ. Press, 1974.

Ernestine Friedl, *Women and Men: An Anthropologist's View*. Holt, 1975.

Rae Lesser Blumberg, *Stratification: Socioeconomic and Sexual Inequality*. Wm Brown, 1978.

Patricia Caplan and Janet M. Burge, eds., *Women United: Women Divided*. Tavistock, 1978.

Alice Schlegel, ed., *Sexual Stratification: A Cross-Cultural View*. Columbia, 1977.

Ruby Rohrlich-Leavitt, ed., *Women Cross-Culturally*. Mouton, 1975.

Dana Raphael, ed., *Being Female*. Mouton, 1975.

Diana L. Barker and Sheila Allen, eds., *Sexual Divisions and Society*. Tavistock, 1976.

June Nash and Eleanor Leacock, "Ideologies of Sex: Archetypes and Stereotypes," *Annals of the New York Academy of Science*, 1977, vol. 285.

B. EVOLUTIONARY APPROACHES

In Rayna R. Reiter, ed., *Toward an Anthropology of Women*. Monthly Review Press:

Kathleen Gough, "The Origin of the Family," 51-57;

Leila Leibowitz, "Perspectives on the Evolution of Sex Differences," 20-35.

Nancy Tanner and Adrienne Zihlman, "Women in Evolution, Part 1: Innovation and Selection in Human Origins," *Signs* 1 (3, pt. 1), spring 1976, 585-608.

Adrienne Zihlman, "Women in Evolution, Part 2: Subsistence and Social Organization Among Early Hominoids," *Signs* 4 (1), autumn 1978, 4-20.

Donna Haraway, "Animal Sociology and a Natural Economy of the Body Politic," *Signs* 4 (1), autumn 1978, 21-60.

C. SOCIOBIOLOGICAL ACCOUNTS, AND CRITICISMS OF SOCIOBIOLOGY

Alice S. Rossi, "A Biosocial Perspective on Parenting," *Daedalus* 106 (2), spring 1977, 1-32.

Nancy Chodorow, "Considerations on a Biosocial Perspective on Parenting," *Berkeley Journal of Sociology* 22 (1977-78), 179-197.

Marian Lowe, "Sociobiology and Sex Differences," *Signs* 4(1), autumn 1978, 118-125.

Harriet Engel Gross et. al., "Considering 'A Biosocial Perspective on Parenting," *Signs* 4(4), summer 1979: 695-717.

R.C. Lewontin, "Sociobiology as an Adaptionist Program," *Behavioral Science* 24, 1979: 5-14.

Arthur L. Caplan, ed., *The Sociobiology Debate*. Harper & Row, 1978.

Ruth Hubbard and Marion Lowe, eds., *Genes and Gender II*. Gordian Press, 1979.

D. MALE BIAS IN ANTHROPOLOGY

In Rayna R. Reiter, ed., *Toward an Anthropology of Women*. Monthly Review Press: Sally Slocum, "Women the Gatherer: Male Bias in Anthropology," pp. 36-51; Ruby Rohrlich-Leavitt et. al., "Aboriginal Women: Male and Female Anthropological Perspectives," pp. 110-26.

E. SEXUAL INEQUALITY AND CAPITALIST ECONOMIC DEVELOPMENT IN THIRD WORLD COUNTRIES

Ester Boserup, *Women's Role in Economic Development*. St. Martin's, 1974.

In Rayna R. Reiter, ed., *Toward an Anthropology of Women*: Susan E. Brown, "Love Unites Them and Hunger Separates Them: Poor Women in the Dominican Republic," pp. 322-332; Anna Rubbo, "The Spread of Capitalism in Rural Colombia: Effects on Poor Women," 333-57; Dorothy Remy, "Underdevelopment and the Experience of Women: A Nigerian Case Study," 358-71.

Mina Caulfield, "Imperialism, the Family, and Cultures of Resistance," *Socialist Revolution* 4(2), Oct. 1974: 67-85.

"Women and National Development," special issue of *Signs* 3(1), autumn 1977.

Nici Nelson, *Why Has Development Neglected Rural Women? A Review of the Southeast Asian Literature*. Pergamon, 1980

Irene Tinker and Michele Bo Bramsen, eds., *Women and World Development*. Overseas Development Council, 1976.

II. MARXIST AND FEMINIST THEORIES OF SEXUAL INEQUALITY, AND EFFORTS TO COMBINE THEM

A. ENGELS' *ORIGINS OF THE FAMILY* (THE ONLY PRIMARY MARXIST SOURCE DEALING EXTENSIVELY WITH THE SUBJECT OF WOMEN AND SEXUAL INEQUALITY) AND RECENT INTERPRETERS AND CRITICS

Frederick Engels, *The Origin of the Family, Private Property and the State* (1898). The 1972 International Publishers paperback edition is the best to use, because of the introduction by Leacock. (Skim through the book; the other readings also summarize Engels' argument.)

Eleanor Burke Leacock, Introduction to Engels (see above), pp. 7-67.

Ann J. Lane, "Woman in Society: A Critique of Frederick Engels," in Berenice A. Carroll, ed., *Liberating Women's History*. Univ. of Illinois Press, 1976, 4-25.

Karen Sacks, "Engels Revisited: Women, the Organization of Production and Private Property," in Rayna R. Reiter, ed., *Toward an Anthropology of Women*. Monthly Review Press, 1975, 211-234.

Kathleen Gough, "The Origin of the Family," in Reiter, ibid., pp. 252-282.

Kathleen Gough, "An Anthropologist Looks at Engels," in Nona Glazer-Malbin and Helen Y. Waehrer, eds., *Woman in a Manmade World*. Rand McNally, 1972, 107-118.

Rayna Rapp, "Gender and Class: An Archaeology of Knowledge Concerning the Origin of the State," *Dialectical Anthropology* 2(4), Dec. 1977: 309-16.

B. MARXIST-FEMINIST THEORIES

Juliet Mitchell, "Women: The Longest Revolution," *New Left Review* 40 (Nov.-Dec. 1966), 11-37. (New England Free Press reprint).

Juliet Mitchell, *Woman's Estate*. Vintage, 1973.

Gayle Rubin, "The Traffic in Women: Notes on the 'Political Economy' of Sex," in Rayna Reiter, ed., *Toward an Anthropology of Women*, 157-210.

In Zillah R. Eisenstein, ed., *Capitalist Patriarcy and the Case for Socialist Feminism*. Monthly Review Press, 1979: Heidi Hartmann, "Capitalism, Patriarchy, and Job Segregation by Sex," 206-247; Rosalind Petchesky, "Dissolving the Hyphen: A Report on Marxist-Feminist Groups 105," 373-390; Batya Weinbaum and Amy Bridges, "The Other Side of the Paycheck: Monopoly Capital and the Structure of Consumption," 190-205.

Joan Kelly, "The Doubled Vision of Feminist Theory: A Postscript to the 'Women and Power' Conference," *Feminist Studies* 5(1), spring 1979, 216-227.

Margaret Benston, "The Political Economy of Women's Liberation," *Monthly Review* 21 (Sept. 1969), 13-29. New England Free Press reprint.

Renate Bridenthal, "The Dialectics of Production and Reproduction in History," *Radical America* 10(2), March-April 1976, 3-11.

Charnee Guettel, *Marxism and Feminism*. The Women's Press.

Jane Flax, "Do Feminists Need Marxism?" *Quest* 3(1), summer 1976, 46-58.

Barbara Ehrenreich, "What is Socialist Feminism?" *Win*, June 3, 1976, 4-7.

Annette Kuhn and AnnMarie Wolpe, *Feminism and Materialism*. Routledge & Kegan Paul, 1978.

Amy B. Bridges and Heidi I. Hartman, "The Unhappy Marriage of Marxism and Feminism," *Capital and Class*, 8. 1979.

Lydia Sargent, ed., *Women and Revolution: A Discussion of the Unhappy Marriage of Marxism and Feminism*. South End Press, 1980.

Batya Weinbaum, *The Curious Courtship of Women's Liberation and Socialism*. South End Press, 1978.

Michele Barrett, *Women's Oppression Today: Problems in Marxist Feminist Analysis*. Shocken, 1981.

C. HISTORICAL PERSPECTIVES ON RELATIONS OF PRODUCTION AND REPRODUCTION; WORK AND FAMILY

Eli Zaretsky, *Capitalism, the Family, and Personal Life*. Harper & Row, 1973.

In Barrie Thorne, with Marilyn Yalom, eds., *Rethinking the Family: Some Feminist Questions*. Longman, 1981: Barrie Thorne, "Feminist Rethinking of the Family: An Overview"; Eli Zaretsky, "The Place of the Family in the Origins of the Welfare State"; Renate Bridenthal, "The Family: The View from a Room of Her Own."

Zillah Eisenstein, *The Radical Future of Liberal Feminism*. Longman, 1981.

Rayna Rapp, Ellen Ross, and Renate Bridenthal, "Examining Family History," *Feminist Studies* 5(1), spring 1979: 174-200.

"Sexuality in History," special issue of *Radical History Review* #20, spr./summer 1979.

Angela Davis, "The Black Woman's Role in the Community of Slaves," *Black Scholar*, Dec. 1971. New England Free Press reprint.

Mary Ryan, *Womanhood in America: From Colonial Times to the Present*. 2nd ed. New Viewpoints, 1979.

Nancy Cott, *The Bonds of Womanhood: 'Women's Sphere' in New England, 1780-1835*. Yale Univ. Press, 1977.

Louise A. Tilly and Joan W. Scott, *Women, Work, and Family*. Holt, 1978.

Elizabeth H. Pleck, "Two Worlds in One: Work and Family," *Journal of Social History*, winter 1976, 178-195.

Barbara Welter, "The Cult of True Womanhood: 1820-1860," *American Quarterly* 18 (2, part 1, 1966), 151-174, reprinted in Gordon, below.

Michael Gordon, ed., *The American Family in Social-Historical Perspective*. St. Martins, 1978.

Stuart Ewen, *Captains of Consciousness: Advertising and the Social Roots of Consumer Culture*. McGraw Hill, 1976.

D. SEXUAL INEQUALITY IN PRODUCTION, CONTEMPORARY U.S. SOCIETY

THE WAGE-PAID ECONOMY

Natalie J. Sokoloff, 'Bibliography on the Sociology of Women's Work: 1970's," *Resources for Feminist Research* (Toronto), Vol. 8, no. 4, 1979: 48-74.

Veronica Beechey, "Women and Production: A Critical Analysis of Some Sociological Theories of Women's Work," in Annette Kuhn and AnnMarie Wolpe, eds., *Feminism and Materialism*. Routledge & Kegan Paul, 1978.

Joan Acker, "Women and Stratification: A Review of Recent Literature," *Contemporary Sociology* 9(1), Jan. 1980: 25-34.

Richard Edwards, Michael Reich, and Thomas Weisskopf, eds., *The Capitalist System*, 2nd ed. (ch. 9, "Sexism"), Prentice-Hall, 1978.

Alice Kessler-Harris, "Stratifying by Sex: understanding the History of Working Women," in Richard Edwards, Michael Reich, and David Gordon, eds., *Labor Market Segmentation*. D.C. Heath, 1975.

Martha Blaxall and Barbara B. Reagan, eds., *Women and the Workplace*. Chicago, 1976.

Robert W. Smuts, *Women and Work in America*. Shocken, 1971.

Valerie Kincade Oppenheimer, *The Female Labor Force in the United States*. Greenwood Press, 1976 (reprint of 1970 publication).

U.S. Dept. of Labor, Bureau of Labor Statistics, *Monthly Labor Review*, regularly has issues with articles on women in the labor force, and recent statistics.

Louise Kapp Howe, *Pink Collar Workers*. Avon, 1978.

Rosabeth Moss Kanter, *Men and Women of the Corporation*. Basic Books, 1977.

Cynthia F. Epstein, *Woman's Place: Options and Limits in Professional Careers*. Univ. of California Press, 1970.

Ann H. Stromberg and Shirley Harkess, eds., *Women Working*. Mayfield, 1978.

HOUSEWORK AND CONSUMPTION WORK

Batya Weinbaum and Amy Bridges, "The Other Side of the Paycheck: Monopoly Capital and the Structure of Consumption," in Eisenstein, ed., *Capitalist Patriarchy*.

Nona Glazer-Malbin, "Review Essay: Housework," *Signs* 1(4), Summer 1976, 905-921.

Margaret Benston, "The Political Economy of Women's Liberation," *Monthly Review* 21 (Sept. 1969), 13-29. New England Free Press reprint.

Peggy Morton, "A Woman's Work is Never Done," in Edith H. Altbach, ed., *From Feminism to Liberation*. Schenkman, 1971, 211-227.

Jean Gardiner, "Women's Domestic Labor," *New Left Review* 89 (Jan.-Feb. 1975), 47-58; reprinted in Eisenstein, op. cit.

Lise Vogel, "The Earthly Family," *Radical America* 7 (July-Oct. 1973), 9-50.

Ira Gerstein, "Domestic Work and Capitalism," *Radical America*, ibid., 101-128.

Mariarosa Della Costa, *Women and the Subversion of the Community*. Falling Wall Press, 1973.

Ann Oakley, *Women's Work: The Housewife, Past and Present*, Vintage, 1974: and *The Sociology of Housework*. Pantheon, 1974.

III. RADICAL FEMINIST THEORY: MEN'S CONTROL OF WOMEN'S BODIES

A. BASIC THEORETICAL WRITINGS

Adrienne Rich, *On Lies, Secrets, and Silence*. W.W. Norton, 1979.

Adrienne Rich, *Of Woman Born*. W.W. Norton, 1976.

Shulamith Firestone, *The Dialectic of Sex*. Wm. Morrow, 1970.

Mary Daly. *Gyn/Ecology: The Metaethics of Radical Feminism*. Beacon Press, 1978.

Ti-Grace Atkinson. *Amazon Odyssey*. Links, 1974.

Andrea Dworkin. *Woman Hating*. E.P. Dutton, 1974.

B. MALE CONTROL OF FEMALE SEXUALITY AND REPRODUCTION

Adrienne Rich, "Compulsory Heterosexuality and Lesbian Existence," *Signs* 5(4), summer 1980: 631-60.

Adrienne Rich, "The Meaning of Our Love for Women is What We Have Constantly to Expand," in *On Lies, Secrets, and Silence*. Norton, 1979, 223-30.

"Women—Sex and Sexuality," special issues of *Signs*, vol. 5(4), summer 1980; vol. 6(1), autumn 1980.

Linda Gordon, *Woman's Body, Woman's Right*. Penguin, 1975.

Linda Gordon, "The Struggle for Reproductive Freedom: Three Stages of Feminism," in Eisenstein, ed., *Capitalist Patriarchy*, 107-35.

Rosalind Petchesky, "Reproductive Freedom: Beyond 'A Woman's Right to Choose,'" *Signs* 5(4), summer 1980: 661-85.

Barbara Ehrenreich and Deirdre English, *For Her Own Good*. Anchor, 1979.

Claudia Dreifus, ed., *Seizing Our Bodies*. Vintage, 1977.

Catharine A. MacKinnon, *Sexual Harrassment of Working Women*. Yale Univ. Press, 1979.

Kathleen Barry, *Female Sexual Slavery*.

C. THE INSTITUTION OF MOTHERHOOD

Adrienne Rich, "Husband-Right and Father-Right" (pp. 215-222); "Motherhood: The Contemporary Emergency and the Quantum Leap" (pp. 259-74), in *On Lies, Secrets, and Silence*, Norton, 1979.

Adrienne Rich. *Of Woman Born: Motherhood as Experience and Institution*. Norton, 1976.

Nancy Chodorow, *The Reproduction of Mothering*. Univ. of Calif. Press, 1978.

Nancy Chodorow and Susan Contratto, "The Fantasy of the Perfect Mother," in Barrie Thorne, with Marilyn Yalom, eds., *Rethinking the Family: Some Feminist Questions*. 1981.

Sara Ruddick, "Maternal Thinking," *Feminist Studies* 6(2), summer 1980, reprinted in ibid.

D. MALE VIOLENCE AGAINST WOMEN

Susan Griffin, "Rape: The All-American Crime," *Ramparts*, Sept. 1971.

Menachem Amir, *Patterns of Forcible Rape*. Univ. of Chicago Press, 1971.

Susan Brownmiller. *Against Our Will: Men, Women and Rape*. Simon & Schuster, 1975.

Colleen McGrath, "The Crisis of Domestic Order," *Socialist Review* 43 (9, no. 1), Jan-Feb, 1979, 11-30.

R. Emerson Dobash and Russell Dobash, *Violence Against Wives*. Free Press, 1979.

IV. THE INTERIOR DYNAMICS OF SEXUAL INEQUALITY

A. PSYCHOANALYTIC APPROACHES TO GENDER AND PATRIARCHY

Nancy Chodorow, "Family Structure and Feminine Personality," in Michelle Z. Rosaldo and Louise Lamphere, eds., *Woman, Culture and Society*. Stanford, 1974, 43-66.

Nancy Chodorow, "Oedipal Asymmetries and Heterosexual Knots," *Social Problems* 23 (April 1976), 454-468.

Nancy Chodorow, *The Reproduction of Mothering: Psychoanalysis and the Social Organization of Gender*. Univ. of Calif. Press, 1978.

Teresa Bernardez-Bonesatti, "Women and Anger: Conflicts with Aggression in Contemporary Women," *Journal of the American Medical Women's Assoc.* 35(5), 1978:215-9.

Peter Lyman, "The Politics of Anger: On Silence, Ressentiment, and Political Speech," *Socialist Reveiw*, in press.

Evelyn Fox Keller, "Feminist Critique of Science: A Forward or Backward Move?" *Fundamenta Scientiae*, vol. 1, 1980: 341-9.

Evelyn Fox Keller, "Gender and Science," *Psychoanalysis and Contemporary Thought*," 1(3), 1978: 409-33.

Gayle Rubin, "The Traffic in Women: Notes on the 'Political Economy' of Sex," in Reiter, ed., *Toward an Anthropology of Women*, 157-210.

Juliet Mitchell, *Psychoanalysis and Feminism*. Vintage, 1976.

Dorothy Dinnerstein, *The Mermaid and the Minotaur*. Harper, 1976.

Batya Weinbaum, *The Curious Courtship of Women's Liberation and Socialism*. South End Press, 1978.

Jessica Benjamin, "Authority and the Family Revisited: or, A World without Fathers?" *New German Critique* #13, vol. 4 (3), winter 1978: 35-57.

Jessica Benjamin, "The Bonds of Love: Rational Violence and Erotic Domination," *Feminist Studies* 6, no. 1 (spring 1980): 144-74.

B. SEX SIMILARITIES AND DIFFERENCES: SOCIAL PSYCHOLOGICAL APPROACHES

Suzanne J. Kessler and Wendy McKenna, *Gender: An Ethnomethodological Approach*. John Wiley, 1978.

Rhoda K. Unger, *Female and Male: Psychological Perspectives*. Harper, 1979.

Mary Brown Parlee, "Review Essay: Psychology," *Signs* 1(1), 1975: 119-38; "Psychology and Women," *Signs* 5(1), 1979: 121-33.

Eleanor E. Maccoby and Carol N. Jacklin, *The Psychology of Sex Differences*. Stanford, 1974.

Jeanne H. Block, "Issues, Problems, and Pitfalls in Assessing Sex Differences: A Critical Review of The Psychology of Sex Differences," *Merrill-Palmer Quarterly* 22(4), 1976: 283-308.

Carol Tavris and Carole Offir, *The Longest War: Sex Differences in Perspective*. Harcourt Brace Jovanovich, 1977.

V. SEXUAL INEQUALITY IN EVERYDAY LIFE: VERBAL AND NONVERBAL COMMUNICATION

Nancy M. Henley, *Body Politics: Power, Sex and Nonverbal Communication*. Prentice-Hall, 1977.

Barrie Thorne and Nancy Henley, eds., *Language and Sex: Difference and Dominance*. Newbury House, 1975 (contains lengthy annotated bibliography).

Sally McConnell-Ginet, Ruth Borker, and Nelly Furman, eds., *Women and Language in Literature and Society*. Praeger, 1980.

Cheris Kramarae, *Women and Men Speaking*. Newbury House, 1981.

Dale Spender, *Man Made Language*. Routledge & Kegan Paul, 1981.

Cheris Kramer, Barrie Thorne, and Nancy Henley, "Review Essay: Language and Communication," *Signs* 3(3), spring 1978.

Pamela Fishman, "Interaction: The Work Women Do," *Social Problems*, April 1978: 397-406.

Erving Goffman, "The Arrangement Between the Sexes," *Theory and Society* 4(3), 1977: 301-31. Also *Gender Advertisements*. Harper.

VI. VARIATIONS IN THE ORGANIZATION OF SEX AND GENDER—ESPECIALLY IN RELATIONS OF PRODUCTION, REPRODUCTION, SEXUALITY—IN CONTEMPORARY WESTERN SOCIETIES (ISSUES OF SOCIAL CLASS AND RACE)

Rayna Rapp, "Family and Class in Contemporary America: Notes Toward an Understanding of Ideology," *Science and Society* 4(3), 1978: 278-310.

Ann Whitehead, "Sexual Antagonism in Herefordshire," in Diana L. Barker and Sheila Allen, eds., *Dependence and Exploitation in Work and Marriage*. Longman, 1976: 169-203.

Arlie R. Hochschild, "Inside the Clockwork of Male Careers," in Florence Howe, ed., *Women and the Power to Change*. McGraw-Hill, 1975: 25-40.

Carol B. Stack, "Sex Roles and Survival Strategies in an Urban Black Community," in Michelle Z. Rosaldo and Louise Lamphere, eds., *Woman, Culture and Society*. Stanford, 1974: 113-128.

Carol B. Stack, *All Our Kin: Strategies for Survival in a Black Community*. Harper, 1976.

Angela Davis, "The Black Woman's Role in the Community of Slaves," New England Free Press reprint. *Black Scholar*, Dec. 1971.

Elliott Currie, Robert Dunn, and David Fogarty, "The New Immiseration: Stagflation, Inequality, and the Working Class," *Socialist Review* 54 (Vol. 10, no. 6), 1980: 7-32.

Lillian B. Rubin, *Worlds of Pain: Life in the Working Class Family*. Basic, 1976.

Mirra Komarovsky, *Blue-Collar Marriage* (1962). Vintage, 1967.

Rosabeth Moss Kanter, *Men and Women of the Corporation*. Basic, 1977.

Rosabeth Moss Kanter, *Work and Family in the U.S.* Russell Sage, 1977.

Hanna Papanek, "Men, Women, and Work: Reflections on the Two-Person Career," *American Journal of Sociology* 78 (Jan 1973), 852-872.

VII. THE FEMINIST MOVEMENT IN THE U.S. AND REACTIONS TO CHANGE

In Zillah Eisenstein, ed., *Capitalist Patriarchy and the Case for Socialist Feminism*: "The Berkeley-Oakland Women's Union Statement," pp. 355-361; "The Combahee River Collective: A Black Feminist Statement," pp. 362-72.

Barbara Ehrenreich and Deirdre English, "Afterword: The End of the Romance," *For Her Own Good*. Anchor, 1978, pp. 313-24.

Laurie Davidson and Laura Kramer Gordon, *The Sociology of Gender*. Rand McNally, 1979.

Jean Stockard and Miriam M. Johnson, *Sex Roles: Sex Inequality and Sex Role Development*. Prentice-Hall, 1980.

Ann Oakley, *Sex, Gender and Society*. Harper & Row, 1972.

Evelyne Sullerot, *Woman, Society and Change*. McGraw-Hill, 1971.

Judith Long Laws, *The Second X*. Elsevier, 1979.

Laurel Richardson and Verta Taylor, eds., *Readings in Sex and Gender*. Heath, 1981.

Meredith Gould, "Review Essay: The New Sociology," *Signs* 5(3) spring 1980: 459-67.

Barrie Thorne, "Guidelines for Incorporating Information on Sex and Gender into Introductory Sociology Courses," Women's Educational Equity Act project/publication, 1981 (Judith M. Gappa and Janice Pearce, *Sex and Gender in the Social Sciences*).

3. GENERAL RESOURCES IN WOMEN'S STUDIES

Women's Studies Abstracts. Published quarterly starting winter, 1972 (from P.O. Box 1, Rush, N.Y. 14543); the M.S.U. library subscribes. Arranged by topic; also occasional articles reviewing areas of research (e.g. women and politics; sex stereotyping in instructional material).

KNOW, Inc. P.O. Box 86031, Pittsburgh, Pa. 15221. Provides a large number of reprints which are a great help for teaching, and for personal reading. They also distribute other feminist materials, and will send a catalogue.

The Feminist Press (Box 334, Old Westbury, N.Y. 11568) publishes a growing number of original books and pamphlets, as well as the *Women's Studies Newsletter* and feminist curricular material for elementary, high school, and college levels. *Female Studies* I through X (a series) includes helpful compilations of syllabi from women's studies courses around the country. *Female Studies VII* is an especially well-selected group of syllabi.

University of Michigan Women's Studies Curriculum Series: four interdisciplinary courses ("Women and Identity,"; "Women's Art and Culture"; "A Cross Cultural Study of Women"; "New Woman, New World: The American Experience") with lecture outlines and annotated bibliographic materials. Each course costs $2.50, from the Women's Studies Program, Univ. of Michigan, Ann Arbor, Michigan.

The review essays in each issue of *Signs: Journal of Women in Culture and Society* (Univ. of Chicago Press) are a very good way to keep up with new developments in varied fields, and to gain entre to the literature of other disciplines.

4. A BIBLIOGRAPHY OF BIBLIOGRAPHIES:

Patricia K. Ballou, "Review Essay: Bibiographies for Research on Women," *Signs* 3(2), winter 1977, 436-450.

Red Apple Collective, "Socialist-Feminist Women's Unions: Past and Present," *Quest* 4(1), 1977; reprinted in Socialist Review 38 (March-April 1978), 37-57.

Jo Freeman, *The Politics of Women's Liberation*. David McKay, 1975.

Sara Evans, *Personal Politics*. Knopf, 1979.

Recent and back issues of *Off Our Backs* (Washington, D.C.); *Sojourner* (Boston);*Quest*; *Sinister Wisdom*; *Conditions*; *Heresies* (The Book Coop has these and other feminist periodicals and newspapers.)

Linda Gordon and Allen Hunter, "Sex, Family and the New Right: Anti-feminism as a Political Force," *Radical America*, Nov. 1977/Feb. 1978 combined issue; New England Free Press reprint.

Rosalind Petchesky, "Anti-Abortion, Anti-Feminism, and the Rise of the 'New Right,'" *Feminist Studies* 7(2), Fall 1981.

VIII. SEXUAL INEQUALITY IN SOCIALIST SOCIETIES

In Zillah Eisenstein, ed., *Capitalist Patriarchy and the Case for Socialist Feminism*: Carollee Bengelsdorf and Alice Hageman, "Emerging from Underdevelopment: Women and Work in Cuba," 271-295; Margaret Randall, "Introducing the Family Code," 296-298; Judith Stacey, "When Patriarchy Kowtows: The Significance of the Chinese Family Revolution for Feminist Theory," 299-354.

Norma Diamond, "Collectivization, Kinship, and the Status of Women in Rural China," in Reiter, ed., *Toward an Anthropology of Women*, 372-395.

Sheila Rowbotham, *Women, Resistance, and Revolution*. Vintage, 1973.

Sheila Rowbotham, *Women's Liberation and Revolution: A Bibliography*. Falling Wall Press, 1973. Distributed by Feminist Press.

Hilda Scott, *Does Socialism Liberate Women? Experiences from Eastern Europe*. Beacon, 1974.

APPENDIX: BIBLIOGRAPHY ON OTHER TOPICS

Marcia Millman and Rosabeth Kanter, eds., *Another Voice: Feminist Perspectives on Social Life and Social Science*. Anchor, 1975.

Julia Sherman and Evelyn Beck, eds., *The Prism of Sex: Essays in the Sociology of Knowledge*. Univ. of Wisconsin Press, 1979 (including Dorothy Smith, "A Sociology for Women").

Dorothy Smith, "Women's Perspective as a Radical Critique of Sociology," *Sociological Inquiry* 4(1), Jan. 1974, pp. 7-13.

Margrit Eichler, *The Double Standard: A Feminist Critique of Feminist Social Science*. St. Martin's, 1980.

Evelyn Shapiro and Barry Shapiro, *The Women Say/The Men Say*. Delta, 1979.

Laurel Richardson Walum, *The Dynamics of Sex and Gender*. Rand McNally, 1977.

Issues in Social Policy: The Sexual Division of Labor

Julie A. Matthaei*
Wellesley College
Economics
Undergraduate
Fall 1980

*Course was developed and first taught with Teresa Amott, Wellesley College, under a Mellon Faculty Development Grant from Wellesley's Center for Research on Women

COURSE DESCRIPTION:

This is a course on the sexual division of labor, the division of social activities into "woman's work" and "man's work." In the first two parts of the course, we will analyze the sexual division of labor from two different theoretical perspectives: first from the traditional neo-classical perspective, and then from the marxist-feminist perspective. In the third part of the course, students will debate strategies for improving the economic and social position of women.

I. INTRODUCTION

1. OVERVIEW OF THE COURSE, AND OF ECONOMIC POSITION OF WOMEN IN THE TWENTIETH CENTURY

Bell, Carolyn Shaw, "Economics, Sex, and Gender," *Social Science Quarterly*, Winter, 1974

U.S. Dept. of Labor, *1975 Handbook on Women Workers*, pp. 3-5, 83-99, 123-137.

Chafe, William, "Looking Backward in Order to Look Forward," in Juanita Kreps, ed., *Women and the American Economy*.

2. COMPETING PARADIGMS AND THE HISTORY OF ECONOMIC THOUGHT

Mundell, Robert A., "The Law of Economy," in Mermelstein, David, ed., *Economics: Mainstream Readings and Radical Critiques*, 3rd edition.

Robinson, Joan, "Introduction," to *Essay on Marxian Economics*.

Sweezy, Paul, Introduction and Chapter 1 in *The Theory of Capitalist Development*.

II. NEO-CLASSICAL ANALYSIS OF THE SEXUAL DIVISION OF LABOR

1. REVIEW OF THE NEO-CLASSICAL ANALYSIS OF THE PERFECTLY COMPETITIVE LABOR MARKET

Chamberlain, Neil, et al, "The Labor Market: Private and Public," from *The Labor Sector*, pp. 317-330 only.

Heilbroner, Robert and Lester Thurow, *The Economic Problem*, Ch. 16, "The Market for Factors of Production."

Mansfield, Edwin, *Microeconomics: Theory and Applications*, Ch. 12, "Price and Employment of Inputs under Perfect Competition."

2. HUMAN CAPITAL THEORY

Bellante, Don and Mark Jackson, *Labor Economics*, Ch. 7, "Human Capital", and Ch. 8, "Long-Run Equilibrium Wage Differences."

Becker, Gary, "Human Capital—A Theoretical and Empirical Analysis," in Lloyd Reynolds, ed., *Readings in Labor Economics*.

3. THE ECONOMICS OF THE FAMILY: MARRIAGE AND CHILDREN

Sawhill, Isabel, "Economic Perspectives on the Family," *Daedalus*, Spring, 1977

Becker, Gary, "A Theory of Marriage," in Theodore Schultz, *The Economics of the Family*, pp. 299-308 (uncat.).

Willis, Robert J., "Economic Theory of Fertility Behavior" in Schultz, *Economics of the Family*, pp. 25-36 only.

Santos, Fredricka P., "The Economics of Marital Status," in Cynthia Lloyd, ed., *Sex, Discrimination, and the Division of Labor* (good diagrams).

Rosenzweig, Mark R., "Child Investment and Women," in Lloyd, *Sex, Discrimination, and the Division of Labor*.

4. THE DIVISION OF LABOR BETWEEN THE SEXES IN MARRIAGE: DIFFERENCES IN LABOR FORCE PARTICIPATION

Lloyd, Cynthia and Beth Niemi, *Economics of Sex Differential*, Ch. 2, "The Economics of Labor Supply: Work in the Market vs. Work at Home," esp. pp. 16-29.

5. THE DIVISION OF LABOR BETWEEN THE SEXES IN MARRIAGE: HUMAN CAPITAL ACQUISITION

Lloyd, and Niemi, *Economics of Sex Differentials*, Ch. 3 "Education, Training, and Occupational Selection," esp. 85-109 and 122-126 AND pp. 156-7 and 169-177 and 232-239.

Mincer, Jacob and Solomon Polachek, "Family Investments in Human Capital: Earnings of Women," in Schultz, *Economics of the Family* (skim).

Blau, Francine and Carol Jusenius, "Economists Approaches...," pp. 185-188 in Blaxall and Reagan, *Women and the Workplace*.

6. SWITCH TO THE DEMAND SIDE: DISCRIMINATION AND CROWDING

LaMond, Annette M., "Economic Theories of Employment Discrimination" in Wallace and LaMond, ed., *Women, Minorities and Employment Discrimination*.

Stevenson, Mary J., "Wage Differences between Men and Women: Economic Theories," in Stromberg and Harkness, eds., *Women Working*.

Lloyd and Niemi, *Economics of Sex Differentials*, Ch. 5, "Discrimination and the Dynamic Determinants of Wages and Unemployment," esp. pp. 193-202.

Arrow, Kenneth, "Models of Job Discrimination" in Pascal, A.H., ed., *Racial Discrimination in Economic Life*.

7. THE NEO-CLASSICAL ANALYSIS OF OCCUPATIONAL SEGREGATION BY SEX: APPLYING ALL THE THEORIES

Amott, Teresa, "A Review of the Literature on Occupational Segregation" and "Conclusion." (Unpublished PhD Dissertation, Boston College, 1979).

Lloyd and Niemi, *Economics of Sex Differentials*, Ch. 7, "Breaking Out of the Vicious Circle."

8. "IN BETWEEN": INSTITUTIONAL AND RADICAL APPROACHES: INTERNAL AND SEGMENTED LABOR MARKETS

Blau and Jusenuis, "Economists' Approaches...," pp. 190-199, in Blaxall and Reagan.

Edwards, Michael, et al, *Labor Market Segmentation*, pp. xi-xii, and 125-55.

Doeringer, Peter and Michael Piore, *Internal Labor Markets and Manpower Analysis*, Ch. 2, "Origins of the Internal Labor Market."

Cain, Glen, "The Challenge of Segmented Labor Market Theories to Orthodox Theory," *Journal of Economic Literature*, Dec., 1976

III. MARXIST-FEMINIST ANALYSIS OF THE SEXUAL DIVISION OF LABOR

1. INTRODUCTION TO MARXIST AND MARXIST-FEMINIST THEORY

Eisenstein, Zillah, "Developing a Theory of Capitalist Patriarch" in *Capitalist Patriarchy and the Case for Socialist Feminism*.

Kuhn, Annette, "Structures of Patriarchy and Capital in the Family" in Kuhn and Wolpe, *Feminism and Materialism*.

Mitchell, Juliet, *Woman's Estate*.

2. THEORY OF THE SEXUAL DIVISION OF LABOR: NATURE, SOCIETY, SEX, AND HISTORY

Levi-Strauss, Claude, "The Family" in Arlene Skolnick and Jerome Skolnick, *The Family in Transition*.

Levine, David and Lynn Levine, *Personality Structure and the Family: Historical and Theoretical Studies*, Ch. 2, "The Family: Historical and Conceptual Aspects," pp. 1-13 (unpublished manuscript, 1978).

Mead, George H., *Mind, Self and Society*, Introduction.

3. THEORY OF THE SEXUAL DIVISION OF LABOR: CONTINUITY AND CHANGE IN SEX ROLES

Rosaldo, Michell, "A Theoretical Overview," pp. 23-35 only, in Louise Lamphere, *Woman, Culture and Society*.

Ortner, Sherry, "Is Female to Male as Nature is to Culture?" in Lamphere, *Woman, Culture and Society*.

Malinowski, Bronislaw, *The Sexual Life of Savages*, pp. 1-50 and 121-129 (skim).

4. AMERICAN PAST: THE SEXUAL DIVISION OF LABOR IN THE COLONIAL FAMILY ECONOMY

Matthaei, Julie, *Womanhood and Economic Life: A Study in American Economic History*, Part I, "Woman's Work in the Colonial Family Economy," Chs. 1-3.**

Freeman, Mary E.W., "The Revolt of Mother" in *The New England Nun*.

**Forthcoming, Schocken Books; book title has been changed to *Womanhood and Capitalism: A Study in the Economic History of the United States*.

5. WOMAN'S WORK UNDER SLAVERY

Matthaei, *Womanhood and Economic Life*, Ch. 4, "Woman's Work and the Sexual Division of Labor under Slavery."

Lerner, Gerda, *Black Women in White America*, Ch. 1, "Slavery," (skim documents).

Davis, Angela, "Reflections on a Black Woman's Role in a Community of Slaves," *Black Scholar* 3.

Genovese, Eugene, *Roll, Jordan, Roll*, "Wives and Mothers," pp. 494-501.

6. THE SEXUAL DIVISION OF LABOR UNDER CAPITALISM: SEPARATE SEXUAL SPHERES AND HOME-MAKING AS A PROFESSION

Matthaei, *Womanhood and Economic Life*, Ch. 5, "The Development of Separate Spheres," Ch. 6, "Home-Making under the Cult of Domesticity: Unity and Diversity," and Ch. 7, "The Development of the Home-Making Profession."

Beecher, Catherine, *Treatise on Domestic Economy*, (skim).

Levine, Lynn, "Masculinity and Femininity" (unpublished papers, 1980).

7. THE SEXUAL DIVISION OF LABOR AS A SEPARATION OF SPHERES: WOMEN IN THE LABOR FORCE UNDER THE CULT OF DOMESTICITY

Hartmann, Heidi, "Capitalism, Patriarchy, and Job Segregation by Sex," in Eisenstein, *Capitalist Patriarchy*, esp. 211-230 (also in Blaxall and Reagan, *Women and the Workplace*).

Matthaei, *Womanhood and Economic Life*, Ch. 8, "Women in the Labor Force under the Cult of Domesticity: Who Were They?" and Ch. 9, "Women in the Labor Force under the Cult of Domesticity: The Sex-Typing of Jobs."

1975 Handbook on Women Workers, Ch. 1, "Women in the Labor Force" and Ch. 2 "Women's Employment by Occupation and Industry," (skim).

8. MARRIED WOMEN ENTER THE LABOR FORCE AS CONSUMERS AND CAREER WOMEN

Matthaei, *Womanhood and Economic Life*, Ch. 10, "The Entrance of Home-Makers Into the Labor Force, As Home-Makers" and Ch. 11, "The Career Girl and the Second Career Girl."

Friedan, Betty, *The Feminine Mystique*, Ch. 1, "The Problem that has No Name," and Ch. 3, "The Crisis in Woman's Identity."

9. THE BREAKDOWN OF THE SEXUAL DIVISION OF LABOR

Matthaei, *Womanhood and Economic Life*, ch. 12, "The Breakdown of the Sex-Typing of Jobs," and Ch. 13, "The Breakdown of the Sexual Division in Marriage."

Komarovsky, Mirra, *Dilemmas of Masculinity*, Introduction, Ch. 2, "Relationships with Women: Intellectual Aspects," and Ch. 5, "Power and Emotional Relationships with Women."

Epstein, *Woman's Place*, pp. 86-150.

Hennig, Margaret and Ann Jardim, *The Managerial Woman*.

Kanter, Rosabeth Moss, *Men and Women of the Corporation*.

10. INDIVIDUAL CHANGE, SOCIAL CHANGE, FEMINISM AND UTOPIAS

Morgan, Robin, ed., *Sisterhood is Powerful*, Introduction and Historical Documents.

Gilman, Charlotte Perkins, *Herland*.

Deckard, Barbara, *The Women's Movement*, Ch. 12, "The New Struggle for Liberation: American Women 1960 to the Present."

Levine, Lynn, "The Limits of Feminism." (unpublished paper, 1977)

Flexner, Eleanor, *Century of Struggle*.

IV. ISSUES IN SOCIAL POLICY: DEBATES

1. UNDERSTANDING THE SEXUAL DIVISIONS OF LABOR: NEO-CLASSICAL OR MARXIST/FEMINIST THEORY?

2. WOMEN'S LIBERATION AND THE HOME-MAKING CAREER: PRESERVE AND UPGRADE IT OR ABOLISH IT?

Edmond, Wendy and Suzie Fleming, *All Work and No Pay: Women, Housework, and the Wages Due*.

Friedan, Betty, *The Feminine Mystique*.

3. THE ROAD TO SEXUAL EQUALITY: ABOLISH THE SEXUAL DIVISION OF LABOR?

4. SEXUAL EQUALITY AND CAPITALISM: REFORM OR REVOLUTION?

1975 Handbook on Women Workers, Part II, "Laws Governing Women's Employment and Status."

Blaxall and Reagan, "Combatting Occupational Segregation" and Gates, Margaret, "Occupational Segregation and the Law."

Wallace, Phyllis, "Impact of Equal Opportunity Laws," in Kreps, *Women and the American Economy*.

Eisenstein, *Capitalist Patriarchy*; Hartsock, "Feminist Theory and the Development of Revolutionary Strategy"; Eisenstein, "Socialist Feminism in America"; Berkeley Oakland Women's Union Statement; Combahee River Collective: Black Feminist Statement.

Lloyd and Niemi, *Economics of Sex Differentials*, Ch. 6, "The Effects of Law and Policy on Sex Differentials."

Women's Life Cycles

Mary Lynn Broe
Sarah Elbert
Joan Smith
State University of New York-Binghamton
English, History, Sociology
Spring 1981

LIFE CYCLE THEORIES AND GENDER

AGES OF LIFE AS HISTORICAL PHENOMENA: DEMOGRAPHY AND SOCIAL FORMATIONS

Phillipe Aries, *Centuries of Childhood*, Chap. 1

Robert V. Wells, "Women's Lives Transformed: Demographic and Family Patterns in America, 1600-1970," in Berkin & Norton, *Women of America, a History*.

HERLAND: THE GREAT FEMALE INDOORS IN MYTH AND REALITY

Charlotte Perkins Gilman, *Herland*.

Carole Berkin, "Private Woman, Public Woman..." in Berkin & Norton, Woman of America, A History, pp. 151-76.

Adrienne Rich, "Diving into the Wreck" (Handout)

Recommended:

Mary Ellman, "Phallic Criticism" in *Thinking About Women* (WSR)

Rita Mae Brown, *Six of One*.
Virginia Woolf, *A Room of One's Own*.

CHILDHOOD AND FEMALE IDENTITY

THE MINIATURE ADULT: FEUDAL AND HOUSEHOLD PRODUCTION

Phillippe Aries, *Centuries of Childhood*, Chs. 2 & 5.

THE ROMANTIC DISCOVERY OF CHILDHOOD AND INDIVIDUALISM

Williams Wordsworth, "Ode to Immortality."
Charles Strickland, "A Transcendental Father, The Child Rearing Practices of Bronson Alcott."

Recommended:

Philip Greven, Jr. *Child Rearing Concepts, 1628-1861*.
Michael B. Katz, *Education in American History, Readings in the Social Issues*, see Zuckerman "Socialization in Colonial New England," pp. 28-36.
Lazerson, "Urban Reform and the Schools: Kindergartens in Massachusetts," pp. 220-236.
Harriet Beecher Stowe, *Uncle Tom's Cabin*.

"REGARDE" SIDO'S WORLD, COLETTE'S LIFE.

Colette, *Earthly Paradise*, pp. 3-78.
Annis Pratt, "Women and Nature in Modern Fiction."

Recommended Readings:

A. Rich, *Of Woman Born*, Chaps. 4, 9.
Yvonne Michell, *A Taste of Life* (on Colette).
W. Gass, "Three Photographs," (from *World Within the Word*).
Annette Kolodny, *The Lay of the Land*.
Susan Griffin, *Woman and Nature: The Roaring Inside Her*.

EDUCATION AND FEMINITY

Berkin and Norton, *Women of America, A History*, pp. 69-91.
Tillie Olsen, "Oh Yes," pp. 48-71, in Olsen, *Tell Me a Riddle*.
Barbara Brensel, "Lancaster Industrial School of Girls," in *Feminist Studies*, Vol. 3, No. 1/2, Fall '75, pp. 40-54.
Alice Deveaux, "The Riddles of Egypt Brownstone," in Washington, *Midnight Birds*, pp. 19-31.

Recommended Readings:

Marks, "Femininity in the Classroom," in Michell & Oakley, *The Rights and Wrongs of Women*.
A.S. Neill, *Summerhill*.

FEMALE ADOLESCENCE IN FACT AND FANTASY

DOMESTICITY, FEMINISM AND FEMALE ADOLESCENCE

Louisa May Alcott, *Little Women*.
Kathryn K. Sklar, "The Founding of Mt. Holyoke" pp. 177-98, in Berkin & Norton, *Women of America, A History*.

Recommended Readings:

Michael Katz, *Education in American History*, Jos. Kett, "Adolescence and Youth in 19th C. America," pp. 51-61.
Madeleine B. Stern, *Louisa May Alcott*.
The Journal of Charlotte L. Forten, A Free Negro in the Slave Era, ed. by Ray Allen Billington.

KISS SLEEPING BEAUTY GOODBYE: ADOLESCENCE AND DISPLACEMENT

Louisa May Alcott, *Little Women*.
Rosemary Minard, ed., *Folk and Fairy Tales*: "Mollie Whuppie," "Kate Crackernuts," "The Woman Who Flummoxed the Fairies," "Three Sisters Who were Entrapped in a Mountain," (Handout).
Mary McCarthy, "Figures in a Clock."

Recommended Readings:

Sarah Orne Jewett, "A White Heron."
Katherine Mansfield, "Her First Ball."
Poems: Eden if a Aoo," and "Advice to a Girl" (anthology R).
Charlotte Perkins Gilman, *Herland*.

EDUCATION FOREVER: ADOLESCENCE AND THE MODE OF PRODUCTION

Harry Braverman, *Labor and Monopoly Capital*, Pt. V.
M. Davis, "Feminization of the Clerical Labor Force."

WORKING GIRLS AND *LITTLE WOMEN*

Shirley Anne Williams, "Meditations on History," pp. 195-248 in Washington, ed., *Midnight Birds*.
Carol R. Berkin, "Not Separate, Not Equal," pp. 273-288 in Berkin & Norton, *Women of America*.
Susan Reverby, "From Aide to Organizer," pp. 288-317 in Berkin & Norton, *Women of America*.

CONTINUATION OF WORKING GIRLS AND *LITTLE WOMEN*

T. Dublin, "Women, Work and Family."
N.S. Dye, "Feminism or Unionism."
Carole Turbin, "And We Are Nothing But Women...", pp. 203-219 in Berkin & Norton, *Women of America*.
Tess of the D'Urbevilles.
Film: "Rosie the Riveter."

WOMEN, WORK AND FAMILIES

WORKING WOMEN AND PURE WOMEN

Thomas Hardy, *Tess of the D'Urbevilles*.

TESS: ON MORAL POISE, RARE CREATURES AND 'NATURAL GIRLS'

Hardy, *Tess of the D'Urbevilles*.

Recommended:

Irving Howe, from *Thomas Hardy* (handout).
Selected Essays from Norton, Critical Ed. of *Tess...*
Mitchell and Oakley, *The Rights and Wrongs of Women*, pp. 217, 255, 139-175.

BEYOND THE AUTHORIAL FATHER: HARDY AND CATHER'S HEROINES

Hardy, *Tess...*
Willa Cather, "The Gold Slipper," and "A Wagner Matinee," from *Youth and the Bright Medusa*.

Recommended:

Selected essays on *Tess...*
Bernard Evslin, "Perseus and the Medusa" chapter in *Mythology*.

BREADMAKING AND BREADWINNING

Anzia Yesierska, *The Breadgivers*.

Recommended Reading:

Alice Kessler Harris, *Women Have Always Worked*, Feminist Press, 1980.
Carole R. Berkin, "Not Separate, Not Equal," pp. 273-288, in Berkin and Norton, *Women of America*.
Rosalind Rosenberg, "The Academic Prism: A New View of American Women," pp. 318-341 in Berkin and Norton, *Women of America*.

MARRIAGE AND THE PRODUCTION OF HOUSEHOLDS

Eli Zaretsky, *Capitalism, the Family and Personal Life*.
Linda Gordon and Allen Hunter, "Sex, Family and the New Right." (WSR)
Leila Rupp, "Women's Place Is in the War...", pp. 342-359, in Berkin and Norton, *Women of America*.

SEX SEGREGATION AND WOMEN'S LIFE CYCLE

Louise Kapp Howe, *Pink Collar Workers*.
Susan Reverby, "From Aide to Organizer," pp. 289-309, in Berkin and Norton.
Frenchy Hodges, "Requiem for Willie Lee," in Washington, ed., *Midnight Birds*, pp. 97-108.

FROM BROADS TO BRIDES: WOMAN'S SEXUALITY AND WOMAN'S PLACE

HIS MARRIAGE AND HERS

Jessamyn West, "The Vase."
Agnes Smedley, "Hsu Meiling" from *Portraits of Chinese Women in Revolution*.
Toni Morrison, "Eva Peace," pp. 156-167, in Washington, ed., *Midnight Birds*.
Toni Cade Bambara, "Medley," pp. 255-274, in Washington, ed., *Midnight Birds*.
Sarah Orne Jewett, "Tom's Husband."
Djuna Barnes, "The Doctors," from *Spillway and Other Stories*.

Recommended:

Marylynn Salmon, "Equality or Submersion? Feme Covert Status in Early Pennsylvania," pp. 92-113, in Berkin and Norton, *Women of America*.
Colette, *Earthly Paradise* ("Willy" Selections).
Hortense Calisher, "The Rabbi's Daughter."

A NEW PRIME: GOOD SPORTS AND FALLEN WOMEN

Jean Rhys, *Good Morning Midnight*.
Jean Harris, Trial Report (New York Magazine Handout).

Recommended:

Frederick Lewis Allen, "Manners and Mores," from *Only Yesterday*.
Dorothy Parker, "Big Blonde."

THE DIRTY GODDESS OR THE RISE OF THE FALLEN WOMAN

Alice Walker, "Laurel" and "Advancing Luna and Ida B. Wells," in Washington, ed., *Midnight Birds*, pp. 48-63.
Paulette Childress White, "The Bird Cage," in Washington, ed., *Midnight Birds*, pp. 31-47.
Jacqueline Dowd Hall, "A Truly Subversive Affair, Women Against Lynching in 20th Century South," Berkin and Norton, *Women of America*, pp. 360-388.

Recommended:

Shulamith Firestone, *Dialectics of Sex*.
Alex K. Shulman, *Memoirs of an Ex Prom Queen*.
_____, *Burning Questions*.
Judith Rossner, *Emmeline*.
Philip Roth, *Portnoy's Complaint*.
Norman Mailer, *Marilyn Monroe, An American Dream*.
Midge Decter, *The New Chastity*.

WHOSE BODY IS IT ANYWAY?

Carasa Handbook.
John Paul Harpur, "Be Fruitful and Multiply: The Origins of Legal Restrictions on Planned Parenthood...", pp. 245-272, in Berkin and Norton, *Women of America*.

Recommended:

Linda Gordon, *Women's Body, Women's Right*.
Lillian Rubin, *Women of a Certain Age*.

ON A CLEAR DAY YOU CAN SEE YOUR MOTHER

Tillie Olsen, Tell Me A Riddle, pp. 9-47.
Toni Morrison, "Eva Peace," in Washington, ed., *Midnight Birds*.
Consumer Reports: "Cutting the Risk of Childbirth After 35," (May 1979).
Carol Gilligan, "In a Different Voice: Women's Conception of the Self and of Morality."

Recommended:

Harriet Arnow, *The Dollmaker*.

Joan Didion, *Play It As It Lays*.
Adrienne Rich, *Of Woman Born*.
Dorothy Dinnerstein, *Of Woman Born*.
Maria Pier, *Infanticide*.
Margaret Llewelyn Davies, *Maternity Letters from Working Women*.
Maud Pember Reeves, *Round About A Pound a Week*.
Jane Lazarre, *The Mother Knot*.
Nancy Chodorow, *The Reproduction of Mothering*.

MOTHERHOOD: INSTITUTION VS. EXPERIENCE

Charlotte Perkins Gilman, *Herland*.
Plath and Sexton (Handout).
Djuna Barnes, "Aller et Retour."
Recommended:
Colette, *Earthly Paradise*.
Rich, *Of Woman Born*, Chaps. 5, 6, 7.
Tillie Olsen, "I Stand Here Ironing," from *Tell Me A Riddle*.

AGING AS A POLITICAL EVENT

Mimeo Paper: "The Political Economy of Old Women," Smith.

NUMBER OUR DAYS: GREY PANTHERS AND OLD LADIES

Tillie Olsen, "Tell Me A Riddle."
Barbara Meyerhoff, "Jewish Comes Up in You From the Roots," from *Number Our Days*.
Theodore Roethke, "Meditations of an Old Woman."
Djuna Barnes, "The Passion" from *Spillway*.
Recommended:
Katherine Anne Porter, "The Jilting of Granny Weatherall." (Anthology R).
Doris Lessing, "An Old Woman and Her Cat."
Mary McCarthy, "Ask Me No Questions" from *Memories of a Catholic Girlhood*.

OLD WOMEN, WITCHES AND OLD MEN'S TALES

Hansel and Gretel, in Lang, ed., *The Blue Fairy Book*.
Grey Papers, #6, Displaced Homemakers, and Compounding Impact of Age on Sex.
Tillie Olsen, "Tell Me A Riddle."
Recommended:
Laurie Schields, *Displaced Homemakers*.
Boyer and Nissenbaum, *Salem Possessed*.

History and Theory of Sexuality

Ellen DuBois
State University of New York-Buffalo
American Studies
Graduate
Spring 1981

WEEK 1 INTRODUCTION TO COURSE; INTRODUCTORY EXERCISE—WHAT IS SEX? WHAT IS SEXUALITY?

WEEK 2 SOME CONTEMPORARY PERSPECTIVES ON SEXUALITY

Ethel Person, "Sexuality as the Mainstay of Identity: Psychoanalytic Perspectives," *Women: Sex and Sexuality* ed. Catherine Stimson (Signs, v. 5 #4).
Adrienne Rich, "Compulsory Heterosexuality and Lesbian Existence," *Women: Sex and Sexuality*.
Beatrice Campbell, "Feminist Sexual Politics: Now You See It, Now You Don't," *Feminist Review* #5, 1-18.
Jeffrey Weeks, "Movements of Affirmation: Sexual Meanings and Homosexual Identities," *Radical History Review* #20, Spring, 1979, 164-180.

WEEK 3

Linda Gordon, *Woman's Body, Woman's Rights: The Social History of Birth Control in the United States*, parts 1 and 2.

WEEK 4

Gordon, part 3.
Carroll Smith Rosenberg, "The Female World of Love and Ritual," *Signs*, v. 1#1, p. 1-30.
Nancy Cott, "Passionlessness: An Interpretation of Victorian Sexual Ideology, 1790-1850," *Signs*, v. 4 #2, 219-36.

WEEK 5 THE UNDERSIDE OF VICTORIAN SEXUALITY

Peter Cominos, "Late Victorian Sexual Respectability and the Social System," *International Review of Social History*," v. 8, 1963, 13-48, 216-250.

Leonore Davidoff, "Class and Gender in Victorian England: the Diaries of Arthur J. Munby and Hannah Cullwick," *Feminist Studies*, v. 5 #1 1979, 87-141.

"Passing Women," in *Gay American History*, Jonathan Katz ed.

Recommended:

Steven Marcus, *The Other Victorians.*

WEEK 6 REVIEW AND COMPARE, IN SMALL GROUPS, PERSON, RICH, GORDON, DAVIDOFF

WEEK 7 PSYCHOANALYTIC PERSPECTIVES

Sigmund Freud, *Sex, Love and Morality* (collected essays).

Freud, "Femininity," from *New Introductory Lectures*: Lecture 33.

Nancy Chodorow, "Feminism and Difference: Gender, Relation and Difference in Psychoanalytic Perspective," *Socialist Review*, #46, 51-67.

Roy Shafer, "Problems in Freud's Psychology of Women," *Journal of the American Psychoanalytic Association*, monograph series.

Luce Irigiray, "When Our Lips Speak Together," *Signs*, v. 6 #1, 69-79.

WEEK 8

Sigmund Freud, *Dora—An Analysis of a Case of Hysteria*, ed. Philip Rieff, including introduction.

Maria Ramas, "Freud's Dora, Dora's Hysteria: The Negation of a Woman's Rebellion," *Feminist Studies*, v. 6 #3, 47 2-510.

Charlotte Perkins Gilman, *The Yellow Wallpaper.*

WEEK 9

Jeffrey Weeks, *Coming Out: Homosexual Politics in Britain from the Nineteenth Century to the Present.*

WEEK 10 EARLY TWENTIETH CENTURY FEMINIST SEXUAL RADICALISM

Margaret Sanger, "The Sexual Impulse-Part I," *What Every Girl Should Know* (1911), 122-136.

Dora Russell, "Sex Love," in *The Sex Problem in Modern Society* (1931), 122-136.

F.W. Stella Browne, "The Sexual Variety and Variability among Women and their Bearing upon Social Reconstruction," in *A New World for Women*, ed. Sheila Rowbotham (1917), 91-105.

Charlotte Perkins Gilman, "On Monogamy," *Our Changing Morality* (1923), ed. Frieda Kirchwey, 53-66.

Havelock Ellis, "The Play Function of Sex," in *The Sex Problem in Modern Society*, (1931), 95-110.

WEEK 11 LESBIANISM

Gayle Rubin, "Introduction," to *A Woman Appeared to Me*, by Renee Vivien.

Gertrude Stein, *QED.*

J.R. Roberts, "Lesbian Hoboes: Their Lives and Times," *Dyke* #5, 37-49.

Vern and Bonnie Bullough, "Lesbianism in the 1920s and 1930s," *Signs*, v. 2 #4, 895-904.

Blanche Wiesen Cook, "Women Alone Stir my Imagination: Lesbianism and the Cultural Tradition," *Signs*, v. 4 #4 718-739.

Martin Duberman, "I am not Contented: Female Masochism and Lesbianism in Early Twentieth Century New England," in *Women: Sex and Sexuality*, ed. Stimpson.

WEEK 12

Michele Foucault, *The History of Sexuality.*

WEEK 13

Wilhelm Reich, *The Mass Psychology of Fascism.*

Juliet Mitchell, *Psychoanalysis and Feminism*, Part II, chapters 1, 8, 10, 11, 12.

Week 14 CONTEMPORARY ISSUES IN SEXUALITY

Deirdre English, "The Politics of Porn," *Mother Jones* April 1980, 20-23.

Andrea Dworkin, "The Prophet of Perversion," *Mother Jones* April 1980, 24-25.

Richard Goldstein, "Sex on Parole," *Village Voice*, August 21, 1980.

Patricia Califia, "The Secret Side of Lesbian Sexuality," *The Gay Advocate*, December 27, 1979, 19-23.

Tom Reeves, "Of Boys and Baltimore," *Fag Rag*, February-March, 1978, 3-11.

Roles of Women in a Changing World

R. Rohrlich
Anthropology
Borough of Manhattan Community College
The City University of New York

WOMEN IN THE MIDDLE EAST

GENERAL

Antoun, Richard T. "On the Modesty of Women in Arab Muslim Villages," *American Anthropologist*, August, 1968.

Awad, B.A. "The Status of Women in Islam," *Islamic Quarterly*, 8, 1, 2, 1964: 17-24.

Devereux, Robert. "11th Century Muslim Views on Women, Marriage, Love and Sex," *Central Asiatic Journal*, 11, 2, 1966: 134-140.

Hussein, A. "Women in the Muslim World," *World Muslim League Monthly Magazine*, 1, 6, 1965: May, 1964: 22-36.

Vatuk, Vad Prakash. "The Position of Women in Hittite Laws and Manusmurti," *Journal of Asian and African Studies*, 2, 1967, 3, 4: 251-265.

EGYPT

Abu Lugbud, Janet. "Egyptian Marriage Adjustment: Microcosm of a Changing Society," *Marriage and Family Living*, 23, 1961: 127-138.

Dickerman, Lysander, "The Condition of Women in Ancient Egypt," in *Bulletin of the American Geographical Society*, Vol. 26, #4, Part 1, 1894, 494-527.

Douglass, Joseph H., and Katherine W. Douglass. "Aspects of Marriage and Family Living Among Egyptian Peasants," *Marriage and Family Living*, 16, 1954: 45-48.

Nelson, Cynthia. "Changing Roles of Men and Women: Illustrations from Egypt," *Anthropological Quarterly*, 41, 1968: 57-77.

ISRAEL

Agress, Eliya U. *Golda Meir: Portrait of a Prime Minister*.

Bettelheim, Bruno. *The Children of the Dream*.

Barai, Miriam, "Women as Managers in Israel," *Public Administration in Israel and Abroad*, 78-87.

Ben-Josef, A.C. *The Woman in the Kibbutz*.

De Beauvoir, Simone. "On Israeli Woman" *New Outlook*, X, May, 1967, 14-26.

Gottstein, Esther R. *Marriage and First Pregnancy: Cultural Influences on Attitudes of Israeli Women*.

Jacobs, Milton. *A Study of Culture Stability and Change: The Moroccan Jewess*.

Patai, Raphael, *The Hebrew Goddess*.

Rosenfeld, H. "On Determinants of the Status of Arab Village Women," (Israel) *Man*, 60 May, 1960, 66-70.

Rosner, M. "Women in the Kibbutz," *Asian and African Studies*, III, 1967, 35-68.

Spiro, Malford E. *Children of the Kibbutz*.

———, *Kibbutz*.

Stern, Geraldine, *Daughters from Afar: Profiles of Israeli Women*.

Syrkin, Marie, *Golda Meir: Israel's Leader*.

TURKEY

Dobkin, Marlene. "Social Ranking in the Woman's World of Purdah: A Turkish Example," *Anthropological Quarterly*, 40, 1967: 65-72.

Guntekin, Reset Huri, *Autobiography of a Turkish Girl*.

Hansen, H.M. *Daughters of Allah Among the Muslim Women in Kuristan*.

Lewis, Bernard, "Men, Women and Traditions in Turkey," *Geographical Magazine*, 32, 1959, 346-354.

WOMEN IN EUROPE

MEDITERRANEAN COUNTRIES

Aries, Philippe, *Centuries of Childhood: Social History of Family Life*.

Balsdon, J.P. *Roman Woman*.

Campo de Alange, Maria, *La Mujer en Espana*.

De Beauvoir, Simone, *Memoirs of a Dutiful Daughter*.

———, *Force of Circumstance*.

De La Mora, Constancia, *In Place of Splendor* (autobiography of a Spanish Civil War Leader).

Gini, Corradod, and Elio Carant. "The Family in Italy," *Marriage and Family Living*, 15, 1954, 354-361.

Ibarruri, Dolores, *They will not Pass* (autobiography of La Pasionara, Spanish Civil War Leader).

Lambiri, Ioanna, *Social Change in a Greek Country Town: The Impact of Factory Work on the Position of Women*. Research Monograph Series 13.

Moss, Leonard W. and Walter H. Thomson, "The South Italian Family," *Human Organization*, 18, 1959, 35-41.

Riegelhaupt, Joyce F. "Saloio Women: an analysis of informal and formal political and economic roles of Portuguese peasant women," *Anthropological Quarterly*, 40, 1967, 109-126.

Russier, *The Affair of Gabrielle Russier* (tragic affair between woman teacher and male student).

Schein, Muriel, "Only on Sundays," (Greek villages), *Natural History*, LXXX, #4, 1971.

Sweet, Louise E., ed. "Appearance and Reality: Status and Roles of Women in Mediterranean Societies," *Anthropological Quarterly*, 40, 3, 1967.

EASTERN EUROPE

Gorecki, Jan, Divorce in Poland.

Hammel, Eugene A. "The Jewish Mother in Serbia," in Wm. Lockwood, ed. *Essays in Balkan Ethnology*, Kroeber Anthropological Society, Special Publications #1.

Kollontai, Alexandra, Autobiography of a Sexually Emancipated Communist Woman.

Brown, Donald, The Role and Status of Women in the Soviet Union.

Nash, Edmund, "The Status of Women in the U.S.S.R." *Monthly Labor Review*, Vol. 93, #6, 1970.

Tatarinova, Nanazhda, Women in the U.S.S.R.

NORTHERN EUROPE

Aner, Kerstin, Swedish Women Today.

Anthony, Katherine, Feminism in Germany and Scandinavia (1915).

Fleisher, Frederic, The New Sweden.

Hegeler, Inge and Sten, An ABZ of Love (Scandinavian View of Sexuality).

Linner, Birgitta, Sex and Society in Sweden.

Moskin, J. Robert, "The New Contraceptive Society (Sweden)," *Look*, 2/4/69, 50-53.

Puckett, Hugh W. Germany's Women go Forward.

BRITISH ISLES

Arensberg, Conrad M., and Solon T. Kimball, Family and Community in Ireland.

Klein, Viola, Britain's Married Women Workers.

_____, Women's Two Roles.

Messenger, John C. Isle of Ireland.

Mill, John Stuart, The Subjection of Women (1869).

Neff, Wanda, Victorian Working Women, 1832-1850.

Rossi, Alice S., ed. John Stuart Mill and Harriet Taylor: Essays on Sex Equality.

Shaw, George Bernard, "Woman-Man in Petticoats," in Dan H. Laurence, ed. *Platform and Pulpit*.

Wollstonecraft, Mary, Vindication of the Rights of Women (1792).

Woolf, Virginia, A Room of One's Own.

_____ Three Guineas.

WOMEN IN ASIA

GENERAL

Bunch-Weeks, Charlotte, "Asian Women in Revolution," in D. Babcor and M. Belkin, eds., *Liberation Now*.

Goode, William, *World Revolution and Family Patterns*.

Patai, Raphael, ed. *Women in the Modern World*, (section on Asian women).

CHINA

Chao Pu-Wei (Yang), *Autobiography of a Chinese Woman*.

Cusask, Dymphna, *Chinese Women Speak*.

Djamoan, J. *Malay Kinship and Marriage in Singapore*.

_____, *The Muslim Matrimonial Court in Singapore*.

Huang, Jen Lucy, "A Re-evaluation of the Primary Roles of the Communist Chinese Women: The Homemaker or the Worker," *Marriage and Family Living*, 25, 1963, 162-1661.

Levy, H.S. *Chinese Foot-Binding: The History of a Curious Erotic Custom*.

Levy, Marion J. Jr. *The Family Revolution in Modern China*.

Mao, Tse-Tung, Quotations from Chairman Mao! Chapter on Women.

Snow, Helen, *Women in Modern China*.

Treudley, Mary B. *The Men and Women of Chung Ho Ch'ang*.

Van Gulick, R.H. *Sexual Life in Ancient China: A Preliminary Survey of Chinese Sex and Society* from ca. 1500 B.C. until 1644 A.D.

Wolf, Margery, *The House of Lim: A Study of a Chinese Farm Family*.

Wolf, Margery, *Women and the Family in Rural Taiwan*.

INDIA

Habb, Lawrence, "Marriage and Malevolence: The Uses of Sexual Opposition in a Hindu Pantheon," *Ethnology* 9, 1970, 137-148.

Cormak, M.L. *The Hindu Women*.

Berremam, Gerald, "On the Role of Women," (in India and the U.S.A.) *Bulletin of the Atomic Scientists*, 1966.

Cormak, M.L. *The Hindu Woman*.

Goswa , M. and D.N. Majumdar, "A Study of Women's Position among the Garo of Assam," *Man in India*, 45, 1, Jan.-March, 1965, 27-35.

Gough, Kathleen, "Female Initiation Rites on the Malabar Coast," *J. of the Royal Anthropological Institute*, 85, 1955, 45-80.

Ikramullah, S.S. "The Role of Women in the Life and Literature of Pakistan," *Asian Review*, 55, 201, 1959, 14-26.

Kapur, Promilia, *Marriage and Working Women in India*.

Khwaja, B.A. "Attitudes towards Purdah among Muslim Girl Students of Kanpur." *Man in India*, 45, 3, July-Sept., 1965, 223-227.

Muhkerjee, P. "Some Notes on the Study of the 'Woman Question' in Ancient India." *Man in India*, 44, 3, July-Sept., 1965, 264-275.

Nakane, C. *Garo and Khasti: A Comparative Study in Matrilineal Systems.*

Nanda, Savitra D. *The City of Two Gateways: Autobiography of an Indian Girl.*

Pinkham, M. *Women in the Sacred Scriptures of Hinduism.*

Rama, Devi B. "Indian Woman and Her Attitude to Traditional Values," *J. of Psychol. Res.*, 7, 1963, 72-78.

Sengapta, N. *Evolution of Hindu Marriage.*

Vreede-de Stuers, Cora, *Parda: A Study of Muslim Women's Life in Northern India.*

JAPAN

Cressy, E.E. *Daughters of Changing Japan.*

DeVos, George, and Hiroshi Wagatomma, "Value Attitudes Toward Role Behavior of Women in Two Japanese Villages" *Am. Anthropologist.* 63, 1961, 1204-1230.

Geertz, Hildred, *The Japanese Family: A Study of Kinship and Socialization.*

Institute of Advanced Projects, East-West Center, *Women's Movements in Post-War Japan.*

Koyama, Takashi, *The Changing Social Position of Women in Japan.*

Norbeck, Edward, *Changing Japan.*

Tsurumi, Kazuko, *Social Change and the Individual: Japan, Before and After Defeat in W.W. II.*

WOMEN IN AFRICA

Canadian Journal of African Studies, Vol. 6, #2, 1972. Special Issue: African Women.

(Additional journal articles in *Africa, African Women, West African Review*).

Anderson, J.N.D. *Family Law in Asia and Africa.*

Ariwoola, O. *The African Wife* (among the Yoruba in Nigeria).

Beidelman, T.O. *The Kaguru: A Matrilineal People of East Africa.*

Boserup, Ester, *Woman's Role in Economic Development.*

Brandel, M. "The African Career Woman in South Africa," *African Women*, 3, 3, Dec. 1959, 57-59.

Clignet, Rene, *Many Wives, Many Powers.*

Dalton, G. "Bridewealth" vs. "Brideprice", *American Anthropologist* 68, 3, 1966, 732-738.

Douglas, Mary, "A Form of Polyandry among the Lelo," *Africa*, 21, 1951, 1-12.

Gordon, David C. *Women of Algeria: an Essay on Change.*

Herskovits, Melville, "A Note on 'Woman Marriage' in Dahomey," *Africa*, 10, 1937, 3:335-341.

Kaberry, Phyllis M. *Women of the Grassfields.*

Leith-Ross, Sylvia, *African Woman: A Study of the Ibo of Nigeria.*

Levine, Robert Z. "Sex Roles and Economic Change in Africa," *Ethnology*, 1966.

Netting, Robert M. "Marital Relations in the Jos Plateau of Nigeria—Women's Weapons: The Politics of Domesticity among the Kofyar," *American Anthropologist*, Dec. 1969.

Nukunv, G.K. *Kinship and Marriage among the Anlo Ewe.*

Okediji, F.O. "Some Social Psychological Aspects of Fertility among Married Women in an African City," *Nigerian Journal of Economic and Social Studies*, 9, 1, 1967, 67-79.

Okoth, Sonya, "Liberation Must also Include the Women of Africa," in D. Babcox and M. Belkin, eds., *Liberation Now.*

Patai, Raphael, ed. *Women in the Modern World* (section on Africa).

Paulme, Denise, *Women of Tropical Africa.*

Radcliffe-Brown, A.R., and D. Forde, eds., *African Systems of Marriage and Kinship.*

Richards, Audrey I. *Chisunga: A Girl's Initiation Ceremony among the Bamba of Northern Rhodesia.*

Simons, N.J. *African Women: Their Legal Status in South Africa.*

Southall, Aiden, ed. "The Position of Women and the Stability of Marriage," *Social Change in Modern Africa.*

Talbot, D.A. *Woman's Mysteries of a Primitive People: The Ibibios of Southern Nigeria.*

Turnbull, Colin, *The Forest People.*

———, *The Lonely African.*

NOVELS

Aluko, T.M. *One Man, One Wife.*

Amadi, E. *The Concubine.*

Bediako, K.A. *A Husband for Esi Ellua.*

Dipoko, M.S. *Because of Women.*

Easmon, R.S. *The Burnt-out Marriage.*

Konadu, A. *A Women in her Prime.*

———, *Come Back Dora.*

Totuola, Amos, *The Brave African Huntress.*

Smith, Mary R. *Baba of Karo: A Woman of the Muslim Hausa* (Autobiography recorded by Mary Smith).

Earthy, E. Dora, *Valenge Women: The Social & Economic Life of the Valenge. Women of Portugese East Africa.*

Mair, Lucy, *African Marriage and social change.*

WOMEN IN NORTH AMERICA: INDIAN AND ESKIMO

Bennett, Kay, *Kiabah: Recollection of a Navajo Girlhood.*

Briggs, Jean L. "Kaplunga Daughter: Living With Eskimos," *Transaction*, 7, 1970, 12-24.

———, *Never In Anger.*

Hammsey, Leila Shukry, "The Role of Women in a Changing Navaho Society," *American Anthropologist*, 59, 1957, 101.

Landes, Ruth, *Ojibwa Women*.

Marriott, Alice, *Maria: The Potter of San Ildefonso* (Pueblo Indian).

O'Meara, Walter, *Daughters of the Country: The Women of the Fur Traders and Mountain Men* (Indian women on the American frontier).

Qoyawagne, P. *No Turning Back* (Hopi Indian Girl's Struggle to Bridge the Gap between Two Worlds).

Richards, Cara, "Matriarchy or Mistake: The Role of Iroquois Women through Time," in Verne F. Ray, ed. *Cultural Stability and Cultural Change*.

Shipeck, Florence C. *The Autobiography of Delfina Cuero, A Diegueno Indian*.

Spindler, Louise S. *Menomini Women and Culture Change*. *American Anthropologist* Memoir #91.

Qookar, Elizabeth, "Masking and Matrilineality in North America," *American Anthropologist*, Dec. 1968.

Washburne, Heluiz C. *Land of the Good Shadows* (Life story of Ananta, an Eskimo woman).

WOMEN IN THE WEST INDIES

GENERAL

Pescatello, Ann, Female and Male in Latin America.

Otterbein, Keith F. "Caribbean Family Organization: A Comparative Analysis," *American Anthropologist*, 67, 1965, 66-79.

Patai, Raphael, ed. *Women in the Modern World*.

Smith, Raymond T. "Culture and Social Structure in the Caribbean: Some Recent Work on Family and Kinship Studies," in Michael M. Horowitz, ed. *Peoples and Cultures of the Caribbean*.

Smith, Raymond T. "The Family in the Caribbean," in Vera Rubin, ed. *Caribbean Studies: A Symposium*.

Stevens, Evelyn P. "Marianismo: The Other Face of Machismo in Latin America," Paper presented at meeting, Latin American Studies Assn., Dec. 1971.

BAHAMAS

Otterbein, Keith F. *The Andros Islanders: A study of Family Organization*.

CUBA

Berman, Joan, "Women in Cuba," *Women: A Journal of Liberation*, January, 1970.

Camarano, Chris, "On Cuban Women," in D. Babcox and M. Belkin, eds. *Liberation Now*.

Castro, Fidel, and Linda Jenness, Women and the Cuban Revolution.

Gordon, Linda, "Speculations on Women's Liberation in Cuba," *Women: A Journal of Liberation*, Summer, 1970, Vol. 1, #4.

Mulhare, Mirta T. "The Cult of Virginity and the Double Standard," Paper presented at meeting, AAA, Nov., 1971.

Oleson, Virginia, "Context and Posture: Notes on Socio-Cultural Aspects of Women's Role and Family Policy in Contemporary Cuba," *Journal of Marriage and the Family*, August, 1971.

GUYANA

Smith, Raymond T. The Negro Family in British Guiana.

HAITI

Bouchereau, M.G. Haiti et ses Femmes: une Etude d'Evolution Culturelle.

Mintz, Sidney, "The Employment of Capital by Market Women in Haiti" in R. Firth and B.S. Yamey, eds. *Capital, Saving and Credit in Peasant Societies*.

JAMAICA

Blake, Judith, Family Structure in Jamaica.

Clarke, Edith, My Mother Who Fathered Me: A Study of the Family in Three Selected Communities in Jamaica.

Cohen, Yehudi A. "Four Categories of Interpersonal Relationships in the Family and Community in a Jamaica Village," in Michael M. Horowitz, ed. *Peoples and Cultures of the Caribbean*.

Henriques, Fernando, Family and Color in Jamaica.

MARTINIQUE

Horowitz, Michael M. "A Decision Model of Conjugal Patterns in Martinique," *Peoples and Cultures of the Caribbean*.

PUERTO RICO

Hill, Reuben, J.M. Stycos, and K.W. Back, The Family and Population Control.

Landy, David, Tropical Childhood.

Lewis, Oscar, La Vida.

Regler, Lloyd H., and August B. Hollingshead. Trapped: Families and Schizophrenia.

WOMEN IN MEXICO AND CENTRAL AMERICA

Aramoni, Aniceto, "Machismo," *Psychology Today*, January, 1972.

Cancian, Francesca M. "Affection and Dominance in Zinacantan and Cambridge Families," *J. of Marriage and the Family*, Feb., 1971.

Chinas, Beverly, The Isthmus Zapotecs.

Covarrubias, Miguel, Mexico South: The Isthmus of Tehuantepec.

Cruening, Ernest, Mexico and Its Heritage (section on Woman, 623-634).

Cosminsky, Sheila, "Sex Differences in Illnesses of Emotional Origin In a Guatemalan Community." Paper, meeting, AAA, 1971.

Hellbon, Ann-Britta, La Participacion Cultural de las Mujeres Indias y Mestizas en el Mexico precortesano y postrevolucionario. Monograph Series Pub. 10. Stockholm: The Ethnographical Museum, Eng. summary.

Hoyos, Arturo, and G. de Hoyos, "The Amigo System and Alienation of the Wife in the Conjugal Mexican Family," in B. Farber, ed., *Kinship And Family Organization.*

Langner, T.S. "Psychophysiological Symptoms and the Status of Women in Two Mexican Communities," in J.M. Murphy and A. Leighton, eds. *Approaches to Cross-Cultural Psychiatry.*

Lewis, Oscar. Five Families.

————, Pedro Martinez.

————, Children of Sanchez.

Millan, Verna C. Mexico Reborn ("Freedom for Mexican Women," ch. 7).

Minturn, Leigh, et al. Mothers in Six Cultures (includes Mexico).

Morton, Ward M. Woman Suffrage in Mexico.

Gamio de Alba, Margarita, La Mujer Indigena de Centro America, Mexico: Ediciones Especiales del Instituto Indigenista Interamerican.

Macias, Anna, Mexican Women in the Social Revolution, Paper presented at the AHA annual meeting, 1972.

Sattles, J.D. "Jalacingo Woman: An Individual and Her Society," *Phylon,* 16, 1, 1955, 41-55.

Solien, Nancie L. "Some Aspects of Child-Bearing and Child Rearing in a Guatemalan Latino Community," *Southwestern J. of Anthropology,* 19, 1963, 411-423.

Torres de Ianello, Reina. La Mujer Cuna de Panama, Mexico, D.F.: Ediciones Especiales del Instituto Indigenista Interamericana.

WOMEN IN SOUTH AMERICA

GENERAL

Buitron, A. "Situacion Economica, Social y culturel de la Mujer en los paises andionos," American indig., 16, 2, Apr., 1965, 83-92.

Carluci, M.A. La Couvade en Sudamerica," Runa, 6, 1-2, 53-54, 152-174, 1955.

BRAZIL

Biocca, Ettore, Yanoama: The Narrative of a White Girl Kidnapped by Amazonian Indians.

de Jesus, Carolina Maria, Child of the Dark (Woman in Sao Paulo favela).

Landes, Ruth, The City of Women (Negro Women Cult Leaders of Bahia).

Shapiro, Judith, "Male Bonds and Female Bonds: An Illustrative Comparison" (Yanomama and Mindurucu). Paper, AAA meeting, 1971.

ECUADOR

Scrimshaw, Susan C. A Description of Non-Coresidential Polygyny in Spanish Ecuado, Paper, AAA meeting, 1971.

Whitten Norman E. Ritual Enactment of Sex Roles in the Pacific Lowlands of Ecuado-Colombia, Paper, AAA meeting, 1971.

PERU

Bolton Ralph Tawanku: Intercouple Bonds in a Quolla Village, Paper, AAA meeting, 1971.

CHILE

Cha Elsa M. The Mobilization of Women in Allende's Chile.

Class and Gender

Gita Sen
Economics
New School for Social Research
Fall, Spring 1980
Graduate

This sequence deals with the interaction between class relations and gender relations with particular reference to capitalist production and reproduction. This course deals with methodological and conceptual issues in the treatment of gender as a social (as opposed to a biological) category, and develops the connections between different forms of women's work and the process of capital accumulation in the advanced capitalist countries. Problems such as labor force participation, occupational segregation, and domestic work among others will be addressed from both neoclassical and Marxist-feminist perspectives.

PART I

*Required reading

I. THE CONCEPT OF GENDER

*G. Rubin, "The traffic in women: notes on the political economy of sex," in R. Reiter (ed) *Toward an anthropology of women*, Monthly Review Press, New York, 1975.

*M. Rosaldo, "Women, culture and society: a theoretical overview," in M. Rosaldo and L. Lamphere (eds) *Woman, Culture and Society*, Stanford University Press, Stanford, 1974.

II. ORIGINS—PRIVATE PROPERTY AND GENDER RELATIONS

E. Leacock, "Women in egalitarian societies," in R. Bridenthal and C. Koonz (ed) *Becoming visible: women in European history*, Houghton Mifflin, 1977.

*R. Reiter, "The search for origins: unraveling the threads of gender hierarchy," *Critique of Anthropology*, vol 3, #9 & 10, 1977.

*F. Engels, *The origin of the family, private property and the state*, International Publ., NY, 1973, pp. 7-146.

P. Aaby, "Engels and women," *Critique of Anthropology*, vol. 3, #9 & 10, 1977.

*K. Gough, "The origin of the family," in *Reiter*.

K. Sacks, "Engels revisited: women, the organization of production and private property," in *Reiter*.

J.H. Moore, "The exploitation of women in evolutionary perspective," *Critique of Anthropology*, vol. 3, #9 & 10, 1977.

C. Meillassoux, *Femmes, greniers et capitaux*, Maspero, Paris, 1975.

R. Rapp, "Brief review of Meillassoux' Femmes, Greniers et Capitaux," *Dialectical Anthropology*, Dec 1977.

B. O'Laughlin, "Production and reproduction: Meillassoux' F, G, et C," *Critique of Anthropology*, vol. 3, #8, 1977.

*M. Mackintosh, "Reproduction and patriarchy: a critique of Meillassoux' F,G, et C," *Capital and Class*, 2, 1977.

III. CONCEPTS—PRODUCTION, REPRODUCTION AND THE SEXUAL DIVISION OF LABOR

R. Bridenthal, "The dialectics of production and reproduction in history," *Radical America*, March-April, 1976.

J. Kelly-Gadol, "The social relation of the sexes: methodological implications of women's history," *Signs*, Summer 1976.

*Edholm, Harris and Young, "Conceptualising women," *Critique of Anthropology*, vol 3, #9 & 10, 1977.

*L. Beneria, "Reproduction, production and the sexual division of labor," *Cambridge Journal of Economics*, 1979.

G. Sen, "The sexual division of labor and the working class family: towards a conceptual synthesis of class relations and the subordination of women" *Review of Radical Political Economics*, vol 12, #2, Summer 1980.

IV. ALTERNATIVE VIEWS ON GENDER AND CLASS UNDER CAPITALISM

—Structural views

*J. Mitchell, "Four structures in a complex unity," in B. Carroll (ed) *Liberating Women's History*, University of Illinois Press, 1976.

_____, *Woman's Estate*, Vintage Books, NY, 1973, esp Part II.

M.E. Gimenez, "Structuralist Marxism on 'the woman question'," *Science and Society*, Fall 1978.

(For a useful introduction to Althusser, see A. Callinicos, *Althusser's Marxism*, Pluto Press, 1976).

—Patriarchy

*Z. Eisenstein (ed) *Capitalist Patriarchy and the case for Socialist Feminism*, MR Press, NY, 1979, esp chs 1, 2, 3.

L. Phelps, "Patriarchy and capitalism," *Quest*, Fall 1975.

*H. Hartmann, "The unhappy marriage of Marxism and feminism: towards a more progressive union," *Capital and Class*, Summer 1979.

—Housework debate

M. Benston, "The political economy of women's liberation," *Monthly Review*, April 1969.

M. Coulson, B. Magas and H. Wainwright, "The housewife and her labor under capitalism—a critique," *New Left Review*, #89, 1975.

*M. Dalla Costa and S. James, *The power of women and the subversion of the community*, Falling Wall Press, 1973.

T. Fee, "Domestic labor: an analysis of housework and its relation to the production process," *RRPE*, Spring 1976.

J. Gardiner, "Women's domestic labor," *NLR*, #89, 1975.

_____, S. Himmelweit and M. Mackintosh, "Women's domestic labor," *Bulletin of the Conference of Socialist Economists*, #2, 1975.

I. Gerstein, "Domestic work and capitalism," *Radical America*, #4 & 5, 1973.

I. Gough and J. Harrison, "Unproductive labor and housework again," *Bulletin of CSE, #1, 1975.*

*S. Himmelweit and S. Mohun, "Domestic labor and capital," *Cambridge Journal of Economics*, #1, 1977.

W. Seccombe, "The housewife and her labor under capitalism," *NLR, #83, 1974.*

_____, "Domestic labor—a reply to critics," *NLR, #94, 1975.*

*B. Weinbaum and A. Bridges, "The other side of the paycheck—monopoly and the structure of consumption," *Monthly Review*, July-August 1976.

V. LABOR FORCE PARTICIPATION AND SEGREGATION—ORTHODOX APPROACHES

H. Kahne with A.I. Kohen, "Economic perspectives on the roles of women in the American economy," *Journal of Economic Literature*, Dec 1975.

J. Kreps, *Sex in the marketplace: American women at work*, Johns Hopkins Press, 1971.

A.O. Krueger, "The economics of discrimination," *J of Political Economy*, Oct 1963.

J.N. Hedges, "Women workers and manpower demands in the 1970's," *Monthly Labor Review*, June 1970.

H. Zellner, "Discrimination against women, occupational segregation and the relative wage," *American Economic Review*, May 1972.

*J. Madden, *The economics of sex discrimination*, esp ch 2 (survey of empirical studies).

J. Gwartney and R. Stroup, "Measurement of employment discrimination according to sex," *Southern Economic Journal*, April 1973.

*C. Lloyd, *Sex, discrimination and the division of labor*, Columbia U. Press, 1975, esp chs 2, 4, 11.

E. Gross, "Plus ca change....the sexual structure of occupations over time," *Social Problems*, 16 (2), 1968, pp 198-208.

*J. Mincer, "Labor force participation of married women," in NBER, *Aspects of labor economics*, 1962.

*_____ & S. Polachek, "Family investment in human capital: earnings of women," *J of Political Economy*, March-April 1974.

V.K. Oppenheimer, The female labor force in the US, U of Calif., *Berkeley Population Monographs*, #5, 1969.

V. Fuchs, "Recent trends and long run prospects for female earnings," *American Economic Review*, May 1974.

I.V. Sawhill, "The economics of discrimination against women: some new findings," *J of Human Resources*, Summer 1973.

*R.W. Smuts, "The female labor force: a case study in the interpretation of historical statistics," *J of the American Statistical Association*, March 1960.

E.S. Phelps, "The statistical theory of racism and sexism," *AER, vol 62*, 1972.

V.K. Oppenheimer, "The interaction of demand and supply and its effect on the female labor force in the US," *Population Studies* vol 21, #3, 1967.

F. Blau and C. Jusenius, "Economists' approaches to sex segregation in the labor market," in M. Blaxall and B. Reagan (eds) *Women and the Workplace*, Univ of Chicago Press, 1976.

J. Madden, "The development of economic thought on the woman problem," *RRPE*, Summer 1972.

VI. CAPITALISM AND GENDER—HISTORICAL EVIDENCE

A. Western Europe
Wage Labor

(For background, F. Engels, The condition of the working class in England, Panther Books, 1969; and E.P. Thompson, The making of the English working class, Vintage, NY, 1963).

*R.T. Vann, "Toward a new lifestyle: women in preindustrial capitalism," in *Bridenthal and Koonz*.

*M.L McDougall, "Working class women during the industrial revolution, 1780-1914," in *Bridenthal and Koonz*.

*T.M. McBride, "The long road home: women's work and industrialization," in *Bridenthal and Koonz*.

*I. Pinchbeck, *Women workers and the industrial revolution: 1750-1850* Kelley, NY, 1969.

A. Clark, *Working life of women in the 17th century*, Harcourt, Brace and Howe, NY, 1920.

M. Hewitt, *Wives and mothers in Victorian industry*, Rockliff, London 1958.

B.L. Hutchins, *Women in modern industry*, Bell & Sons, London, 1915.

W. Neff, *Victorian working women*, Allen and Unwin, London, 1929.

E. Richards, "Women in the British economy since about 1700: an interpretation," *History*, 59, 1974.

J. Foster, *Class struggle and the industrial revolution: early industrial capitalism in three English towns*," Weidenfeld and Nicolson, London, 1974.

_____, "Nineteenth century towns—a class dimension," in H.J. Dyos (ed) *The study of urban history*, Edward Arnold, London.

*P. Stearns, "Working class women in Britain, 1890-1914," in M. Vicinus (ed) *Suffer and be still: women in the Victorian age*, Indiana U Press, Bloomington, 1972.

F. Clark, *The position of women in contemporary France*, King & Son London, 1937.

R. Jacoby, "Feminism and class consciousness in the British and American Women's Trade Union Leagues, 1890-1925," in *Carroll*.

*B. Taylor, "The men are as bad as their masters: socialism, feminism and sexual antagonism in the London tailoring trade in the early 1830's," *Feminist Studies*, Spring 1979.

I. Pinchbeck and M. Hewitt, *Children in English society*, vol II, esp pp 387-413.

N.J. Smelser, *Social change and the industrial revolution*, chs 9-11.

V. Goddard, "Domestic industry in Naples," *Critique of Anthropology*, vol 3, #9, & 10, 1977.

J. & D. Walkowitz, "We are not beasts of the field: prostitution and the poor in Plymouth and Southampton under the Contagious Diseases Act," *Feminist Studies*, I, 1973.

Working class families and domestic work

H.J. Habbakuk, "Family structure and economic change in 19th century Europe," *Journal of Economic History*, 1955.

*N.J. Smelser, "The industrial revolution and the British working class family," *Journal of Social History*, 1, pp 17-35.

*Lutz K. Berkner, "Recent research on the history of the family in Western Europe," *Journal of Marriage and the Family*, Aug 1973.

*J. Scott and L. Tilly, "Women's work and family in 19th century Europe," *Comparative Studies in Society and History*, 3, 1975.

*_____, *Women, work and family*, Houghton Mifflin, 1978.

*L. Oren, "The welfare of women in working class families; England, 1860-1950," *Feminist Studies*, 1, 1973.

F. Collier, *The family economy of the working classes in the cotton industry, 1784-1833*, Manchester U Press, 1964.

M. Anderson, *Family Structure in 19th century Lancashire*, Cambridge U Press, 1971.

*_____, "Household structure and the industrial revolution: mid 19th century Preston in comparative perspective," in P. Laslett (ed) *Household and family in past time*, Cambridge U Press, 1972.

P. Laslett, "Mean household size in England since the 16th century," in *Laslett*.

J. Humphries, "Class struggle and the persistence of the working class family," *Cambridge Journal of Economics*, Sept 1977.

*_____, "Working class family, women's liberation and class struggle: the case of 19th century British history," RRPE, Fall 1977.

*G. Sen, "Class struggle and the working class family—a comment," mimeo, August 1978.

Nancy Tomes, "A 'torrent of abuse': crimes of violence between working class men and women in London, 1840-75" *Journal of Social History*, Spring 1978.

B. United States

Wage labor

E. Abbott, *Women in industry*, NY, Arno Press, 1969.

*_____, "A history of industrial employment of women in the US," *J of Political Economy*, 14, 1906, pp 461-501.

_____, "Employment of women in industries: cigar making, its history and present tendencies," *JPE*, 15, Jan 1907, pp 1-25.

E.F. Baker, *Technology and women's work*, NY, Columbia U Press, 1964.

W.H. Chafe, *The American woman: her changing social, economic and political roles, 1920-70*. (protective legislation)

E. Beardsley, *Women and the trades*, Arno Press, 1969.

R. Baxandall, L. Gordon and S. Reverby, *America's working women: a documentary history*, Vintage Books, NY, 1976.

_____, "Boston working women protest, 1869," *Signs*, Vol 1, #3, part 1.

M.J. Buhle, "Women and the socialist party, 1910-14," *Radical America* 4, #2, Feb 1970.

W.E. Brownlee and M.M. Brownlee, *Women in the American economy: a documentary history*, Yale Univ Press, 1976.

*P. Branca, "A new perspective on women's work: a comparative typology," *J of Social History*, 9, 1975, pp 129-153.

*G. Kolko, "Working wives: their effects on the structure of the working class," *Science and Society*, Fall 1978.

T. Dublin, "Women, work and protest in the early Lowell mills," *Labor History*, Winter 1975.

P. Foner, *The factory girls*, U of Illinois Press, 1977.

*H. Hartman, "Capitalism, patriarchy and job segregation by sex," *Signs*, vol 1, #3, part 2, pp 137-169; also in *Eisenstein*.

*Meredith Tax, *The Rising of the Women—Feminist solidarity and class conflict, 1880-1917*, NY, MR Press, 1980.

Philip Foner, *Women workers and trade unions* (this is not the exact title, but this is a recently published history).

*M.E.J. Kelly, "Women and the labor movement," *North American Review* March 1898.

G. Lerner, "The lady and the mill girl: changes in the status of women in the age of Jackson," in R.W. Hogeland (ed) *Women and womanhood in America*, D.C. Heath and Co., 1973.

W. O'Neill (ed), *Women at work*, Chicago, Quadrangle Books, 1972.

M.J. Soltow et al, *Women in American labor history: 1825-1935*, Michigan State Univ Press. (annotated bibliography).

A. Wolfe (ed), "Letters of a Lowell mill girl and friends, 1845-46," *Labor History*, vol 17, 1976, pp 96-108.

M. Davies, "The feminization of the clerical labor force," *Radical America*, July-Aug 1974; also in *Eisenstein*.

Dye, "Creating a feminist alliance: sisterhood and class conflict in the New York women's trade union league," *Feminist Studies*, vol 2, #3, 1975, pp 24-38.

Teresa Wolfson, *The woman worker and the trade unions*.

W. Bolin, "The economics of middle income family life: working women in the Great Depression," *Journal of American History*, LXIV, 1978, pp 60-74.

Ruth Milkman, "Woman's work and the economic crisis: some lessons from the Great Depression," RRPE, Spring 1976.

Jane Humphries, "Women: scapegoats and safety valves in the Great Depression," RRPE, Spring 1976.

William Breen, "Black women and the Great War: mobilization and reform in the South," *Journal of Southern History*; LXIV 1978, pp 421-440.

David Katzman, *Seven days a week: women and domestic service in industrializing America*, 1978.

Working class families and domestic work

R. Rapp, "Family and class in contemporary America: notes toward an understanding of ideology," *Science and Society*, Fall 1978.

Nancy Folbre, *Patriarchy and Capitalism in New England, 1650-1900*, unpublished Ph. D. dissertation, Univ. of Massachusetts, May 1979 (also see her article in *RRPE*, Summer 1980).

*C.S. Bell, "Working women's contribution to family income," *Eastern Economic Journal*, April-July 1974.

P. Greven, "The average size of families and households in the province of Massachusetts in 1764 and in the US in 1790: an overview," in *Laslett*.

R.V. Wells, "Demographic change and the life cycle of American families," *J of Interdisciplinary History*, #2, 1971.

T. Hareven, "Family time and industrial time," *J of Urban History*, May 1975.

*L. Glasco, "The life cycles and household structure of American ethnic groups," *J of Urban History*, May 1975.

D.J. Walkowitz, "Working class women in the gilded age: factory, community and family life among the Cohoes, NY cotton workers," *J of Social History*, Summer 1972.

V.Y. McLaughlin, "Patterns of work and family organization: Buffalo Italians," *J of Interdisciplinary History*, Autumn 1971.

A. Gordon, M.J. Buhle and N. Schram, "Women in American society," *Radical America*, July-August 1971.

*R.M. Jacoby, "Feminism and class consciousness in the British and American women's trade union leagues," in *Carroll*.

M. Ryan, *Womanhood in America*, NY, Franklin Watts, 1975.

*B. Welter, "The cult of true womanhood, 1820-1860," in M. Gordon (ed) *The American family in sociohistorical perspective*, NY, St Martin's Press 1973.

E. Pleck, "The two parent household: black family structure in late 19th century Boston," *J of Social History*, 6, 1972.

*L. Rainwater and W.L. Yancey, *The Moynihan report and the politics of controversy*, Cambridge Mass, 1967 (includes the report itself).

Joan Jensen, "Cloth, butter and boarders: women's household production for the market," *RRPE*, vol 12, #2, Summer 1980.

H. Gutman, *The black family in slavery and freedom, 1750-1925*, Vintage, NY, 1977.

A. Billingsley, *Black families in white America*, Englewood Cliffs, NJ, Prentice Hall, 1968.

*R.L. Blumberg and M.P. Garcia, "The political economy of the mother-child family: a cross-societal view," in L. Lenero-Otero (ed) *Beyond the nuclear family model*, London Sage Publ, 1976.

*C. Stack, *All our kin: strategies for survival in a black community*, NY, Harper and Row, 1974.

J. Modell and Hareven, "Urbanization and the malleable household: an examination of boarding and lodging in American families," in T. Hareven (ed) *Family and kin in urban communities, 1700-1930*, NY, Franklin Watts, 1977.

*R. Staples, "Towards a sociology of the black family: a theoretical and methodological assessment," *J of Marriage and the Family* 1971, pp 119-138.

Biological reproduction and control over fertility

Linda Gordon, *Woman's Body, Woman's Right—Birth Control in America*, Penguin Books, 1977.

Nancy Aries, "Abortion clinics and the organization of work—a case study of Charles Circle," *RRPE*, vol 12, #2, Summer 1980.

Kristin Booth Glen, "Abortion in the courts: a laywoman's guide to the new disaster area," *Feminist Studies*, vol 4, #1, Feb 1978, pp 1-26.

Barbara Ehrenreich and John Ehrenreich, *The American health empire: power, profits and politics*, NY, Random House, 1970.

PART II

The second course in this sequence is designed to develop an understanding of the interconnections between social production, reproduction and the sexual division of labor in the context of women in the Third World and in the transition to socialism. Specific emphasis will be placed on the changes in the position of women brought about by such processes of capitalist transition as the differentiation of the peasantry, proletarianization and the penetration of foreign capital. Concepts such as reproduction, household, domestic work, patriarchy will be developed further through a comparison of social change in the Third World and under advanced capitalism. Neoclassical theories of population growth and control will be examined, along with alternative formulations. The interaction between socialism and the liberation of women will be examined.

Signs, Special issue on *Women and National Development*, Autumn 1977.

E. Boserup, *Woman's role in economic development*, St. Martin's Press, NY, 1970.

Latin American Perspectives, Special issue on *Women and class struggle*, 1977.

_____, Special issue on *Population and imperialism*, and *Women in revolution*, Fall 1977.

I. Tinker and B. Bramsen (ed), *Women and world development*, Overseas Development Council, 1976.

June Nash and H. Safa (ed), *Sex and class in Latin America*, Praeger, 1976.

R. Reiter (ed), *Toward an anthropology of women*, MR Press, NY, 1975.

M. Rosaldo and L. Lamphere (ed), *Woman, culture and society*, Stanford U Press, 1974.

L. Iglitzin and R. Ross (ed), *Women in the world: a comparative study*, ABC Clio, Santa Barbara, 1976.

R. Rohrlich-Leavitt (ed) *Women in cross-cultural perspective*, Paris, Mouton, 1975.

I. ORIGINS—PRECAPITALIST PRODUCTION AND GENDER STRATIFICATION

E. Leacock, "Women in egalitarian societies," in R. Bridenthal and C. Koonz (ed) *Becoming visible: women in European history*, Houghton Mifflin, 1977.

R. Reiter, "The search for origins: unraveling the threads of gender hierarchy," *Critique of Anthropology*, vol 3, #9 & 10, 1977.

*F. Engels, *The origin of the family, private property and the state*, International Publ. NY, 1973, pp. 7-146.

*P. Aaby, "Engels and women," *Critique of Anthropology*, vol 3, #9 & 10, 1977.

K. Gough, "The origin of the family," in *Reiter*.

K. Sacks, "Engels revisited: women, the organization of production and private property," in *Reiter*.

J.H. Moore, "The exploitation of women in evolutionary perspective," *Critique of Anthropology*, vol 3, #9 & 10, 1977.

C. Meillassoux, *Femmes, greniers et capitaux*, Maspero, Paris, 1975.

R. Rapp, "Brief review of Meillassoux' Femmes, Greniers et Capitaux," *Dialectical Anthropology*, Dec 1977.

B. O'Laughlin, "Production and reproduction: Meillassoux' F,G, et C," *Critique of Anthropology*, vol 3, #8, 1977.

M. Mackintosh, "Reproduction and patriarchy: a critique of Meillassoux' F,G, et C," *Capital and Class*, 2, 1977.

II. CONCEPTS—PRODUCTION, REPRODUCTION AND THE SEXUAL DIVISION OF LABOR

R. Bridenthal, "The dialectics of production and reproduction in history," *Radical America*, March-April, 1976.

J. Kelly-Gadol, "The social relation of the sexes: methodological implications of women's history," *Signs*, Summer 1976.

Edholm, Harris and Young, "Conceptualising women," *Critique of Anthropology*, vol 3, #9 & 10, 1977.

*L. Beneria, "Reproduction, production and the sexual division of labor," *Cambridge Journal of Economics*, 1979.

*G. Sen, "The sexual division of labor and the working class family: towards a conceptual systhesis of class relations and the subordination of women" mimeo, Dec 1979.

III. WOMEN AND "ECONOMIC DEVELOPMENT"

E. Boserup.

S. Huntington, "Issues in woman's role in economic development: critique and alternatives," *Journal of Marriage and the family*, vol 37, #4, 1975.

L. Beneria and G. Sen, "Modernization or accumulation: Boserup revisited," mimeo.

Articles in *Tinker and Bramsen*—Tinker, Figueroa, Youssef, Childers.

Articles in *Signs*—Elliott, Pala, Papanek, Reflections on the Conference.

D. Remy, "Underdevelopment and the experience of women: a Nigerian case-study," in *Reiter*.

J. van Allen, "African women, 'modernization' and national liberation," in *Iglitzin and Ross*.

IV. CAPITALIST TRANSITION AND THE SEXUAL DIVISION OF LABOR

i) Peasant differentiation and patriarchy

C.D. Deere and A. de Janvry, "A conceptual framework for the empirical analysis of peasants," *American Journal of Agricultural Economics*, Nov 1979.

_____, "Changing social relations of production and Peruvian peasant women's work," *Latin American Perspectives*, 4, 1977.

_____, "The differentiation of the peasantry and family structure: a Peruvian case study," *Journal of Family History*, vol 3, #4, 1978.

K. Young, "Modes of appropriation and the sexual division of labor: a case study from Oaxaca, Mexico," in A. Kuhn and A. Wolpe (eds) *Feminism and Materialism*, Routledge and Kegan Paul, London, 1978.

A. Stoler, "Class structure and female autonomy in rural Java," in *Signs*.

A. Rubbo, "The spread of capitalism in rural Colombia: effects on poor women," in *Reiter*.

G. Sen, "Women workers and agrarian change."

ii) Subsistence production and proletarianization

S. Young, "Fertility and famine: women's agricultural history in Southern Mozambique", in *The Roots of Rural Poverty in Central and Southern Africa* (eds) R. Palmer and N. Parsons, Univ. of California Press, 1977.

*C.D. Deere, "Rural women's subsistence production in the capitalist periphery," *Review of Radical Political Economics*, Spring 1976.

*G. Sen, "Peasant production, domestic labor and the value of labor power", mimeo.

J. Bukh, "The village woman in Ghana", Scandinavian Institute of African Studies, Uppsala, 1979.

*Z. Tadesse, "The impact of land reform on women: the case of Ethiopia", forthcoming in L. Beneria, ed., *Women's Work in rural economies*, ILO.

iii) Migration

E. Jelin, "Migration and labor force participation of Latin American women: the domestic servants in the cities", in *Signs*.

M. Smith, "The female domestic servant and social change: Lima, Peru", in *Rohrlich-Leavitt*.

Y. Moses, "Female status, the family, and male dominance in a West Indian community", in *Signs*.

N. Sudarkasa, "Women and migration in contemporary West Africa" in *Signs*.

K. Young, "Sex-specificity in migration: a case study from Mexico", forthcoming in *Berneria*.

iv) Women's labor force participation in the urban areas

H. Saffioti, "Relationships of sex and social class in Brazil", in *Nash and Safa*.

G.G. Salazar, "Participation of women in the Mexican labor force", in *Nash and Safa*.

N. Aguiar, "The impact of industrialization on women's work roles in Northeast Brazil", in *Nash and Safa*.

E. Jelin, "The Bahiana in the labor force in Salvador, Brazil", in *Nash and Safa*.

*L. Arizpe, "Women in the informal labor sector: the case of Mexico city", in *Signs*.

N.S. Chinchilla, "Industrialization, monopoly capitalism, and women's work in Guatemala", in *Signs*.

V. Piho, "Life and labor of the woman textile worker in Mexico", in *Rohrlich-Leavitt*.

B. Silvestrini Pacheco, "Women as workers: the experience of the Puerto Rican woman in the 1930's", in *Rohrlich-Leavitt*.

N. Lustig and T. Rendon, "Female employment, occupational status, and socioeconomic characteristics of the family in Mexico", *Signs*, Autumn 1979.

M. Navarro, "Research on Latin American women—review essay", *Signs*, Autumn 1979.

H. Safa, "The changing class composition of the female labor force in Latin America", in *Latin American Perspectives*, Fall 1977.

J. Elizaga, "The participation of women in the labor force in Latin America: fertility and other factors", *International Labor Review*, May-June 1974.

v) Multinational firms and women's employment

R. Grossman, "Women's place in the integrated circuit" *Southeast Asia Chronicle*, Jan-Feb 1979.

A. Lin Neumann, "'Hospitality girls' in the Phillipines", *Southeast Asia Chronicle*, Jan-Feb 1979.

D. Elson and R. Pearson, "The internationalization of capital and its implications for women in the Third World", forthcoming in *The Subordination of Women in the Development Process*, Institute for Development Studies, Sussex.

V. POPULATION CONTROL AND BIRTH-CONTROL

*M. Gimenez, "Population and capitalism", *Latin American Perspectives*, Fall 1977.

B. Mass, "Puerto Rico: a case study of population control", *Latin American Perspectives*, Fall 1977.

_____, *Population target: the political economy of population control in Latin America*.

*K. Young, "The social determinants of fertility", mimeo.

M. Mamdani, *The Myth of Population Control*, MR Press, 1972.

R. Meek, ed, *Marx and Engels on the Population Bomb*, Ramparts Press, 1971.

N. Folbre, "Population growth and capitalist development in Zongolica, Veracruz", *Latin American Perspectives*, Fall 1977.

B. White, "Demand for labour and population growth in colonial Java", *Human Ecology* Vol 1, 1973, pp 217-239.

N.S. Kinzer, "Priests, machos and babies: or Latin American women and the Manichaean heresy", *Journal of Marriage and the Family*, 35, no. 2, 1973, pp 300-312.

M. de Lenero, "Women's work and fertility", in *Nash and Safa*.

N. Birdsall, "Women and population studies", *Signs*, Spring 1976.

S. Tangri, "A feminist perspective on some ethical issues in population programs", *Signs*, Summer 1976.

D. Nortman, "Population and family planning programs: a factbook" in *Reports on Population/Family Planning*, No. 2, 5th ed., New York, Population Council.

L. Gordon, "Are the interests of men and women idenitcal?" *Signs*, Summer 1976.

_____, "The politics of population: birth control and the eugenics movement", *Radical America*, July-Aug 1974.

VI. GENDER RELATIONS AND FORMS OF STRUGGLE

H. Safa, "Class consciousness among working-class women in Latin America: Puerto Rico", in *Nash and Safa*.

V. Mota, "Politics and feminism in the Dominican Republic: 1931-45 and 1966-74", in *Nash and Safa*.

I.P. Vidal, "The history of women's struggle for equality in Puerto Rico", in *Nash and Safa*.

M. Mattelart, "Chile: the feminine version of the coup d'etat", in *Nash and Safa*.

*M. Crummett, "El poder feminino: the mobilization of women against socialism in Chile", *Latin American Perspectives*, Fall 1977.

C. Andreas, "The Chilean woman: reform, reaction, and resistance", *Latin American Perspectives*, Fall 1977.

N. Chinchilla, "Mobilizing women: revolution in the revolution", *Latin American Perspectives*, Fall 1977.

X. Bunster, "The emergence of a Mapuche leader: Chile", in *Nash and Safa*.

J. Nash, "Resistance as protest: women in the struggle of Bolivian tin-mining communities", in *Rohrlich-Leavitt*.

D. Barrios de Chungara with M. Viezzer, *Let Me Speak!* MR Press, 1978 (testimony of Domitila, a woman of the Bolivian mines).

*J. van Allen, "'Aba riots' or 'Igbo women's war'? Ideology, stratification, and the invisibility of women", in *Women in Africa*, N. Hafkin and E. Bay, eds, 1976.

———, "'Sitting on a man': colonialism and the lost political institutions of Igbo women", *Canadian Journal of African Studies*, vol 6, no. 2, 1972.

S. Urdang, *Fighting two colonialisms: women in Guinea-Bissau*, MR Press, 1979.

S. Jackson, "Hausa women on strike", *Review of African Political Economy*, May-August, 1978.

*G. Omvedt, "Women and rural revolt in India", *Journal of Peasant Studies*, April 1978.

LABOR

Transformation of Work in 19th and 20th Century America

Maurice Isserman
Department of History
Oberlin College
Fall 1979
Undergraduate

This course examines the cultural and social impact of industrialization as experienced by American workers, both in the workplace and in the family. Preindustrial work patterns, centered on household and artisanal production, were disrupted by the rise of the factory system, the increasing division of labor and technological innovations in the 19th century. "Scientific management" sought to wrest control of the work process away from the shop floor in the late 19th and early 20th century. Institutional (trade union, political) and informal community and workplace resistance to these developments sprang up in the 19th century and continued into the 20th century. Particular attention will be paid to the way that new techniques of production and management transformed "women's work" in the workplace and the home.

Harry Braverman, *Labor and Monopoly Capital*.
Alan Dawley, *Class and Community, The Industrial Revolution in Lynn*.
Herbert Gutman, *Work, Culture and Society in Industrializing America*.
Studs Terkel, *Working*.
Rosalynn Baxandall, et al., *America's Working Women*.
Eli Zaretsky, *Capitalism, the Family and Personal Life*.
Gerda Lerner, "The Lady and the Mill Girl" (reprint).
David Montgomery, "The Working Class of the Pre-Industrial American City" (reprint).

I. INTRODUCTION

Studs Terkel, *Working*, pp. 1-10, 17-22, 57-60, 72-82, 221-232; John R. Commons, "Shoemakers" in Commons, *Labor and Administration*, pp. 219-266; Selig Perlman, excerpts from "Theory of the Labor Movement," (Xerox).

II. PREINDUSTRIAL WORK

E.P. Thompson, "Time, work, discipline," (Xerox); Eric Foner, *Tom Paine*, pp. 19-69; Alan Dawley, *Class and Community*, pp. 1-41; David Montgomery, "Working Classes in the Pre-industrial American City."

III. FAMILY AND WORK ON THE EVE OF INDUSTRIALISM

Eli Zaretsky, *Capitalism, The Family and Personal Life*, pp. 13-55; Rosalynn Baxandall, et al., *America's Working Women*, xiii-xxii, pp. 15-23; Elizabeth Pleck, "Two Worlds in One," (Xerox).

IV. THE MACHINE ENTERS THE GARDEN

Foner, *Tom Paine*, pp. 145-182; Dawley, *Class and Community*, pp. 42-96; Gerda Lerner, "Lady and the Mill Girl"; Baxandall, *Working Women*, pp. 41-53.

V. "DARK SATANIC MILLS" AND THEIR CRITICS

Bruce Laurie, "Nothing on Impulse," (Xerox and in Milton Cantor, *American Working Class Culture*); Paul Faler, "Cultural Aspects of the Industrial Revolution," (Xerox and in Cantor); Dawley, pp. 97-148; Baxandall, pp. 57-68.

VI. A DIVIDED WORKING CLASS: IMMIGRATION AND SLAVERY

David Montgomery, "Shuttle and the Cross," (Xerox); Eugene Genovese, "Black Work Ethic," in *Roll, Jordan, Roll*; Baxandall, pp. 24-35.

VII. AMERICA'S RISE TO INDUSTRIAL SUPREMACY: FROM THE CIVIL WAR TO WORLD WAR ONE

Herbert Gutman, *Work, Culture and Society*, pp.

3-78; 209-233; Dawley, pp. 149-172; Baxandall, pp. 85-103, 128-141.

VIII. TRADE UNIONISM: CLASS CONSCIOUSNESS OR JOB CONSCIOUSNESS?

Gutman, pp. 79-117; 234-292; Dawley, pp. 173-193; William Tuttle, "Labor Conflict and Racial Violence," in Herbert Gutman, *Many Pasts*; Baxandall, pp. 104-125, 187-209.

IX. STRUGGLE ON THE SHOP FLOOR, PART ONE

David Montgomery, "Workers Control of Machine Production," (Xerox); Harry Braverman, *Labor and Monopoly Capital*, pp. 3-123.

X. STRUGGLE ON THE SHOP FLOOR, PART TWO

Braverman, pp. 144-248; Loren Baritz, *Servants of Power*, pp. 77-116.

XI. THE TRANSFORMATION OF "WOMEN'S WORK"

Zaretsky, pp. 56-77; Susan J. Kleinberg, "Technology and Women's Work," (Xerox); Barbara Ehrenreich and Deirdre English, "The Manufacture of Housework," (Xerox); Braverman, pp. 293-358; Baxandall, pp. 223-228, 232-235; Terkel, 396-405.

XII. THE REDISCOVERY OF THE UNHAPPY WORKER

Terkel, pp. 91-103, 158-161, 232-266, 344-351, 384-389, 451-456; Braverman, pp. 424-449; Barbara Garson, "Luddites in Lordstown," (Xerox); Judson Gooding, "Blue Collar Blues," (Xerox).

XIII. CONCLUSION: "AND WAS JERUSALEM BUILDED HERE?"

Christopher Lasch, *The New Narcissism*, pp. 218-236; Dawley, pp. 220-241; Stanley Aronowitz, "The Labor Movement and the Left in the United States," (Xerox).

Labor Economics

David M. Gordon
Graduate Faculty, New School
for Social Research
Department of Economics
Fall and Spring 1981-1982
Graduate

OUTLINE

I. The Creation of the Topic
A. The Emergence of Labor Markets and the Labor Process
B. A Preview of the "History of Thought" of "Labor Economics"

II. The Demand for Labor//The Allocation of the Means of Production and the Organization of the Labor Process
A. The Firm as a Unit of Accumulation
B. The Allocation of the Means of Production among Firms and Industries
C. The Organization of the Capitalist Labor Process
D. The Derived Demand for Labor

III. The Supply of Labor//The Production and Reproduction of Labor Power
A. The Household and Labor Power
B. Factors Affecting the Quantity of Labor Power Supplied
C. Factors Affecting the Quality of Labor Power Supplied

IV. The Mechanisms of the Labor Market
A. Competitive Labor Markets
B. Labor Markets with Imperfections

V. Labor Market Outcomes
A. The Determination of Wages, Income, and Employment
B. Inequalities in the Distribution of Wages, Income, and Employment

VI. Collective Efforts to Shape the Labor Process and Labor Markets
A. Collective Worker Efforts and Trade Unions
B. Collective Corporate Efforts and Trade Associations

VII. Class Efforts to Shape the Labor Process and Labor Markets
A. Working Class Struggle
B. Capitalist Class Struggle
C. Government Policy Affecting the Labor Process and Labor Markets

READING LIST

This bibliography aims toward a comprehensive, comparative syllabus in labor economics.

The starred readings are the most important. Those marked with a "#" represent further elaborations or, in many cases, examples of applied empirical work within the respective topics.

There are many holes in this syllabus—despite its length and breadth. In particular, I have dropped any attempt to provide coverage on specific policy issues like unemployment compensation or income maintenance. I would appreciate hearing from any readers who would be interested in trying to improve the coverage of this list.

I. THE CREATION OF THE TOPIC

A. The Historical Emergence of Labor Markets and the Labor Process

*Karl Marx, *Capital*, Vol. I, Chs. 13-15.

*Stephen A. Marglin, "What Do Bosses Do?" *Review of Radical Political Economics*, Summer 1974.

*William Lazonick, "The Subjugation of Labor to Capital: The Rise of the Capitalist System," *Review of Radical Political Economics*, Spring 1978.

*John R. Hicks, *A Theory of Economic History* (Oxford Univ. Press, 1967), Chs. 1-3.

*Heidi Hartmann, "Capitalism, Patriarchy, and Job Segregation by Sex," *Signs*, Spring 1976.

B. INTRODUCTION TO THE "HISTORY OF THOUGHT" IN LABOR ECONOMICS

Clark Kerr, "Industrial Relations Research: A Personal Retrospective," *Industrial Relations*, May 1978.

Michael J. Piore, "Introduction," in Piore, ed., *Unemployment and Inflation: Institutionalist and Structuralist Views* (Sharpe, 1979).

David M. Gordon, *Theories of Poverty and Underemployment* (Health, 1972), Chs. 1-2.

#John T. Dunlop et al., *Industrialism and Industrial Man Reconsidered* (Inter-University Study of Labor Problems in Economic Development, 1975).

#James L. Cochrane, *Industrialism and Industrial Man in Retrospect: A Critical Review....*(Ford Foundation, 1979).

II. THE DEMAND FOR LABOR/THE ALLOCATION OF THE MEANS OF PRODUCTION AND THE ORGANIZATION OF THE LABOR PROCESS

A. THE FIRM AS A UNIT OF ACCUMULATION

1. Marxian Perspectives

*Richard C. Edwards, *Contested Terrain* (Basic Books, 1979), Ch. 5.

Paul Baran and Paul Sweezy, *Monopoly Capital* (Monthly Review, 1966), pp. 1-13.

David Levine, "The Theory of the Growth of the Capitalist Economy," *Economic Development and Cultural Change*, October 1975.

#Joseph Steindl, *Maturity and Stagnation in American Capitalism* (Monthly Review, 1976), reprint of 1952 ed., Intro., Chs. 13-14.

2. Neoclassical Perspectives

*Ronald Coase, "The Nature of the Firm," *Economica*, November 1937.

Nina Shapiro, "The Neoclassical Theory of the Firm," *Review of Radical Political Economics*, Winter 1976.

3. Institutionalist Perspectives

*Robert Averitt, *The Dual Economy* (Norton, 1968), Chs. 1-3.

B. THE ALLOCATION OF THE MEANS OF PRODUCTION AMONG FIRMS AND INDUSTRIES

1. An Historical/Institutional Overview

Stanley Lebergott, *Manpower in Economic Growth* (McGraw-Hill, 1964), Chs. 2-3.

Alfred Chandler, *The Visible Hand* (Harvard, 1977), Intro., Chs. 12-14.

#Victor Fuchs, *The Service Economy* (NBER, 1968), Ch. 2.

#Richard Barnett and Ronald Muller, *Global Reach* (Simon & Schuster, 1974), Part I.

#Michael Reich, "The Development of the Wage-Labor Force," in R.C. Edwards et al., eds., *The Capitalist System* (Prentice-Hall, 1978).

2. The Theory of the Allocation of the Means of Production

a. Marxian Perspectives

*Ernest Mandel, *Late Capitalism* (New Left Books, 1975), Chs. 3, 7, 10.

Samir Amin, *The Law of Value and Historical Materialism* (Monthly Review, 1978), Chs. 5, Conclusion.

b. Neoclassical Perspectives

*J.R. Hicks, *The Theory of Wages* (St. Martin's, 1964, 2nd ed., Chs. 4, 6.

#George Stigler, *Capital and Rates of Return in Manufacturing* (Princeton Univ. Press, 1963), Chs. 1-3.

#B.R. Williams, "Types of Competition and the Theory of Employment," *Oxford Economic Papers*, January 1949.

c. Institutionalist/Post-Keynesian Perspectives

Alfred Eichner, *Megacorp and Oligopoly* (Cambridge, 1976), Chs. 1-2.

C. THE ORGANIZATION OF THE CAPITALIST LABOR PROCESS

1. General Analysis

a. Marxian Perspectives

*Karl Marx, *Capital*, Vol. I, Chs. 6-15 and Supp. to Ch. 6 in Penguin edition.

*Harry Braverman, *Labor and Monopoly Capital* (Monthly Review, 1974) Chs. 1-10.

*David M. Gordon, "Capitalist Efficiency and Socialist Efficiency," *Monthly Review*, July-August 1976.

*Herbert M. Gintis, "The Nature of the Labor Exchange and the Theory of Capitalist Production," *Review of Radical Political Economics*, Summer 1976.

*Michael Reich and James Devine, "The Microeconomics of Conflict and Hierarchy in Capitalist Production," *Review of Radical Political Economics*, Winter 1981.

Herbert M. Gintis and Samuel Bowles, "Structure and Practice in the Labor Theory of Value," *Review of Radical Political Economics*, Winter 1981.

Samuel Bowles, "A Model of Competitive Wage Determination...," 1981, unpublished paper.

#Michael Burawoy, "Toward a Marxist Theory of the Labor Process: Braverman and Beyond," *Politics and Society*, 8: 3-4, 1978.

#Brighton Labour Process Group, "The Capitalist Labour Process," *Capital and Class*, #1, Spring 1977.

b. Neoclassical Perspectives

*Edward J. Nell, "Property and the Means of Production: A Primer on the Cambridge Controversy," *Review of Radical Political Economics*, Summer 1972.

T.C. Koopmans, *Activity Analysis of Production and Allocation* (Wiley, 1971), pp. 33-97.

#S. Carlson, *Study on the Pure Theory of Production* (Kelley, 1939).

c. Post-Keynesian Perspectives

John Eatwell, *Theories of Value, Employment and Distribution* (Thames Studies in Political Economy).

2. Specific Topics

a. Technology, Hierarchy, and the Division of Labor

Andre Gorz, ed., *The Division of Labour: The Labour Process and Class Struggle in Modern Capitalism* (Humanities Press, 1977).

#Donald D. Weiss, "Marx vs. Smith on the Division of Labor," *Monthly Review*, July-August 1976.

#Nathan Rosenberg, "Marx as a Student of Technology," *Monthly Review*, July-August 1976.

*R. Coase, "The Nature of the Firm," *Economica*, November 1937.

*A.A. Alchian and H. Demsetz, "Production, Information Costs, and Economic Organization," *American Economic Review*, December 1972.

#Joseph Stiglitz, "Incentives, Risk, and Information: Notes toward a Theory of Hierarchy," mimeo, 1975.

#G.A. Calvo and S. Willisz, "Hierarchy, Ability, and Income Distribution," *Journal of Political Economy*, October 1979.

b. Productive and Unproductive Labor

*Harry Braverman, *Labor and Monopoly Capital*, op. cit., Chs. 18-19.

*Ian Gough, "Marx's Theory of Productive and Unproductive Labor," *New Left Review*, November-December 1972.

James O'Connor, "Productive and Unproductive Labor," *Politics and Society*, 5:3, 1975.

David Laibman, "Theories of Productive and Unproductive Labor," 1979, unpublished paper.

Anwar Shaikh, "National Income Accounts and Marxian Categories," 1978, unpublished paper.

c. Labor Productivity

*David M. Gordon, "Capital-Labor Conflict and the Slowdown in Productivity Growth," *American Economic Review*, May 1981.

*Richard R. Nelson, "Research on Productivity Growth and Differences," *Journal of Economic Literature*, September 1981.

Kim B. Clark, "Unionization and Productivity: Micro-Econometric Evidence," *Quarterly Journal of Economics*, December 1980.

3. Historical Studies

*Work Relations Group, "Uncovering the Hidden History of the Workplace," *Review of Radical Political Economics*, Winter 1978.

*Richard C. Edwards, *Contested Terrain* (Basic Books, 1979).

*David M. Gordon, Richard Edwards, and Michael Reich, *Segmented Work, Divided Workers: The Historical Transformation of Labor in the United States* (Cambridge Univ. Press, 1982).

Katherine Stone, "The Origins of Job Structures in the Steel Industry," *Review of Radical Political Economics*, Summer 1974.

Michel Aglietta, *Theory of Capitalist Regulation* (New Left Books, 1979).

#David Noble, *America by Design: Science, Technology, and the Rise of Corporate Capitalism* (Knopf, 1977).

#Joan Greenbaum, *In the Name of Efficiency* (Temple Univ. Press, 1979).

#Andrew Friedman, *Industry and Labour: Class Struggle and Monopoly Capitalism* (Macmillan, 1977).

#Dan Clawson, *Bureaucracy and the Labor Process* (Monthly Review, 1980).

#Andrew Zimbalist, ed., *Case Studies on the Labor Process* (Monthly Review, 1979).

#Michael Burawoy, *Manufacturing Consent: Changes in the Labor Process under Monopoly Capitalism* (Univ. of Chicago Press, 1979).

#J. Zeitlin, "Craft Control and the Division of Labour: Engineers and Compositors in Britain, 1890-1930," *Cambridge Journal of Economics*, September 1979.

#B. Elbaum and F. Wilkinson, "Industrial Relations and Uneven Development: A Comparative Study of the American and British Steel Industries," *Cambridge Journal of Economics*, September 1979.

#W. Lazonick, "Industrial Relations and Technical Change: The Case of the Self-Acting Mule," *Cambridge Journal of Economics*, September 1979.

#B. Elbaum, et al., "The Labour Process, Market Structure, and Marxist Theory," *Cambridge Journal of Economics*, September 1979.

#Jill Walker, "Markets, Industrial Process, and Class Struggle: The Evolution of the Labor Process in the U.K. Engineering Industry," *Review of Radical Political Economics*, Winter 1981.

D. THE DERIVED DEMAND FOR LABOR

1. Neoclassical Perspectives

a. Marginal Productivity Theory

*Allan M. Cartter, *Theory of Wages and Employment* (Irwin, 1959), Chs. 2-3.

J.R. Hicks, *The Theory of Wages* (St. Martin's, 1964), 2nd ed., Chs. 1-2.

b. Neoclassical Critiques and Re-assessments

*Cartter, *Theory of Wages and Employment*, op. cit., Ch. 4.

*Hicks, *Theory of Wages*, 2nd ed., op. cit., pp. 305-384.

#R.A. Lester, "Shortcomings of Marginal Analysis for Wage-Employment Problems," *American Economic Review*, March 1946; reprinted in McCormick and Smith, eds., *The Labor Market* (Penguin, 1971).

#F. Machlup, "Marginal Analysis and Economic Research," *American Economic Review*, September 1946, reprinted in ibid.

#R.A. Lester, "Reply," *American Economic Review*, September 1946, in ibid.

#F. Machlup, "On the Meaning of the Marginal Product," in W. Fellner and B. Haley, eds., *Readings in the Theory of Income Distribution* (Irwin, 1965).

#D.H. Robertson, "Wage Grumbles," in Fellner and Haley, ibid.

c. The Derived Demand for Labor

*Cartter, *Theory of Wages and Employment*, op. cit., Chs. 5-6.

Melvin Reder, "A Partial Survey of the Theory of Income Size Distribution," in L. Soltow, ed., *Six Papers on the Size Distribution of Income and Wealth* (National Bureau of Economic Research, 1969), pp. 214-223.

R.B. Freeman, "An Empirical Analysis of the Fixed Coefficient 'Manpower Requirements' Model, 1960-1970," *Journal of Human Resources*, Spring 1980.

K.B. Clark and R.B. Freeman, "How Elastic is the Demand for Labor?" *Review of Economics and Statistics*, November 1980.

#J.M. Malcomson, "The Measurement of Labour Cost in Empirical Models of Production and Employment," *Rev. of Econ. and Stat.*, November 1980.

2. Marxian Perspectives

*Erik Olin Wright, "The Value Controversy and Social Research," *New Left Review*, No. 116, July-August 1979.

*Maurice Dobb, *Wages* (Cambridge Univ. Press, 1946), rev. ed., Chs. 4-5.

David M. Gordon, *Theories of Poverty and Underemployment*, op. cit., Ch. 5.

S.A. Marglin, *Growth, Distribution and Prices* (Harvard, 1982), Chs. 3, 9, 10.

#R.C. Edwards, "Individual Traits and Organizational Incentives: What Makes a 'Good' Worker?" *Journal of Human Resources*, Winter 1976.

3. Institutionalist Perspectives

*Peter B. Doeringer and Michael J. Piore, *Internal Labor Markets and Manpower Analysis* (Heath, 1971), Chs. 1-3.

*Michael J. Piore, ed., *Unemployment and Inflation: Institutionalist and Structuralist Views* (Sharpe, 1979), essays by Thurow and Appelbaum and introduction by Piore in Part II.

S.A. Marglin, *Growth, Distribution and Prices*, op. cit., Chs. 4, 9, 10.

III. THE SUPPLY OF LABOR/THE PRODUCTION AND REPRODUCTION OF LABOR POWER

A. THE HOUSEHOLD AND LABOR POWER

1. An Historical Overview

Edward A. Wrigley, *Population and History* (McGraw-Hill, 1969).

Richard A. Easterlin, *Population, Labor Force, and Long Swings in Economic Growth* (Columbia Univ. Press, 1968), Ch. 2.

Neil J. Smelser, "The Industrial Revolution and the British Working Class Family," *Journal of Social History*, Vol. I, 17-35.

Heidi Hartmann, "Capitalism, Patriarchy and Job Segregation by Sex," *Signs*, Spring 1976.

B. Lutz and K. Berkner, "Recent Research on the History of the Family in Western Europe," *Journal of Marriage and the Family*, Aug. 1973.

2. Marxian Perspectives

*L. Beneria, "Reproduction, Production and the Sexual Division of Labour," *Cambridge Journal of Economics*, September 1979.

Nancy Folbre, "The Reproduction of Labor Power," mimeo, 1980.

Nancy Folbre, "Of Patriarchy Born: The Political Economy of Fertility Decisions," mimeo, 1980.

#Terry Fee, "Domestic Labor: An Analysis of Housework and Its Relation to the Production Process," *Rev. of Radical Political Economics*, Spring 1976.

#S. Himmelweit and S. Mohun, "Domestic Lobor and Capital," *Cambridge Journal of Economics*, March 1977.

3. Neoclassical Perspectives

a. The Household and Time Allocation

*Gary Becker, "A Theory of the Allocation of Time," *Economic Journal*, Sept. 1965.

*Gary Becker, *A Treatise on the Family* (Harvard, 1981), Chs. 1-2, 5-6, 10-11.

T.W. Schultz, ed., *Economics of the Family* (Univ. of Chicago Press, 1975), especially articles by Becker, Gronau, and Nerlove.

Reuben Gronau, "Home Production: A Forgotten Industry," *Review of Economics and Statistics*, August 1980.

#Ray Fair, "A Theory of Extramarital Affairs," *Journal of Political Economy*, February 1978.

#T.J. Wales and A.D. Woodland, "Estimation of the Allocation of Time for Work, Leisure, and Housework," *Econometrica*, January 1977.

b. The Economics of Fertility

*R.J. Willis, "Economic Theory of Fertility Behavior," in T.W. Schultz, ed., *Economics of the Family*, op. cit.

Marc Nerlove, "Household and Economy: Toward a New Theory of Population and Economic Growth," *Journal of Political Economy*, March-April 1974.

#M.R. Rosenzweig and K.I. Wolpin, "Life-Cycle Labor Supply and Fertility: Causal Inferences from Household Models," *Journal of Political Economy*, April 1980.

#M.P. Ward and W.P. Butz, "Completed Fertility and Its Timing," *Journal of Political Economy*, October 1980.

B. FACTORS AFFECTING THE QUANTITY OF LABOR POWER SUPPLIED

1. Marxian Perspectives

*S. Castels and G. Kozack, *Immigrant Workers and Class Structure in Western Europe* (Oxford Univ. Press, 1973).

History Task Force, Centro de Estudios Puertorriquenos, *Labor Migration under Capitalism: The Puerto Rican Experience* (Monthly Review Press, 1979), Chs. 1-2.

2. Institutionalist Perspectives

*M.J. Piore, *Birds of Passage and the Promised Land* (Cambridge Univ. Press, 1979).

Charles Sabel, "Marginal Workers in Industrial Society," in M.J. Piore, ed., *Unemployment and Inflation*, op. cit.

3. Neoclassical Perspectives

a. The Work-Leisure Choice and the Supply of Labor

*W. Henderson and R. Quandt, *Microeconomic Theory* (McGraw-Hill, 1958), pp. 23-24.

*A. Rees, *The Economics of Work and Pay*, op. cit., Ch. 2.

A.S. Blinder, "Human Capital and Labor Supply: A Synthesis," *Journal of Political Economy*, June 1976.

John D. Owen, *Working Hours: An Economic Analysis*, Lexington 1979, Part I Chs. 1-6.

J. Heckman and O. Ashenfelter, "Estimating Labor Supply Functions," in G. Cain and H. Watts, eds., *Income Maintenance and Labor Supply*.

#D.O. Parsons, "Health, Family Structure, and Labor Supply," *American Economic Review*, September 1977.

#T.J. Kneisner, "The Full-Time Workweek in the U.S. 1900-1970," *Labor Relations Review*, October 1976.

b. Labor Force Participation

William G. Bowen and T. Aldrich Finegan, *The Economics of Labor Force Participation* (Princeton Univ. Press, 1969).

*Jacob Mincer, "The Labor Force Participation of Married Women," in *Aspects of Labor Economics* (National Bureau of Economic Research, 1962).

Michael Wachter, "Intermediate Swings in Labor Force Participation," *Brookings Papers on Economic Activity*, 1977; 2.

#J.J. Heckman, "A Partial Survey of Recent Research on the Labor Supply of Women," *American Economic Review*, May 1978.

#C.B. Lloyd and B. Niemi, "Sex Differences in Labor Supply Elasticity: The Implications of Sectoral Shifts in Demand," *American Economic Review*, May 1978.

#J.A. O'Neill, "A Time-Series Analysis of Women's Labor Force Participation," *American Economic Review*, May 1981.

c. Labor Migration

*M.J. Greenwood, "Research on Internal Migration in the United States: A Survey," *Journal of Economic Literature*, June 1975.

L.A. Sjaastad, "Costs and Returns of Human Migration," *Journal of Political Economy*, Supplement, 1962; reprinted in Burton *et al.*, eds., *Readings in Labor Market Analysis*, op. cit.

#G.S. Fields, "Labor Force Migration, Uemployment, and Job Turnover," *Review of Economics and Statistics*, November 1976.

C. FACTORS AFFECTING THE QUALITY OF LABOR POWER SUPPLIED

1. Marxian Perspectives

a. Schooling and Training

*Samuel Bowles, "Unequal Education and the Reproduction of the Social Division of Labor," *Review of Radical Political Economics*, Summer 1971.

*Samuel Bowles and Herbert Gintis, *Schooling in Capitalist America* (Basic Books, 1975), Chs. 3-6.

b. Abstract Labor and Heterogeneous Labor

*Samuel Bowles and Herbert Gintis, "The Marxian Theory of Value and Heterogenous Labour: A Critique and Reformulation," *Cambridge Journal of Economics*, June 1977.

#M. Morishima, "Comment on Bowles and Gintis," and Bowles and Gintis, "Reply," *Cambridge Journal of Economics*, December 1978.

2. Neoclassical Perspectives

a. Human Capital Theory of Investment

*Gary Becker, *Human Capital* (National Bureau of Economic Research, 1975) 2nd ed.

Sherwin Rosen, "Learning and Experience in the Labor Market," *Journal of Human Resources*, June 1972.

#Jacob Mincer and Solomon Polachek, "Family Investments in Human Capital: Earnings of Women," *Journal of Political Economy*, March-April 1974.

#James J. Heckman, "A Life Cycle Model of Earnings, Learning, and Consumption," *Journal of Political Economy*, August 1976.

#J.S. Akin and I. Garfinkel, "School Expenditures and the Economic Returns to Schooling," *Journal of Human Resources*, Fall 1977.

#J.M. Ritzler and D.R. Winkler, "The Production of Human Capital over Time," *Review of Economics and Statistics*, November 1977.

#C. Brown, "Education and Jobs: An Interpretation," *Journal of Human Resources*, Summer 1978.

b. Critiques of Human Capital Theory

*Mark Blaug, "The Empirical Status of Human Capital Theory: A Slightly Jaundiced Survey," *Journal of Economic Literature*, September 1976.

*Samuel Bowles and Herbert Gintis, "The Problem of Human Capital Theory: A Marxian Critique," *American Economic Review*, May 1975.

Michael Carter, "To Abstain or Not to Absain (Is that the Question?): A Critique of Human Capital Concept," in J. Schwartz, ed., *The Subtle Anatomy of Capitalism* (Goodyear, 1977).

Ivar Berg, *Education and Jobs: The Great Training Robbery* (Praeger, 1970).

c. Signalling and Screening Theory

A.M. Spence, "Job Market Signalling," *Quarterly Journal of Economics*, August 1974.

A.M. Spence, *The Theory of Signalling* (Harvard University Press, 1974).

Joseph Stiglitz, "The Theory of 'Screening,' Education, and the Distribution of Income," *American Economic Review*, June 1975.

J.G. Riley, "Testing the Educational Screening Hypothesis," *Jo. Pol. Econ.*, Part 2, October 1979.

W.R. Johnson, "A Theory of Job Shopping," *Quarterly Journal of Economics*, May 1978.

IV. MECHANISMS OF THE LABOR MARKET

A. COMPETITIVE LABOR MARKETS

1. The Theory of Labor Market Competition

*Lloyd Reynolds, *Labor Economics and Labor Relations*, Chs. 4-6.

*Simon Rottenberg, "On Choice in Labor Markets," *Industrial and Labor Relations Review*, January 1965.

2. Search Theory

*George Stigler, "Information in the Labor Market," *Journal of Political Economy* Supplement, October 1962.

John J. McCall, "Economics of Information and Job Search," *Quarterly Journal of Economics*, February 1970.

S.A. Lippman and J.J. McCall, "The Economics of Job Search: A Survey," *Economic Inquiry*, September 1976.

#T.F. Bradshaw and J.L. Scholl, "The Extent of Job Search during Layoff," *Brookings Papers on Economic Activity*, 1976:2.

#J.M. Barron and S. McCafferty, "Job Search, Labor Supply and the Quit Decision: Theory and Evidence," *American Economic Review*, September 1977.

#G.M. MacDonald, "Person-Specific Information in the Labor Market," *Journal of Political Economy*, June 1980.

3. Contract Theory

*Arthur Okun, "Inflation: Its Mechanics and Welfare Costs," *Brookings Papers on Economic Activity*, 1975:2.

R.E. Hall and David M. Lilien, "Efficient Wage Bargains under Uncertain Supply and Demand," *American Economic Review*, December 1979.

R.E. Hall, "Employment Fluctuations and Wage Rigidity," *Brookings Papers on Economic Activity*, 1980:1.

B. Holmstrom, "Contractual Models of the Labor Market," *American Economic Review*, May 1981.

B. LABOR MARKETS WITH IMPERFECTIONS

1. General Analysis

*Cartter, *Theory of Wages and Employment*, Chs. 7,8.

*A. Rees and G. Schultz, *Workers and Wages in an Urban Labor Market* (Univ. of Chicago Press, 1974).

#Mark S. Granovetter, *Getting a Job: A Study of Contacts and Careers* (Harvard Univ. Press, 1974).

2. Internal Labor Markets

*Peter B. Doeringer and Michael Piore, *Internal Labor Markets and Manpower Analysis*, Chs. 2-3.

#Lawrence M. Kahn, "Internal Labor Markets: San Francisco Longshoring," *Industrial Relations*, October 1976.

3. Secondary Labor Markets

Lloyd Fisher, *The Harvest Labor Market in California* (Harvard, 1953).

Peter B. Doeringer et al., *Low-Income Labor Markets and Urban Manpower Programs: A Critical Assessment* (U.S. Dept. of Labor, 1972).

Bennett Harrison, *Education, Training, and the Ghetto* (Johns Hopkins, 1972).

#Teresa Sullivan, *Marginal Workers, Marginal Jobs: The Underutilization of American Workers* (Univ. of Texas Press, 1978).

V. LABOR MARKET OUTCOMES

A. THE DETERMINATION OF WAGES, INCOME, AND EMPLOYMENT

1. Wages and Income

a. Neoclassical Theories

  i. Overview

*Sian Singh Sahota, "Theories of Personal Income Distribution: A Survey," *Journal of Economic Literature*, March 1978.

Alan Blinder, *Toward an Economic Theory of Income Distribution* (MIT, 1974).

ii. Traditional Theories of Wage Differentials

*Lloyd Reynolds, *Labor Economics and Labor Relations*, chs. 9-10.

Melvin Reder, "Wage Differentials: Theory and Measurement," in *Aspects of Labor Economics* (National Bur. of Econ. Research, 1962).

C. Brown, "Equalizing Differences in the Labor Market," *Quarterly Journal of Economics*, February 1980.

#R.E.B. Lucas, "Hedonic Wage Equations and Psychic Wages in the Returns to Schooling," *American Economic Review*, September 1977.

  iii. Human Capital Theories

*Gary Becker, "Human Capital and the Personal Distribution of Income: An Analytical Approach," in *Human Capital*, 2nd ed., 94-144.

*Jacob Mincer, *Schooling, Age, and Earnings* (National Bur. of Econ. Research, 1975).

#G. Becker and N. Tomes, "An Equilibrium Theory of the Distribution of Income and Intergenerational Mobility," *Journal of Political Economy*, October 1979.

#E.P. Lazear, "Age Experience and Wage Growth," *American Economic Review*, September 1976.

#S. Bartlett, "Education, Experience and Wage Inequality: 1939-1969," *Journal of Human Resources*, Summer 1978.

#R.B. Freeman, "The Effect of Demographic Factors on Age-Earnings Profiles," *Journal of Human Resources*, Summer 1979.

iv. Critiques

*D.M. Gordon, *Theories of Poverty and Underemployment*, Chs. 3,7.

Mark Blaug, "The Empirical Status of Human Capital Theory: A Slightly Jaundiced Survey," *Journal of Economic Literature*, September 1976.

J.L. Medoff and K.G. Abraham, "Experience, Performance, and Earnings," *Quarterly Journal of Economics*, December 1980.

v. Traditional Theories of Labor's Share

S. Lebergott, "Factor Shares in the Long Term: Some Theoretical and Statistical Aspects," in *The Behavior of Income Shares* (National Bureau of Economic Research, 1964).

J. Marchal and B. Duclos, eds., *The Distribution of National Income* (St. Martin's Press, 1968), especially papers by Bronfenbrenner and Solow.

b. Institutionalist Perspectives

*P. Doeringer and M. Piore, *Interal Labor Markets...*, ch. 4.

*D.M. Gordon, *Theories of Poverty and Underemployment*, Ch. 4.

*M. Piore, ed., *Unemployment and Inflation*, especially pieces by Dunlop and Thurow.

#Marcia K. Freedman, *Labor Markets: Segments and Shelters* (Montclair, 1976).

#J.R. Maroney and B.T. Allen, "Monopoly Power and the Relative Share of Labor," *Industrial and Labor Relations Review*, January 1969.

c. Marxian/Radical Perspectives

  i. General Views

*Maurice Dobb, *Wages* (Cambridge Univ. Press, 1946), rev. ed.

*D.M. Gordon, *Theories of Poverty and Underemployment*, Chs. 5,7.

*Erik Olin Wright, *Class Structure and Income Determination*, (Academic Press, 1979), Chs. 1-4.

ii. The Segmentation of Labor

*R. Edwards et al., eds., *Labor Market Segmentation* (Heath, 1975), especially articles by Edwards, Piore, Wachtel, and Birnbaum.

*R. Edwards, *Contested Terrain*, Chs. 9-10.

*D.M. Gordon, "Segmentation by the Numbers," unpublished paper, June 1982.

*R.W. Rumberger and M. Carnoy, "Segmentation in the U.S. Labor Market: Its Effects on Mobility and Earnings of Whites and Blacks," *Cambridge Journal of Economics*, June 1980.

#Martin Carnoy, "Segmented Labour Markets," in *Education, Work, and Employment* (Paris: International Inst. for Ed. Planning, 1980).

#Paul Ryan, "Some Empirical Issues in the Analysis of Labour Market Segmentation," in F. Wilkinson, *Low Pay and Labour Market Segmentation* (Cambridge Univ. Press, forthcoming).

#Sam Rosenberg, "A Survey of Empirical Work in Labor Market Segmentation," in Wilkinson, ibid.

#Jill Rubery, "Structured Labour Markets, Worker Organization, and Low Pay," *Cambridge Journal of Economics*, 1978.

iii. Critiques

*Glen Cain, "The Challenge of Segmented Labor Market Theories to Orthodox Theory: A Survey," *Journal of Economic Literature*, December 1976.

Michael Wachter, "Primary and Secondary Labor Markets: A Critique of the Dual Approach," *Brookings Papers on Economic Activity*, 1974:3.

d. Comparative Empirical Studies

i. The Effect of Wealth

John Brittain, The Inheritance of Economic Status (Brookings, 1977).

Y. Weiss, "The Wealth Effect in Occupational Choice," *International Economic Review*, June 1976.

ii. The Relative Effect of Family Background

Christopher Jencks et al., *Who Gets Ahead?* (Basic Books, 1979).

Mary Corcoran et al., "The Effects of Family Background on Earnings," *American Economic Review*, May 1976.

Barry Chiswick, "Sons of Immigrants: Are They at an Earnings Disadvantage?" *American Economic Review*, February 1977.

iii. Personal, Industrial, and Class Characteristics

E.O. Wright, *Class Structure and Income Determination*, chs. 5-10.

Barry Bluestone et al., *Low Wages and the Working Poor* (Michigan, 1973).

I. Garfinkel and R. Havemann, "Earnings Capacity, Economic Status, and Poverty," *Journal of Human Resources*, Winter 1977.

2. The Determination of Employment

a. Neoclassical Perspectives

i. Macroeconomic Foundations

E. Roy Weintraub, "The Microfoundations of Macroeconomics: A Critical Survey," *Journal of Economic Literature*, March 1977.

*Anthony Santomero and John J. Seater, "The Inflation-Unemployment Trade-Off: A Critique of the Literature," *Journal of Economic Literature*, June 1978.

#W. Vroman, "Worker Upgrading and the Business Cycle," *Brookings Papers on Economic Activity*, 1977:1.

#M.N. Baily, "On the Theory of Layoffs and Unemployment," *Econometrica*, July 1977.

ii. The Distribution of Employment and Unemployment

George Perry, "Unemployment Flows in the U.S. Labor Market," *Brookings Papers on Economic Activity*, 1972:3.

K.B. Clark and L.H. Summers, "Labor Market Dynamics and Unemployment: A Reconsideration," *Brookings Papers on Economic Activity*, 1979:1.

#Clair Vickery, "The Impact of Turnover on Group Unemployment Rates," *Review of Economics and Statistics*, November 1977.

#R.H. Frank and R.T. Freeman, "The Distribution of the Unemployment Burden: Do the Last Hired Leave First," *Review of Economics and Statistics*, August 1978.

b. Institutional Perspectives

P. Doeringer and M. Piore, *Internal Labor Markets...*, Ch. 5.

M. Piore, ed., *Unemployment and Inflation*, article by Wheeler.

#R.N. Bloch, "The Impact of Senority Provisions on the Manufacturing Quit Rate," *Industrial and Labor Relations Review*, July 1978.

#C.L. Betsey, "Differences in Unemployment Experience between Blacks and Whites," *American Economic Review*, May 1978.

c. Radical/Marxian Perspectives

*A. Shaikh, "An Introduction to the History of Crisis Theories," in URPE, *U.S. Capitalism in Crisis* (URPE, 1978).

*R. Boddy and J. Crotty, "Class Conflict, Macropolicy, and the Political Business Cycle," *Review of Radical Political Economics*, Winter 1975.

L. Kahn, "Bargaining Power, Search Theory, and the Phillips Curve," *Cambridge Journal of Economics*, September 1980.

G. Oster, "Labour Relations and Demand Relations: A Case Study of the 'Unemployment Effect'," *Cambridge Journal of Economics*, Dec. 1980.

D. Furth et al., "On Marx's Theory of Unemployment," *Oxford Economic Papers*, July 1978.

B. INEQUALITIES IN LABOR MARKET OUTCOMES

1. Theories of Inequality

a. Neoclassical Perspectives

H. Phelps Brown, *The Inequality of Pay* (Univ. of California Press, 1977).

Barry Chiswick, *Income Inequality: Regional Analyses within a Human Capital Framework* (National Bureau of Economic Research, 1974).

R.E.B. Lucas, "Is There a Human Capital Approach to Income Inequality?" *Journal of Human Resources*, Summer 1977.

#B. Chiswick and J. Mincer, "Time-Series Changes in Personal Income Inequality in the United States since 1939, with Projections to 1985," *Journal of Political Economy*, May/June 1972.

b. Marxist Perspectives

*M. Kalecki, "Class Struggle and the Distribution of Income," *Kyklos*, 1974.

*M. Reich, *Racial Inequality: A Political Economic Analysis* (Princeton Univ. Press, 1981), Ch. 6.

John Roemer, "Toward a General Theory of Exploitation," forthcoming in *Politics and Society*, 1982.

S. Bowles and H. Gintis, "On the Class-Exploitation-Domination Reduction," forthcoming in *Politics and Society*, 1982.

2. Theories of Discrimination
a. Neoclassical Perspectives

J. Stiglitz, "Theories of Discrimination and Economic Policy," in G. von Furstenberg et al., eds., *Patterns of Racial Discrimination* (Lexington Books, 1974).

*E.S. Phelps "The Statistical Theory of Racism and Sexism," *American Economic Review*, September 1972.

#D.J. Aigner and G.C. Cain, 'Statistical Theories of Discrimination in Labor Markets," *Industrial and Labor Relations Review*, January 1977.

b. Marxian Perspectives

*Oliver C. Cox, *Caste, Class, and Race* (Monthly Review Press, 1959), originally published in 1948.

Batya Weinbaum, "Redefining the Question of Revolution," *Review of Radical Politcal Economics*, Fall 1977.

Paddy Quick, "The Class Nature of Women's Oppression," *Review of Radical Political Economics*, Fall 1977.

Nancy Folbre, "Patriarchy and Capitalism in New England, 1620-1900," Unpublished Ph.D. dissertation, U. Mass-Amherst, 1979, Chs. 1-3.

3. Discrimination by Sex
a. Neoclassical Perspectives

*Cynthia B. Lloyd and Beth Niemi, *Women and Work* (Columbia Univ. Press, 1982).

Alice Amsden, ed., *The Economics of Women and Work* (Penguin, 1980), Chs. 3,5.

Isabel V. Sawhill, "The Economics of Discrimination against Women: Some New Findings," *Journal of Human Resources*, Summer 1973.

Jacob R. Mincer and Solomon Polachek, "Family Investments in Human Capital: Earnings of Women," *Journal of Political Economy*, March/April 1974.

Francine Blau and Carol Jusenius, "Economists' Approaches to Sex Segregation in the Labor Market: An Assessment," *Signs*, Spring 1976.

#Ronald Oaxaca, "Sex Discrimination in Wages," in O. Ashenfelter and A. Rees, eds., *Discrimination in Labor Markets* (Princeton, 1974).

#A.G. King, "Is Occupational Segregation the Cause of the Flatter Experience-Earnings Profiles of Women?" *Journal of Human Resources*, Fall 1977.

#E.M. Landes, "Sex Differences in Wages and Employment: A Test of the Specific Capital Hypothesis," *Economic Inquiry*, October 1977.

#R.H. Frank, "Why Women Earn Less: The Theory and Estimation of Differential Overqualification," *American Economic Review*, June 1978.

#R.J. Gordon, "Structural Unemployment and the Productivity of Women," *Journal of Monetary Economics*, Supplement, 1977.

b. Marxist-Feminist Perspectives

Francine Blau, "Women's Place in the Labor Market," *American Economic Review*, May 1972.

Mary Stevenson, "Women's Wages and Job Segregation," in Edwards et al., eds., *Labor Market Segmentation*.

*Lourdes Beneria, "The Production and Reproduction of Labor and the Sexual Division of Labor," *Cambridge Journal of Economics*, September 1979.

*G. Sen, "The Sexual Division of Labor and the Working Class Family: Toward a Conceptual Synthesis of Class Relations and the Subordination of Women," *Review of Radical Political Economics*, Summer 1980.

#Mary Corcoran, "The Structure of Female Wages," *American Economic Review*, May 1978.

#Sheldon Danziger, "Do Working Wives Increase Family Income Inequality?" *Journal of Human Resources*, Summer 1980.

#Robert Buchele, "Sex Discrimination and Labor Market Segmentation," unpublished paper, Smith College, 1980.

4. Discrimination by Race
a. Neoclassical Perspectives

*Gary Becker, *The Economics of Discrimination* (Chicago, 1971), rev. ed.

*F. Ray Marshall, "The Economics of Racial Discrimination; A Survey," *Journal of Economic Literature*, September 1974.

#Kenneth Arrow, "The Theory of Discrimination," in O. Ashenfelter and A. Rees, eds., *Discrimination in Labor Markets*.

#Richard Freeman, "Changes in the Labor Market for Black Americans, 1948-1972," *Brookings Papers on Economic Activity*, 1973:1.

#Stanley Masters, *Black-White Income Differentials* (Academic Press, 1975), Chs. 1-5.

#J.P. Smith and F.R. Welch, "Black-White Male Wage Ratios, 1960-70," *American Economic Review*, June 1977.

#R.J. Flanagan, "Discrimination Theory, Labor Turnover, and Racial Unemployment Differentials," *Journal of Human Resources*, Spring 1978.

#D.O. Parsons, "Racial Trends in Male Labor Force Participation," *American Economic Review*, December 1980.

b. Institutionalist Perspectives

*P. Doeringer and M. Piore, *Internal Labor Markets...*, Ch. 7.

*F. Ray Marshall, "The Economics of Racial Discrimination: A Survey," *Journal of Economic Literature*, September 1974.

#Vernon Briggs et al., *The Chicano Worker* (Univ. of Texas Press, 1977).

c. Radical/Marxian Perspectives

*Michael Reich, *Racial Inequality: A Political Economic Analysis* (Princeton University Press, 1981) entire.

John Helmer, *Drugs and Minority Oppression* (Seabury, 1975).

Robert Allen, "Racism and the Black Nation Thesis," *Socialist Revolution*, January-February 1976.

#William K. Tabb, "Capitalism, Colonialism, and Racism," *Review of Radical Political Economics*, Summer 1971.

#Donald J. Harris, "The Black Ghetto as Colony: A Theoretical Critique and Alternative Formulation," *Review of Black Political Economy*, Summer 1971.

VI. COLLECTIVE EFFORTS TO SHAPE THE LABOR PROCESS AND LABOR MARKETS

A. TRADE UNIONS

1. A Selective History of the Formation of Unions and Workers' Movements in the U.S.

U.S. Department of Labor, *The American Worker* (U.S. Government Printing Office, 1976) includes excellent selections by Morris and Montgomery.

Harry Millis and Royal Montgomery, *Organized Labor* (McGraw-Hill, 1945), Chs. 1-5.

Joseph Rayback, *A History of American Labor* (Macmillan, 1959).

David M. Gordon, Richard Edwards, and Michael Reich, *Segmented Work, Divided Workers: The Historical Transformation of Labor in the United States* (Cambridge Univ. Press, 1982), entire.

#Richard Morris, *Government and Labor in Early America* (Harper, 1965).

#David Montgomery, "The Working Classes of the Pre-Industrial American City,' *Labor History*, 1968, Vol. 9.

#Norman Ware, *The Industrial Worker, 1840-1860* (Quadrangle, 1964).

#David Montgomery, *Beyond Equality: Labor and the Radical Republicans, 1860-1872* (Vintage, 1968).

#Jeremy Brecher, *Strike!* (South End Press 1978) originally published in 1972.

#James Green, *The House of Labor* (Hill & Wang, 1981).

#Stanley Aronowitz, *False Promises* (McGraw-Hill, 1974), Ch. 4.

#David Brody, "The Old Labor History and the New: In Search of an American Working Class," *Labor History*, Winter 1979.

#David Montgomery, "To Study the People: The American Working Class," *Labor History*, Fall 1980.

#Mike Davis, "Why the U.S. Working Class Is Different," *New Left Review*, Sept.-Oct. 1980.

2. Theories of the Rise of Labor Unions

Selig Perlman, *A Theory of the Labor Movement* (Macmillan, 1928).

Lloyd Ulman, *The Rise of National Labor Unions* (Harvard, 1957).

Richard A. Lester, *As Unions Mature: An Analysis of the Evolution of American Unionism* (Princeton, 1958).

#Richard Hyman, *Industrial Relations: A Marxist Introduction* (Macmillan, 1975).

Tom Clarke and Laurie Clements, *Trade Unions under Capitalism* (Humanities Press, 1978), especially Parts 1-3.

3. The Structure and Behavior of Labor Unions

Philip Taft, *The Structure and Government of Labor Unions* (Harvard, 1954).

*R. Freeman and J. Medoff, *What Do Unions Do?* (Basic Books, forthcoming 1982).

W. Atherton, *Theory of Union Bargaining Goals* (Princeton, 1973).

#M.O. Reynolds, "Whatever Happened to the Monopoly Theory of Labor Unions?" *Journal of Labor Research*, Spring 1981.

*David M. Gordon, "The Best Defense Is a Good Defense: Toward a Marxist Theory of Labor Union Structure and Behavior," in M. Carter and W. Leahy, eds., *New Directions in Labor Economics* (Notre Dame, 1982).

4. The Effects of Labor Unions

a. Theory

*Allan Cartter, *Theory of Wages and Employment*, Chs. 7-8.

*Albert Rees, *The Economics of Trade Unions*, passim.

#John T. Dunlop, *Wage Determination under Trade Unions* (Harvard, 1944), 28-94.

#F.R. Warren-Boulton, "Vertical Control by Labor Unions," *American Economic Review*, June 1977.

#C. Brown and J. Medoff, "Trade Unions in the Production Process," *Journal of Political Economy*, June 1978.

#J.S. Pettengill, "Labour Unions and the Wage Structure: A General Equilibrium Approach," *Review of Economic Studies*, Oct. 1979.

b. Empirical Analyses

i. Overview

*George E. Johnson, "Economic Analysis of Trade Unionism," *American Economic Review*, May 1975.

ii. Wage Effects

*C.J. Parsley, "Labor Unions and Wages: A Survey," *Journal of Economic Literature*, March 1980.

*Daniel B. Mitchell, *Unions, Wages, and Inflation* (Brookings, 1980).

P. Sylos-Labini, *Trade Unions and Inflation* (Harvard, 1976).

#O. Ashenfelter and G.E. Johnson, "Unionism, Relative Wages, and Labor Quality in U.S. Manufacturing," *International Economic Review*, October 1972.

#R.J. Flanagan, "Wage Interdependence in Unionized Labor Markets," *Brookings Papers on Economic Activity*, 1976:3.

#L.M. Kahn, "The Effect of Unions on the Earnings of Nonunion Workers," *Industrial and Labor Relations Review*, January 1978.

#G.J. Duncan and R. P. Stafford, "Do Union Members Receive Compensating Wage Differentials?" *American Economic Review*, June 1980.

#R.B. Freeman, "Unionism and the Dispersion of Wages," *Industrial and Labor Relations Review*, October 1980.

iii. Employment Effects

L.M. Kahn, "Unions and the Employment Status of Nonunion Workers," *Industrial Relations*, May 1978.

R. Freeman, "The Exit-Voice Tradeoff in the Labor Market: Unionism, Job Tenure, Quits, and Separations," *Quarterly Journal of Economics*, June 1980.

W.K. Viscusi, "Union, Labor Market Structure, and the Welfare Implications of the Quality of Work," *Journal of Labor Research*, Spring 1980.

R. Freeman, "The Effect of Unionism on Worker Attachment to Firms," *Journal of Labor Research*, Spring 1980.

iv. Strike Incidence

O. Ashenfelter and G.E. Johnson, "Bargaining Theory, Unions, and Strike Activity," *American Economic Review*, March 1969.

Douglas Hibbs, Jr., "Industrial Conflict in Advanced Industrial Societies," *American Political Science Review*, December 1976.

Colin Crouch and A. Pizzorno, eds., *The Resurgence of Class Conflict in Western Europe since 1968* (Macmillan, 1978), Vol. I.

#H.S. Farber, "Bargaining Theory, Wage Outcomes, and the Occurrence of Strike: An Econometric Analysis," *American Economic Review*, June 1978.

#J. Shorey, "An Inter-Industry Analysis of Strike Frequency," *Economica*, November 1976.

v. Union Membership

H.S. Farber and D.H. Saks, "Why Workers Want Unions: The Role of Relative Wages and Job Characteristics," *Journal of Political Economy*, April 1980.

B.T. Hirsch, "The Determinants of Unionization: An Analysis of Interarea Differences," *Industrial and Labor Relations Review*, January 1980.

VII. CLASS EFFORTS TO SHAPE THE LABOR PROCESS AND LABOR MARKETS

A. CLASS CONFLICT

1. A Reminder!

J.R. Prickett, "Anti-Communism and Labor History," *Industrial Relations*, October 1976.

2. The Sources of Working-Class Consciousness

C. Castoriadis, "On the History of the Workers' Movement," *Telos*, Winter 1976-77.

Barrington Moore, Jr., *Injustice: The Social Bases of Obedience and Revolt* (Shape, 1978), Chs. 4-9.

Herbert Gutman, "Work Culture, and Society in Industrializing America, 1815-1919," *American Historical Review*, June 1973.

A. Przeworski, "Proletarians into a Class," *Politics and Society*, 7:4, 1977.

F. Piven and R. Cloward, *Poor People's Movements* (Vintage, 1978.)

3. The Structure of Class Conflict

Charles Tilly, *From Mobilization to Revolution* (Addison-Wesley, 1978).

D.E. Booth, "Collective Action, Marx's Class Theory, and the Union Movement," *Journal of Economic Issues*, Symposium, Part 2, March 1978.

Anthony Giddens, *Class Structure in Advanced Capitalist Societies*.

B. Silverman and M. Yanowitch, eds., *The Worker in 'Post-Industrial' Capitalism* (Free Press, 1974), especially Parts I-IV.

URBAN

Urban Economics

William K. Tabb
University of California
Department of Economics
Fall Quarter, 1977

Urban Economics as a field of study is rooted in classic location theory (a spatial application of micro), the theory of public choice including discovery of market failure, externalities, and the difficulties of collective decision making. It is also an amorphous field--everything that happens in cities, which is to say almost all important economic questions of our urban society, are considered. Typically a course begins with a theory section, meaning applied price theory, and then considers a series of separate problem areas: urban poverty, housing congestion, pollution and so on. This terms' offering supplements this approach by examining spatial organization and social processes as part of a larger capitalistic socioeconomic formation. The state will loom larger as a mediator of class conflicts, rather than as attempting to maximize some social utility function. An effort will be made to contrast marxist views to traditional mainstream positions. Both in matters of analysis of problems and policy discussions the goal will be to understand the underlying assumptions of the different paradigms and models within each framework. Attention will be given to static allocation models using a market framework, modified neo-classical approaches which take into account externalities, cost benefit studies, the distribution of gains and losses, and the political economy of decision making.

BOOKS

Edel and Rothenberg, *Readings in Urban Economics*
Grieson, *Urban Economics*
Callow, *American Urban History*
O'Connor, *Fiscal Crisis of the State*
Tabb, *The Political Economy of the Black Ghetto*

1. INTRODUCTION TO THE COURSE AND THE APPROACH

Thompson, "The City as a Distorted Price System," in Grieson, pp. 4-14.

Anthony Downs, "Alternative Forms of Future Urban Growth," in Downs, *Urban Problems and Prospects*, pp. 6-25.

Sjoberg, "Origin and Evolution of the Cities," *Scientific American*, September 1965, pp. 54-6 also in Callow, pp. 6-16.

Tabb and Sawers, "Introduction," in Tabb and Sawers, *Marxism and the Metropolis*, pp. 1-16.

2. THE GROWTH OF CITIES IN THE U.S.

Handlin, "The Modern City as a Field of Historical Study," in Callow, pp. 17-34.

Schlesinger, "The City in American Civilization," in Callow, pp. 35-52.

Gordon, "Capitalism and the Roots of Urban Crisis," in Alcaly and Mermelstein, *The Fiscal Crisis of American Cities*, pp. 82-112.

Scheiber, "Urban Rivalry and Internal Improvements in the Old Northwest, 1820-1860," in Callow, pp. 135-145.

Wade, "Competition Between Western Cities," in Wade, in Callow, pp. 109-121.

3. THE SPATIAL ECONOMY: NEO-CLASSICAL APPROACHES TO LOCATION THEORY AND MODELING URBAN LOCATION

Alonso, "Location Theory," in Edel and Rothenberg, pp. 16-37.

Alonso, "A Theory of Urban Land Markets," in Edel and Rothenberg, pp. 104-112.

Moses and Williamson, "The Location of Economic Activities in Cities," in Edel and Rothenberg, pp. 124-134.

Tiebout, "A Method of Determining Incomes and Their Variation in Small Regions," in Grieson, pp. 19-25, and in Edel and Rothenberg, pp. 84-90.

Lowry, "Seven Models of Urban Development: A Structural Comparison," in Edel and Rothenberg, pp. 151-178.

4. CITY SIZE AND INTRA—METROPOLITAN DISPARITIES

Richardson, "Optimality in City Size, Systems of Cities and Urban Policy: A Skeptic's View," *Urban Studies*, Feburary 1972, pp. 29-48.

Gilbert, "The Arguments for Very Large Cities Reconsidered," *Urban Studies*, February 1976, pp. 27-34.

Brazer, "Economic and Social Disparities Between Central Cities and Their Suburbs," *Land Economics*, August 1967.

Murry, "Metropolitan Interpersonal Income Inequality," *Land Economics*, February 1969.

Meyer, Kain and Wohl, "Economic Change and the City: A Qualitative Evolution of Some Hypotheses," in Grieson, pp. 55-72.

Chinitz, "Contrasts in Agglomeration: New York and Pittsburgh," in Edel and Rothenberg, pp. 90-103.

5. THE CHANGING DISTRIBUTION OF JOBS AND URBAN DISINVESTMENT

Kain, "The Distribution and Movement of Jobs and Industry," in Wilson, *The Metropolitan Enigma* (Cambridge, Harvard University Press, pp. 1-31 or 1-43 in 1970 Anchor paperback edition).

Vernon, "The Changing Function of the Central City," in Wilson, ed., *Urban Renewal*, pp. 3-23.

Harrison and Kanter, "The Great State Robbery," *Working Papers*, Spring 1976, pp. 57-66.

Muller, "The Declining and Growing Metropolis: A Fiscal Comparison in Sterlieb and Hughes, *Post-Industrial America: Metropolitan Decline and Inter-Regional Job Shifts*, pp. 197-218.

Steinlieb and Hughes, "Prologue," in *Post-Industrial America: Metropolitan Decline and Inter-Regional Job Shifts*, pp. 1-28.

Leone, "The Fiscal Decline of Older Cities: Causes and Cures," *National Tax Journal*, September 1976, pp. 257-260.

6. UNEVEN DEVELOPMENT AND CLASS STRUGGLE

Sawers, "Urban Form and the Mode of Production," *Review of Radical Political Economics*, Spring 1975, pp. 59-68.

Hill, "State Capitalism and the Urban Fiscal Crisis in the United States," *International Journal of Urban and Regional Research*, March 1977, pp. 76-100.

Harvey, "Social Processes, Spatial Form and the Redistribution of Real Income in an Urban System," in Chisholm, Frey and Hagget, *Regional Forecasting*, Butterworth, 1971.

7. THE SPATIAL ECONOMY, TAKE TWO: MARXIAN URBAN THEORY

Castells, "The Wild City," *Capitalistate*, Summer 1976, pp. 2-30.

Markusen, "Class Rent and the State Uneven Development in Western Boomtowns," Manuscript, April 1977.

Mollenkopf, "The Post-War Politics of Urban Development," *Politics and Society*, 1975, pp. 247-295.

Fahri, "Urban Economic Growth and Conflict: A Theoretical Approach," *Papers of the Regional Science Association*, 1973.

Santos, "Space and Domination: A Marxist Approach," *International Social Science Journal* no. 2, 1975.

8. TRANSPORTATION: PRICING AND INVESTMENT

Vickery, "Pricing in Urban and Suburban Transport," in Grieson, pp. 106-118.

Vickery, "Congestion Theory and Transportation Investment," in Grieson, pp. 119-132.

Meyer, "Urban Transportation," in Grieson, pp. 88-105.

9. THE POLITICAL ECONOMY OF TRANSPORTATION

Wingo and Perloff, "The Washington Transportation Plan: Technics or Politics?" in Edel and Rothenberg, pp. 486-500.

Webber, "The Bart Experience—What Have We Learned? *Public Interest*, Fall 1976.

Ives, et. al., "Mass Transit and the Power Elite," *Review of Radical Political Economics*, Summer 1972, pp. 68-77.

Ketcham, "Societal Cost Accounting: A New Tool for Planners," mimeo October 1976.

10. HOUSING MARKETS

Achtenberg, "The Social Utility of Rent Control," in Pynos, Schager and Hartman, *Housing Urban America*, pp. 434-447.

Smith, "A Theory of Filtering," Edel and Rothenberg, pp. 193-204.

Edel, "Filtering in a Private Housing Market," in Edel and Rothenberg, pp. 204-214.

Muth, "Urban Residential Land and Housing Markets," in Grieson, pp. 177-199.

Mollenkopf and Pynos, "Broadway and Park Place: Property Ownership, Political Structure and Housing Policy at the Local Level," in Pynoos, Schafer and Hartman, *Housing Urban America*, pp. 55-74.

Stone, "Federal Housing Policy: A Political-Economic Analysis," in Pynos, Schafer and Hartman, eds., *Housing Urban America*, pp. 423-433.

11. URBAN RENEWAL

Nieburg, "The Equity Package," *Society*, November/December 1975, pp. 41-47.

Castels, "Urban Renewal and Social Conflict in Paris," *Social Science Information II.*, (2).

Krumholz, Cogger and Linner, "The Cleveland Policy Planning Report," *Journal of the American Institute of Planners*, September 1975, pp. 298-304.

Kessler and Hartman, "The Illusion and Reality of Urban Renewal: A Case Study of San Francisco's Yerba Buena Center," *Land Economics* 1973, pp. 440-453.

Rothenberg, "Urban Renewal Programs," in Edel and Rothenberg, pp. 215-226.

Davis and Whiaston, "The Economics of Urban Renewal," in Grieson, pp. 163-176.

12. RACIAL DISCRIMINATION AND RACIAL SEGREGATION

Shelling, "The Practice of Residential Segregation: Neighborhood Tipping," in Pascal, ed., *Racial Discrimination in Economic Life*.

Harrison, "Education and Unemployment in the Urban Ghetto," *American Economic Review*, December 1972, pp. 796-812.

Muth, "Residential Segregation and Discrimination," in von Furstenberg, et al., eds., *Patterns of Racial Discrimination*, Vol. I (Lexington, Mass.: Lexington Books, 1973), pp. 121-138.

13. URBAN POVERTY: HUMAN CAPITAL APPROACH

Thurow, *Investment in Human Capital*, pp. 1-43.

Thurow, "The Causes of Poverty," *Quarterly Journal of Economics*, February, 1967, pp. 39-57.

Adams and Nestel, "Interregional Migration, Education and Poverty in the Urban Ghetto: Another look at Black-White Earnings Differentials," *Review of Economics and Statistics*, May 1976.

Feldstein, "The Economics of the New Unemployment," *Public Interest*, Fall 1973.

Borus, Brennan and Rosen, "A Benefit-Cost Analysis of the Neighborhood Youth Corps," *Journal of Human Resources*, Spring 1970, pp. 139-159.

14. URBAN POVERTY: RADICAL APPROACHES

Wachtel, "Capitalism and Poverty in America: Paradox or Contradiction?, *Monthly Review*, June 1972, pp. 51-64.

Bluestone, "Capitalism and Poverty in America: A Discussion, *Monthly Review*, June 1972, pp. 65-71.

Gordon, "American Poverty: Functions, Mechanisms, and Contradictions," *Monthly Review*, June 1972, pp. 72-79.

Bowles, "Unequal Education and the Reproduction of the Social Division of Labor," *Review of Radical Political Economics*, Fall/Winter 1971, pp. 1-30.

Tabb, *The Political Economy of the Black Ghetto*, Chapters 2, 5, and 6.

15. LOCAL PUBLIC FINANCE: MARKET CRITERIA FOR PUBLIC CHOICE

Bator, "Government and the Sovereign Consumer," in Phelps, ed., *Private Wants and Public Needs* (New York: W.W. Norton, 1965), pp. 118-133.

Stigler, "The Tenable Range and Function of Local Government," in Phelps, ed., *Private Wants and Public Needs*, pp. 167-176.

Tiebout, "A Pure Theory of Local Expenditures," *Journal of Political Economics*, October 1956, pp. 416-424, in Edel Rothenberg, pp. 513-523.

Fitch, "Metropolitan Finance Problem," and Netzer, "Financing Urban Government," in Grieson, pp. 415-442.

16. FISCAL CRISIS: A MARXIST VIEW

O'Connor, *The Fiscal Crisis of the State*.

17. STATE INVERVENTION AND THE URBAN FISCAL CRISIS

Peppard, "Toward a Radical Theory of Fiscal Incidence," *Review of Radical Politcal Economics*, Winter 1976, pp. 1-11.

Sclar, Behr, Torto, and Edid, "Taxes, Taxpayers and Social Change: The Political Economy of the State Sector," *Review of Radical Political Economy*, Spring, 74, pp. 134-53.

Greer, "Racial Biases in the Property Tax System," *Review of Radical Political Economics*, Fall 1975, pp. 22-32.

18. MARKET AND MARXIST VIEWS: THE CASE OF CRIME

Becker, "Crime and Punishment: An Economic Approach," *Journal of Political Economy*, March/April 1968.

Stigler, "The Optimum Enforcement of Laws," *Journal of Political Economy*, May-June 70.

Cantor, "New Laws for a New Society," *Crime and Social Justice*, Fall-Winter 1974.

Judge G.W. Crockett, "Crime and Criminal Justice in Communist China."

19. ECOLOGY: TWO PERSPECTIVES

Mills, "Economic Incentives in Air Pollution Control," in Grieson, pp. 229-244, and in Edel and Rothenberg, pp. 357-363.

Mishan, "Property Rights and Amenity Rights," in Grieson, pp. 245-250.

Ridker, "Strategies for Measuring the Cost of Air Pollution," in Edel and Rothenberg, pp. 364-375.

d'Arge and Hunt, "Environmental Pollution, Externalities, and Conventional Wisdom: A Critique," pp. 266-286.

England and Bluestone, "Ecology and Class Conflict," *Review of Radical Political Economy*, Fall-Winter 1971.

Hardesty, Clement and Jencks, "Political Economy and Environmental Destruction," *Review of Radical Political Economy*, Fall-Winter 1971.

20. CITIES AND SOCIALISM

Acosta and Hardoy, *Urban Reform in Revolutionary Cuba*.

Armstrong and McGee, "Revolutionary Change and the Third World City: A Theory of Urban Involution," in McGee, ed., *The Urbanization Process in the Third World.*

Sawers, "Urban Planning in the U.S.S.R. and China," *Monthly Review,* March 77, pp. 34-39.

Fisher, "Urban Planning in the Soviet Union and Eastern Europe," in *Taming Metropolis,* Vol. II., pp. 1068-1099.

Committee of Concerned Asian Scholars, *China!,* Chapter 4, "Cities," pp. 104-149.

Kopkind, "Model City," (on Bologna, Italy) *Working Papers,* Summer 1976, pp. 32-40.

The Nation's Housing

Undergraduate
Michael Stone
College of Public and Community Service
University of Massachusetts/Boston
Fall 1979

Goals of the Course:
1. To develop familiarity with national data on households, the housing stock, housing production, and housing finance.
2. To develop an understanding of the institutions and dynamics of housing production and housing finance.
3. To develop an understanding of the various forms of government intervention in housing and the impact of these interventions.
4. To develop an understanding of the relationship between housing, the economy, and the social system.

BIBLIOGRAPHY

Frieden, Bernard J. and Arthur P. Solomon. *The Nation's Housing: 1975 to 1985.* Cambridge, MA: Joint Center for Urban Studies, 1977.
Hartman, Chester W. *Housing and Social Policy.* Englewood Cliffs, N.J.: Prentice-Hall, Inc., 1975.
Hartman, Chester, and Michael Stone. "Housing: A Socialist Alternative." In Marcus Raskin, *et al.,* eds. *The Federal Budget and Social Reconstruction,* New Brunswick, N.J.: Transaction Books, 1978.
Stone, Michael E. "Federal Housing Policy: A Political-Economic Analysis." In Jon Pynoos, Robert Schafer, and Chester Hartman, eds. *Housing Urban America,* Chicago: Aldine Publishing Company, 1973.
Stone, Michael E. "The Housing Crisis, Mortgage Lending, and Class Struggle." In Richard Peet, ed. *Radical Geography.* Chicago: Maaroufa Press, 1977.
Stone, Michael, and Emily Achtenberg. *Hostage! Housing and the Massachusetts Fiscal Crisis.* Boston: Community School, 1977.
U.S. Department of Housing and Urban Development (HUD). *Housing in The Seventies.* Washington D.C.: Government Printing Office, 1974.
U.S. League of Savings Associations. *Savings and Loan Fact Book: 79.* Chicago: U.S. League of Savings Associations, 1979.

1. INTRODUCTION AND NATIONAL HOUSING GOALS

2. THE HOUSING PROBLEM

Hartman, *Housing and Social Policy,* Chapter 1, pp. 1-18.

Frieden and Solomon, *The Nation's Housing,* Chapter 4, pp. 80-98.

3. FORECASTING RESIDENTIAL CONSTRUCTION: HOUSEHOLD GROWTH

Frieden and Solomon, Chapter 2, pp. 12-46.

4. FORECASTING RESIDENTIAL CONSTRUCTION: OTHER NEEDS

Frieden and Solomon, Chapter 3, pp. 47-79.

5. THE HOUSING MARKET AND HOMEOWNERSHIP

Stone, "Federal Housing Policy," Section on *The Price of Housing*, pp. 424-425.

Savings and Loan Fact Book, pp. 36-45.

Frieden and Solomon, Chapter 5, pp. 99-130.

6. THE RESIDENTIAL CONSTRUCTION INDUSTRY

Housing in the Seventies, Chapter 7, pp. 185-203.

7. CONSTRUCTION COSTS AND HOUSING PRODUCTION

Hartman, *Housing and Social Policy*, Chapter 2, pp. 33-52.

Savings and Loan Fact Book, pp. 16-25.

8. HOUSING FINANCE

Housing in the Seventies, Chapter 3, pp. 54-59, 69-73.

Stone, "The Housing Crisis," Section on *Mortgage Lending*, pp. 160-174.

Savings and Loan Fact Book, pp. 26-35.

9. THE FEDERAL GOVERNMENT AND HOUSING FINANCE

Stone, "Federal Housing Policy," Section on *The State and the Housing Sector*, pp. 429-433.

Housing in the Seventies, Chapter 3, pp. 59-65, 73-80.

Savings and Loan Fact Book, pp. 110-117.

10. FEDERAL HOUSING SUBSIDY PROGRAMS

Housing in the Seventies, Chapter 1, pp. 5-30.

Hartman, *Housing and Social Policy*, Chapter 4, pp. 106-108, 110-129; Chapter 5, pp. 136-145, 153-163.

11. HOUSING AND THE FEDERAL INCOME TAX

Hartman, *Housing and Social Policy*, Chapter 4, pp. 108-110; Chapter 5, pp. 145-151.

Housing in the Seventies, Chapter 2, pp. 33-44.

12. HOUSING POLICIES OF STATE GOVERNMENTS

Housing in the Seventies, Chapter 5, pp. 139-152.

Stone and Achtenberg, *Hostage!* Chapter 2, pp. 7-15: Chapter 4, pp. 27-34.

13. THE FUTURE OF HOUSING

Hartman and Stone, "Housing: A Socialist Alternative."

THE CORPORATION

The Capitalist Enterprise

William H. Lazonick
Stephen A. Marglin
Department of Economics
Harvard University
Fall 1980
Undergraduate

I. INTRODUCTION

II. ALTERNATIVE APPROACHES

A. General Background

S. Marglin, *Growth, Distribution and Prices*, ch. 15.

B. Neoclassical

G. Stigler, *The Theory of Price*, ch. 5, 6.

R. Coase, "The Nature of the Firm," *Economica*, 1937.

A. Alchian and H. Demsetz, "Production, Information Costs and Economic Organization," *American Economic Review*, December 1972.

C. Marxian

R. Edwards, M. Reich and T. Weisskopf, *The Capitalist System*, revised edition, pp. 38-49, 74-105.

*H. Gintis, "The Labor Exchange and the Theory of Capitalist Production," *Review of Radical Political Economics* (RRPE), Vol. 8, No. 2, Summer 1976.

*K. Marx, *Capital*, Vol. I, ch. 13, 14, 15.

D. Keynesian

J.M. Keynes, *The General Theory of Employment, Interest, and Money*.

*J. Robinson, *Essays in the Theory of Economic Growth*, ch. 2.

E. Behavioral

R.M. Cyert and J.G. March, *A Behavioral Theory of the Firm*, ch. 2, 6.

*H. Leibenstein, "Allocative Efficiency vs. 'X-Efficiency,'" *American Economic Review*, Vol. 56, June 1966.

*G. Stigler, "The Xistence of X-Efficiency," *American Economic Review*, No. 66, Dec. 1976.

*H. Leibenstein, "X-inefficiency Xists-Reply to an Xorcist," HIER Discussion Paper No. 522, Dec. 1976.

F. Institutional

A. Chandler, *Strategy and Structure*, Introduction.

*A. Berle and G. Means, *The Modern Corporation and Private Property*, Revised Edition, preface.

*T. Veblen, *The Theory of Business Enterprise*.

III. AN EXERCISE IN CONTRAST: MEDIEVAL ENTERPRISES

G. Duby, "Medieval Agriculture," in C. Cipolla (ed.), *The Fontana History of Europe*, Vol. I, *The Middle Ages*.

S. Thrupp, "Medieval Industry," in C. Cipolla (ed.), *The Fontana History of Europe*, Vol. I.

and one of the following:

H.S. Bennett, *Life on the English Manor*, ch. 1-10.

or

E. Carus-Wilson, "The Woolen Industry," in M. Postan and H. Habakkuk (general eds.), *The Cambridge History of Europe*, Vol. II, *Trade and Industry in the Middle Ages*.

IV. THE ORIGINS OF THE CAPITALIST ENTERPRISE

A. Introduction

E. Hobsbawm, *Industry and Empire*, ch. 2-4.

P. Mantoux, *The Industrial Revolution in the 18th Century*, Introduction, Part I, ch. 1; Part II, ch. 1-2.

B. The Creation of the Wage Labor Force

W. Lazonick, "Karl Marx and Enclosures in England," *RRPE*, Vol. 6, No. 2, 1974.

C. Division of Labor and the Rise of the Factory

S. Marglin, "What Do Bosses Do?," *RRPE*, Vol. 6, No. 2, 1974.

E. Thompson, "Time, Work Discipline, and Industrial Capitalism," *Past and Present*, Vol. 38, Dec. 1967.

*N. McKendrick, "Josiah Wedgwood and Factory Discipline," *Historical Journal*, Vol. 4, 1961; reprinted in D. Landes (ed.), *The Rise of Capitalism*.

*S. Pollard, *The Genesis of Modern Management*, ch. 5.

V. FROM SIMPLE PYRAMID TO COMPLEX FORMS OF HIERARCHICAL CONTROL

A. The Growth of the Enterprise

R. Edwards, *Contested Terrain*, pp. 43-46.

A. Chandler, *Strategy and Structure*, pp. 19-36.

A. Chandler, *The Visible Hand*, ch. 7-11.

*J. Blair, *Economic Concentration*, Parts II and III.

B. Case Studies in Control

K. Stone, "The Origins of Job Structures in the Steel Industry," *RRPE*, Vol. 6, No. 2, 1974.

W. Whyte, *Money and Motivation*, ch. 1-9.

C. "Worker Control" in the 19th Century

D. Montgomery, "Worker Control of Machine Production in the 19th Century," *Labor History*, Vol. 17, 1976.

J. Buttrick, "The Inside Contract System," *Journal of Economic History*, Vol. 12, Summer 1952.

D. The Development of Management and Managerial Technique—Separation of Management from Entrepreneurship

*S. Pollard, *The Genesis of Modern Management*, pp. 40-126, 147-159.

A. Chandler, *Strategy and Structure*, pp. 1-18, 36-51.

*F. Taylor, *Scientific Management*.

*F. Roethlisberger and W. Dickson, *Management and the Worker*, Part V.

*H. Braverman, *Labor and Monopoly Capital*, Parts I and II.

E. The Development of New Forms of Control: Technology, Bureaucracy, and Paternalism

R. Edwards, *Contested Terrain*, ch. 6-8.

F. A Comparative Perspective

*R. Dore, *British Factory, Japanese Factory*, ch. 8-10.

K. Yamamura, "A Compromise With Culture" in H. Williamson (ed.), *Evolution of International Management Structures*, pp. 159-192.

VI. THE MULTINATIONAL CORPORATION

S. Hymer, "The Multinational Corporation and the Law of Uneven Development," in J. Bhagvati (ed.), *Economics and the World Order*, pp. 113-140.

R. Muller, "The Multinational Corporation and the Underdevelopment of the Third World," in C. Wilber (ed.), *The Political Economy of Development and Underdevelopment*, pp. 151-178.

R. Barnet and R. Muller, *Global Reach*, ch. 1-3.

J. Hawley, "International Banking and the Internationalization of Capital," in Union for Radical Political Economics, *U.S. Capitalism in Crisis*, pp. 124-137.

R. Vernon, *Storm over the Multinationals*, ch. 1,2,6,7.

VII. WHO CONTROLS THE ENTERPRISE? AND TO WHAT ENDS?

A. The Case for Managerial Control

A. Berle and G. Means, *The Modern Corporation and Private Property*, Book I.

*J. Burnham, *The Managerial Revolution*.

R. Larner, "Ownership and Control of the 200 Largest Non-Financial Corporations," *American Economic Review*, September 1966.

*A. Chandler, *The Visible Hand*, ch. 12-14.

A. Chandler, *The Visible Hand*, Conclusion.

B. The Case for the Technostructure

J.K. Galbraith, *The New Industrial State*, ch. 1-8.

C. The Case for the Shareholders

R. Solow, "The New Industrial State of Son of Affluence," *Public Interest*, Fall 1967.

*S. Peterson, "Corporate Control and Capitalism," *Quarterly Journal of Economics*, February, 1965.

*B. Hindley, "Separation of Ownership and Control in the Modern Corporation," *Journal of Law and Economics*, April 1970.

D. The Case for Banks and other Financial Institutions

D. Kotz, "Finance Capital and Corporate Control," in R. Edwards, M. Reich and T. Weisskopf (eds.), *The Capitalist System*, 2nd edition.

*D. Kotz, *Bank Control of Large Corporations in the United States*.

E. What Difference Does it Make?

J.K. Galbraith, *The New Industrial State*, ch. 9-20.

*J. Williamson, "Profit Growth and Sales Maximization," *Economica*, 1966.

*R. Wong, "Profit Maximization and Alternative Theories: A Dynamic Reconciliation," *American Economic Review*, September 1975.

M. DeVroey, "The Separation of Ownership and Control in Large Corporations," *RRPE*, Vol. 7, No. 2, 1975.

VIII. CORPORATIONS AND THE STATE

M. Best and W. Connolly, *The Political Economy*, ch. 1,2,4.

J. O'Connor, *The Corporations and the State*, ch. 5.

J. Crotty and L. Rapping, "Class Struggle, Macropolicy and the Business Cycle" in Edwards, Reich and Weisskopf, *The Capitalist System*, pp. 461-469.

M. Kalecki, "Political Aspects of Full Employment" in Kalecki, *Selected Essays on the Dynamics of the Capitalist Economy*, pp. 138-145.

P. Sweezy and H. Magdoff, "Keynesian Chickens Come Home to Roost," *Monthly Review*, Vol. 25, No. 11, April 1974, pp. 1-12.

*Dollars and Sense, *Special Issue on Inflation*.

*Dollars and Sense, *The Energy Crisis* (available from 38 Union Square, Room 14, Somerville, MA 02143).

R. Barnet and R. Muller, *Global Reach*, ch. 4, 10.

R. Vernon, *Storm over the Multinationals*, ch. 8,9.

IX. SAVING AND INVESTMENT

A. Personal and Corporate Saving

P. David and J. Scadding, "Private Saving, Corporate Saving, Ultra-Rationality, Aggregation, and Denison's Law," *Journal of Political Economy*, 1974.

M. Feldstein, "Tax Incentives, Corporate Saving, and Capital Accumulation in the United States," *Journal of Political Economy*, 1973.

S. Marglin, *Growth, Distribution, and Prices*, ch. 16.

B. Investment

D. Jorgenson, "Optimal Capital Accumulation and Corporate Investment Behavior," *Journal of Political Economy*, Nov./Dec. 1968.

D. Jorgenson and C. Siebert, "A Comparison of Alternative Theories of Corporate Investment Behavior," *American Economic Review*, Sept. 1968.

J.M. Keynes, *The General Theory of Employment, Interest and Money*, ch. 11-12.

M. Kalecki, *Selected Essays on the Dynamics of Capitalist Economy*, ch. 1 and 10.

J. Steindl, *Maturity and Stagnation in American Capitalism*, ch. 9-11.

R. Marris and A. Wood, *The Corporate Economy*, ch. 1.

X. THE DETERMINANTS OF TECHNICAL CHANGE

A. General Approaches

E. Mansfield, *The Economics of Technical Change*, ch. 4.

N. Rosenberg, *Perspectives on Technology*, ch. 6. 11.

M. Kamien and N. Schwartz, "Market Structure and Innovation: A Survey," *Journal of Economic Literature*, Vol. XII, No. 1, March 1975.

A. Heertje, *Economics and Technical Change*.

J. Schumpeter, *Capitalism, Socialism and Democracy*, ch. VII-X.

P. Sweezy, "Professor Schumpeter's Theory of Innovation," *Review of Economics and Statistics*, Vol. XXV, Feb. 1943, pp. 93-96.

C. Kerr, "Productivity and Labour Relations" in Australian Institute of Political Science, *Productivity and Progress*, pp. 35-69.

National Academy of Sciences, *Technology: Processes of Assessment and Choice*, ch. 2.

B. A Case Study

L. Sandberg, "American Rings and English Mules: The Roles of Economic Rationality," *Quarterly Journal of Economics*, Vol. 83, No. 1, Feb. 1969.

W. Lazonick, "Industrial Organization and Technological Change: The Decline of the British Cotton Industry," xerox, Harvard University, September 1980.

XI. THE STRUCTURE AND FUNCTIONS OF REWARDS

A. Human Capital Theory

J. Mincer, *Schooling, Experience and Earnings*, ch. 1,5.

B. What Does Experience Do?

J. Medoff and K. Abraham, "Experience, Performance and Earnings," Harvard Institute of Economic Research Discussion Paper No. 654, October 1978.

R. Edwards, "Individual Traits and Organizational Incentives: What Makes a Good Worker?," *Journal of Human Resources*, Winter, 1976.

C. What Does Schooling Do?

M. Spence, *Market Signalling*, Ch. 1 and 2.

S. Bowles, "Unequal Education and the Reproduction of the Social Division of Labor," in R. Edwards, M. Reich and T. Weisskopf (eds.), *The Capitalist System*, 2nd edition.

D. Distribution at the Enterprise Level

E. Livernash, "The Internal Wage Structure" in G. Taylor and F. Pierson (eds.), *New Concepts in Wage Determination*.

P. Doeringer and M. Piore, *Internal Labor Markets and Manpower Analysis*, ch. 4.

H. Lydall, *The Structure of Earnings*, pp. 125-133.

D. Starrett, "Social Institutions, Imperfect Information and the Distribution of Income," *Quarterly Journal of Economics*, May 1976, pp. 261-284.

W. Lazonick, "Social Institutions, Imperfect Information and the Distribution of Income: A Comment," and D. Starrett, "Reply," *Quarterly Journal of Economics*, Feb. 1978, pp. 179-186.

XII. QUALITY OF WORK LIFE: CAUSES AND CONSEQUENCES

R. Blauner, *Alienation and Freedom*, ch. 1 and 8.

E. Shorris, "Scenes from Corporate Life," *Harpers Magazine*, March 1980.

D. Bell, *The Coming of Post-Industrial Society*, pp. 123-168.

HEW Task Force, *Work in America*, pp. 13-17, ch. 4.

S. Marglin, "Catching Flies with Honey," *Economic Analysis and Workers' Management*, Vol. XIII, No. 4, 1979, pp. 473-485.

M. Kohn, *Class and Conformity*, Preface and ch. 11.

S. Bowles and H. Gintis, *Schooling in Capitalist America*, ch. 5, 8-9.

C. Pateman, *Participation and Democratic Theory*, ch. 4, pp. 67-85.

XIII. ALTERNATIVES TO CAPITALIST ENTERPRISE

D. Ellerman, "What is a Workers' Cooperative?" xerox.

R. Oakeshott, *The Case for Workers' Cooperatives*.

K. Frieden, *The Effect of Workers' Ownership and Workers' Participation on Productivity*

C. Riskin, "Incentive Systems and Work Motivation: The Experience of China," *Working Papers*, Vol. I, No. 4, Winter 1974, pp. 27-31, 77-92.

J. Case and R. Taylor, *Co-ops, Communes, and Collectives*

G. Hunnius, "Workers' Self-Management in Yugoslavia," in G. Hunnius, G. Garson, and J. Case (eds.), *Workers' Control*, pp. 268-321.

Structure of American Industry

David Kotz
Department of Economics
University of Massachusetts
Fall 1979
Undergraduate

TEXTS

Adams, Walter (ed.), *Structure of American Industry*, 5th edition, 1977.

Blair, John, *Economic Concentration*, 1972.

Galbraith, J.K., *New Industrial State*, 2nd ed., 1971.

Goldschmid, Harvey J.; Mann, H.M.; and Weston, J.F., *Industrial Concentration: The New Learning*, 1974.

Tanzer, Michael, *The Energy Crisis*, 1974.

COURSE OUTLINE AND READINGS

Note: An asterisk (*) means that a reading is optional. GMW is the abbreviation for the book by Goldschmid et. al. (See above).

I. OVERVIEW OF U.S. INDUSTRIAL STRUCTURE

Adams, Ch. 14.
Blair, Ch. 1-4.
Averitt, Robert, The Dual Economy, Ch. 1,4,5.

II. THE DEVELOPMENT OF THE LARGE CORPORATION

Blair, Ch. 5,7,8.
Sweezy, Paul, Theory of Capitalist Development, Ch. 14.
Galbraith, Ch. 1-4.
*Scherer, F.M., *Industrial Market Structure and Economic Performance*, pp. 72-103.
Josephson, Matthew, *The Robber Barons*, Ch. 5, 12.
Blair, Ch. 11, pp. 257-69.
Kotz, D., *Bank Control of Large Corporations in the U.S.*, pp. 23-51.
Edwards, Richard, "Capital Accumulation and Corporate Power in the Transition to Monopoly Capitalism," photocopy on reserve.
*Nelson, Ralph, *Merger Movement in American Industry*, Ch. 3, 4.
*GMW, Ch. 2.
*Kolko, Gabriel, *Triumph of Conservatism*.

III. THE EVOLUTION OF CONTROL OVER INDUSTRY

Berle, Adolf A., and Means, G., *The Modern Corporation and Private Property*—Book I, ch. 1,6; and Book IV, Ch. 1-4.
Kaysen, Carl, "The Social Significance of the Modern Corporation," *American Economic Review*, May 1957.
Galbraith, Ch. 5-15 (skim ch. 10-13).
Mermelstein, David (ed.), *Economics: Mainstream Readings and Radical Critiques*, 2nd edition, Ch. 5,6,7.
Baran and Sweezy, *Monopoly Capital*, Ch. 2.
Kotz, D., *Bank Control of Large Corporations*, pp. 51-89, 96-101, 119-149.
*U.S. Congress, Senate Governmental Affairs Committee, *Interlocking Directorates Among Major U.S. Corporations*, 1978.
*Baumol, William, "On the Theory of Expansion of the Firm," *American Economic Review*, December 1962.
*Berle, Adolf A., *Power Without Property*.
*Marris, Robin, *Economic Theory of 'Managerial' Capitalism*.
*Menshikov, S., *Millionaires and Managers*.

IV. BUSINESS BEHAVIOR IN CONCENTRATED INDUSTRIES

A. Pricing Behavior

Blair, Ch. 18,19.
Bain, Joe, *Industrial Organization*, 2nd ed., pp. 304-322.
Baran and Sweezy, *Monopoly Capital*, pp. 52-66.
Galbraith, Ch. 16,17.
Adams, Ch. 2,3,5,8.
*Scherer, *Industrial Market Structure and Economic Performance*, Ch. 5-7.
*Bain, *Industrial Organization*, Ch. 8.
*Smith, R., "The Incredible Electrical Conspiracy," *Fortune*, April and May 1961.
*Blair, Ch. 14.
*Koller, Roland, "The Myth of Predatory Pricing," photocopy on reserve.

B. Market Power and Inflation

GMW, Ch. 6.
Galbraith, Ch. 22.
*Blair, Ch. 16,17.
*Scherer, *Industrial Market Structure and Economic Performance*, pp. 288-303.

C. Advertising

GMW, Ch. 3.
Galbraith, Ch. 18-20.
Baran and Sweezy, *Monopoly Capital*, Ch. 5.
Adams, Ch. 7.
*Blair, Ch. 13.

D. Technical Progress

Blair, Ch. 9,10.
Baran and Sweezy, *Monopoly Capital*, pp. 67-72, 91-99.
Galbraith, Ch. 1-3 (review).
GMW, Ch. 5.
*Scherer, *Industrial Market Structure and Economic Performance*, Ch. 15.
Sylos-Labini, *Oligopoly and Technical Progress*.

V. CASE STUDY: THE PETROLEUM INDUSTRY

Tanzer, Ch. 1-4, 8.
Blair, John, *Control of Oil*, Ch. 6,7,11,12.
Adams, Ch. 4.
Vernon, Raymond (ed.) *The Oil Crisis*, pp. 39-57, 159-78.
Ruttenberg, S.H., "Control of Competing Energy Sources," photocopy.
Teece, David, "Divestiture and the Economics of Energy Supply," photocopy.
Mancke, R.B., "Competition in the Oil Industry," photocopy.

VI. SUMMARY: THE CONSEQUENCES OF MARKET POWER AND CORPORATE GIANTISM

Blair, Ch. 20.
Galbraith, Ch. 29-32.
Adams, Ch. 14 (review).
GMW, pp. 162-201; 231-245.
Baran and Sweezy, *Monopoly Capital*, Ch. 11.

VII. SOLUTIONS TO THE MONOPOLY PROBLEM

Galbraith, Ch. 25-28, 32-35.
GMW, pp. 360-400.
*Blair, Ch. 22.

RACISM

The Political Economy of Discrimination

Economics
Guy C.Z. Mhone
New School of Social Research/Howard
University, School of Human Ecology
Spring 1981
Graduate

The first two times I taught this course it was primarily a critique of neoclassical and dual labor market theories of discrimination. Basing our investigation on a 30 page bibliographic outline, we explored taste theories, risk aversion theories, statistical theories, labor participation theories, job search theories, monopolistic theories, and dual labor market theories of discrimination; we discussed mediating influences such as education, spatial factors and institutional and public policies; and finally we reviewed the empirical literature on differences in black/white incomes and returns to education, and spatial discrimination. We found these theories inadequate, and quite circumscribed from the point of view of political economy. However, it was increasingly apparent to us that despite our extreme dissatisfaction with the preceding theories we could not counterpose an adequate Marxist (historical materialist) theory of discrimination as an alternative.

Fortunately, in the second semester the course was taught, we were able to arrive at the methodological requirements for a historical materialist approach to the analysis of discrimination. It is as a result of these requirements that a new outline and reading list was developed. The bibliographic outline given below is a revised and extended version of the one used in the Spring of 1981. In this semester we decided to forego the usual 'running' critique of traditional theories in favor of a total concentration on evolving a historical materialist understanding of discrimination in the tradition of political economy. Not only did we find this approach immensely more illuminating and satisfying, but we also found it to be pregnant with significant implications for developing a Marxist comparative and general theory of discrimination that synthesizes class and race.

The following are the historical materialist postulates we used as a guide in our investigation:

a) No group of people is inherently or innately inclined to discriminate or to be discriminated against, and, as such, the origin of discrimination should not be located in the superstructure or genetic make-up of a particular group.

b) Under capitalism the need to discriminate should be historically located in the need to maximize surplus through the differential exploitation of labor.

c) The historical conditions under which such differential exploitation of labor arises and is possible should be identifiable in the determinants of the differences in levels of the socially necessary reproduction costs of the labor of different groups prior to and at the advent of capitalism.

d) The market and extra market mechanisms (mediating factors) used to ensure a differential supply and utilization of labor should be identifiable. Such labor utilization and activities by capitalists are said to constitute primary discrimination.

e) Since the labor needs of capitalists are not homogeneous the conflicts among fractions of the capitalist class arising from primary discrimination should be identifiable and predictable on the basis of their technical production requirements and interests in maximizing the rate of surplus accumulation.

f) The impact of primary discrimination on different fractions of the working class should be identifiable and predictable on the basis of whether primary discrimination (i.e. use of "cheap" labor) materially affects their incomes and employment positively or negatively.

g) The attempts by some fractions of labor to react to primary discrimination through economic and extra economic discriminatory measures designed to safeguard their incomes and employment can be said to constitute secondary discrimination.

h) Intra and inter class interest group configurations around the issues of primary versus secondary discrimination should be identifiable at the political level. The impact on the economy of attempts to arrive at compromise combinations of the two types of discrimination will manifest itself as a contradiction and as a fetter on accumulation.

i) Racist ideologies rationalizing primary and secondary discrimination separately or jointly should be identifiable and traceable to the material interests of particular configurations of fractions of capitalist and labor interests.

g) The conditions under which a discriminatory ideology becomes all embracing and semi-autonomous in the superstructural sphere sould be identifiable in the degree to which mediating factors enhance its diffusion and internalization by discriminators and the discriminated alike and hence, should be manifested in seemingly 'autonomous' and 'rational' behavior of the type generally assumed as given in traditional theories of discrimination (e.g. taste, risk aversion/statistical, job search, and labor force participation theories).

The procedure entailed periodizing U.S. economic history according to the resource (inputs or factors of production) utilization patterns dominant in each period. For each period we found it necessary to disaggregate the capitalist and working classes into different fractions; and the material interests of each fraction in primary and secondary discrimination were identified. We also found it important to place racial discrimination within a comparative perspective and within the context of other forms of discrimination such as those relating to sex, ethnic and age discrimination. Finally we were compelled to recognize that since discrimination qualitatively affects the relative costs of inputs as perceived from the point of view of capitalist accumulation, it cannot be viewed as a peripheral phenomenon. Once discrimination has begun it becomes both a significant cause and effect of emerging resource utilization patterns in succeeding periods for the economy as a whole.

BIBLIOGRAPY

I. THE MARXIST THEORY OF EXPLOITATION AND HETEROGENEOUS LABOR

a) Labor as a commodity.

b) Accumulation through absolute and relative surplus.

c) Role of the reserve army.

Bowles, S. and Herbert Gintis. "The Marxian Theory of Value and Heterogeneous Labour: A Critique and Reformation", *Cambridge Journal of Economics*, Vol. 1, 1977, pp. 173-192.

Marx, Karl, *Capital*, Vol. 1, Parts III, IV, V, Chapter 25.

_____, *Grundrisse*, (Vintage Books, Random House, 1973), "The Chapter on Capital", pp. 250-401, 459-471.

_____, *Theories of Surplus Value*, (Progress Publishers, Moscow, 1963), Vol. 1, Chapter IV.

Mhone, Guy C.Z. "Discrimination and Labor Market Segmentation Under Capitalism: A General and Comparative Marxist Approach", (Unpublished paper used for class discussion).

Roemer, J.E. "Divide and Conquer: Microfoundations of a Marxian Theory of Wage Discrimination", *Bell Journal of Economics*, Vol. 10, pp. 695-705, Aut. 1979.

II. SLAVERY UNDER CAPITALISM AND THE ORIGINS OF DISCRIMINATION

a) Economic basis of slavery.

b) Inter and intra class contradictions within context of regional, national and world capitalist economy.

c) Superstructural rationalization and the evolution of an ideology of racism.

Anderson, Ralph V. "Labor Utilization and Productivity, Diversification and Self Sufficiency, Southern Plantations, 1800-1840", Doctoral Dissertation, University of North Carolina, 1974.

Aufhauser, Keith, "Slavery and Scientific Management", *Journal of Economic History*, Vol. 33, 1973.

Bernstein, Barton J. "Southern Politics and Attempts to Reopen the African Slave Trade", *Journal of Negro History*, Vol. 51, 1961.

Daniel, Pete, *The Shadow of Slavery: Peonage in the South 1901-1969*, Urbana: University of Illinois Press, 1972.

David, Paul A., Herbert Gutman, Richard Sutch, Peter Temin and Gavin Wright, *Reckoning With Slavery*, (Oxford University Press, New York, 1976).

Domar, Evsey, "The Causes of Slavery or Serfdom: A Hypothesis", *Journal of Economic History*, Vol. 30, 1970.

Fleisig, Heywood, "Slavery, the Supply of Agricultural Labor and Industrialization in the South", *Journal of Economic History*, Vol. 36, 1976.

Fogel, R.W. and Stanley L. Engerman, *Time on the Cross: The Economics of American Negro Slavery* (Little-Brown, Boston, 1974).

Genovese, Eugene, *The Political Economy of Slavery*, (Random House, 1967).

Jordan, W.D. *White Over Black*, (Penquin Books, 1968).

Patterson, Orlando, "On Slavery and Slave Formations", *New Left Review*, No. 117, 1979, pp. 31-67.

Soltow, Lee, "Economic Inequality in the United States in the Period from 1790 to 1860", *Journal of Economic History*, Vol. 31, 1971.

Wallerstein, Immanuel, "American Slavery and the Capitalist World Economy", *American Journal of Sociology*, Vol. 81, 1976.

Williams, Eric, *Capitalism and Slavery*, (Capricorn Books, G.P. Putnam's Sons, N.Y., 1966).

Wright, G.J. "Cheap Labor and Southern Textiles before 1880", *Journal of Economic History*, Vol. 39, pp. 655-680, 1979.

III. THE POST-EMANCIPATION PERIOD TO THE TURN OF THE CENTURY

a) The rise of tenancy and share-cropping and a Black Proletariat.

b) The rise of secondary discrimination and its coexistence with primary discrimination and the emergence of Jim Crow.

c) Emerging contradictions in imperatives of regional and national expansion.

Higgs, Robert, *Competition and Coercion: Blacks in the American Economy*, (Cambridge University Press, 1977).

———, "Race, Tenure and Resource Allocation in Southern Agriculture, 1910", *Journal of Economic History*, Vol. 33, 1973.

Mandle, Jay R. *The Roots of Black Poverty: The Southern Plantation Economy After the Civil War*, (Duke University Press, 1978).

———, "The Re-establishment of the Plantation Economy in the South, 1865-1910", *Review of Black Political Economy*, Vol. 3, No. 2, 1973, pp. 68-88.

Ransom, Rogert L. *One Kind of Freedom: The Economic Consequences of Emancipation*, (Cambridge University Press, Cambridge, 1977).

Reid, Joseph D., Jr. "Sharecropping as an Understandable Market Response", *Journal of Economic History*, Vol. 33, 1973.

Shugg, Roger W. *Origins of Class Struggle in Louisiana*, (Louisiana State University Press, Baton Rouge, 1939).

Weiner, Jonathan M. "Planter-Merchant Conflict in Reconstruction Alabama", *Past and Present*, Vol. 68, 1975.

Woodward, C. Vann, *The Strange Career of Jim Crow*, (Oxford University Press, 1966).

Wright, Gavin, *The Political Economy of the Cotton South*, (Norton, N.Y., 1978).

IV. MODERN INDUSTRIAL CAPITALISM: APPROACH TO TECHNICAL RELATIONS

a) The technical division of labor and industrial structure.

b) The technical division of labor occupational structure and labor market segmentation.

c) Labor-market segmentation and heterogeneous labor.

Baron, H. "The Demand for Black Labor", *Radical America*, Vol. 9, No. 2, 1971.

Batra, Ravandva and Gerald W. Scully, "Technical Progress, Economic Growth, and the North-South Wage Differential", *Journal of Regional Science*, Vol. 12, No. 3, 1972, pp. 375-386.

Beck, E.M. et al. "Industrial Segmentation and Labor Market", *Social Problems*, Vol. 28, pp. 113-130, 1980.

Bellante, D. "North-South Differential and the Migration of Heterogeneous Labor", *American Economic Review*, Vol. 69, pp. 166-175, March, 1979.

Braverman, Harry, *Labor and Monopoly Capital: The Degradation of Work in the Twentieth Century*, (Monthly Review Press, N.Y., 1974).

Chivers, T.S. "The Proleterianisation of a Service Worker", *Sociological Review*, Vol. 21, No. 4, Nov. 1973, pp. 633-656.

Doeringer, Peter B. and Michael J. Piore, *Internal Labor Markets and Manpower Analysis*, (U.S. Dept. of Labor, Office of Manpower Administration, Washington, D.C., May 1970).

Edwards, Richard, *Contested Terrain: The Transformation of the Workplace in the Twentieth Century*, (Basic Books, Inc., N.Y., 1979).

Edwards, R. et al. *Labor Market Segmentation*, (Leviton Books, 1975).

Glenn, E. Nakaro and Roslyn L. Feldberg, "Degraded and Diskilled: The Proletarization of Clerical Work", *Social Problems*, Vol. 25, No. 1, 1977, pp. 51-64.

Gustman, Alan L. and Martin Segal, "The Skilled-Unskilled Wage Differential in Construction", *Industrial and Labor Relations Review*, Vol. 27, No. 2, January 1974, pp. 261-275.

Hammerman, Herbert, "Minority Workers in Construction Referral Unions", *Monthly Labor Review*, Vol. 95, No. 5, May 1972, pp. 17-26.

Hodson, R. "Labor in the Monopoly, Competitive, and State Sectors of Production", *Politics and Society*, Vol 8, Numbers 3-4, pp. 429-480, December 1978.

Johnson, D.B. and J.L. Stern, "The Shift from Blue-Collar to White Collar Jobs", *Monthly Labor Review*, Vol. 92, No. 10, October 1969, pp. 7-13.

Knight, J.B. "Job Competition, Occupational Production Functions, and Filtering Down", *Oxford Economic Papers*, Vol. 31, pp. 187-204, July 1979.

Lowell, Ruth Jabrican, "Testing a Dual Labor Market Classification of Jobs", *Journal of Regional Studies*, Vol. 18, No. 1, 1978, pp. 95-103.

Mattila, J. Peter, "The Effect of Extending Minimum Wages to Cover Household Maids", *Journal of Human Resources*, Vol. 8, No. 3, 1973, pp. 365-382.

Oaxaca, Ronald L., "Estimation of Union/Non-Union Wage Differentials Within Occupation/Regional Subgroups", *Journal of Human Resources*, Vol. 10, No. 4, Fall 1975, pp. 529-537.

O'Conner, James, *The Fiscal Crisis of the State*, (St. Martins Press, N.Y., 1973).

Orton, Eliot S. "Changes in the Skill Differential: Union Wages in Construction 1907-1972", *Industrial and Labor Relations Review*, Vol. 30, No. 1, 1976, pp. 16-24.

Parcel, T.L. "Race, Regional Labor Markets and Earnings", *American Sociological Review*, Vol. 44, pp. 262-279, April 1979.

Singh, R. and J. Hefner, "Relative Job Discrimination and Technology in Basic Industries", *Review of Black Political Economy*, Vol. 6, pp. 29-40, Fall 1975.

Wool, Harold, *The Labor Supply for Lower-Level Occupations*, (Praeger Publishers, N.Y., 1976).

V. MODERN INDUSTRIAL CAPITALISM AND THE UTILIZATION OF BLACK LABOR

a) The demand for and utilization of Black labor through primary discrimination.

b) The emergence of secondary discrimination in industrial areas and intra working class conflict.

Adams, Arvil V. "Black-White Occupational Differentials in Southern Metropolitan Employment", *Journal of Human Resources*, Vol. 7, No. 4, Fall 1972, pp. 500-517.

Bonavicich, E. "Advanced Capitalism and Black/White Race Relations in the United States: A Split Labor Market Interpretation", *American Sociological Review*, Vol. 41, pp. 34-51, 1976. Reply with rejoinder K. Oehler, Vol. 44, pp. 339-344, '79.

Bracey, J.H. et al. *Black Workers and Organized Labor*, (Wadsworth Publishing Company, 1971).

Cayton, H.R. and George Mitchell, *Black Workers and the New Unions*, (McGrath Publishing Company, 1969).

Christiansen, J.B. "Split Labor Market Theory and Filipino Exclusion: 1927-1934", *Phylon*, Vol. 40, 66-74, March 1979.

Crawford, V.P. and E.M. Knoer. "Job Matching with Heterogeneous Firms and Workers", *Econometrica*, Vol. 49, pp. 437-49, 1981.

Cummings, S. "White Ethnics, Racial Prejudice, and Labor Market Segmentation", *American Journal of Sociology*, Vol. 85, pp. 938-950, 1980.

Dick, T. and M.H. Medoff, "Filtering by Race and Education in the U.S. Manufacturing Sector: Constant-Ratio Elasticity of Substitution Evidence", *Review of Economic Statistics*, Vol. 58, pp. 148-155, May 1976.

Foner, P.S. *Organized Labor and the Black Worker*, (International Publishers, N.Y., 1976).

Gordon, David M., Editor, *Problems in Political Economy: An Urban Perspective*, (D.C. Heath and Co., Lexington, Massachusetts, 1977).

Gould, W.B. *Black Workers and White Unions*, (Cornell University Press, Ithaca, 1977).

Hill, Herbert, "Labor Union Control of Job Training: A Critical Analysis of Apprenticeship Outreach Programs and Hometown Plans", Howard University Institute of Urban Affairs, Washington, D.C., 1974.

Hogan, Lloyd and Harry Hains, "The Occupational-Industrial Structure of Black Employment in the United States", *Review of Black Political Economy*, Vol. 6, No. 1, 1975, pp. 8-28.

Jacobson, Julius, *The Negro and the American Labor Movement*, (Anchor Books, 1968).

Johnson, W.R. "Racial Wage Discrimination and Industrial Structure", *Bell Journal of Economics*, Vol. 9, No. 1, 1978, pp. 70-81.

Leggett, *Class, Race and Labor*, (Oxford University Press, 1968).

Niemi, Albert W., Jr. "Wage Discrimination Against Negroes and Puerto Ricans in the New York SMSA: An Assessment of Educational and Occupational Differences", *Social Science Quarterly*, Vol. 55, No. 1, 1975, pp. 112-120.

Northrup, H.R. and Richard Rowan, *Negro Employment in Southern Industry*, (Industrial Resource Unit, Wharton School of Finance and Commerce, University of Pennsylvania, 1970).

Perlo, Victor, *Economics of Racism U.S.A.: Roots of Black Inequality*, (International Publishers, N.Y., 1975).

Reich, Michael, "Persistence of Racial Inequality in Urban Areas and Industries 1950-1970", *American Economic Review Papers and Proceedings*, Vol. 70, pp. 128-131, 1980.

Rhee, Jongmo, "The Redistribution of the Black Work Force in the South by Industry", *Phylon*, Vol. 35, No. 3, September 1974, pp. 293-300.

Spero and Harris, *The Black Worker*, (Columbia University Press, 1931).

Snyder, D. and P.M. Hudis, "Occupational Income and the Effects of Minority Competition and Segregation: A Reanalysis and Some Evidence," *American Sociological Review*, Vol. 41, pp. 209-234, April 1976.

Swinton, David H. "A Labor Force Competition Theory of Discrimination Over Time", *American Economic Review*, Vol. 67, No. 1, February 1977.

Szymanski, A. "Racism and Sexism as Functional Substitutes in the Labor Market", *Sociological Quarterly*, Vol. 17, pp. 65-73, Winter, 1976.

Weeks, G.C. "Labor Markets, Class Interests, and the Technology of Production", *Journal of Economic Issues*, Vol. 14, pp. 553-566, June 1980.

Wilson, W.J. *The Declining Significance of Race*, (University of Chicago Press, Chicago, 1978).

Winegarden, C.R. "Barriers to Black Employment in White-Collar Jobs: A Quantitative Approach", *Review of Black Political Economy*, Vol. 2, No. 3, 1972, pp. 13-24.

Wise, D.E. "Effect of the Bracero on Agricultural Production in California", *Economic Inquiry*, Volume 12, pp. 547, 558, 1974.

Wright, Ohlin, *Class Structure and Income Determination*, (Academic Press, 1979).

VI. SOME COMPARATIVE STUDIES IN THE POLITICAL ECONOMY OF DISCRIMINATION

a) Review of studies illustrating or utilizing historical materialist interpretation of experiences in Southern Africa, Western Europe and England.

b) For further study approach can be extended to study of discrimination on the basis of sex, ethnicity and age.

Burawoy, Michael, "The Functions and Reproduction of Migrant Labor: Comparative Material from Southern Africa and the United States", *American Journal of Sociology*, Vol. 81, No. 5, pp. 1050-1087.

Castales, Stephen and Godula Kosack, "The Function of Labor Immigration in Western European Capitalism", *New Left Review*, No. 73, May 1972.

_____, *Immigrant Workers and Class Structure in Western Europe*, (Oxford University Press, London, 1973).

Cox, Oliver, *Caste, Class and Race*, (Doubleday and Company, 1948).

Feit, E. and R.G. Stokes, "Racial Prejudice and Economic Pragmatism: A South African Case-Study", *Journal of Modern African Studies*, Vol. 14, pp. 487-506, Spring 1976.

Johnstone, Frederick A. *Class, Race and Gold: A Study of Class Relations and Racial Discrimination in South Africa*, (Routledge and Kegan Paul, 1976).

Mhone, Guy C.Z. *The Political Economy of a Dual Labor Market in Africa*, (Fairleigh Dickinson University Press/Associated University Presses, New Brunswick, 1982).

_____, "Factor Combinations and the Distribution of Product in a Dominance Subjugation System: An Approach to the Allocation of Resources in the Apartheid Economy of South Africa", *Journal of Southern African Affairs*, Vol. 1, October 1976, pp. 31-52.

Robinson, R.V. and J. Kelley, "Class as Conceived by Marx and Dahrendorf: Effects on Income Inequality and Politics in the U.S. and Great Britain", *American Sociological Review*, Vol. 44, pp. 38-58, 1979.

Simons, J.J. and R.E. *Class and Color in South Africa*, (Penquin Books, 1969).

Stanley, Greenberg, *Race and State in Capitalist Development*, Yale University Press, New Haven, 1980.

Stewart, J.B. "Contemporary Patterns of Black-White Political Economic Inequality in the United States and South Africa", *Review of Black Political Economy*, Vol. 9, pp. 359-391, 1979.

Thompson, E.P. *The Making of the English Working Class*, (Random House, 1966).

LAW AND CRIME

Sociology of Law

David Greenberg
New York University
Department of Sociology
Spring 1982

The course deals primarily with the relationship between a society's social organization and its legal system. Such topics as the social sources of law and the social functions of law are examined in a comparative, historical framework. Although legal systems will be examined in a variety of settings, including the acephalous societies studied by anthropologists, the city-states and empires of classical antiquity, and the feudal societies of medieval Europe, particular attention will be given to the relationship between law and the development of capitalism. What role has law played in the rise of capitalism? How is it implicated in the reproduction of capitalist social relations today? What are its possibilities and its limits as an instrument of social change? The course will also include an introduction to the sociology of the legal profession, taking up such issues as the effects of law school socialization, professional self-regulation, stratification within the legal profession, relationships between lawyers and clients, the problems of combining radical politics with legal practice.

ASSIGNED TEXTS

Lawrence M. Friedman and Stewart Macauley (eds.), *Law and the Behavioral Sciences* (denoted by FM below)

Max Weber, *On Law in Economy and Society*

Edwin Schur, *Law and Society: A Sociological View*

John Commons, *Legal Foundations of Capitalism*

J. Willard Hurst, *Law and the Conditions of Freedom in Nineteenth Century America*

Marc Green and Bruce Wasserstein (ed.), *With Justice for Some* (GW below)

Jerold Auerbach, *Unequal Justice: Lawyers and Social Change in Modern America*

RECOMMENDED TEXTS

Vilhelm Aubert (ed.), *Sociology of Law*

Lawrence Friedman, *A History of American Law*

Roberto Unger, *Law in Modern Society*

Michael E. Tigar and Madeleine R. Levy, *Law and the Rise of Capitalism*

Piers Beirne and Richard Quinney, *Law, State and Capital: Readings for a Marxist Theory of Law*

I. OVERVIEW OF THE COURSE. THE MEANING OF LAW, LEGALITY AND THE RULE OF LAW

This introductory session will review the historical development of the sociology of law and an overview of its scope. The debate between normative and positivist approaches to the definition of law will be reviewed.

Edwin Schur, *Law and Society*, pp. 17-67.

Lawrence Friedman, "Legal Culture and Social Development," pp. 1028-1031 im FM.

Philip Selznick, "The Sociology of Law," pp. 11-17 in FM.

Marc Galanter, "Notes on the Future of Social Research in Law," pp. 18-20 in FM.

Donald Black, *The Behavior of Law*, pp. 1-10.

Supplementary Readings

Stanley Diamond, "The Rule of Law versus the Order of Custom," in Robert Paul Wolff, *The Rule of Law*

Ronald Dworkin, "Philosophy and the Critique of Law," in Wolff.

Lon Fuller, "Human Interaction and the Law," in Wolff.

Georg Simmel, *The Sociology of Georg Simmel* (K. Wolff, ed.), pp. 186-189, 250-67.

Carl A. Auerbach, "Legal Tasks for the Sociologist," 1 *Law and Society Review* 91, 1966.

Jerome Skolnick, "Social Research on Legality: A Reply to Auerbach," 1 *Law and Society Review* 105, 1966.

Philippe Nonet, "For Jurisprudential Sociology," *Law and Society Review* 10, 515-46, 1976.

Richard Posner, *Economic Analysis of Law*.

II. A COMPARATIVE AND HISTORICAL ANALYSIS OF LAW AND SOCIAL ORGANIZATION

1. LAW IN STATELESS SOCIETIES

Drawing on the anthropological literature on dispute-processing in stateless, "primitive" societies, we will ask whether such societies have law, and if so, what characteristics it possesses and how it interfaces with other social institutions. How does the primitive state arise, and in what way does its law differ from the law of stateless societies?

Paul Bohannan, *Justice and Judgment among the Tiv* (excerpt in FM, pp. 994-99).

William Felstiner, "Influences of Social Organization on Dispute Processing," 9 *Law and Society Review*, 1974 (reprinted in FM, pp. 1013-1027).

Richard D. Schwartz and James C. Miller, "Legal Evolution and Societal Complexity," *American Journal of Sociology* 70, pp. 159-169, 1964, reprinted in FM, pp. 1032-1045.

Emile Durkheim, "Types of Law in Relation to Types of Social Solidarity," pp. 17-29 in Aubert.

Supplementary Readings

Max Gluckman, *The Judicial Process among the Barotse of Northern Rhodesia* (excerpt in Aubert, pp. 161-170).

Takeyoshi Kawashima, "Dispute Resolution in Contemporary Japan," in A. von Mehren (ed.), *Law in Japan* (excerpt in Aubert, pp. 182-193).

E.A. Hoebel, *The Law of Primitive Man*.

A.S. Diamond, *Primitive Law, Past and Present*.

H.D. Siebel, "Social Deviance in Comparative Perspective," in Robert A. Scott and Jack D. Douglas, *Theoretical Perspectives on Deviance*.

Michael Barkun, *Law without Sanctions*.

Laura Nader (ed.), *Law in Culture and Society*.

Leopold Pospisil, *Anthropology of Law: A Comparative Theory*.

Sally Falk Moore, *Law as Process: An Anthropological Approach*.

Elman Service, *Origins of the State and Civilization*.

Lucy Mair, *Primitive Government*.

Morton Fried, *The Evolution of Political Societies*.

Lawrence Krader, *Formation of the State*.

2. LAW IN CLASSICAL ANTIQUITY, AND IN FEUDAL EUROPE

"Legal Texts from Mesopotamia," in James B. Pritchard, *The Ancient Near East*, vol. 1, 33-72; vol. 2, pp. 70-86.

Hebrew Law, Exodus 20-23, Leviticus 17-26, Deuteronomy 5-28; I Kings 3:16-28.

Marc Bloch, *Feudal Society*, vol. 1, pp. 109-133, 219-240; vol. 2, pp. 359-374, 320-331.

Supplementary Readings

a. Ancient Law

Robert Nisbet, "Kinship and Political Power in First Century Rome," pp. 257-271 in *Sociology and History*, reprinted in Donald Black and Maureen Mileski, *The Social Organization of Law*, pp. 161-177.

S.N. Eisenstadt, *The Political Systems of Empires*.

Roberto Unger, *Law in Modern Society: Toward a Criticism of Social Theory*, ch. 2.

W.J. Jones, *Law and Legal Theory of the Greeks*.

George Calhoun, *The Growth of Criminal Law in Ancient Greece*.

Wolfgang Kunkel, *An Introduction to Roman Legal and Constitutional History*.

John Crook, *Law and Life of Rome*.

b. Marc Kennedy, "Beyond Incrimination," Catalyst No. 6, 1970, reprinted in Charles Reasons, *The Criminologist: Crime and the Criminal*.

S.F.C. Milson, *Historical Foundations of the Common Law*.

R.C. van Caenegem, *The Birth of the Common Law*.

Marc Bloch, *Feudal Society*, pp. 134-218, 241-279 in vol. 1; 375-440 in vol. 2.

3. LAW AND EARLY CAPITALIST ECONOMIC DEVELOPMENT. THE CIVIL LAW AND COMMON LAW TRADITIONS.

The late middle ages sees the growth of cities, revival of trade, centralization of political authority, and religious schisms. How are these processes reflected in law? What contributions does law make to these changes? Does the Reformation play a role in the development of a capitalist economy and legal system?

Max Weber, *On Law in Economy and Society*, chs. 9-14.

John Commons, *Legal Foundations of Capitalism*, chs. 6, 7.

Supplementary Readings

Jerome Hall, *Theft Law and Society*, chs. 1-3.

David Trubeck, "Max Weber on Law and the Rise of Capitalism," 1972 *Wisconsin Law Review* 170, 1972.

John Merryman, *The Civil Law Tradition*.

Michael Tigar and Madeleine Levy, *Law and the Rise of Capitalism*, Parts 2, 3.

George Rusche and Otto Kirchheimer, *Punishment and Social Structure*, ch. 2.

Judith Koffler, "The Contribution of Edward I in the Capitalist Transformation of England," pp. 107-126 in Steven Spitzer (Ed.), *Research in Law and Sociology*, vol. 3.

David Little, *Religion, Order and Law: A Study in Pre-Revolutionary England*.

Jan Smith, "Violence, Property Rights and Economic Growth in Pre-Industrial Europe," pp. 87-106 in Steven Spitzer (ed.), *Research in Law and Sociology*, vol. 3.

Alan MacFarlane, *The Origins of English Individualism: The Family, Property, and Social Transformation*.

4. LAW, INDIVIDUAL FREEDOM AND THE STATE: LIBERAL THEORY AND MARXIST CRITIQUE

In 18th century England, the doctrine of economic liberalism or individualism proposed a radically new conception of the relationship between individual and state, with profound implications for the scope and form of law.

Franz Neumann, *The Democratic and the Authoritarian State*, esp. chs. 1, 2, 6.

Maureen Cain, "The Main Themes of Marx' and Engels' Sociology of Law," 1 *British Journal of Law and Society*, reprinted in FM. pp. 653-662.

Milton Mankoff, "Power in Advanced Capitalist Society: A Review Essay on Recent Elitist and Marxist Criticism of Pluralist Theory," 17 *Social Problems* 418, 1970, reprinted in FM, pp. 663-75.

William Chambliss, "The State, the Law, and the Definition of Behavior as Criminal or Delinquent," pp. 7-43 in Daniel Glaser (ed.), *Handbook of Criminology*.

Friedrich Engels, "Letter to Conrad Schmidt," pp. 401-407 in L. Feuer (ed.), *Marx and Engels: Basic Writings*.

Isaac Balbus, "Commodity Form and Legal Form: An Essay on the 'Relative Autonomy' of the Law," *Law and Society Review* (1977) 11:529-570.

Supplementary Readings

Roberto Unger, *Law in Modern Society*, ch. 3.

Otto Kirchheimer, "The Rechtstaat as Magic Wall," pp. 428-452 in Burin and Schell (eds.), *Politics, Law and Social Change: Selected Essays of Otto Kirchheimer*.

Karl Marx, "On the Jewish Question," and "Relation of the State and Law to Property," in *The German Ideology*. Reprinted in Lloyd D. Easton and Kurt H. Guddat, *Writings of the Young Marx on Philosophy and Society*.

Peter Gabel, "Reification in Legal Reasoning," pp. 25-51 in Steven Spitzer (ed), *Research in Law and Sociology*, vol. 3.

Eugene Genovese, "The Hegemonic Function of the Law," in *Roll, Jordan Roll*, pp. 35-49.

Piers Beirne and Robert Sharlett, *Pashukanis: Selected Writings on Marxism and the Law*.

Maureen Cain and Alan Hunt, *Marx and Engels on Law*.

Bob Fine et al., *Capitalism and the Rule of Law*.

David Greenberg and Nancy Anderson, "Recent Marxisant Work on Law," *Contemporary Crises* 5 (1981): 293-322.

Piers Beirne and Richard Quinney (eds.), *Law, State and Capital: Readings for a Marxist Theory of Law*.

Paul Phillips, *Marx and Engels on Law and Laws*.

Paul Hirst, *On Law and Ideology*.

Bernard Edelman, *Ownership of the Image*.

Thomas Mathiesen, *Law, Society and Political Action*, chs. 1-4.

Bob Jessop, "On Recent Marxist Theories of Law, the State and Jurido-Political Ideology," *International Journal of the Sociology of Law* 8 (1980): 339-368.

Mark Tushnet, "A Marxist Analysis of American Law," *Marxist Perspectives* 1 (1978): 96-116.

5. WEIMAR LAW AND NAZI LAW

Although Weber viewed the nineteenth century German civil codes as the culmination of a long process of rationalization in law, German law began to develop in the last years of Weber's life, and following his death, in the Weimar Republic, and then in Nazi Germany, in a very different direction from early tendencies. We will examine the nature and social sources of legal change in the Weimar Republic and during the Nazi years.

Otto Kirchheimer, "Weimar—and What Then? An Analysis of a Constitution," in Burin and Schell.

Otto Kirchheimer, "The Legal Order of National Socialism," in Burin and Schell.

Roberto Unger, *Law in Modern Society*, pp. 192-220.

Franz Neumann, *The Democratic and the Authoritarian State*, chs. 11, 12.

Supplementary Readings

Franz Neumann, *Behemoth: The Structure and Practice of National Socialism*.

Mihaly Vajda, *Fascism*.

6. FUNCTIONALISM, LAW, AND THE UNIVERSAL PROBLEM OF SOCIAL ORDER.

With this topic we interrupt our historical and comparative approach to examine the place of law in

Parsonian functionalist theory. We will be particularly concerned with a confrontation between Parsonian theory and Marxist theory, and between Parsonian theory and the evidence regarding Nazi law.

Edwin Schur, *Law and Society*, pp. 79-85.

Harry Bredemeier, "Law as an Integrative Mechanism," pp. 52-68 in Aubert.

Supplementary Readings

Emile Durkheim, "Types of Law in Relation to Types of Social Solidarity," in Aubert, pp. 17-29.

Talcott Parsons, *Politics and Social Structure*, ch. 2.

Talcott Parsons, *Sociological Theory and Modern Society*, pp. 92-97.

George Herbert Mead, "The Social Psychology of Punitive Justice," *American Journal of Sociology* 23 (1928): 577-602.

Jonathan H. Turner, "A Cybernetic Model of Legal Development," *Western Sociological Review* 5 (1974): 3-16.

7. LAW AND INDUSTRIAL CAPITALISM

Industrialization in the context of competitive capitalism in the nineteenth century United States was accompanied by major legal changes. We will examine the nature of these changes, the role of law in allocating the costs of industrialization among classes, and the new institutions of legal social control that developed in this period, particularly the prison and the salaried public police force.

J. Willard Hurst, *Law and the Conditions of Freedom in Nineteenth Century America*.

John Commons, *Legal Foundations of Capitalism*, ch. 8.

Lawrence M. Friedman and Jack Ladinsky, "Social Change and the Law of Industrial Accidents," 67 *Columbia Law Review* 50 (1967), reprinted in FM, 629-652.

David J. Rothman, *The Discovery of the Asylum*, chs. 1-4.

Supplementary Readings

Wex Malone, "The Formative Era of Contributory Negligence," 41 *Illinois Law Review* 151-182 (1946).

L.M. Friedman, *History of American Law*, part 3; also chs. 1, 3, 4, 6.

————, *Contract Law in America*.

Morton Horowitz, *The Transformation of American Law 1780-1860*.

William Nelson, *Americanization of the Common Law: The Impact of Legal Change on Massachusetts Society 1760-1830*.

Mark Tushnet, "A Marxist Analysis of American Law," *Marxist Perspectives* 1 (1978): 96-116.

8. REGULATORY LAW: PROBLEMS OF RATIONALITY AND LEGITIMATION.

The growth of the large corporation in late nineteenth-century America led to demands for the regulation of economic affairs. How did the courts respond to these demands? What contribution did the corporations themselves make to the demand for regulation? What can we learn about the so called "partial autonomy" of law by studying the judicial response to regulatory legislation? We will look at the growth of regulatory agencies and the development of administrative law as attempts to solve problems of rationality that arise in an unregulated capitalist economy, and as expressions of class interest. What economic consequences have these efforts had? What problems do they pose for legitimation of capitalism through rule by law? How can personal freedom be preserved in a regulated society?

John Commons, *Legal Foundations of Capitalism*, ch. 9.

Upton Sinclair, *The Jungle* (excerpt) and "Background of the First Food and Drug Act, 1906" in FM, 610-13.

Yehezkiel Dror, "Law as a Tool of Directed Social Change," in *American Behavioral Scientist* 13(4), 1970, reprinted in Aubert, pp. 90-9.

Charles Reich, "The Law of the Planned Society," *Yale Law Journal* 75, July 1966.

————, "The New Property," 73 *Yale Law Journal*, 1964.

Robert Fellmuth, "The Regulatory-Industrial Complex" in Green and Wasserstein.

G. Kolko, "Railroads and Regulation 1877-1916" and preceding comments, in FM, pp. 457-463.

Walton H. Hamilton, *The Politics of Industry* (excerpt in FM, pp. 465-6).

Louis L. Jaffe, "The Effective Limits of the Administrative Process: A Re-Evaluation," 67 *Harvard Law Review* 1105, 1954, reprinted in FM, pp. 467-77.

Supplementary Readings

Michael Levine, "Is Regulation Necessary? California Air Transportation and National Regulatory Policy," 74 *Yale Law Journal* 1416, 1965.

Sheldon J. Plager and Joel F. Handler, "The Politics of Planning for Urban Redevelopment: Strategies in the Manipulation of Public Law," 1966 *Wisconsin Law Review* 724, 1966.

NOTE: The articles by Levine and Plager-Handler are reprinted in the *first* edition of FM but have been deleted from the second edition.

David Lilienthal, *TVA—Democracy on the March*.

George H. Miller, *Railroads and the Granger Laws*.

Barry M. Mitnick, *The Political Economy of Regulation*.

Franklin D. Roosevelt, "The Commonwealth Club Address, 1932," in *Public Papers and Addresses*, vol. 1, 742-56.

Arthur S. Miller, *The Supreme Court and American Capitalism*.

Milton Friedman, *Capitalism and Freedom*.

James J. Jimmerson and Robin C. Campbell, "Cities Fight to Stem Population Growth: Constitutional Crisis from *Ramapo* to *Petaluma*," *Columbia Human Rights Law Review* 7, 313.

A.S. Miller, "Science Challenges Law," in *American Behavioral Scientist* 13(4), March/April 1970.

Ralph Nader, "The Case for Federal Chartering," in Nader and Green (eds.), *Corporate Power in America*.

Daniel Bell, "Comment" (on Michael Harrington's Revolution) in Eugene V. Rostow (ed.), *Is Law Dead?*

Robert Fellmuth, "The Regulatory-Industrial Complex," in Green and Wasserstein.

Walter Adams, "The Anti-Trust Alternative," in Nader and Green.

Alan Wolfe, *The Limits of Legitimacy*, chs. 3-5.

Richard Quinney, *Class, Crime and State*, chs. 3-5.

Nicholas Kittrie, *The Right to be Different*, chs. 1, 10.

AFSC Working Party, *Struggle for Justice*.

9. THE ROLE OF LAW IN THIRD WORLD DEVELOPMENT

A number of legal scholars have argued that the introduction of Western law into the third world facilitates economic growth and democratic political development, and helps to protect human rights. The basis for this belief will be considered and the perspective criticized from the standpoint of dependence theory/world-Systems theory.

Marc Galanter, "The Modernization of Law," in FM, pp. 1046-56.

Lawrence M. Friedman, "The Legal System: A Social Science Perspective," pp. 218-222, excerpt reprinted in FM, pp. 1056-61.

Supplementary Readings

Rheinstein, "Problems of Law in the New Nations of Africa," in Clifford Geertz (ed.), *Old Societies and New States*.

R. David, "A Civil Code for Ethiopia," 37 *Tulane Law Review* 187, 1963.

Rosenn, "The Reform of Legal Education in Brazil," 21 *Journal of Legal Education* 251, 1969.

Mendelson, "Law and the Development of Nations," 32 *Journal of Politics* 223, 1970.

Steiner, "Legal Education and Socio-Economic Change; Brazilian Perspectives." 19 *American Journal of Comparative Law* 39, 1971.

Seidman, "Law and Development: A General Model," 6 *Law and Society Review* 311, 1972.

Steinberg, "Law, Development and Korean Society," 3 *Journal of Comparative Administration* 215, 1971.

John Beckstrom, "Transplantation of Legal Systems: An Early Report on the Reception of Western Laws in Ethiopia," *American Journal of Comparative Law* 22, 697-712, 1974.

Seidman, "Law and Economic Development in Independent, English-Speaking, Sub-Saharan Africa," in T. Hutchison (ed.), *Africa and the Law*, 1968.

Peter Fitzpatrick, *Law and State in Papua New Guinea*.

Francis Snyder, *Capitalism and Legal Change: An African Transformation*.

John Gardner, *Legal Imperialism*.

Marc Galanter and David Trubeck, "Scholars in Self-Estrangement: The Crisis in Law and Development Studies," 1974 *Wisconsin Law Review* 1062, 1974.

David F. Greenberg, "Law and Economic Development in Light of Dependency Theory," pp. 129-59 in Steven Spitzer (ed.), *Research in Law and Sociology*, vol. 3.

10. LAW AND SOCIAL INEQUALITY IN ADVANCED CAPITALIST SOCIETY

Here we will examine the role of legal strategies in attempts to ameliorate the social disadvantages of poverty and discrimination. How successful have these efforts been? What limitations are entailed in this approach?

Wasserstein and Green, *With Justice for Some* (articles by Green, Hiestand, Murphy and Ross, Brown, Riley, Berlin et al.)

Earl Johnson, Jr., *Justice and Reform: The Formative Years of the OEO Legal Services Program* (excerpt in FM, pp. 521-32).

Ronald Dworkin, "Why Ronald Bakke Has No Case," *New York Review of Books*, November 10, 1977.

Marc Galanter, "Why the 'Haves' Come Out Ahead: Speculations on the Limits of Legal Change," *Law and Society Reivew* 9 (1974):95.

Klare, Karl, "Judicial Deradicalization of the Wagner Act and the Origins of Modern Legal Consciousness, 1937-1941," *Minnesota Law Review* 62: 265-339.

Supplementary Readings

Kalman Silvert, *Man's Power*, pp. 99-143.

Marvin Frankel, "An Immodest Proposal," *New York Times Magazine*, Dec. 4, 1977, p. 92.

Jerome Carlin and Jan Howard, "Legal Representation and Class Justice," 12 *UCLA Law Review* 381-431 (excerpt in Aubert, pp. 332-50).

Robert Lefcourt, "Law Against the People," in Lefcourt (ed.), *Law Against the People* (reprinted in Richard Quinney, *Criminal Justice in America: A Critical Understanding*).

DeFunis Symposium, *Columbia Law Review* 75, 1975.

Jean and Edgar Cahn, "The War on Poverty: A Civilian Perspective," *Yale Law Journal*, 1964.

Gregory Barak, *In Defense of Whom*, ch. 3.

Jeffrey M. Fitzgerald, "The Contract Buyers League and the Courts: A Case Study of Poverty Litigation," 9 *Law and Society Review* 165, 1975.

Marc Galanter, "The Abolition of Disabilities—Untouchability and the Law," pp. 241-91 in J. Michael Mahar (ed.), *The Untouchables in Contemporary India*.

11. LAWYERS

Here we will take an overview of the sociological literature on the legal profession, examining such issues as socialization into the profession, forms of work organization, stratification within the profession, political ideologies and activism among lawyers.

Readings by Rueschemeyer, Abel-Smith and Stevens, Dahrendorf, Moriodono, Blumberg in Aubert, pp. 265-331.

Wasserstein and Green (eds.), *With Justice for Some* (articles by Hiestand, Moore, Van Loon).

Edwin Schur, *Law and Society*, ch. 4.

Robert Lefcourt, *Law Against the People* (articles by Lefcourt, Rockwell, Kennedy, Rutgers Report, G. Lefcourt, Kunstler and Kinoy).

Jerold S. Auerbach, *Unequal Justice: Lawyers and Social Change in Modern America*.

Supplementary Readings

Erwin Smigel, *The Wall Street Lawyer*.

Jack Ladinsky, "Careers of Lawyers, Law Practice and Legal Institutions," *ASR* 28, 47-54, 1963; also reprinted in Rita Simon (ed.), *Sociology of Law*.

Lawrence M. Friedman, *A History of American Law*, chs. 11, 12.

Beryl H. Levy, *The Corporation Lawyer: Saint or Sinner?*

Ralph Nader and Mark Green, *Verdicts on Lawyers*, 1976.

John D. Donnell, *The Corporate Counsel: A Role Study*.

H. Stumpf, Henry Shroerluke, and F. Dill, "The Legal Profession and Legal Services: Explorations in Local Bar Politics." *Law and Society Review* 6, 46-67, 1971.

W.I. Wardell, "The Extra-Professional Role of the Lawyer," *AJS* 61, January 1956.

Joseph Zelan, "Social Origins and the Recruitment of American Lawyers," *British Journal of Sociology* 18, March 1967.

M. Tigar and M. Levy, Part 6.

Special Issue on the Movement and the Lawyer, *Guild Practitioner*, Winter 1969.

Jonathan Black (ed.), *Radical Lawyers*.

Articles on Indian Legal Profession in 3 *Law and Society Review* 1968.

Von Mehren, "Law and Legal Education in India: Some Observations," 78 *Harvard Law Review* 1180, 1965.

Robert L. Kidder, "Formal Litigation and Professional Insecurity: Legal Entrepreneurship in South India," 9(1) *Law and Society Review* 11 (Fall, 1974).

Abram Chayes, "The Role of the Judge in Public Law Litigation," 89 *Harvard Law Review* 1281-1316, 1976.

Dietrich Rueschemeyer, "The Legal Profession in Comparative Perspective," *Sociological Inquiry* 47, 97-127, 1977.

D.D. Barry and H.J. Berman, "The Soviet Legal Profession," 82 *Harvard Law Review*, 1-41, 1968.

J.E. Carlin, *Lawyers on their Own: A Study of Individual Practitioners in Chicago*. (Excerpt in FM, 944-954.)

―――, *Lawyers' Ethics: A Survey of the New York City Bar*.

H. Eulau and J.D. Sprague, *Lawyers in Politics: A Study in Professional Convergence*.

Lawrence M. Friedman, and Z.L. Zile, "Soviet Legal Profession: Recent Developments in Law and Practice," *Wisconsin Law Review*, 1964, 32-77.

J.F. Handler, *The Lawyer and His Community: The Practicing Bar in a Middle-Sized City*.

Q. Johnstone and D. Hopson, Jr., *Lawyers and Their Work: An Analysis of the Legal Profession in the United States and in England*.

Arthur L. Wood, *Criminal Lawyer*.

Hubert J. O'Gorman, *Lawyers and Matrimonial Cases: A Study of Informal Pressures in Private Professional Practice*.

Jack Ladinsky, "The Impact of Social Backgrounds of Lawyers on Law Practice and the Law." 16 *Journal of Legal Education* 127, 1963.

Vern Countryman, Ted Finman and Theodore J. Schneyer (ed.), *The Lawyer in Modern Society*.

John H. Merryman, "Legal Education There and Here: A Comparison." 27 *Stanford Law Review* 859, 1975.

Green, Schmidhauser, Berg and Brady, "Lawyers in Congress: A New Look at Some Old Assumptions," 26 *Western Political Quarterly* 440, 1973.

Brian Abel-Smith and Robert Stevens, *Lawyers and the Courts: A Sociological Study of the English Legal System 1750-1965*.

Mogens N. Pedersen, "Lawyers in Politics: The Danish Folketing and United States Legislatures," in Paterson and Wahlke (eds.), *Comparative Behavior: Frontiers of Research*.

Hain and Pierson, "Lawyers and Politics Revisited: Structural Advantages of Lawyer-Politicians," 19 *American Journal of Political Science* 41, 1975.

Douglas E. Rosenthal, *Lawyer and Client: Who's in Charge?*

Arthur A. Murphy, "The Army Defense Counsel: Unusual Ethics for an Unusual Advocate," pp. 955-962 in FM.

Robert Stevens, "Two Cheers for 1870: The American Law School," in Donald Fleming and Bernard Bailyn, *Law in American History*.

Nancy E. Anderson, "Demystifying Demystification: A Study of the Radical Bar," *Contemporary Crises* 5 (1981): 227-46.

Theory and Topics in the Economics of Crime

Harold Barnett
Department of Economics
University of Rhode Island
Fall 1979
Undergraduate

The purpose of this course is to consider orthodox and radical analyses of crime in the United States. Emphasis is placed on determinants of individual participation in illegal activity (broadly defined), the causal role of market and state institutions and the purposes and methods of crime control within the context of a capitalist economic system. An understanding of the significance of class, race and sex is deemed central to an explanation of crime and punishment.

The course will be divided into two main sections. The first will focus on the micro and macro economics of crime and the political economy of punishment. The second will focus on the relationships of women to illegal activity and state control.

Statistical and background information may be obtained from the following sources:

Sutherland and Cressey, *Principles of Criminology*, Lippincott, 1970.

Richard Quinney, *Criminology: Analysis and Critique of Crime in America*, Little, Brown, 1979.

The President's Commission on Law Enforcement and Administration of Justice, U.S. Government Printing Office, 1967 (this consists of a Commission Report, *The Challenge of Crime in a Free Society* and nine task force reports).

Federal Bureau of Investigation, *Uniform Crime Reports*, Washington, Annual.

COLLECTIONS AND TEXTS

Gary Becker and William Landes (eds.), *Essays in the Economics of Crime and Punishment*, National Bureau of Economic Research, 1974.

Simon Rottenberg (ed.), *The Economics of Crime and Punishment*, American Enterprise Institute for Public Policy Research, 1973.

Robert Lefcourt (ed.), *Law Against the People*, Vintage, 1971.

Daryl Hellman, *The Economics of Crime*, St. Martin's 1980.

Lee McPheters and W.B. Strong, *The Economics of Crime and Law Enforcement*, Charles Thomas, 1976.

Employment and Crime project, *Crime and Employment Issues*, U.S. Department of Labor, 1978.

Erik Olin Wright, *The Politics of Punishment*, Harper Torch Books, 1973.

Richard Quinney, *Class, State and Crime*, David McKee, 1978.

Freda Adler and Rita James Simon, *The Criminology of Deviant Women*, Houghton Mifflin, 1979.

MONOGRAPHS

Lee S. Friedman, *The Economics of Crime and Justice*, General Learning Press, 1976.

Timothy Bates, *Economic Man as Politician: Neoclassical and Marxist Theories of Government Behavior*, General Learning Press, 1976.

Key: * denotes required reading.

I. THE POLITICAL ECONOMY OF CRIME—AN ANALYSIS OF CRIME AND CRISES

A. THE PROBLEM POSED—DIMENSIONS, DEFINITION AND MEANINGS OF CRIME.

Challenge of Crime in a Free Society, pp. 1-15.

E.O. Wright, *The Politics of Punishment*, pp. 3-21.

*R. Quinney, *Class State and Crime*, ch. 1 and pp. 31-34.

*Lee Friedman, *The Economics of Crime and Justice*, pp. 1-18.

*D. Hellman, *The Economics of Crime*, ch. 1

B. MODELS OF CRIMINAL BEHAVIOR

Hypotheses regarding the conditions under which individuals will engage in illegal activity. Consideration given to historical and contemporary views of economists and criminologists.

*R. Quinney, *Class State and Crime*, ch. 2.

*D. Hellman, *The Economics of Crime*, ch. 3.

*McKenzie and Tullock, "The Economic Versus the Sociological View of Crime" in McKenzie and Tullock, *The New World of Economics*, Irwin, 1975, 1979.

*Radzinowicz and Wolfgang, *Crime and Justice, Vol. 1, The Criminal in Society*, pp. 391-476.

R. Sullivan, "The Economics of Crime: Introduction to the Orthodox Literature," *Crime and Delinquency*, April 1973, pp. 138-144.

C. ECONOMIC STRUCTURE, CRIME AND THE STATE

1. Crime and the Structure of American Capitalism

Consideration of crime in relationship to production and distribution. Examination of causal role of competition, inequality, materialism, discrimination, inflation and unemployment.

*Isaac Ehrlich, "Participation in Illegal Activity: A Theoretical and Empirical Investigation," *Journal of Political Economy*, May/June 1973 (in Becker and Landes).

*S. Danziger and D. Wheeler, "The Economics of Crime: Punishment or Income Redistribution," *Review of Social Economy*, Oct. 1975.

"The Economics of Crime: Comments by Tullock, Clear and Barnett," *Review of Social Economy*, April 1976.

*David Gordon, "Class and the Economics of Crime," *Review of Radical Political Economics*, Summer 1971.

*Phillips, Votey and Maxwell, "Crime, Youth and the Labor Market," *Journal of Political Economy*, May/June 1972.

Belton Fleisher, "The Effect of Income on Delinquency," *American Economic Review*, March 1966.

*Crime and Employment Project, "Crime and Employment Issues," pp. 13-18, 53-59, 85-96, 119-138.

Roger Hood and Richard Sparks, "Subculture and Gang Delinquency," in Radzinowicz and Wolfgang, *The Criminal in Society*, pp. 477-501.

Harvey Brenner, *Estimating the Social Costs of National Economic Policy: Implications for Mental and Physical Health and Criminal Aggression*, prepared for Joint Economic Committee, Oct. 26, 1976, U.S. Government Printing Office, 1976.

2. Political Economy of Law and the State

a. Neoclassical Analysis

*T. Bates, "Economic Man as Politician," pp. 1-19.

Gary Becker, "Crime and Punishment: An Economic Approach," *Journal of Political Economy*, March/April 1968 (in Becker and Landes).

*L. Friedman, "The Economics of Crime and Justice," pp. 18-39.

*Daryl Hellman, *Economics of Crime*, chs. 4-5.

*Lester Thurow, "Equity and Efficiency in Law Enforcement," *Public Policy*, Summer 1970.

William Landes, "An Economic Analysis of the Courts," *Journal of Law and Economics*, April 1971 (in Becker and Landes).

John Harris, "On the Economics of Law and Order," *Journal of Political Economy*, Jan/Feb 1970.

b. Marxian Analysis

*T. Bates, "Economic Man as Politician," pp. 19-39.

*R. Quinney, *Class, State and Crime*, chs. 3-5.

R. Lefcourt, "Law Against the People," in Lefcourt (ed.), *Law Against the People*.

Eric Ohlin Wright, *The Politics of Punishment*, pp. 221-241.

*Kenneth Cloke, "'The Economic Basis of Law and the State," in Lefcourt, *Law Against the People*.

*H. Barnett, "Wealth, Crime and Capital Accumulation," *Contemporary Crises*, April 1979.

3. Crime and Markets

a. Corporate and Other White Collar Crime

*Marshall Clinard, *Illegal Corporate Behavior*, chs. 1-3, 8, 11-12.

*C. Geis, *White Collar Criminal*, no. 3, 4, 7, 14, 28-32.

*Ermann and Lindman, *Corporate and Governmental Deviance*, no. 1, 15-19.

Richard Posner, "The Behavior of Administrative Agencies," *Journal of Legal Studies*, June 1972 (in Becker and Landes).

August Bequai, *White Collar Crime: A 20th Century Crisis*.

Edwin Sutherland, *White Collar Crime*.

Theodore Sorenson, "Improper Payments Abroad: Perspectives and Proposals," *Foreign Affairs*, 54 (July).

H. Barnett, "Corporate Capitalism, Corporate Crime," Xerox, 1980.

b. Organized Crime

*William Chambliss, *On the Take*, Indiana University Press, 1978.

*Daryl Hellman, *Economics of Crime*, ch. 10.

Paul Rubin, "The Economic Theory of the Criminal Firm," in Rottenberg (ed.), *The Economics of Crime and Punishment*.

Thomas Schelling, "Economics and Criminal Enterprise," *The Public Interest*, Spring 1976.

James Buchanan, "A Defense of Organized Crime," in Rottenberg.

Donald Cressey, "Organized Crime: Demand, Supply and Profits," in David Gordon (ed.), *Problems in Political Economy*.

David Bell, *The End of Ideology*, pp. 127-150.

II. WOMEN, CRIME AND LAW

A. PERSPECTIVES ON CRIME AND THE STATUS OF WOMEN

Freda Adler, *Sisters in Crime*, McGraw-Hill, 1975, pp. 1-54.

Freda Adler and Rita James Simon (eds.), *The Criminology of Deviant Women*, Houghton Mifflin, 1979, pp. 1-94.

Carol Smart, *Women, Crime and Criminology: A Feminist Critique*, Routledge and Kegan Paul, pp. 1-76, 1976.

Carol Smart and Barry Smart, *Women, Sexuality and Social Control*, Routledge and Kegan Paul, 1978.

B. SEX AND THE LAW

DeCrow, Karen, *Sexist Justice*, Vintage Books, New York, 1975.

Kanowitz, Leo, *Women and the Law*, University of New Mexico Press, Albuquerque, 1969.

Ann M. Garfinkle et al., "Women's Servitude Under Law" in R.Lefcourt (ed.), *Law Against the People*, Vintage, 1971.

"Equality on Paper, Not on the Job," *Dollars and Sense*, no. 28, July 1977.

Gilbert Geis, *Not the Law's Business*, Schocken Books, 1979, pp. 15-104.

Kaye Archiprete et al., *The Abortion Business: A Report on Free-Standing Abortion Clinics*, Women's Research Action Project, 1975.

C. VIOLENCE AS SEX

1. Sexual Harassment and Abuse

Diana E.H. Russell and Nicole Van de Ven (eds.), *Crimes Against Women*, Proceedings of the International Tribunal, Les Femmes, Millbrae CA, 1976.

Catherine A. MacKinnon, *Sexual Harassment of Working Women*, Yale University Press, 1979.

Del Martin, *Battered Wives*, Pocket, 1976.

2. Rape

Amir, Menachem, *Patterns in Forcible Rape*, The University of Chicago Press, Chicago and London, 1971.

Lisa Brodyaga, et al., *Rape and Its Victims*, LEAA, U.S. Department of Justice, 1975.

Drapkin, Israel and Viano, Emilio(eds.), *Victimology: A New Focus* (Volume III), Lexington Books, Lexington, Mass. 1975.

Griffin, Susan, "Rape The All-American Crime," *Ramparts*, Volume 10, No. 3, September 1971. Reprinted in Warner Module, reprint 528, 1973.

Susan Griffin, *Rape: The Power of Consciousness*, Harper and Row, 1979.

Leo Carrol, "Race and Sexual Assault in a Maximum Security Prison," *Urban Life and Culture*, Summer 1976.

Connell, Noreen and Wilson, Cassandra (eds.), *Rape: The First Sourcebook for Women*, New American Library, New York, 1974.

Julia R.Schwendinger and Herman Schwendinger, "A Review of the Rape Literature," *Crime and Social Justice*, 6, Fall/Winter, 1976.

Julia R. Schwendinger and Herman Schwendinger, "Rape Myths: In Legal, Theoretical and Everyday Practice," *Crime and Social Justice*, 1, Spring/Summer 1974.

Susan Brownmiller, *Against Our Will: Men, Women and Rape*, Simon and Schuster, New York, 1975.

Davis, Angela, "Joanne Little—The Dialectics of Rape," *Ms*, Volume III, No. 2, June 1975.

Carol Smart, *Women, Crime and Criminology*, pp. 77-107.

Harold Barnett, "The Political Economy of Rape and Prostitution," *Review of Radical Political Economy*," Vol. 8, No. 1, spring 1976.

D. WOMEN AS CRIMINALS

1. Prostitution

Goldman, Emma, "The Traffic in Women," in Miriam Schneir (ed.), *Feminism: The Essential Historical Writings*, Vintage Books, Random House, New York 1972.

Gayle Rubin, "The Traffic in Women: Notes on the Political Economy of Sex," in Rayna Reiter (ed.), *Toward An Anthropology of Women*, Monthly Review Press, 1975.

Winick, Charles and Kinsie, Paul M., *The Lively Commerce*, New American Library, New York, 1972.

Adler/Simon, *The Criminology of Deviant Women*, pp. 196-222.

Adler, *Sisters in Crime*, pp. 55-84.

Daryl Hellman, *Economics of Crime*, ch. 8.

Gilbert Geis, *Not the Law's Business*, pp. 173-221.

Millet, Kate, *The Prostitution Papers*, Avon Books, New York, 1973. Originally in Gornick and Moran (eds.), *Women in a Sexist Society*, Basic Books, New York, 1971.

Sheehy, Gail, *Hustling*, Dell, New York, 1974.

Roby, Pamela, "Politics and Criminal Law: Revision of the New York State Penal Law on Prostitution," *Social Problems*, Vol. 17, No. 1, Summer 1969.

Women Endorsing Decriminalization, "Prostitution: A non-victim crime," *Issues in Criminology*, 8:2, Fall, 1973.

2. Perspectives on the Emerging Female Criminal

Adler, *Sisters in Crime*, pp. 85-110, 133-170.

Rita James Simon, *Women and Crime*, Lexington Books, 1975.

Adler/Simon, *The Criminology of Deviant Women*, pp. 387-418.

Laura Crites, *The Female Offender*, Lexington Books, D.C. Heath & Co., 1976.

Ann P. Bartel, "Women and Crime: An Economic Analysis," *Economic Inquiry*, Vol. XVII, No. 1, January 1979.

Joseph G. Weis, "Liberation and Crime: The Invention of the New Female Criminal," *Crime and Social Justice*, 6, Fall/Winter, 1976.

3. Women and Criminal Justice

Adler, *Sisters in Crime*, pp. 171-245.

Adler/Simon, *The Criminology of Deviant Women*, pp. 249-386.

Carol Smart, *Women, Crime and Criminology*, pp. 108-175.

SOCIAL CLASS

Stratification and Power

John. D. Stephens
Sociology
Brown University
Undergraduate

This course will focus on the structure of social inequality and distribution of power in western capitalist societies. It is not intended to be an overview of the field of stratification. In addition to excluding the "socialist" societies of Eastern Europe, premarket societies of the present and preindustrial Europe; some topics such as ethnic and sexual inequality will not be covered in depth. This is not to indicate that these topics are not important. Rather by limiting the scope of the course, we can explore the theoretical issues and empirical research on the topic in greater detail.

The first half of the course will cover the main theoretical perspectives in stratification theory beginning with the two main classic views, that of Marx and Weber. Weberian theory subsequently evolved in two directions. In the U.S., it was combined with functional theory and interest in mobility leading to an emphasis on "occupational prestige" as the main object of analysis. The European variant, recently developed by Parkin and Giddens, on the other hand, focused on the market as the main stratifying force. Marxist theory has continued to focus on production relation rather than the market per se, but recently many Marxists have broken away from simple repetition of orthodoxy to produce new theoretical insights as well as empirical research.

The second half of the course will deal with the developments of the class structure and its consequences for political action in advanced capitalist societies and then contrast these societies to dependent capitalist societies, primarily in Latin America.

Five main themes in stratification theory and research will be emphasized throughout the semester. 1) What are the main causes of variation in material reward? (e.g., differences in the distribution of marketable resources, relation to production, relation to political power). 2) What are the main causes of the distribution of control in the enterprise and in the economy at large? 3) The state: the determinants of political power and the policy output of the state. For the democratic societies under examination, we will try to answer the difficult question of why state power is not routinely used to destratify society given that the majority of people would benefit in relative terms from such a policy. 4) Social mobility: What are the determinants of social mobility within a country, and what causes variations across countries? Is it most appropriate to view mobility as movement between a very large number of ranks (occupations) or are there clear mobility blocks in the class structure? 5) Class Formation, Class Consciousness and Action: How, when and to what degree does the class structure become the basis for collective social action to change (or maintain) it?

1. MARX'S THEORY

Try to do the reading before class since we will discuss Marx in the first class. (Note: the average reading load will be about 150 pages/week, but it will be concentrated in the middle third of the course, so you should get started on some of the later books now. *White Collar* and *The Affluent Worker* are good candidates.)

Marx and Engels, *The Communist Manifesto*, Section I

Dahrendorf, *Class and Class Conflict in Industrial Society*, 9-18

Stephens, *The Transition from Capitalism to Socialism*, Ch. I.

Giddens, *The Class Structure of Advanced Societies*, 9-40.

Recommended:

Marx, *The German Ideology*, Part I (on Feuerbach)

_____, *The Eighteenth Brumaire*

_____, *Value, Price and Profit*

_____, *Capital I* (esp. Chapter X)

2. WEBER

Weber, "Class Status, and Party" in *Economy and Society*, *From Max Weber*, and almost any stratification reader.

"Status Groups and Classes" in *Economy and Society*, pp. 302-307.

"Bureaucracy" in *Economy and Society* or *From Max Weber*.

Giddens, *The Class Structure...*, pp. 41-52.

Recommended:

Weber, *Economy and Society*, esp. Chapters III, X, XII, XIII.

_____, *From Max Weber*, "Politics as a Vocation."

_____, "The Development of Caste" in Lipset and Bendix, *Class, Status and Power*.

3. POST WORLD WAR II AMERICAN THOUGHT

Davis and Moore, "Some Principles of Stratification."

Giddens, *The Class Structure...*, pp. 53-82.

Horan, "Is Status Attainment Research Atheoretical," *ASR* 1978: pp. 534-540.

Reiss, *Occupations and Social Status*, pp. 19-23, 31-42, 53, 58, 83-88, 105-132, 190-195.

Recommended:

Lenski, *Power and Privilege*

Dahrendorf, *Class and Class Conflict...*

Blau and Duncan, *The American Occupational Structure*

Trieman, *Occupational Prestige in Comparative Perspective*

Barber, *Social Stratification*

Post war American work has revolved around the concept of "occupational prestige." The concept itself lies on theoretical assumptions that are rarely scrutinized. This is unfortunate, since the validity of all of the methodologically sophisticated mobility research in the Blau-Duncan tradition depends on the validity of these assumptions. A second widely held view in American thought is that the stratification system can be conceived of as "three dimensional." In our session this week, we will examine both of these theoretical bases of American stratification work and discuss what implications the questioning of these assumptions might have for future empirical research.

4. NEO WEBERIAN THOUGHT

Giddens, *The Class Structure...*, pp. 83-117.

Parkin, *Class Inequality and Political Order*, pp. 9-78.

Recommended:

Giddens, *The Class Structure...*, pp. 139-176, 275-294.

Parkin (ed.), *The Social Analysis of Class Structure*

Collins, *The Credential Society*

Much recent British stratification theory has drawn heavily on both Marx and Weber. But since it takes the market as the principal stratifying force and considers property purely as an aspect of "market situation," the stream of British thought represented by Giddens and Parkin has to be considered Weberian rather than Marxist despite the leftist orientation of the authors. Particularly impressive is this school's attempt to provide comprehensive stratification theories covering almost all aspects (distribution, control, political power, class formation and class action, and mobility) of structured inequality.

5. RECENT MARXIST THEORIES OF SOCIAL CLASS

Poulantzas, "On Social Class," *New Left Review (NLR)* 78.

Wright, "Class Boundaries in Advanced Capitalist Societies," *NLR* 98

_____ and Perrone, "Marxist Class Categories and Income Inequality," *ASR* 42.

Carchedi, "On the Economic Identification of the New Middle Class," *Economy and Society* 4.

Stephens, *The Transition...*, pp. 15-38.

Recommended:

Poulantzas, *Class in Contemporary Capitalism*.

Wright, *Class, Crisis and the State*.

_____, *Class Structure and Income Inequality*.

Carchedi, *On the Economic Identification of Social Class*.

Recent Marxist theory has broken from repetition of orthodoxy into innovative theoretical developments in a number of areas. This week we look at a number of attempts to deal with the problem of the new middle class. In America, some younger Marxists have broken with the tradition of hostility to statistical analysis and brought a whole new dimension into Marxist social science. The Wright and Perrone piece is a case in point.

6. RECENT MARXIST THEORIES OF THE STATE

Poulantzas, "The Problem of the Capitalist State," *NLR* 58.

Miliband, "The Capitalist State," *NLR* 59.

_____, "Poulantzas and the Capitalist State," *NLR* 82.

Gold et al., "Recent Developments in Marxist Theories of the State," *Monthly Review*, Oct. 1975 (Two Parts).

Whitt, "Toward a Class-Dialectical Model of Power," *ASR* 44.

Alavi, "The State in Post-Colonial Societies," *NLR* 74.

Esping-Andersen et al, "Modes of Class Struggle in the Capitalist State," *Kapitalistate* 4-5.

Recommended:

Leclau, "The Specificity of the Political: Around the Poulantzas-Miliband Debate," *Economy and Society* 5.

Miliband, *The State in Capitalist Society*.

Poulantzas, *Political Power and Social Classes*.

_____, "The Capitalist State," *NLR* 95.

Offe, "Advanced Capitalism and the Welfare State," *Politics and Society* 2.

"The Theory of the Capitalist State and the Problem of Policy Formation" in Lindberg et al., *Stress and Contradiction in Modern Capitalism*.

"Structural Problems of the Capitalist State."

"Political Authority and Class Structure," *International Journal of Sociology*.

Wright, *Class, Crisis, and the State*

Reich and Edwards, "Political Parties and Class Conflict in the United States," *Socialist Review* 39.

Korpi, *The Working Class in Welfare Capitalism*, Ch. 2.

Stephens, *The Transition...*, pp. 47-48, 74-81.

Domhoff, *Who Rules America?*

Friedland, *Class Power and the City*.

Hicks et al, "Class Power and State Policy," *ASR* 43.

Gramsci, *Selections from the Prison Notebooks*. esp. pp. 206-276.

Anderson, *The Antinomies of Antonio Gramsci*, *NLR* 100.

Marxist theories of the state have become more differentiated in the last twenty years, but virtually all of them agree that state policy serves the interest of the economically dominant class. The question is what mechanisms insure this is so. A particularly difficult point for Marxists is that policies which they claim are in the long run interests of the capitalists (e.g., Keynesian policies and welfare state expansion) were passed against the will of the overwhelming majority of businessmen. The Marxist debate on this point (the so-called "relative autonomy of the state") and others will be discussed this week.

7. NON MARXIST VIEWS OF POLITICAL POWER AND THE STATE

Lukas, *Power: A Radical View*

Stepan, *The State and Society*, pp. 3-7, 40-46, 66-113.

Giddens, *The Class Structure*, pp. 156-177.

Parkin, *Class Inequality...*, pp. 79-102.

Recommended:

Dahl, *Who Governs?* (Also see Domhoff's critique of Dahl using Dahl's own data on New Haven: *Who Really Rules?*)

Mills, *The Power Elite*

Parsons, "On the Concept of Political Power" in *Sociological Theory and Modern Society*.

The debate between pluralist theory and elite theory cuts across the Marxist/Non-marxist dimension, since some elite theorists such as Mills are left Weberians rather than Marxists. The debate between Marxists, elite theorists, and pluralists revolves around the question of which groups in society the state represents. Given their focus on the state in developed capitalist democracies, this is not surprising. But if we turn to less developed societies where all forces in civil society are weak, the state can be an autonomous and independent force.

8. THE DEVELOPMENT OF THE CLASS STRUCTURE OF ADVANCED CAPITALIST SOCIETIES I: THE WORKING CLASS

Goldthorpe et al., *The Affluent Worker in the Class Structure*.

Hamilton, *Class and Politics in the United States*, pp. 22-63, 152-180, 188-225.

Giddens, *The Class Structure...*, pp. 198-222.

Recommended:

Mann, *Consciousness and Action Among the Western Working Class*.

Hamilton, *Class and Politics...*, pp. 308-329.

Affluence and the French Worker in the Fourth Republic.

Korpi, *The Working Class...*

Braverman, *Labor and Monopoly Capital*

Lipset, "The Changing Class Structure of Contemporary European Politics," *Daedalus* 63.

Hill, "Sources of Variation in the Class Consciousness of the British Working Class," Brown diss. 1978.

Butler and Stokes, *Political Change in Britain*.

Stephens, "Class Formation and Class Consciousness," *British Journal of Sociology*, 1979.

The controversy on the working class centers on the question of material affluence and its consequences for working class politics: can the working class still be considered an agent working for the transformation of capitalism? The question of class consciousness and class action thus becomes the focus of our interest.

9. THE DEVELOPMENT OF THE CLASS STRUCTURE II: THE NEW MIDDLE CLASS

Mills, *White Collar*, pp. 3-13, 20-28, 34-40, 54-81, 100-115, 119-121, 136-142, 161-166, 169-174, 178-184, 189-198, 204-215, 224-233, 235-250, 251-258, 262-282, 289-355.

Giddens, *The Class Structure...*, pp. 177-197, 255-274.

Recommended:

Low-Beer, *Protest and Participation: The New Working Class in Italy*.

Hamilton, *Class and Politics*, pp. 336-361.

Crozier, *The World of the Office Worker*.

Lockwood, *The Blackcoated Worker*.

Bell, *The Coming of the Post Industrial Society*, esp. pp. 165-267.

Touraine, *The Post Industrial Society*, pp. 26-87.

The most dramatic change in the class structure of all developed capitalist democracies in the post war period has been the growth of the proportion of non-manual employees. Is the new middle class an extension of the working class, a new ruling class based on the control of knowledge, or something else entirely? Where will this class line up in political struggles between labor and capital?

10. CLASS CONFIGURATIONS IN LESS-DEVELOPED CAPITALIST SOCIETIES

Stevenhagen, "Classes, Colonialism, and Acculturation," in Kahl, *Comparative Perspectives on Stratification*.

Gonzalez-Casanova, "Dynamics of the Class Structure," in Kahl, *Comparative Perspectives...*

Frank, "Economic Dependence, Class Structure, and Underdevelopment Policy," in Cockcroft et al, *Dependence and Underdevelopment*.

Cardoso, "Dependency and Development in Latin America," *NLR* 74.

Bornschier, "Cross-national Evidence of the Effects of Foreign Investment and Aid on Economic Growth and Inequality," *AJS* 84.

Zeitlin et al, "Class Segments," *ASR* 41.

Recommended:

Petras and Zeitlin (eds.), *Latin America: Reform or Revolution*.

Horowitz (ed.), *Masses in Latin America*.

Lipset and Solari (eds.), *Elites in Latin America*.

Wallerstein, *The Modern World System*.

Kahl, *Modernization, Exploitation and Dependency*.

This week we will contrast class configurations in less developed capitalist economies with those found in the developed countries we examined the last two weeks. Two primary points of contrast are: 1) lower levels of development per se which is associated with a larger peasant class and a larger and politically more significant landholding class. On this point, it is inviting to compare less developed countries to pre World War I Europe (e.g., Latin America and Germany). 2) Here a comparison with pre World War I Europe yields differences rather than similarities.

11. THE DEVELOPMENT OF THE WELFARE STATE AND EQUALITY IN COMPARATIVE PERSPECTIVE

Stephens, *The Transition...*, pp. 39-209.
Parkin, *Class Inequality...*, pp. 103-137.

Recommended:

Anderson, "Antinomies of Antonio Gramsci," *NLR* 100.

Wilensky, *The Welfare State and Equality*.

————, *The "New Corporatism," Centralization, and the Welfare State*.

Martin, *The Politics of Economic Policy in the United States*.

Gorz, *Strategy for Labor*.

Burnham, *Critical Elections and the Mainspring of American Politics*.

O'Brien, *Allende's Chile*.

In our final session we will discuss my own research and similar research by others on the past and future movements toward destratification in developed capitalist democracies. Then, drawing on our discussion of last week, we will try to assess to what extent the West European experience is relevant for movements for destratification in less developed countries. In particular, lessons of Allende Chile, the closest case to the European model, will be examined.

EDUCATION

Higher Education in the United States

Sherry Gorelick
Livingston College
Rutgers University
Department of Sociology
Spring 1982
Undergraduate

REQUIRED

W.E.B. DuBois, *The Education of Black People*
S. Gorelick, *City College and the Jewish Poor*
David N. Smith, *Who Rules the Universities?*
C. Jencks and D. Riesman, *The Academic Revolution*

RECOMMENDED

Halsey, Floud and Anderson, *Education, Economy and Society*

OUTLINE OF THE COURSE

I. INTRODUCTIONS

First Assignment: Written Essay—a *sociological* analysis of why you are in this classroom.

II. HIGHER EDUCATION: WHAT IT'S LIKE

One Description of Higher Education: *Crisis at CUNY*, Chapter 1.

III. HOW IT GOT THAT WAY

A. Class Conflict and the Development of Higher Education

Gorelick, *City College and the Jewish Poor*, Chapter 3.

Recommended:

Gorelick, *City College*, Chapter 4; *Crisis at CUNY*, Chapter 2.

B. From Elite to Mass Education?

Either: Smith, *Who Rules the Universities?* Chapters 5 & 6. Or: *Crisis at CUNY*, Chapters 2 & 3.

C. The Development of Higher Education: An Alternative View

C. Jencks & D. Riesman, *The Academic Revolution*, Chapter 1.

IV. SOCIAL CLASS AND HIGHER EDUCATION

A. Class and Access: Who Goes to College and Why?

Jencks & Riesman, *Academic Revolution*, pp. 67-107; 146-154.

Either: Mills, *The Power Elite*, pp. 62-70 (on reserve). Or: Domhoff, *Who Rules America*, pp. 12-19 (on reserve).

Short materials to be handed out in class.

Recommended:

Bowles, "Unequal Education and the Reproduction of the Social Division of Labor."

Shostak, *Blue Collar Life*, Ch. 9 & 10.

B. Class and Power: Who Controls the University?

Smith, *Who Rules the University* Ch. 2 "The Academic Marketplace" in Halsey, Floud, et al, *Education Economy & Society*.

"College vs. Business: The Versus Declines, *New York Times*, Jan. 25, 1974. Several other clippings from the *Times*, to be distributed in class.

"Memorandum to the Faculty and Administrative Staff of the University" (to be distributed in class).

Review

Jencks, *The Academic Revolution*, ch. 1.

V. CONTRADICTORY FORCES IN HIGHER EDUCATION

A. Contradictions of the Equal Opportunity Ideal: Raising Aspirations...

Either: R. Turner, "Modes of Social Ascent through Education," in Halsey, et al, *Education Economy and Society* (on reserve).
Or: R.K. Merton, "Social Structure and Anomie" in Robert Merton, *Social Theory and Social Structure*. (on reserve).

...And Cooling Out: Equal Opportunity to be Unequal

Clark, "The Cooling Out Function in Higher Education."

Halsey, Floud, *Education Economy and Society* (on reserve).

B. Contradictions of Vocationalism and Credentialism: Education and Jobs:

(Question: Has education expanded because "the economy needs people with more training," or are people overeducated for the available jobs? Can both be true?)

J. O'Connor, "The University and the Political Economy."

Ivar Berg, "Rich Man's Qualifications for Poor Man's Jobs."

C. Contradictions of Social Control and Student Revolt

Skolnick, *The Politics of Protest*, pp. 79-105.

Sewell, "Students and the University" (Xerox on reserve).

Recommended

Kirk, "The University and Revolution: An Insane Conjunction," in Gary Weaver, ed., *The University and Revolution* (on reserve).

(Question: Is the student revolt dead history? Why did it start and why did it end? Are the conditions which caused it gone?)

VI. THE PURPOSES OF HIGHER EDUCATION—WHAT IS A COLLEGE EDUCATION FOR?

W.E.B. Dubois, *The Education of Black People* (Note: these essays cover a span of 54 years, during which DuBois changed his views very dramatically. Read the whole book, but especially the first 3 essays, the essay on "Education and Work," Editor's Note, and the last 3 Essays. This book is not just about the education of Black people and it is not just about history. It raises issues faced by *ALL* students today—issues which are being hotly debated throughout academia, at Harvard, Yale, New Paltz, CUNY, Rutgers, and throughout the nation. A major conference was held in 1981 on the liberal arts vs. vocationalism, and new books and articles are about to be published on these questions. So read it as though it is about YOU. It is.)

VII. "HIGHER CULTURE"—WHAT IS LEARNED AND TAUGHT?

Gorelick, *City College and the Jewish Poor*, Chapter 7, "Dominant Culture" and Chapter 8, The City College in an Age of Cultural Conflict."

Adrienne Rich, "Claiming an Education" in Rich, *On Lies, Secrets, and Silence* ("Claiming an Education" was a talk which Rich gave at the Douglass College Convocation in 1977. She was teaching at Douglas at the time. You may also want to read the next essay, "Taking Women Students Seriously." The book is on reserve).

"Puerto Rican Studies: Notes for the 80s" (To be Distributed in Class).

Recommended

Dale Spender, *Men's Studies Modified: The Impact of Feminism on the Academic Disciplines*. Also, Gloria Hull, et al, *But Some of Us Are Brave: Black Women's Studies*; Jencks & Riesman, *Academic Revolution*, Chapters VII-X; Ballard, *Education of Black Folk*, Chapter 3 "It's Just that Our Entire College is White."

VIII. ACADEMIC FREEDOM AND LIBERAL CULTURE

Excerpt from Rutgers University Regulations, Section 3.90, and a Case Study, to be distributed in class).

IX. THE CURRENT CRISES IN HIGHER EDUCATION

A. Enrollment and Employment

Gorelick, "Boom and Bust in Higher Education" (To be distributed in class).

Recommended

Carnegie Commission, *Priorities for Action: Final Report of the Carnegie Commission on Higher Education* (on reserve).

B. Affirmative Action or Resurgent Discrimination?

Materials on Affirmative Action at Rutgers University to be handed out in class.

Recommended

Nathan Glazer, *Affirmative Discrimination*; Materials on the Bakke case, available from me.

C. Militarization of the University

New York Times, "R.O.T.C., Butt of the 70s, is on Target Again" January, 1982.

X. LIVINGSTON COLLEGE: A LIVING HISTORY

We will use Livingston as a case study. Materials to be announced.

GOVERNMENT REGULATION

Assessing the Costs and Benefits of Social Regulation

William K. Tabb
Department of Economics
Queens College
Spring 1980

Social regulation or government interventions in health, safety and environmental issues is the subject of major controversy. We shall look at the methodological, data, ideological and policy issues raised by the proponents of deregulation and of those who urge the restricting role of government in quality of life areas.

1. INTRODUCTION

Paul H. Wasver, "Regulation, Social Policy and Class Conflict," *The Public Interest*, Winter 1978, pp. 45-53.

Robert Crawford, "You are Dangerous to Your Health: The Ideology and Politics of Victim Blaming," *International Journal of Health Services*, Vol. 7, No. 4, pp. 663-680.

Murray Weidenbaum, "The High Cost of Government Regulation," *Challenge*, November-December 1979, pp. 32-39.

R.C. D'Arge and E.K. Hunt, "Environmental Pollution, Externalities, and Conventional Economic Wisdom: A Critique," *Environmental Affairs*.

2. THE COST OF REGULATION

Robert A. Leone, "The Real Cost of Regulation," *Harvard Business Review*, November-December 1977.

William Lilley XXI and James C. Miller III, "The New 'Social Regulation," *The Public Interest*, Spring 1977, pp. 49-62.

Warren J. Samuels, "Normative Premises in Regulatory Theory," *Journal of Post-Keynesian Economics*.

3. ENVIRONMENTAL IMPACT STATEMENTS AND THEIR ECONOMIC IMPACT

Eugene Bardach and Lucian Puglieresi, "The Environmental-Impact Statement vs the Real World," *Public Interest*, Fall 1977, pp. 22-38.

Richard Walker, Michael Storper and Ellen Garsh, "The limits of Environmental Control: The Saga of Dow in the Delta," *Antipode*, Vol. 11, No. 2, 1979, pp. 48-60.

Dow Chemical Company, "Summary Background Report on Dow Projects in Northern California," 10 pp., N.D.

Dow, "Summary Statement of the Dow Petrochemical Project," January 24, 1977 with Summary of Permits Required Chronology and Speech by Jack Jones, Manager, Public Affairs, Dow Chemical Company.

4. CRITICISMS OF COST-BENEFIT ANALYSIS

Baruch Fishoff, "Cost-Benefit Analysis and the Art of Motorcycle Maintenance," *Policy Science*, 1977.

Richard J. Hammond, "Convention and Limitation in Benefit-Cost Analysis," *Natural Resources Journal*, April 1966.

Frank Muller, "Benefit Cost Analysis: A Questionable Part of Environmental Decisioning," *Journal of Environmental Systems*, Winter 1974.

5. CASE STUDY: ASBESTOS

Russell F. Settle, "Benefits and Costs of the Federal Asbestos Standard," mimeo, March 1975.

"Dying for Work: Occupational Health and Asbestos," *NACLA Report on the Americas*.

6. TECHNOLOGY RISKS, TECHNOLOGY FORCING AND POLITICS

Helen Ingram, "The Political Rationality of Innovation: The Clean Air Act Amendment of 1970," in Ann Friedlander, ed., *Approaches to Controlling Air Pollution*, MIT Press, 1978, pp. 12-67.

Baruch Fishoff, et al., "How Safe is Safe Enough? A Psychometric Study of Attitudes Towards Technology Risks and Benefits," *Policy Sciences*, April 1978.

Dean Mann, "Political Incentives in U.S Water Policy: Relationships Between Distributive and Regulatory Policies," in Matthew Holden and Dennis Dresang, *What Government Does*, Sage 71975, pp. 94-123.

Richard Walker and Michael Storper, "Erosion of the Clean Air Act of 1970: A Study in the Failure of Government Regulation and Planning," *Boston College Environmental Affairs*, Vol. 7, No. 2, 1978, pp. 189-250.

7. VALUE OF HUMAN LIFE

J. Linnirooth, "Value of Human Life: A Review of the Models," *Economic Inquiry*, Vol. 17, 1979.

Steven Rhodes, "What is Life Worth? How Much Should We Spend to Save a Life?" *Public Interest*, Spring 1978, pp. 74-92.

Max Singer, "What is Life Worth: How to Reduce Risks Rationally," *Public Interest*, Spring 1978, pp. 93-112.

W. Kip Vigcusi, "Labor Market Valuations of Life and Limb: Empirical Evidence and Policy Implication," *Public Policy*, Summer 1978, pp. 359-386.

Richard Thaler and Shervein Rosen, "The Value of Saving a Life: Evidence from the Labor Market," in *Household Production and Consumption*, edited by Destor E. Terleckyj, pp. 265-296.

8. OSHA

Albert L. Nichols and Richard Zeckhauser, "Government comes to The Workplace: An Assessment of OSHA," *The Public Interest*, Fall 1977.

Robert Ullman, "GM and Auto Workers: OSHA Reshuffles the Deck," and Les Boden and David Wegman, "Increasing OSHA's Clout: Sixty Million New Inspectors," *Working Papers For a New Society*, May/June 1978, pp. 43-49 and 50-54.

Robert Stewart Smith, "The Impact of OSHA Inspection on Manufacturing Injury Rates," *Journal of Human Resources*, Spring 1979, pp. 145-170.

James Chelius, "The Control of Industrial Accidents: Economic Theory and Empirical Evidence," *Law and Contemporary Problem*, Vol. 38, 1974, pp. 700-729.

9. AUTO SAFETY

Lester Lane and Warren Webber, "A Benefit-Cost Analysis of Auto Safety Features," *Applied Economics*, 1970, pp. 265-275.

Sam Peltzman, "The Effects of Automobile Safety Regulation," *Journal of Political Economy*, 1975, pp. 677-726.

Leon S. Robertson, "A Critical Analysis of Peltzman's "The Effects of Auto Safety Regulation," *Journal of Economic Issues*, September 1977.

10. CONSUMER PROTECTION

Elizabeth H. Dole, "Cost-Benefit Analysis Versus Protecting the Vulnerable: The FTC's Special Interest Groups," *Antitrust Law and Economics Review*, 1977.

Daryl M. Freedman, "Reasonable Certainty of No Harm: Reviewing the Safety Standard for Food Additives, Color Additives, and Animal Drugs," *Ecology Law Quarterly*, Vol. 7, No. 2, 1978.

Walter W.O., "The Economics of Product Safety," *Bell Journal of Economics and Management*, Spring 1973, pp. 3-28.

Robert Pitorsky, "Beyond Nader: Consumer Protection and the Regulation of Advertising," *Harvard Law Review*, February 1977, pp. 661-701.

11. CASE STUDY: DRUGS

Sam Peltzman, "An Evaluation of Consumer Protection Legislation: The 1962 Drug Amendments: A Reply." *Journal of Political Economy*, June 1975, pp. 1049-1093.

Thomas McGuire, Richard Nelson and Thomas Spavins, "An Evaluation of Consumer Protection Legislation: The 1962 Drug Amendments: A Comment." *Journal of Political Economy*, June 1975, pp. 655-662.

Don G. Rushing, "Picking Your Poison: The Drug Efficacy Requirement," *UCLA Law Review*, February 1978, pp. 578-618.

Supplementary Reading

David Seidman, "The Politics of Policy Analysis: Protection or Overprotection in Drug Regulation," *Regulation*, July/August 1977, pp. 22-37.

12. TOXIC SUBSTANCES

Jeffrey Lewis Berger and Steven D. Riskin, "Economic and Technological Feasibility in Regulating Toxic Substances Under the Occupational Safety and Health Act," *Ecology Law Quarterly*, Vol. 7, No. 2, 1978.

Michael H. Brown, "Love Canal and Poisoning of America," *the Atlantic Monthly*, December 1979.

R. Jeffrey Smith, "Toxic Substances: EPA and OSHA and Reluctant Regulators," *Science*, January 5, 1979, pp. 28-29.

13. CASE STUDY: VINYL CHLORIDE

David D. Doniger, "Federal Regulation of Vinyl Chloride: A Short Course in the Law and Policy of Toxic Substances Control," *Ecology Law Quarterly*, Vol. 7, No. 2, 1978.

14. INTERNATIONAL ASPECTS OF HEALTH AND SAFETY

Barry I. Castleman, "The Export of Hazardous Factories to Developing Nations," *International Journal of Health Services*, Vol. 9, No. 4, 1979, pp. 569-606.

J.D. Richardson and J.E. Mutti, "Industrial Displacement Through Environmental Controls: The International Competitive Aspects," *Studies in International Environmental Economics*.

A.. Cristine Laurall, "Work and Health in Mexico," *International Journal of Health Services*, Vol. 9, No. 4, 1979, pp. 543-568.

ENERGY

The Economics of Energy

Andrew Zimbalist
Smith College
Department of Economics
Spring 1981
Undergraduate

E. Mitchell, *U.S. Energy Policy: A Primer*
J. Blair, *The Control of Oil.*
Stobaugh and Yergin (eds.), *Energy Future.*
B. Commoner, *The Politics of Energy.*

OPTIONAL BOOKS:
H. Landsberg, et. al., *Energy: The Next Twenty Years.*
National Academy of Sciences, *Energy in Transition, 1985-2010.*
A. Gyorgy, et. al., *No Nukes.*

* denotes optional reading.
** denotes both optional reading and oral review.

I. THE "ENERGY CRISIS"

A. OVERVIEW

Stobaugh and Yergin, *Energy Future*, Chs. 1 and 2, pp. 1-64.

Landsberg, et. al., *Energy: The Next Twenty Years*, Ch. 2, pp. 77-91.

***The Budget of the U.S. Government, FY 1981*, pp. 129-153.

*M. Adelman, *The World Petroleum Market*, pp. 24-42, 76-77.

*W. Keene, "The Energy Information Administration's Oil and Gas Reserves Program—The First Year's Report," *Monthly Energy Review* (D.O.E.), June, 1980, pp. i-vii.

*S. McDonald, *Petroleum Conservation in the United States: An Economic Analysis*, pp. 9-28.

*E. Marshall, "Energy Forecasts: Sinking to New Lows," *Science*, June 1980, pp. 1353-1356.

B. METHODOLOGY AND THEORY

Optimizing over time and non-renewable resources:
Griffin and Steele, *Energy Economics and Policy*, pp. 65-86.

*S. McDonald, *op. cit.*, pp. 75-92.

*Webb and Ricketts, *The Economics of Energy*, pp. 27-73.

Net energy analysis:
Baumol and Blackman, "Unprofitable Energy is Squandered Energy," *Challenge: The Magazine of Economic Affairs*, July/August 1980, pp. 28-35.

*Odum and Odum, *Energy Basis for Man [sic] and Nature.*

Modelling:
Stobaugh and Yergin, *op. cit.*, "Limits to Models," pp. 305-338.

Measurement problems:
E. Mitchell, *op. cit.*, Appendix A: "Measuring Energy Consumption and Prices," pp. 75-84.

II. OIL AND ECONOMIC POLICY

E. Mitchell, *op. cit.*, pp. 1-74, 85-103.

J. Wetzler, "Energy Excise Taxes as Substitutes for Income Taxes," *National Tax Journal*, Fall 1980.

**Joint Committee on Taxation, U.S. Congress, "Summary of H.R. 3919: The Crude Oil Windfall Profit Tax Act of 1980."

**J. Sweeney, "Energy Regulation—Solution or Problem?" in Carnesale et. al., *Options for U.S. Energy Policy*, pp. 179-209.

**Stobaugh and Yergin, *op. cit.*, pp. 65-92.

*Arrow and Kalb, "Why Oil Prices Should be Decontrolled," *Regulation*, Sept./Oct. 1979, pp. 13-17.

*P. MacAvoy (ed.), *Federal Energy Administration Regulation: Report of the Presidential Task Force.*

*U.S. Dept. of Energy, Energy Information Administration, Energy Policy Studies on Regulation, Subsidies and Taxation (see me for more info.).

*Stobaugh and Yergin, op. cit., pp. 339-351.

*Batelle Pacific Northwest Laboratories, "An Analysis of Federal Incentives to Stimulate Energy Production," for D.O.E., March 1978.

III. MARKET POWER AND RESOURCE ALLOCATION

J. Blair, The Control of Oil, pp. 3-23, 98-120, 125-204, 276-330, 355-395, **pp. 29-97, **pp. 211-275.

R. Engler, The Brotherhood of Oil, pp. 199-237, **pp. 1-92, **pp. 139-198.

R. Sherrill, "Where is the Cry of Protest?," The Nation, Oct. 25, 1980.

F. Cook, "The Natural Gas Boom," The Nation, July 12, 1980.

F. Cook, "Somebody Doesn't Like Hy-Fuel," The Nation, Oct. 4, 1980.

*R. Sherrill, "The Case Against the Oil Companies," New York Times Sunday Magazine, October 14, 1979.

*F. Cook, "Big Oil Primes a New Crisis at the Pumps," The Nation, April 12, 1980.

*F. Cook, "Runaway Heating Oil Profits," The Nation, March 22, 1980.

*F. Cook, "Mobil-izing Against Gasohol," The Nation, July 19, 1980.

*F. Cook, "Behind the Great DOE Stonewall," The Nation, May 31, 1980.

*FTC, Concentration Levels and Trends in the Energy Sector of the U.S. Economy.

*M. Tanzer, The Energy Crisis: World Struggle for Power and Wealth.

IV. MACRO AND INTERNATIONAL DIMENSIONS OF THE ENERGY CRISIS

H. Landsberg, et. al., op. cit., "Economic Management of the Energy Problem," pp. 155-184.

Congressional Budget Office, "Oil and the Value of the Dollar," The World Oil Market in the 1980s: Implications for the U.S., pp. 39-52.

M. Moffitt, "The Third World: Deeper in Debt," The Nation, July 5, 1980.

P. Volcker, "The Recycling Problem Revisited," Challenge: The Magazine of Economic Affairs, July/August 1980.

*H. Wachtel, The New Gnomes: Multinational Banks in the Third World.

*P. Erdman, The Crash of '79.

*F. Block, The Origins of International Economic Disorder.

*C.I.A., "Non-OPEC LDCs: External Debt Positions," Jan. 1980.

V. NUCLEAR ENERGY

Stobaugh and Yergin, op. cit., "The Nuclear Stalemate," pp. 127-166.

National Academy of Sciences, op. cit., pp. 24-39.

C. Komanoff, "Cost Escalation at Nuclear and Coal Power Plants."

A. Gyorgy, No Nukes, "The Economics of Nuclear Power," pp. 149-185 (**189-207), or Nader and Abbotts, The Menace of Nuclear Power, "Nuclear Economics," pp. 212-233 and pp. 261-292 (*370-382).

**"Low Level Radiation and Mancuso Affair," Science, April 13, 1979, pp. 150-164.

**Kemeny Commission, The Accident at TMI.

**A. Gyorgy, et. al., No Nukes, pp. 1-224, or Nader and Abbotts, pp. 9-14, 25-31, 69-183.

**Landsberg, et. al., op. cit., pp. 413-466; or **National Academy of Sciences, op. cit., pp. 210-344.

*D.O.E., Energy Information Administration, Nuclear Safety Regulation.

*C. Komanoff, Power Plant Escalation: Nuclear and Coal Capital Costs and Economics.

*S. Miller, The Economics of Nuclear and Coal Power.

*I. Bupp and J. Derian, Light Water.

*E. Douglass, "The D.O.E.'s Hazardous Waste," The Nation, Dec. 27, 1980.

*Union of Concerned Scientists, The Nugget File.

*R. Lipschutz, Radioactive Waste: Politics, Technology and Risk.

*J. Bowring, Federal Subsidies to Nuclear Power: Reactor Design and the Fuel Cycle, D.O.E., March 1980.

*A. Lovins, et. al., "Nuclear Power and Nuclear Bombs," Foreign Affairs, Summer 1980.

VI. COAL, SYNFUELS AND OIL SHALE

Stobaugh and Yergin, op. cit., pp. 93-126.

R. Howard, "Coal," Parts 1 and 2, In These Times, Dec. 19, 1979 and Jan. 8, 1980.

J. Blair, The Control of Oil, pp. 330-341.

**Landsberg, et. al., op. cit., pp. 271-372 or **National Academy of Sciences, op. cit., pp. 146-205.

*M. Yarrow, "The Labor Process in Coal Mining," in A. Zimbalist (ed.), Case Studies on the Labor Process.

*Office of Technology Assessment (U.S. Congress), An Assessment of Oil Shale Technologies, June 1980.

*H. Caudill, "Coal—The Pall in the Panacea," The Nation, Nov. 22, 1980.

VII. SOLAR AND CONSERVATION

A. Lovins, *Soft Energy Paths*, pp. 3-60, 161-170 (*147-160).

Stobaugh and Yergin, *op. cit.*, pp. 167-269.

B. Commoner, *The Politics of Energy*, pp. 24-82.

S. Denman, "Big Business Reaches for the Sun," *The Nation*, Sept. 13, 1980.

*Kendall and Nadis, *Energy Strategies: Toward a Solar Future*.

*B. Commoner, *Poverty of Power*, pp. 221-249.

*F. Cook, "Time for Gasohol: America's Home-Grown Fuel," *The Nation*, Sept. 27, 1980.

*Timmer and Mullen, "Corn: Food and Fuel?," *New York Times*, op. ed. A15, Dec. 31, 1980.

*Office of Technology Assessment, *Energy from Biological Processes*, July 1980.

*A. MacRobert, "Who Owns the Sun," *Valley Advocate*, October 17, 1979.

*National Academy of Sciences, *op. cit.*, Chs. on solar (345-384), fusion (385-396), geothermal (397-421).

*Landsberg, et. al., *op. cit.*, pp. 467-510.

*Office of Technology Assessment, *Gasohol* (September 1979).

*P. Donvito, "Gasohol: The Real Issue is BTUs," *New York Times* Sunday, Business Section, July 13, 1980, p. 18.

*K. O'Banion, "Reagan's Energy Program: A Time for Conservation," *The Nation*, Jan. 3, 1981.

HEALTH

The Political Economy of Health

Meredeth Turshen
International Studies Program
School of Human Ecology
Howard University
Graduate

A political and economic analysis of the ecology of disease in underdeveloped countries; the problems of industrialized countries are introduced when needed to explain developments in the Third World.

The textbook for the course is L. Doyal, *The Political Economy of Health*; an American edition is published by South End Press, Boston.

I. INTRODUCTION TO THE POLITICAL ECONOMY OF HEALTH

Doyal, L. *The Political Economy of Health*, Part One, 'Understanding medicine and health' pp. 11-46.

Suggested readings:

T. McKeown, *The Role of Medicine: Dream, Mirage or Nemesis*, Preface and Introduction, pp. ix-10.

J. Tudor Hart, "McKeown's The Role of Medicine: Advancing Backwards" Milbank Memorial Fund Quarterly, Summer 1977, pp. 383-388.

1. CRITICISM OF HEALTH CARE UNDER CAPITALISM

J. Powles, "On the limitations of modern medicine" *Science, Medicine and Man*, 1973, 1, 1, pp. 1-30.

Suggested readings:

M. Turshen, "The political ecology of disease" *Review of Radical Political Economics*, 1977, 9, 1, 45-60.

HealthPAC, The American Health Empire, 'Introduction: the system behind the chaos' pp. 3-28.

2. RE-EVALUATION OF CLINICAL MEDICINE—IATROGENESIS AND EFFICACY

Ivan Illich, *Medical Nemesis*, chapter 1, 'the epidemics of modern medicine' pp. 3-27.

Suggested readings:

V. Navarro, "The industrialization of fetishism: a critique of Ivan Illich" *Medicine under Capitalism*.

Lopate, C. Review of Medical Nemesis by Ivan Illich, *HealthPAC Bulletin*, No. 65, July/Aug 1975, pp. 26-32.

J. Eyer, Review of Assessing the efficacy and safety of medical technologies by Office of Technology Assessment, Congress of US, *HealthPAC Bulletin*, 1979, Nos. 83/85, pp. 54-63.

3. DEBATES ON THE NATURE OF HEALTH AND DISEASE

H. Berliner, "Emerging ideologies in medicine" *Review of Radical Political Economics*, Spring 1977, 9, 1, pp. 116-124.

Suggested readings:

S. Kelman, "The social nature of the definition problem in health" *International Journal of Health Services*, 1975, 5, 4.

S. Guttmacher, "Whole in body, mind and spirit: holistic health and the limits of medicine" *The Hastings Center Report*, 1979, 9, 2, pp. 15-21.

II. SOCIAL DETERMINANTS OF HEALTH AND DISEASE

L. Doyal, *The Political Economy of Health*, Chapter 3, 'Health, Illness and Underdevelopment' pp. 96-137.

Suggested readings:

H.P. Dreitzel, 'Introduction' *The Social Organization of Health* pp. v-xvii.

Ivan Illich, *Medical Nemesis*, Part II. Social Iatrogenesis, pp. 31-118.

4. PREVENTIVE AND CURATIVE MEDICINE; VICTIM-BLAMING AND SOCIAL CONTROL

I.K. Zola, "Medicine as an institution of social control" *The Sociological Review*, 1972, 20, 4 (new series), pp. 487-509.

Suggested readings:

R. Crawford, "You are dangerous to your health: the ideology and politics of victim-blaming" *International Journal of Health Services* 1977, 7, 4, 663-680.

Holtzman, N. "Prevention: rhetoric and reality" *International Journal of Health Services*, 1979, 9, 1, 25-39.

5. SOCIAL CLASS AND THE DISTRIBUTION OF DISEASE

N. Hart, Health and Inequality, Part II: The Evidence of Inequality in Health, pp. 39-105.

Suggested readings:

Sussor, M.W. & Watson, W. *Sociology in Medicine*, chapter: 3 & 4, 'Social class and disorders of health', pp. 105-176.

Abel-Smith, B. & Leisserson, A. Poverty, Development and Health Policy, WHO Public Health Paper 69, chapter 1, 'The inequity of past development', pp. 13-20.

6. PUBLIC HEALTH AND TROPICAL MEDICINE

J.S. Horn, *Away with All Pests*, chapter 10, 'The fight against schistosomiasis', 94-106.

Suggested readings:

Sandbach, F.R. "Preventing schistosomiasis: a critical assessment of present policy" *Social Science and Medicine*, 1975, 9, 517-527.

III. DEVELOPMENT, ENVIRONMENTAL AND OCCUPATIONAL HEALTH

Dasmann, R.F., Milton, J.P. & Freeman, P.H. *Ecological Principles for Economic Development*, chapter 7, esp. pp. 197-204.

Suggested readings:

Farvar, T. & Milton, J.P. (eds) *Careless Technology*, MIT Press; Brokensha, D. (ed) *Ecology and Economic Development in Tropical Africa*, University of California Press, Berkeley.

7. DISEASE AND DEVELOPMENT—ECOLOGICAL IMPACTS

Hughes, C.C. & Hunter, J.M. "Disease and Development in Africa" in H.P. Dreitzel (ed) *The Social Organization of Health*, chapter 7, pp. 150-214.

Suggested readings:

Patterson, K.D. "Bibliographical essay" in Hartwig & Patterson, *Disease in African History*.

Patterson, K.D. & Hartwig, G.W. "The disease factor: an introductory overview" in Hartwig & Patterson, *Disease in African History*.

8. WORK-RELATED DISEASE—DEFINITIONS OF WORK AND OF OCCUPATIONAL DISEASE

Khogali, M. "Types of risk and their prevention" in Proceedings of the Symposium on the Health Problems of Industrial Progress in Developing Countries, London School of Hygiene and Tropical Medicine, Sept 1970.

Suggested readings:

International Labour Conference, "Safety and Health and the Working Environment" Report VII(a), 1980, pp. 33-41 'Action taken in developing countries'.

NACLA, 'International hazards: occupational health and asbestos' *NACLA Bulletin*, 1978, XII, 2, 21-29.

Castleman, B. "The export of hazardous factories to developing nations" *International Journal of Health Services*, 1979, 9, 4, pp. 561-606.

IV. WOMEN'S HEALTH, WOMEN'S STATUS AND BIRTH CONTROL

Blumberg, R.L. "Fairy tales and facts: economy, family, fertility and the female " in *Women & World Development*, ODC, Wash. DC. 1976.

Suggested readings:

H. Rodriguez-Trias, "Childbearing rights and economic imperatives" HMO Packet #6, 1979, pp. 25-33.

ISIS, "Women and Health" 1978, 7, 'Who controls reproduction?' pp. 20-35.

Pala. A.O. "Definitions of women and development: an African perspective" in *Women & National Development*, University of Chicago Press, 1976.

9. WOMEN'S STATUS, CLASS, MORTALITY AND MORBIDITY

WHO, Report on the meeting on women and family health, Geneva, 1979.

Suggested readings:

Elizabeth Reid, "Women at a standstill: the need for radical change" *International Labour Review*, 1975, 6, pp. 459-486.

L. Doyal, *The Political Economy of Health*, chapter 6, "Women, medicine and social control: the case of the NHS" p. 215.

10. WOMEN AS USERS AND PROVIDERS OF HEALTH SERVICES

Bui Dang Ha Doan, "Women in the health professions," *World Health Statistics Quarterly*, 1979, 32, 2, 154-170.

Suggested reading:

URPE Women's Work Project, *Women in Health*, 1976.

11. WOMEN'S REPRODUCTIVE RIGHTS AND POPULATION CONTROL

Bonnie Mass, *Population Target:* The Political Economy of Population Control in Latin America, "Birth control and political demography," pp. 141-162.

Suggested readings:

CARASA, Women under attack: Abortion, sterilization abuse, and reproductive freedom, 1979.

Bangladesh People's Health Center, ISIS *International Bulletin*, 1978, 8, pp. 8-10.

V. MEDICINE AND IMPERIALISM

D. Banerji, "Political dimensions of health and health services" *Economic and Political Weekly*, June 3, 1978.

Suggested readings:

V. Navarro, "The underdevelopment of health or the health of underdevelopment", *International Journal of Health Services*, 1974, 4, 1, 5-27.

L. Doyal, *The Political Economy of Health*, chapter 7, Medicine and Imperialism, pp. 239-290.

12. COLONIAL MEDICAL SERVICES

J. Paul, "Medicine and Imperialism" *Health Politics*, 1975, 4, 3-9.

Suggested readings:

M. Turshen, "The impact of colonialism on health and health services in Tanzania" *International Journal of Health Services*, 1977, 7, 1, 7-35.

V. Navarro, "The political and economic origins of the underdevelopment of health in Latin America" *Medicine under Capitalism* pp. 3-32.

13. THE PHARMACEUTICAL INDUSTRY

M. Turshen, "An analysis of the medical supply industries" *International Journal of Health Services*, 1976, 6, 2, 271-293.

Suggested readings:

Sanjay Lall, "The international pharmaceutical industry and less developed countries with special reference to India" *Oxford Bulletin of Economics and Statistics*, 1974, 36, pp. 143-172.

Gish, O. & Feller, L.L. Planning pharmaceuticals for primary health care: the supply and utilization of drugs in the third world.

14. MEDICAL EDUCATION AND BRAIN DRAIN

Mejia, A. Pizurki, H. & Royston, E., *Physician and Nurse Migration*, Chapter 4, -Consequences of Migration, pp. 101-170. Chapter 3, Determinants of Migration (WHO, 1979).

Suggested readings:

Gish, O. "Medical brain drain revisited" *International Journal of Health Services*, 1976, 6, 2, pp. 231-237.

Brown, E.R. "Exporting medical education: professionalism, modernization and imperialism" *Social Science & Medicine*, 1979, 13A, 6, pp. 585-595.

15. PRIMARY HEALTH CARE

England, R. "More myths in international health planning", *American Journal of Public Health*, 1978, 68, 2, 153-159.

Suggested readings:

WHO/UNICEF, Alma Ata Declaration on Primary Health Care Thebaud, A. & Turshen, M. "Vers la medicalisation du sous-developpement?" *Le Monde Diplomatique*, Avril 1981 (English version in preparation).

16. TRADITIONAL MEDICINE AND HOLISTIC MEDICINE

D. Banerji, "Place of the indigenous and western systems of medicine in the health services of India" *International Journal of Health Services*, 1979, 9, 3, p. 511.

Suggested readings:

Maclean, U. *Magical medicine, A Nigerian Case Study*, Penguin, 1974 Berliner, H.S. & Salmon, J.W. "Toward a political holistic medicine" *Socialist Review*, 1979, 43.

17. INTERNATIONAL MEDICAL AID

World Bank, Health Sector Policy Paper, Feb. 1980.

Suggested readings:

John Briscoe, "Are voluntary agencies helping to improve health in Bangladesh?" *International Journal of Health Services*, 1980, 10, 1, 47-69.

O. Gish, *Planning the Health Sector*, chapters 10 and 11, pp. 178-199.

VI. NATIONAL HEALTH PLANNING

Abel-Smith, B & Leisserson, A. Poverty, Development and Health Policy, WHO 1978, chapter 4, planning national health policy and chapter 8, low-cost services.

Suggested readings:

Gish, O. *Planning the Health Sector: The Tanzanian Experience*, Chapter 2, The Health Plan.

Gish, O. "Resource allocation, equality of access and health" *International Journal of Health Services*, 1973, 3, 2, 37-44.

VII. THE SOCIALIST EXPERIENCE

18. USSR

V. Navarro, *Social Security and Medicine in the USSR: A Marxist Critique*, D.C. Heath, Lexington, 1977.

19. CHINA, VIETNAM

Sidel, V.W. & Sidel, R. "The health care delivery system in the People's Republic of China" in Newell, K. (ed), *Health by the People*, WHO 1975, pp. 1-12.

McMichael, J.K. (ed) *Health in the Third World, Studies from Vietnam*, Spokesman Books, 1976.

20. CUBA, TANZANIA

Tejeiro Fernandez, A.F. "The national health system in Cuba" in Newell, K. (ed) *Health by the People*, pp. 13-29.

Chagula, W.K. & Tarimo, E. "Meeting basic health needs in Tanzania" in Newell, K. (ed) *Health by the People*, p. 145-168.

SUPPLEMENTARY BIBLIOGRAPHY ON THE PHARMACEUTICAL INDUSTRY

1. EXPOSES

Mintz, M. *By prescription only*, Beacon Press, Boston, revised ed. 1967. Covers Congressional investigations by Estes Kefauver, Hubert Humphrey, et al., which see; the most recent is:

Subcommittee on Monopoly and Anticompetitive Activities of the Select Committee on Small Businesses, U.S. Senate, 95th Congress, Hearings: "Competitive Problems in the Drug Industry", Part 33, Nov. 14, 15, 16, 1977.

Klass, Alan, *There's Gold in them thar Pills*, An inquiry into the medical-industrial complex, Penguin Books 1975.

Klaw, Spencer, *The Great American Medicine Show*, Penguin Books, 1976, Chapter 7.

Sjostrom, H. & Nilsson, R. *Thalidomide and the Power of the Drug Companies*, Penguin Books, 1972.

Sunday Times Insight Team, *Suffer the Children*, the story of thalidomide, Futura Publications, 1979, London (UK).

2. INVESTIGATIONS

Levinson, Charles, *The Multinational Pharmaceutical Industry*, International Chemical Federation, Geneva undated (c. 1975?).

Segall, M. & Barker, C. Two papers on pharmaceuticals in developing countries, IDS(Institute for Development Studies) Communication 119, University of Sussex, 1975.

Lall, Sanjaya, "The international pharmaceutical industry and less-developing countries, with special reference to India" *Oxford Bulletin of Economics and Statistics*, 1974, 56, 5, 143-172.

UNCTAD (United Nations Conference on Trade and Development), Major Issues in Transfer of Technology to Developing Countries: A case study of the pharmaceutical industry, TD/B/C.6/4, 8 October 1975.

UNCTAD, Case studies in the transfer of technology: Pharmaceutical policies in Sri Lanka, TD/B/C.6/21, 27 June 1977.

UNCTAD, Case studies in the transfer of technology: the pharmaceutical industry in India, TD/B/C.6/20, 11 Oct. 1977.

Haslemere Group, Who needs the Drug Companies? Third World Publications, Brimingham (UK) no date (c. 1976?).

Summers, R.S. "International Health Care and Pharmacy: Current implications with particular refernce to developing communities" University of the North, Pietersburg, South Africa, Apr. 1977.

Dupuy, J.-P. & Karsenty, S. *L'invasion pharmaceutique*, Editions du Seuil, Paris, 1977.

Chaulet, P. et al. "Results of the international cooperative inquiry into the cost of anti-tuberculosis drugs" *Bulletin of the International Union Against Tuberculosis*, 1978, 53, 4, 237-253.

Chudnovsky, D. "The challenge by domestic enterprises to the transnational corporations' domination: A case study of the Argentine Pharmaceutical industry" *World Development*, 1979, 7, 45-58.

Medawar, Charles, *Insult or Injury?* An enquiry into the marketing and advertising of British food and drug products in the Third World, Social Audit, 9 Poland St, London, 1979.

Gish, Oscar & Feller, Lee, *Planning Pharmaceuticals for Primary Health Care*: The supply and utilization of drugs in the Third World, American Public Health Assn, Monograph Series No. 2, 1979, Washington, D.C.

In addition, the International Journal of Health Services regularly publishes studies on the pharmaceutical industry, e.g.

Murray, M. "The Pharmaceutical Industry: A

study in corporate power" I.J.H.S., 1974, 4, 4, 625-640.

Turshen, M. "An analysis of the medical supply industries" I.J.H.S. 1976, 6, 2, 271-294.

Yudkin, J.S. "The economics of pharmaceutical supply in Tanzania" I.J.H.S., 1980.

3. RAW MATERIALS

Federal Trade Commission, Pharmaceutical Industry: A Selected Bibliography, Bibliography Series No. 3, April 1979, Washington, DC (annotated).

WHO Regional Office for Europe, *National Drug Policies*, Public Health in Europe No. 12, Copenhagen, 1979.

Wardell, W.M. & Lasagna, L. "Regulation and Drug Development" American Enterprise Institute, Washington, DC, 1975.

Commission of the European Communities, Concentration in the Pharmaceutical Industry—studies of Denmark, Italy, Belgium, France, U.K., Netherlands, 1975, P.O. Box 1003, Luxemburg.

World Health Organizaition, *The Selection of Essential Drugs*, Technical Report Series No. 615, Geneva, 1977, and Report of the Second Expert Committee, 1980.

Also see documents of the Organization of Economic Cooperation and Development, Paris and, United Nations Industrial Development Organization, Vienna (especially reports of their recent meetings in Cancun, Mexico (1979) and Vienna (1980)).

HUNGER

The Political Economy of Hunger

Meredeth Turshen
International Studies Program
School of Human Ecology
Howard Universy
Graduate

This is a course about famine and malnutrition in underdeveloped areas of Africa, Asia and Latin America. In it we explore the economic, social and political determinants of hunger, using as our framework a structural analysis of underdevelopment in the Third World.

The text for the course is Lappe, F.M. & Collins, J., *Food First*, Ballantine Book edition, 1979.

I. INTRODUCTION: STUDENT GOALS AND OBJECTIVES OF THE COURSE; EVALUATION PROCEDURES

II. FAMINE—CAUSES AND REMEDIES: CASE STUDY OF THE SAHEL

1. DROUGHT, DESERTIFICATION; OVERGRAZING, DEFORESTATION

The Coup, a novel by John Updike.
Additional readings:

Ball, N. "Drought and dependence in the Sahel", *International Journal of Health Services*, 1978, 8, 2, 271-298.

Meillassoux, C. "Development or exploitation: is the Sahel famine good business?" *Review of African Political Economy*, 1974, 1, pp 27-33.

Comite information Sahel, "Qui se nourrit de la famine en Afrique?" Le dossier politique de la faim au Sahel. Maspero, Paris, 1974.

2. THE COLONIAL LEGACY OF UNDERDEVELOPMENT: THE CASE OF TANZANIA

a. Neglect of food production for domestic consumption, discouragement of local marketing.

b. Ecological change, population growth.

c. Introduction of money economy.

Kjekshus, H. *Ecology Control and Economic Development in East African History*, Heinemann, London, 1977.

Turshen, M. "The impact of colonialism on health and health services in Tanzania", *International Journal of Health Services*, 1977, 7, 1, 7-35.

Nnoli, O. "Political will and the margin of autonomy in Tanzania for policy" *Africa Quarterly*, 1977, 17, 1, 5-36.

Allan, W. *The African Husbandman*, Oliver & Boyd, Edinburgh, 1965.

3. SHIFT FROM FOOD CROP PRODUCTION TO CASH CROP PRODUCTION; PROBLEM OF DEPENDENCY ON WORLD MARKET PRICES FOR EXPORT CROPS: THE CASE OF NORTHEAST BRAZIL.

de Castro, J. *Geopolitics of Hunger*, Monthly Review Press, N.Y., 19

de Castro, J. *Death in the Northeast*, Random House, N.Y. 1966.

Linhart, R. *Le sucre et la faim*, Les editions de minuit, Paris, 1980.

Juliao, F. *Cambao, The Yoke: The Hidden Face of Brazil*, Pelican Books, London, 1972.

4. EMERGENCY FOOD AID; TRADITIONAL COPING MECHANISMS

Lappe, F.M. & Collins, J. *Food First: Beyond the Myth of Scarcity*, Ballantine paperbacks, N.Y. 1979 ($2.75) Part IX, Chapter 40, 'Food aid for whom?'

George, S. *How the other half dies: the real reasons for world hunger*, Allanheld, Osman & Co Publishers, Montclair, 1977 ($5.95 paper) Chapter 8 'Food aid? or weapon?' pp. 164-183.

Plommer, L. 'The disaster game' *New York Times*, Nov 17, 1978.

III. MALNUTRITION—FORMS AND CONSEQUENCES

1. UNDERNUTRITION, OVERNUTRITION, SPECIFIC DEFICIENCIES; THE ECONOMIC DETERMINANTS OF NUTRITION

Behar, M. "European diets vs. traditional foods" *Food Policy*, 1976, 1, 5, 432-435.

Hartmann, B. & Boyce, J. *Needless Hunger: Voices from a Bangladesh Village*, Institute for Food & Development Policy, San Francisco, 1979, ($3.00 paper).

2. VARIATIONS IN NUTRITIONAL STATUS (E.G. SEASONAL, URBAN/RURAL); PROBLEMS OF FOOD SUPPLY AND DEMAND.

Scofield, S. "Seasonal factors affecting nutrition in different age groups and especially preschool children" *Journal of Development Studies*, 1974, 11, 1, 22-40.

Escudero, J. "The magnitude of malnutrition in Latin America" *International Journal of Health Services*, 1978, 8, 3, 465-490.

3. GOVERNMENT INTERVENTION (E.G. TO CONTROL FOOD SUPPLIES, PRICES): THE CASE OF CHILE

Hakim, P. & Solimano, G. *Development, Reform, and Malnutrition in Chile*, M.I.T. Press, Cambridge, 1978.

Hakim, P. & Solimano, G. "Nutrition and National Development: establishing the connection" *Food Policy*, May 1976.

4. MULTINATIONAL FOOD CORPORATIONS AND TECHNOLOGICAL SOLUTIONS

Muller, M. *The Baby Killer*, War on Want, 1975, London.

Greiner, T. "The promotion of bottle feeding by multinational corporations: how advertising and the health professions have contributed" Cornell International Nutrition Monograph Series No. 2, 1975, Cornell University, Ithaca, N.Y.

Cottingham, J. (ED.) "Bottle babies: a guide to the baby foods issue" ISIS, Geneva, 1976.

Garson, B. "The bottle baby scandal: milking the third world for all its worth" *Mother Jones*, December 1977.

Lappe, F.M. & Collins, J. *Food First*, Part VIII, Chapter 37, 'Do they really kill babies?'

5. CONSEQUENCES TO HEALTH AND POPULATION

E cudero, J. "The magnitude of malnutrition in Latin America" *International Journal of Health Services*, 1978, 8, 3, 465-490.

Turshen, M. "The impact of colonialism on health and health services in Tanzania" *International Journal of Health Services*, 1977, 7, 1, 7-35.

IV. LAND, LABOR AND CAPITAL

1. LAND TENURE SYSTEMS

Allan, W. The African Husbandman, Oliver & Boyd, Edinburgh, 1965 *Poverty and Landlessness in Asia*, International Labor Office, Geneva, 1978.

2. THE AGRICULTURAL LABOR FORCE AND THE ROLE OF WOMEN

Boserup, E. *Woman's Role in Economic Development*, Allen & Unwin, 1970.

Pala, A.O. "The role of African women in rural development: research priorities" Institue of Development Studies, University of Nairobi, Discussion paper no. 203, 1975.

Davin, D. *Woman work: Women and the party in revolutionary China* Clarendon Press, Oxford, 1976.

3. PRIVATE AND PUBLIC INVESTMENT

a. International Agribusiness

George, S. *How the other half dies*, Allanheld, Osmun & Co., 1977, Chapter 7, 'There's no business like agribusiness' pp. 132-163.

Lappe, F.M. & Collins, J. *Food First*, Part VIII, "World Hunger as Big Business" Chapters no 33-36.

b. International Development Aid

Taussig, M. "Nutrition, Development, and Foreign Aid: Acase study of U.S.-directed health care in a Colombian plantation zone" *International Journal of Health Services*, 1978, 8, 1, 101-121.

George, S. *Feeding the Few: Corporate Control of Food*, Institute for Policy Studies, Washington, DC, undated ($3.95).

George, S. *How the other half dies*, Part Three chapter 10, pp. 205-232.

4. THE NEW AGRICULTURAL TECHNOLOGY; THE 'GREEN REVOLUTION'

Palmer, I. *Food and the new agricultural technology*, 1972, United Nations Research Institute for Social Development, Geneva.

Cleaver, H.M. "The contradictions of the green revolution", *American Economic Review*, 1972, LXII, 2, 177-186.

V. SUMMATION

1. CLASS STRUCTURES AND WORLD NUTRITION

Behar, M. "Nutrition and the future of mankind" *International Journal of Health Services*, 1976, 2, 315-320.

World Agricultural Research Project, "The Political Economy of Food and Agriculture", *International Journal of Health Services*, 1980, 10, 1, 161-170.

SUPPLEMENT: THE GREEN REVOLUTION— BIBLIOGRAPHY

Cleaver, Harry, "The contradictions of the green revolution", *American Economic Review*, 1972, LXII, 2, 177-186. Also reprinted in Wilbur, C.K. (ed.) *The Political Economy of Development and Underdevelopment*, Random House, N.Y. 1973, pp. 187-197.

Gough, Kathleen, "The green revolution in South India and North Vietnam", *Monthly Review*, 1978, 29, 8, 10-21.

Lappe, F.M. & Collins, J. *Food First*, Part V, "Modernizing Hunger" chapters 15-22.

George, Susan, *How the other half dies*, chapter 5, 'The green revolution'

Palmer, Ingrid, *Food and the new agricultural technology*, United Nations Research Institute for Social Development (UNRISD), Geneva, 1972.

Palmer I. *Science and Agricultural Production*, UNRISD, Geneva 1972.

Palmer, I. *The new rice in the Philippines*, UNRISD, Geneva, 1975.

Palmer, I. *The new rice in Asia: Conclusions from four country studies*, UNRISD, Geneva, 1976.

Dasgupta, Biplab, *Agrarian Change and the New Technology in India*, UNRISD, Geneva, 1977.

Pearse, Andrew, *Seeds of Plenty, Seeds of Want*, Oxford University Press, 1980.

Griffin, Keith, "The political economy of agrarian change: An essay on the green revolution", Macmillan, 1974.

Abdul Hameed, N.D. et al. *Rice revolution in Sri Lanka*, UNRISD, 1976, Geneva.

Bhati, U.N., "Some social and economic aspects of the introduction of new varieties of paddy in Malaysia: A village case study" UNRISD, Geneva, 1976.

WHAT IS URPE?

The Union for Radical Political Economics is an interdisciplinary educational association founded in 1968 by a group of socialist intellectuals and activists. The primary work of the organization, publications and conferences, is oriented toward the development and application of political-economic analysis to social problems. We intend to provide a forum for debate and education in which divergent and often conflicting interpretations can be critically presented and compared.

DEVELOPMENT OF ALTERNATIVE THEORY & PRACTICE

We encourage the development of radical political-economic theory and its application. Emphasis is on a continuing critique of the capitalist system and of all forms of exploitation and oppression, the construction of progressive social policy, and the creation of socialist alternatives.

EDUCATION

We work in educational institutions to provide students with critiques of, and alternatives to, traditional economics, and to aid those teaching and developing this curriculum.

A long-standing and very successful tradition in URPE has been the encouragement and support of study groups. Some have been created with a short-term goal in mind, such as specific policy analysis, while others have a longer-range focus, including the special writing collectives formed as part of the URPE Economic Education Project.

COOPERATION WITH OTHER ORGANIZATIONS

We work with a wide variety of progressive, community, labor, feminist, and educational organizations by holding joint conferences, providing technical resources, and sharing educational materials.

Within URPE we are consciously struggling against the sexism, racism, elitism, and competitiveness in our lives which are stimulated and reinforced in a capitalist society. We are attempting to construct democratic and collective social relationships that will assist in reaching our goals.

OUR ACTIVITIES INCLUDE:

PUBLICATIONS

The Review of Radical Political Economics (RRPE)—A quarterly journal which encourages and disseminates radical political economic theory and applied analysis. Special issues based on topical themes appear regularly. Some past special issues have been on Health, Racism, the Political Economy of Women, and Contemporary Imperialism. URPE members serve on the Editorial Board and elect the Editorial Board and its coordinator.

The URPE Newsletter—Published bimonthly by a collective of members, serves as a vehicle for internal discussion and communication and also contains brief articles on current political and economic issues.

Dollars and Sense—A monthly magazine published by URPE members which offers interpretations of current economic events written in a popular style.

SPECIAL PROJECTS

Special materials issued as single publications or as part of long-term, multi-product projects initiated by URPE members:

The Women's Work Project published a series of pamphlets on women and the economy.

The Economic Education Project (EEP) prepares clear and accessible material to serve the wider progressive movement. It has published *U.S. Capitalism in Crisis, Crisis in the Public Sector: A Reader*, jointly published with Monthly Review Press, and *Reading Lists in Radical Social Science*, with the cooperation of the Radical Historians' Organization (MARHO) and Monthly Review Press.

CONFERENCES

Every year we hold two national conferences. Our annual summer conference is held at a low-cost camp and is designed to provide an informal setting where URPE members and their friends can discuss their current academic and political work, make major URPE organizational policy and budgetary decisions, and socialize.

A second conference is held each year at the annual meeting of the Allied Social Science Association (ASSA), an association of social scientists, where we offer critiques of, and alternatives to, mainstream economic analyses. We also engage in actions over issues which the leadership of the ASSA has evaded or ignored. Some of our past sessions have centered on the role economists play in American society, on the Vietnam War, the ERA, Milton Friedman, "advice" to the Chilean Junta, and Reaganomics.

Regions, local chapters, and the Women's Caucus also sponsor occasional conferences, classes, and teach-ins. Some topics in recent years have been: Energy, The Rise of the Right, the Future of the Soviet Union, the Political Economy of the Third World, and Political Economics for Left Journalists.

WORKING GROUPS / NETWORKING

The Women's Caucus—A multi-faceted support network, the Women's Caucus helps women within URPE to make contact with others doing related academic and community work and to learn about and further develop work on the political economy of women. The Caucus supports the recognition of class and gender as a principal aspect of political economics and works to overcome the sexism that students and faculty face. Members have coordinated and contributed to special issues of the *RRPE* on the political economy of women and regularly present papers and panels at URPE conferences. The Caucus also works to ensure that feminist concerns are embodied in all of URPE's work.

Working Groups—Working groups are now being established regionally. These groups will engage in ongoing collective work aimed at bringing about systematic connections between our theoretical perspectives and political life. Some proposed topics are: Race and Class, Health Care, Class and Gender, and Crisis Theory.

JOIN URPE!

MEMBER
- ☐ $10 Membership only—This category is for those who wish to be part of URPE, but do not want to receive *The Review of Radical Political Economics*.
  - Six issues of the Newsletter
  - Voting rights
  - 20% discount on EEP literature
- ☐ $20 Membership plus low income subscription to *Review*.
- ☐ $35 Membership plus regular income subscription to *Review*.
- ☐ $50 Membership plus contributor's subscription to *Review*.

  Foreign Postage Charges: Surface mail—add $5.00.

SUBSCRIBER
- ☐ $45 Libraries/Institutions
- ☐ $25 Regular Subscription
- ☐ $6 *Newsletter*

  Foreign Postage Charges: Surface mail—add $5.00.

I wish to enclose a contribution of $_____ .

- ☐ $500.00 Lifetime supporting member/subscriber.

  (URPE is a non-profit, tax-exempt organization.)

  Enclosed is a check or money order for $_____ . *(U.S. currency only.)*

Name_____

Address_____

City _____

State _____ Zip _____

(1982 rates)

Members of the Editorial Board 1981-82

Nancy Breen, The New School for Social Research, 65 Fifth Avenue, New York, N.Y. 10011
Carol Brown, Department of Sociology, Occidental College, 1600 Campus Road, Los Angeles, CA 90041
Fikret Ceyhun, Economics Department, University of North Dakota, Grand Forks, ND 58201
Jim Devine, Department of Economics, Occidental College, 1600 Campus Road, Los Angeles, CA 90041
Richard England, The Whittemore School of Business and Economics, McConnel Hall, University of New Hampshire, Durham, NH 03824
Marshall Feldman, Cross-Disciplinary Program in Behavioral and Social Sciences, San Francisco State University, 1600 Holloway Avenue, San Francisco, CA 94132
Susan Himmelweit, 47 Canonbury Park South, London N12JL, United Kingdom
E.K. Hunt, Department of Economics, University of Utah, Salt Lake City, UT 84112
Chuck Levenstein, 126 Sumner Street, Newton Centre, MA 02159
Arthur MacEwan, University of Massachusetts, Boston, MA 02125
Peter Meyer, College of Community Development, The Pennsylvania State University, University Park, PA 16802
Gary Nickerson, 245 W. 107 Street, Apt. 9D, New York, NY 10025
Laurie Nisonoff, Social Science, Hampshire College, Amherst, MA 01002
Mary Perkins, 4201 Massachusetts Ave., N.W., Washington, DC 20014
Michael Perlman, Department of Economics, College of Liberal Arts & Sciences, University of Connecticut, Storrs, CT 06268
Mary Sternberg, 2928 Derby Street, Berkeley, CA 94705
Estagrul A. Tonak, The New School for Social Research, 65 Fifth Avenue, New York, NY 10011
John Willoughby, Department of Economics, American University, Washington, DC 20016
Andy Winnick, Antioch College, Yellow Springs, OH 45307

Alternates:

Cyrus Bina, Department of Economics, American University, Washington, DC 20016
Jim Cypher, Department of Economics, California State University, Fresno, CA 93740
Raul Fernandez, Program in Comparative Culture, University of California, Irvine, CA 92717
David Gleicher/Paul Swanson, Department of Economics, Columbia University, New York, NY 10027
Tom Michl, Department of Economics, New School for Social Research, 65 Fifth Avenue, New York, NY 10011
Sandy Schilen, 127 West Lowther, Carlisle, PA 17013

Book Review Editor:

Herbert Gintis, Department of Economics, Harvard University, Cambridge, MA 02138

URPE National Office Staff:

Joyce Bressler
Luis Prado
Margi Robison
URPE National Office
41 Union Square West, Room 901
New York, NY 10003

Editorial Board Coordinator:

Kim Edel
Department of Urban Studies
Queens College
Flushing, NY 11367
Phone: (212) 520-7613